# Quasi-Constitutionality and Constitutional Statutes



This book examines the interstices among statutory enactment, constitutional convention and formal constitution in which quasi-constitutionality exists. It provides a focal resource that can serve as a point of reference for scholars interested in quasi-constitutionality, from national and transnational perspectives, expanding on its many forms, functions, and applications with recourse to comparative insights. The book is divided in three main Parts, each preceded by a separate critical introduction in which an informed scholar contextualizes the chapters and offers reflections on the themes they develop. The first Part, titled 'Forms', is composed of chapters that address, from a theoretical and comparative perspective, questions related to the recognition of constitutional statutes and quasi-constitutional legislation. The second Part is titled 'Functions', and contains chapters that explore the explanatory power of quasi-constitutionality in different institutional contexts. The third Part, titled 'Applications', considers the ways in which constitutional statutes and quasi-constitutionality operate in relation to particular tensions and debates present in various jurisdictions.

**Richard Albert** is the William Stamps Farish Professor of Law at The University of Texas at Austin, USA.

**Joel I. Colón-Ríos** is an Associate Professor at the Faculty of Law, Victoria University of Wellington, New Zealand.

# Comparative Constitutional Change

Comparative Constitutional Change has developed into a distinct field of constitutional law. It encompasses the study of constitutions through the way they change and covers a wide scope of topics and methodologies. Books in this series include work on developments in the functions of the constitution, the organization of powers and the protection of rights, as well as research that focuses on formal amendment rules and the relation between constituent and constituted power. The series includes comparative approaches along with books that focus on single jurisdictions, and brings together research monographs and edited collections which allow the expression of different schools of thought. While the focus is primarily on law, where relevant the series may also include political science, historical, philosophical and empirical approaches that explore constitutional change.

*Series editors:*

Xenophon Contiades is Professor of Public Law, Panteion University, Athens, Greece and Managing Director, Centre for European Constitutional Law, Athens, Greece.

Thomas Fleiner is Emeritus Professor of Law at the University of Fribourg, Switzerland. He teaches and researches in the areas of Federalism, Rule of Law, Multicultural State; Comparative Administrative and Constitutional Law; Political Theory and Philosophy; Swiss Constitutional and Administrative Law; and Legislative Drafting. He has published widely in these and related areas.

Alkmene Fotiadou is Research Associate at the Centre for European Constitutional Law, Athens.

Richard Albert is Professor of Law at the University of Texas at Austin.

*Also in the series:*

**The Law and Legitimacy of Imposed Constitutions**
*Edited by Richard Albert, Xenophon Contiades and Alkmene Fotiadou*

**Quasi-Constitutionality and Constitutional Statutes**
Forms, Functions, Applications
*Edited by Richard Albert and Joel Colón-Ríos*

For more information about this series, please visit: www.routledge.com/Comparative-Constitutional-Change/book-series/COMPCONST

# Quasi-Constitutionality and Constitutional Statutes

## Forms, Functions, Applications

**Edited by Richard Albert and Joel I. Colón-Ríos**

Routledge
Taylor & Francis Group
LONDON AND NEW YORK

First published 2019
by Routledge
2 Park Square, Milton Park, Abingdon, Oxon OX14 4RN

and by Routledge
52 Vanderbilt Avenue, New York, NY 10017

First issued in paperback 2020

*Routledge is an imprint of the Taylor & Francis Group, an informa business*



*British Library Cataloguing-in-Publication Data*
A catalogue record for this book is available from the British Library

*Library of Congress Cataloging-in-Publication Data*
A catalog record has been requested for this book

ISBN 13: 978-0-367-66078-9 (pbk)
ISBN 13: 978-0-8153-8534-9 (hbk)

Typeset in Galliard
by Swales & Willis, Exeter, Devon, UK

# Contents

# Contributors

**Richard Albert** is the William Stamps Farish Professor of Law at the University of Texas at Austin.

**Franciska Coleman** is a Visiting Assistant Professor at the University of Kansas School of Law.

**Joel I. Colón-Ríos** is an Associate Professor at the Faculty of Law, Victoria University of Wellington.

**Oran Doyle** is an Associate Professor and former Head of School at Trinity College Dublin School of Law.

**James C. Fisher** is a Project Associate Professor at the Faculty of Law & Graduate Schools for Law and Politics, University of Tokyo.

**Claudia Geiringer** is a Professor of Law at Victoria University of Wellington, where she holds the Chair in Public Law and is the co-Director of the New Zealand Centre for Public Law.

**Jonathan Hafetz** is a Professor of Law at Seton Hall Law School.

**John Helis** holds a PhD from the Faculty of Law, Queen's University in Kingston, Ontario.

**Mark Hickford** is Pro Vice-Chancellor and Dean of Law at Victoria University of Wellington.

**Dean Knight** is an Associate Professor at the Faculty of Law, Victoria University of Wellington, and is the co-Director of the New Zealand Centre for Public Law.

**Sir Geoffrey Palmer QC** is a Barrister, Distinguished Fellow at Victoria University of Wellington, Faculty of Law and New Zealand Centre for Public Law, and a Global Affiliated Professor at the University of Iowa College of Law.

**Sofia Ranchordas** is Professor of European and Comparative Public Law and Rosalind Franklin Fellow at the Faculty of Law, University of Groningen.

**Nikos Skoutaris** is a Senior Lecturer in EU Law at the University of East Anglia.

**Scott Stephenson** is a Senior Lecturer at Melbourne Law School, The University of Melbourne.

**Sergio Verdugo** is a Professor of Constitutional Law at the Universidad del Desarrollo School of Law.

**Rivka Weill** is a Senior Research Scholar at Yale Law School and a former Visiting Professor at Cardozo, Chicago and Yale Law Schools. Professor Weill is a tenured member of Radzyner Law School, IDC.

**Lael Weis** is a Senior Lecturer at Melbourne Law School, The University of Melbourne.

# Preparing a written, codified Constitution for New Zealand

## Is there a need that can be met?

*Sir Geoffrey Palmer QC**

### Introduction

It is interesting, and perhaps significant, that the conference on quasi-constitutionality that gave rise to this symposium took place in New Zealand. For New Zealand has a Constitution and structure of government that is unusual and exceptional. It has no written codified constitution and much of its constitution is not law, but based on constitutional conventions or customs. More than most constitutions, New Zealand's is political. There is no supreme law in New Zealand lying down the constitutional norms. The Constitution is contained in a number of statutes that are ordinary law, some of which were enacted in the United Kingdom. Some of its important elements are to be found in such documents as the Standing Orders of the House of Representatives. And there is but one house in the New Zealand Parliament. It is possible to make the case that the New Zealand Constitution as it now exists is largely quasi-constitutional. That, however, is not the task undertaken in this chapter. The purpose here is to raise questions about the nature of the New Zealand Constitution as it now exists. The conclusion is that it is problematic in many ways and there is a case for changing it and embarking on a process to produce a codified written constitution.

In short, this chapter aims to embark on a journey away from quasi-constitutionality for New Zealand.

The chapter is in the nature of a report upon work in progress of a constitutional project in New Zealand. The project that Dr Andrew Butler[1] and I are engaged on, with the support of a grant from the New Zealand Law Foundation, will produce a draft written, codified Constitution for New

* Barrister, Distinguished Fellow Victoria University of Wellington, Faculty of Law and New Zealand Centre for Public Law, Global Affiliated Professor University of Iowa College of Law. This is a revised version of a keynote address delivered on 19 May 2016 to the Symposium on Quasi-Constitutionality and Constitutional Statutes at the Victoria University of Wellington.

1 Dr Andrew Butler was born and educated in Ireland, a country with a written Constitution. He settled in New Zealand many years ago and was an academic lawyer at the Victoria University of Wellington before becoming a Senior Crown Counsel. He is now a partner with Russell McVeagh, barristers and solicitors, Wellington.

Zealand. At the time of the conference, the book containing the constitution supporting commentary was in press to be published by the Victoria University Press.

The project has no official status. The project was borne of the conviction that the desultory nature of constitutional discussions in New Zealand over the past 30 years were handicapped by the lack of a developed model to discuss. The constitutional arrangements have been reviewed twice without any tangible result, first in 2005 and then in 2013. Effective public discourse requires some concrete proposals to focus on.[2] We aim to provide a model and stimulate the debate. New Zealand's Constitution needs to be modernised.

The New Zealand Constitution Act 1852 (UK) enacted for New Zealand what amounted to a written Constitution to a large extent, but over the years it was whittled away by amendments. Its life petered out after the abolition of Provincial Governments in 1876, provided for in the 1852 Act. So it ended up, before being repealed and replaced by the Constitution Act 1986, with only about 12 provisions and these provided almost no guidance on how the country was governed.

The Constitutional Society, following the abolition of the Legislative Council in 1950, (an unelected upper house) developed a proposal for a written constitution. Later they added a bill of rights and a package was offered by the National Party in its 1960 election policy. The proposal was dropped after a Select Committee examination.[3] The issue was re-examined by Parliament in 1963 but not taken up.

Since that time there have been significant constitutional developments:

- The Official Information Act 1982.
- The Constitution Act 1986, which you may think sounds like a Constitution. It sets out the main features of the system. But it is skeletal and does not look like a written Constitution as that term is generally understood.
- The New Zealand Bill of Rights Act 1990.
- Various parliamentary reforms.
- The introduction of the mixed-member proportional system of electing Members of Parliament based on the German model;
- Development of measures to recognise the Treaty of Waitangi between Māori and Crown and to provide for redress of grievances suffered by New Zealand's indigenous people.

2 Constitutional Arrangements Committee *Inquiry to review New Zealand's existing constitutional arrangements* (10 August 2005); Constitutional Advisory Panel *New Zealand's Constitution: A Report on a Conversation* (November 2013).

3 *Report of the Public Petitions M to Z Committee* [1961] AJHR I 2-12A. The Society tried again in 1963 again this was rejected after a report of a Select Committee: *Report of the Constitutional Reform Committee* [1964] AJHR I 14.

## New Zealand's Constitutional profile

New Zealand is a constitutional monarchy in which Queen Elizabeth II is the head of state. A Governor-General nominated by the New Zealand Government carries out her functions here. The Queen has many legal powers that are in practice exercised on the advice of responsible Ministers. It has been authoritatively stated that the underlying principle of the New Zealand Constitution is democracy: the Queen reigns, but the government rules so long as it has the support of the House of Representatives.[4] The House has 121 members elected under a mixed-member proportional representation electoral system. New Zealand is unicameral—the House of Representatives is the only house.

Seven political parties are currently represented there. Under the electoral system that came into effect in 1996, usually no party can form a majority single party government as was formerly the case under the first-past-the-post electoral system. The habit has developed that a minority government governs with confidence and supplies agreements with minor parties, representatives of whom may occupy ministerial roles outside Cabinet.

The Parliament is elected every three years and enjoys what is known in Westminster systems as "parliamentary sovereignty." It has full power to make laws assented to by the Governor-General. The Executive comprises Cabinet, headed by the Prime Minister with 20 Cabinet Ministers, seven ministers outside Cabinet and one parliamentary under-secretary. The public service carries out the instructions of Cabinet. There is in addition a wider state sector, including the New Zealand Police and armed forces comprising a navy, army and air force.

There is an independent judiciary with the Supreme Court sitting at the top of the judicial pyramid. The Constitution Act 1986 is the main constitutional statute, but very short.

The New Zealand Bill of Rights Act 1990 is not entrenched. It can be and is overridden by legislation. The courts have no power in New Zealand to strike down statutes. Neither of these two statutes are protected from amendment by a simple majority in the House except for the three-year term of Parliament.

It is fair to say that New Zealand's Constitution is highly flexible, that it evolves with political developments, it has few fixed anchors and it is very hard to find. In this respect the New Zealand Constitution shares many of the problems of indeterminacy exhibited by the phenomenon of quasi-constitutionality. What authority do the various elements have? How binding are they? When will they be followed and when not?

Compared with other Constitutions New Zealand's is highly unusual, most resembling that of the United Kingdom. But the resemblances are becoming increasingly distant and the political cultures are quite distinct from one another.

4 Cabinet Office, Department of Prime Minister and Cabinet, *Cabinet Manual 2008* (Wellington, 2008) at 3.

## The sources of New Zealand's Constitution

A key difficulty with the New Zealand Constitution is that it cannot be found in one place. The difficulties in this regard are marked. Dr Matthew Palmer QC (now Palmer J) found in 2006 that the New Zealand Constitution is located in 45 Acts of Parliament, including six passed in England, 12 international treaties, nine areas of common law, eight constitutional conventions, three and a half executive instruments, one prerogative instrument, one legislative instrument and half a judicial instrument.[5]

The list raises the issue of exactly what measures are to be regarded as constitutional and what aren't. At the heart of New Zealand's existing constitutional arrangements is a large area of vagueness and lack of clarity. In this it strongly resembles quasi-constitutionality. No doubt there are those who would argue that such a situation has advantages. On the contrary, the argument made in this project is that such a situation poses constitutional dangers. No authoritative methods exist under New Zealand's constitutional arrangements to say what comprises the constitution and what does not. So in New Zealand saying a step is "unconstitutional" is a political statement not a legal one. The search for normative standards in such a constitutional context is fraught.

The current New Zealand Constitution consists of a hodge-podge of rules, some legally binding, others not. It is formed by a jumble of statutes, some New Zealand ones and some very old English ones; a plethora of obscure conventions, letters patent and manuals, and a raft of decisions of the courts. There has also been much academic and professional commentary on constitutional practice. Other than parts of the Cabinet Manual, which has no legal status, no attempt has been made to bring the sum of the parts together. An interested person cannot find a clear and coherent statement of the whole framework within which political decisions are made.

In short, accessing the basic material required to understand the current New Zealand Constitution is both arduous and frustrating. It is unsurprising then that New Zealanders speak little of their Constitution and think about it even less. Indeed, it might seem that the Constitution is deliberately kept something of a mystery so people will not bother about it. New Zealand's existing Constitution is so widely dispersed as to be a serious problem.[6]

Concern about the inaccessibility of the most basic rules of how we govern ourselves is neither new nor idiosyncratic. One of New Zealand's leading historians, Professor J C Beaglehole, warned as far back as 1944 of the New Zealand Constitution being "some silk-wrapped mystery, laid in an Ark of the Covenant

5 Matthew SR Palmer "What is New Zealand's constitution and who interprets it? Constitutional realism and the importance of public office holders"(2006) 17 PLR 133 at 142–145.

6 Matthew SR Palmer above, found the New Zealand Constitution to be located in 45 Acts of Parliament, including six passed in England, 12 international treaties, nine areas of common law, eight constitutional conventions, three and a half executive instruments, one prerogative instrument, one legislative instrument and half a judicial instrument.

round which alone the sleepless priests of the Crown Law Office tread with superstitious awe".[7] Fast forward 70 years and that concern remains valid. Two recent official inquiries—one by a parliamentary Select Committee chaired by the Honourable Peter Dunne in 2005 and the other by a Government-appointed panel on constitutional issues in 2013[8]—agreed that New Zealanders do not understand their own Constitution.[9] Inaccessibility is a major contributor to that sorry state of affairs.

The Constitution is the foundation of law and politics in any country. It should be easy to find, so that people know the basic rules by which they are governed and public power is regulated. New Zealand is one of the few countries in the world where a citizen cannot go to a single source of those rules. In the modern age it is frankly shocking that that is so. There are only two other countries in the world that have constitutions as fragmented, unorganised and uncodified as we have.[10] This alone suggests that putting all the rules in one place is the minimum that needs to happen.

The most fundamental aim of this project is to state the Constitution in one place so that it is certain and accessible for everyone. This would move us away from a constitutional system that could be described as operating within a framework of quasi-constitutionality. The unfilled spaces in the New Zealand Constitution need to be coloured in. People should be able to know and see the rules that govern those carrying out public duties. People should know what their fundamental rights are and how to enforce them. A single basic law, accessible to all, allows that to occur. In this regard we echo the words of Professor Robert Blackburn of King's College London, who has been of great assistance to us in this project[11]:

7 JC Beaglehole *New Zealand and the Statute of Westminster* (Victoria University College, Wellington, 1944) at 50.

8 Constitutional Arrangements Committee *Inquiry to review New Zealand's existing constitutional arrangements* (10 August 2005); Constitutional Advisory Panel *New Zealand's Constitution: A Report on a Conversation* (November 2013). Two private attempts have also been made to discuss and conceptualise some of the issues facing our constitutional system, see Colin James (ed.) *Building the Constitution* (Victoria University of Wellington Institute of Policy Studies, Wellington, 2000); and Caroline Morris, Jonathan Boston and Petra Butler (eds) *Reconstituting the Constitution* (Springer, London, 2011). See also Mai Chen *Public Law Toolbox: Solving Problems with Government* (LexisNexis, Wellington, 2014) Chapter 28 for a discussion of the prospects for change.

9 Constitutional Advisory Panel, above, at [9].

10 The United Kingdom and Israel.

11 Robert Blackburn "Enacting a written Constitution for the United Kingdom" (2015) 36 Stat. L.R. 1 at 3. Professor Blackburn was the lead adviser to the House of Commons, Political and Constitutional Committee, *A New Magna Carta?* Second Report of Session 2014–15, HC 463,10 July 2014. This is work that has been invaluable to us in a New Zealand context. Professor Blackburn was good enough to conduct a seminar of interested constitutional lawyers at King's College, London in February 2016 to consider and comment upon a draft of our work.

> The primary argument for a written Constitution is that it would enable everyone to know and see what the rules and institutions were that governed and directed ministers, parliamentarians, civil servants and all senior state officials and public office holders, in performing their public duties.

The time has come for New Zealand to make its Constitution clear and accessible. That need is now compelling in contemporary New Zealand. The ethnic and cultural composition of the people who live here is fundamentally different from what it was 50 years ago. It will change further in the future. Nowadays so many of us who call New Zealand home were born and bred overseas in very different constitutional systems. Twenty-five per cent of the people who live here were not born here. It is only right that we make our system known and knowable.

While New Zealand is exceptionally unusual compared with other nations in not having a written codified Constitution, many New Zealanders probably feel they have more pressing matters with which to be concerned. No public clamour exists for such a development. We will need to persuade people that while New Zealand is a successful country, it would be more successful and better governed if there were constitutional change. Our proposal is not meant as a simple restatement of our constitutional framework as it is now. There are also important aspirational and reformist aims in this project.

The changes we are putting forward in Constitution Aotearoa we believe are a necessary part of preserving democratic freedom in New Zealand, and of protecting the fundamental principles that anchor public power and strengthen government accountability.

So the first point upon which it is necessary to prevail is the demonstration that the current situation is unsatisfactory. The New Zealand Constitution is neither accessible nor certain, echoing the confusion that quasi-constitutionality can engender. So we aim to set out the rules, principles and processes about government in one document so they are accessible, available and clear. That will involve eliminating the need for significant unwritten constitutional conventions and customs which are in important respects unclear. So the first aim of the project will be to remove the mystery and provide an accurate map about how we govern ourselves.

## Existing constitution too flexible?

Accessibility is not the only problem with our current arrangements. New Zealand's present Constitution is dangerously incomplete, obscure, fragmentary and far too flexible. It remorselessly evolves with political developments and is subject to few limits. It evolves in obscure and unpredictable ways that are not transparent. That is the trouble with such a political constitution. It can be compared with the idea of quasi-constitutionality. The Constitution is not fully fit for purpose in the political and social realities of modern New Zealand. That needs to change. New Zealand needs a Constitution fit for the modern age.

Unlike almost all other countries, nearly all of New Zealand's constitutional rules can be altered easily. That is because:

- In New Zealand a simple majority of MPs in Parliament has the power to make, repeal or amend almost any law that it pleases, including any constitutional law.[12] Unlike the position in most other representative and participatory democracies like ours New Zealand judges cannot invalidate any such law on the ground that it is unconstitutional.
- We have a unicameral Parliament, in that our Parliament consists of one House only, the House of Representatives. This means laws can be made at great speed as there is no second House to act as a check. And there is no requirement at all for the Government to consult with anyone before bringing a Bill before Parliament, and it can use numbers in the House to prevent the Bill, once introduced, from being sent out for public submissions. In short, all of the usual legislative practices can be, and are, overridden where it suits the Government of the day.

It would be legally possible for our Parliament to repeal the Constitution Act 1986 or the New Zealand Bill of Rights Act 1990 in a single sitting day of the House under urgency, without any public input. Such an occurrence is unlikely, but abuses have occurred.

For example, in 2013 Parliament enacted the New Zealand Public Health and Disability Amendment Act (No 2) in a single sitting day. Its principal effects were first to prevent anyone ever making a complaint to the Human Rights Commission or bringing a court proceeding against any Government family carer policy no matter how discriminatory, and second, to exclude retrospectively the provision of remedies for past discrimination. It followed a decision of the Court of Appeal that had upheld human rights of some of the most vulnerable people in our community—the disabled and family members who cared for them.[13] There was no warning that the Bill was to be introduced; there was no public consultation on it; there was no Select Committee consideration of it. By any measure, it was a shocking piece of legislation that ousted well-known constitutional protections and removed New Zealand citizens' rights to be free from discrimination in certain cases. Yet it passed in a single sitting day despite an almost immediate public outcry about it. Only another Act of Parliament can alter or remove it. That is how fragile the New Zealand constitutional system currently is.

12 With the exception of six provisions of the Electoral Act 1993, set out in section 268.

13 *Ministry of Health* v *Atkinson* [2012]NZCA 184,[2012] 3NZLR 456,(2012) HRNZ 572. For a detailed discussion of these events see Andrew Butler, Petra Butler *The New Zealand Bill of Rights Act-A Commentary* (2nd ed., LexisNexis, Wellington, 2015) at 853–857.

## The dangers of claiming too much

New Zealand has one great advantage over some other countries in fashioning a written, codified constitution. It is a unitary state, not a federation. Federations, such as Australia and the United States, have states. These states have complicated power relationships with the federal government. The powers of each have to be made clear and there is extensive and continuing argument over which unit of government should be carrying out various functions.

This often takes the form of frequent and contentious litigation in federations. While we propose strengthening local government in New Zealand, we think New Zealand should remain a unitary state. We are only 4.5 million souls and federalism would not be a congenial form of government for us.

No Constitution can give an accurate description of every feature of the complicated nature of modern government in New Zealand. What a Constitution can do is to state the principles upon which governance is based and allocate the division of powers between the principal institutions of government. It must state and settle the most basic issues about how to organise the government. It needs to define the sources of power and their location. It should provide a code of normative behaviour for the institutions, officers and agencies of the state.

The manner in which this is accomplished in a proposed Constitution needs to reflect the fact that a Constitution is for the whole community and not merely part of it. It must establish a framework that accommodates as wide a range of political views as possible. The views of people on many issues differ greatly and the Constitution must serve the interests of all of them.

It is tempting to use the Constitution as a vehicle for improvement of policy and to advance particular policy agendas. But Constitutions should confine themselves largely to constitutional policies. In the New Zealand context it is important to recognise the reality of the exercise of political power in the existing political culture. On the other hand what should constitute a "constitutional policy" is a topic upon which reasonable minds will differ.

The restricted range of what can properly be regarded as constitutional issues rules out the inclusion of many pet policy concerns that people may wish to see included. A Constitution needs to leave wide room for governments to change policies and meet new demands. It needs to recognise the reality that matters change and that a constitution must not constitute a strait-jacket preventing a response to challenges not foreseen when it was drawn up. Any Constitution must continue to live.

We need to remember we have in New Zealand approximately 65,000 pages of statute law, as well as numerous other regulations or legal instruments. One cannot expect to include much of what is contained in Acts of Parliament in a Constitution designed to be higher law. If it is not higher law there is little to be gained from enacting it since everything could be altered at any time with a majority of one in the House of Representatives. The selection of subjects that are not appropriate for a Constitution is not an issue we have found to be easy. There is a tendency to put too much in and make it too prescriptive.

It needs also to be appreciated that a written, codified Constitution cannot save New Zealand or any nation from political disasters. A constitution can restrain the use of power but it cannot prevent intolerance, or bad behaviour or cynicism about government. Nor can it stop all abuses of power. And it is worth bearing in mind the warnings of a famous American, Judge Learned Hand who said in 1944[14]:

> A society so riven that the spirit of moderation has gone no court can save; a society where that spirit flourishes, no court need save; and in a society which evades its responsibilities by thrusting upon the courts the nurture of that spirit, that spirit in the end will perish.

While the written, codified Constitution we propose will be higher law, it is likely in the end to give the last word to the House of Representatives. If New Zealanders are determined to go to hell in a hand cart then, in the end, the Constitution will not stop them, although it will slow them down. And we should not undervalue the qualities of sober second thought.

It is then important not to claim too much for a written, codified Constitution, but that does not mean nothing should be claimed for it. Public power ought not to be at large, untethered and without anchors. A Constitution based on history and custom is not sufficient in the modern age. While a written, codified constitution cannot fill in the whole picture concerning the use of power in a democracy, it can place limits upon its exercise.

What we are seeking to design is a New Zealand Constitution that "holds that the exercise of government power must be controlled in order that it should not be destructive of the very values it was intended to promote."[15] It must be a flexible instrument dependent upon the social and political values of the people who live here. It must protect the freedom of responsible individuals. And readjustments must be made in response to the constant drumbeat of social and political change. So the manner in which the norms and values are expressed in the Constitution ought not to be overly prescriptive or restrictive. On the other hand the habit of Westminster styled Parliaments is to enact legislation of a highly prescriptive nature.

So what this Constitution aims to advance are institutions that are open and transparent. It must create efficient mechanisms of accountability. It must provide for free and open democratic elections for MPs and local government members. It should ensure that government should be designed to be effective.

14 Learned Hand "The contribution of an Independent Judiciary to Civilization" in *The Spirit of Liberty* (I. Dilliard ed., 1960) 155 at 164.

15 Lord Steyne "The weakest and least dangerous department of government" (1997) *Public Law* 84 at 87.

Public participation and involvement in decision-making should be encouraged. Having an accessible Constitution, as we propose, should advance this value. We need to ensure that the institutions can be trusted and are legitimate.

## The state and the crown

We plan to include a number of features that are essential in any system of government. The new Constitution in our view needs to provide for the legal establishment of the State. The term the "Crown" is a common, compendious, ambiguous and variable term in New Zealand constitutional law. The terms "Crown", "Majesty", "Sovereign" and "Governor-General" run throughout the statute book and in many different contexts. In literal terms the "Crown" is what the Queen wears on her head on State occasions as a badge of office. And that is not what we mean when we use the term in relation to government.

The Queen is a constitutional monarch. Government is conducted in her name and under her legal authority. In New Zealand virtually the whole of government is carried out in the name of the Queen. The Queen is part of Parliament, she is the head of the judiciary, she is the commander-in-chief of the armed forces. Government bodies that operate under ministerial or departmental authority are connected to the Crown. As the Public Sector Act 1988 puts it "all instruments of the Crown in respect of the Government of New Zealand."

These great legal powers are tempered by the fact that the Queen acts upon the advice of Ministers who must be Members of Parliament. Members of Parliament have to be democratically elected. The royal prerogative that comes from the Queen, is a source of power for her Ministers.

We have inherited all this from English law and we have altered it very little. The Governor-General in New Zealand acts here on behalf of the Queen and in her name. He is her representative. She is Queen of New Zealand, separate from her role as Queen of the United Kingdom. There are complications involving multiple Crowns in different jurisdictions but these cause little practical problem. The Queen is also Head of the Commonwealth, although no legal powers attach to this position. The meanings given to the Crown have shifted over time. Sometimes the Crown has been employed as a means of protecting the government from legal liability by using Crown immunity. "The Queen can do no wrong" is an oft repeated principle of English law. The Queen is Head of State. This is distinct from the Queen personally.

In some ways the term "Crown" is equivalent to the "State" but in some respects there are important differences. In most European countries public administration is carried out in the name of the State but in New Zealand it is under the legal authority of the Crown. English law treats the Crown as what is known as a corporation sole. It is our view that the wide use of the term "the Crown" in New Zealand is confusing and obscures many different realities concerning the use of public power. Matters would be much more straight forward legally and politically if we used the term "State."

A New Zealand Law Professor Janet McLean has written the leading work in English law on this subject.[16] She sums it up in this way:

> There is a state tradition in British legal thought. It is contested, adaptable and complex. These features have given it flexibility to adjust to changes in state institutions and functions. At times, though, we have been at risk of losing useful intellectual resources which could help us face contemporary challenges.

The Crown in New Zealand wears so many hats that it is a source of considerable confusion and obscurity.

What we are contemplating creating the State and sourcing its powers in this way:

I. **The state and nation of Aotearoa New Zealand**

1. The country known as New Zealand in the English language or Aotearoa in te reo Māori is referred to in this Constitution by the composite name of Aotearoa New Zealand.
2. Aotearoa New Zealand is a sovereign, independent, free and democratic state that functions under the rule of law and is committed to the task of building a successful nation.
3. The State of Aotearoa New Zealand (in this Constitution referred to as "the State") is a legal entity and has a legal personality and the rights, powers and capacities of a natural person of full age and capacity.
4. The exact boundaries of the State territory are determined from time to time by or under Act of Parliament.

II. **Source and exercise of governmental powers**

(1) All powers of government, legislative, executive and judicial, derive from the people of Aotearoa New Zealand.

(2) The State is bound by this Constitution and the law for the time being in force, except to the extent it is inconsistent with this Constitution.

(3) The powers of the State may be exercised only by or on the authority of an institution of State recognised by this Constitution or by Act of Parliament.

(4) The Government established under Article 17 has the executive powers of the State that are expressly, or by necessary implication, conferred on it by this Constitution or by Act of Parliament.

(5) However, the rights, powers and capacities of the State that flow from the legal personality of the State conferred by Article 1(3) may be exercised—

16 Janet McLean *Searching for the State in British Legal Thought* (Cambridge University Press, Cambridge, 2015) at 310.

(a) only by or on the authority of the Government; and
(b) only for the purpose of doing anything that is required for, or that is incidental to, or consequential on the performance of a function conferred by law on the Government. (…)

We note that it is possible to retain the monarchy and create the State. The important point here is to ensure that the nature of the powers of the State are clear and the nature of the executive authority exercised by the Government is also clear.

There has been considerable academic and judicial controversy in New Zealand about the so called third source of power. Can the Crown, or now the State do anything that a natural person can do? There is a division of judicial opinion on this issue in New Zealand.

In an important judgment the Chief Justice of New Zealand took the position that had been approved in England initially enunciated by Laws J[17]:

> For private persons, the rule is that you may do anything you choose which the law does not prohibit. It means that the freedoms of the private citizen are not conditional upon some distinct and affirmative justification for which he must burrow in the law books. Such a notion would be anathema to our English legal traditions. But for public bodies the rule is opposite, and so of another character altogether. It is that action to be taken must be justified by positive law.

McGrath J in an earlier case thought the approach in the passage above was restricted to local authorities and he endorsed the view that the Crown has the powers of a natural person that could then be relied upon by the Police.[18] Professor Bruce Harris of the University of Auckland takes the view that the third source of power exists, that allows the Executive Government to act without explicit authority.[19] Professor Phil Joseph from the University of Canterbury argues such a source of power is dangerous to the values of the rule of law and that all public action must be positively authorised by law, that is to say legislation, the royal prerogative or the common law.

This state of affairs raises some difficult issues for constitution drafters in New Zealand. The model that was most influential upon us has been the third of three models put forward in the *A New Magna Carta?* project in the United Kingdom, a written Constitution. This was put forward in the work done for the House of Commons Committee under the supervision of Professor

17 *Hamed v R* [2011] NZSC 101 para 26. [2012] 2 NZLR 304
18 *Ngan* [2007] NZSC 105.
19 B V Harris "The "Third Source" of Authority for Government action Revisited" (2007) 123 LQR 225 and other articles by the same author.

Blackburn.[20] In that draft the Government received the powers of a natural person. So we adopted in in early drafts[21]:

> The Government has all the rights, powers and capacities of a person of full age and capacity, in addition to the rights, powers, and capacities conferred by this Constitution and by or under Act of Parliament, subject to the terms of this Constitution, any Act of Parliament and the judicial principles of public law.

We have taken in our most recent draft a more qualified position as can be seen in the drafted text above. In particular, we think Parliament has to authorise the powers received by the Police. This is an interactive project and we are very open minded. Views are welcome.

## Other topics

There is no space to develop in detail all the other topics that have to be canvassed and provided for in this project. The following are the major components of Constitution Aotearoa to give a flavour of the range of the project.

Preamble
Part 1 The State
Part 2 The Head of State
Part 3 The Government
Part 4 Parliament and the Legislature
Part 5 The Judiciary
Part 6 Law-Making
Part 7 Finance and Taxation
Part 8 International Relations
Part 9 Defence and Security
Part 10 The Treaty of Waitangi
Part 11 The Bill of Rights
Part 12 Other State Institutions
Part 13 Integrity and Transparency
Part 14 Adoption and Amendment
Part 15 Emergencies and suspension of parts of the Constitution
Part 16 Transitional provisions

20 House of Commons, Political and Constitutional Reform Committee, *A new Magna Carta* (Second Report of Session 2014–15, published 10 July 2014).
21 New Magna Carta, above at 290.

## Conclusion

Our project aims to publish a written constitution "that demarcates the institutions and powers of government, the boundaries between executive, legislative, and judiciary, and sets out the rights of ordinary people in their relationship with the bureaucracies of state and in their means of involvement."[22] That is the principle upon which we have selected what to include in the draft Constitution and what to exclude.

Looked at through the lens of quasi-constitutionality it is a project that aims to take the development of New Zealand's Constitution away from quasi-constitutionality and towards clarity, accessibility and certainty of the constitutional values and norms. Constitutional change is a long game. I have been at it for many years during which time the caravan has moved on.[23] Fresh times demand new measures.

Opinions will differ on what precise powers should be distributed where and this is an important reason whereby the project proposes to solicit comments and submissions from the public before we express our final view on what should be in a Constitution for Aotearoa New Zealand. The project has designed a website for that purpose (see https://constitutionaotearoa.org.nz/).

22 Robert Blackburn "Enacting a Written Constitution for the United Kingdom" (2015) 36, No.1, Statute Law Review 1.

23 Geoffrey Palmer "The Bill of Rights after Twenty-one Years: The New Zealand Constitutional Caravan moves on"(2013) 11 JPIL 257.

# Table of cases

# Table of legislation

# The space between ordinary and constitutional law

*Richard Albert and Joel I. Colón-Ríos*

On 3 November 2016, the Queen's Bench Division of the High Court of England and Wales issued its judgement in *R(Miller) v Secretary of State for Exiting the EU*. The judgement, later affirmed by the Supreme Court, was characterized by very strong constitutional language.[1] After stating that the United Kingdom "does not have a constitution to be found entirely in a written document",[2] the court expressed that this was not the same as not having "a constitution or constitutional law".[3] Part of the constitution, the court stated, "is reflected in fundamental rules of law recognized by both Parliament and the courts".[4] Other parts are "written, in the form of statutes which have particular constitutional importance".[5] As courts in any constitutional democracy, English courts "have a constitutional duty fundamental to the rule of law in a democratic state to enforce rules of constitutional law in the same way as the courts enforce other laws".[6] Since the question involved in the proceedings was framed as requiring the court "to apply the constitutional law of the United Kingdom" to determine whether the Crown could use the prerogative to trigger the Article 50 process for withdrawal from the European Union, the court proceeded to identify the relevant constitutional content.[7]

The "most fundamental rule of UK constitutional law" was the principle that the Crown-in-Parliament is sovereign, and another important rule maintains that the constitutional limits of the prerogative powers of the Crown include its inability to "alter the law of the land, whether it be common law or contained in legislation".[8] Moreover, following the House of Lords, the court referred to the *European Communities Act, 1972* as a "constitutional statute", one of those

1 This is of course not the only time that a court in the United Kingdom engaged in this type of discussion; the case is simply offered as a recent example.
2 *R(Miller) v Secretary of State for Exiting the EU* [2016] EWHC 2768, para. 40.
3 ibid., para. 18.
4 ibid.
5 ibid.
6 ibid.
7 ibid., para. 19.
8 ibid., paras 20, 25.

written parts of the constitution "having such importance in our legal system [that] it is not subject to the usual wide principle of implied repeal by subsequent legislation".[9] There is nothing novel about any of these pronouncements; all of them are firmly based in previous judgements or have long been part of the constitutional tradition of the United Kingdom. At the same time, however, they put the idea of "constitutional law" under some strain.

## Conventions and constitutional statutes

In countries with codified constitutions, "constitutional law" is usually said to be contained in a single document, and the rules contained in that document are more difficult to change than ordinary legislation. Of course, the exercise of political power in those countries may be limited, not only by rules of constitutional law, but also by constitutional conventions that political actors treat as obligatory even if they are not judicially enforceable.

In countries with uncodified constitutions, in contrast, the exercise of political power is often regulated by constitutional conventions. But constitutional conventions are not law; indeed, they normally require government officials to abstain from exercising powers that the law clearly confers to them. What some judges have suggested, and what actual constitutional practice in different jurisdictions exemplify, is that there may be forms of constitutional *law* to which the categories of uncodified and codified do not apply. In the United Kingdom, the clearest manifestation of those forms of constitutional law are what some judges have called "constitutional statutes". Even though they are created through the same procedures that are used to bring into existence ordinary laws, constitutional statutes acquire a special importance as a result of their content. For LJ Laws, a constitutional statute is one that "(a) conditions the legal relationship between citizen and State in some general, overarching manner, or (b) enlarges or diminishes the scope of what we would now regard as fundamental constitutional rights".[10] Because they are materially constitutional, these statutes are not to be interpreted by courts in the same ways as ordinary laws. Moreover, as noted earlier, they are not subject to the doctrine of implied repeal.

9 ibid., paras 44, 82; *Thoburn v Sunderland City Council* [2003] QB 151, para. 62.
10 *Thoburn* (n 4) para. 62. Lord Laws added:

> The special status of constitutional statutes follows the special status of constitutional rights. Examples are the Magna Carta, the Bill of Rights 1689, the Act of Union, the Reform Acts which distributed and enlarged the franchise, the HRA, the Scotland Act 1998 and the Government of Wales Act 1998. The ECA clearly belongs in this family. It incorporated the whole corpus of substantive Community rights and obligations, and gave overriding domestic effect to the judicial and administrative machinery of Community law. It may be there has never been a statute having such profound effects on so many dimensions of our daily lives. The ECA is, by force of the common law, a constitutional statute.

For LJ Laws, constitutional statutes are "highly beneficial" since they give the United Kingdom "most of the benefits of a written constitution" while preserving the principle of parliamentary sovereignty.[11] But in countries with written constitutions, one can observe a similar phenomenon. In Canada, as early as 1985, the Supreme Court referred to human rights legislation as "not quite constitutional but certainly more than ordinary".[12] Some years later, in 1992, the court described the Quebec *Charter of Human Rights and Freedoms* as providing "quasi-constitutional protection" to the right to privacy.[13] A similar conclusion was reached by the Federal Court of Appeal, which expressed that the *Official Languages Acts, 1988* was not an ordinary statute, as it reflected "both the Constitution of the country and the social and political compromise out of which it arose". Accordingly, the court concluded, the *Act* "belongs to that privileged category of quasi-constitutional legislation which reflects certain basic goals of our society and must be so interpreted as to advance the broad policy considerations underlying it".[14] Canadian "quasi-constitutional legislation", like English "constitutional statutes", are of course "law". Yet they are not constitutional law in a formal sense since they are not formally different from ordinary statutes.

## Creation and content

From a formal perspective, rules of constitutional law are created according to special procedures and are not amendable through the ordinary law-making process. The content of the rule is irrelevant; what matters is that its adoption and change are subject to specific procedures. Constitutional statutes and quasi-constitutional legislation not only seem to exist in the space between a constitutional convention and a formal constitution, but their status depends precisely on the opposite features of the latter. That is to say, what makes a – not formally constitutional – rule a "constitutional statute" or "quasi-constitutional" seems to be *only* its content. The way it comes into existence or the way it can be changed are irrelevant: as long as they regulate a subject deemed constitutional from a material point of view (according to whatever standards are applied) they may be attributed a status higher than ordinary laws. The implication is that any rule of law considered to be materially constitutional may be treated by courts differently from any other rule of law that deals with a non-constitutional subject (e.g. non-subjection to the doctrine of implied repeal, increased weight to the policy considerations underlying it, subjection to

11 ibid., para. 64.

12 *Ontario Human Rights Commission v Simpson-Sears*, [1985] 2 SCR 536 at 547. For a discussion, see Vanessa McDonnell, "A Theory of Quasi-Constitutional Legislation" (2016) 53(2) Osgoode Hall L.J. 508.

13 *Frenette v Metropolitan Life Insurance Co*, [1992] 1 SCR 647 at 673.

14 *Canada (Attorney General) v Viola*, [1991] 1 FC 373, 386.

particular modes of interpretation). There is an obvious problem with this approach: whoever has the authority to declare a statute constitutional or quasi-constitutional is able to frustrate the goals of other, even more recently adopted, legislation.

## Surveying the field

Despite the importance of quasi-constitutionality, there still remains a void in the literature. To this day, there is no major scholarly resource addressing the nature of these norms, their functions, and the ways they are being applied (or could be applied) in different jurisdictions.

To be sure, there exists scholarship on quasi-constitutionality and constitutional statutes. One such contribution is the theory of "Super-Statutes", advanced by William Eskridge and John Ferejohn.[15] Their work identifies the intermediate legal terrain, between constitutional and ordinary law, as quasi-constitutional law. They argue that certain statutes exist in this space, and rise to this level as a result of their political salience and importance in the legal infrastructure.[16]

In her chapter "A Theory of Quasi-Constitutional Legislation", Vanessa McDonnell seeks to define comprehensive criteria for recognizing a quasi-constitutional statute or regulation within Canadian law.[17] She concludes that quasi-constitutional legislation should be understood as laws that implement a constitutional imperative, defining those imperatives as constitutional obligations that are derived from rights within the Constitution itself.

Adam Perry and Farrah Ahmed's work, both "The Quasi-Entrenchment of Constitutional Statutes"[18] and "Constitutional Statutes",[19] analyze how constitutional statutes in the United Kingdom have taken on a separate role from ordinary statutes in a quasi-constitutional way. Due to their "fundamental constitutional status", they write, these statutes have become un-repealable – and thus have become entrenched fixtures within UK law.

But in general, the scholarship in this field, until now, has been jurisdictionally-bound in its scope. Rather than analyzing quasi-constitutionality as an independent concept, many scholars have been more focused on identifying quasi-constitutional laws within specific political systems. Scholars have correctly identified that in many countries quasi-constitutionality law fills the gap between constitutional law and original law, but have yet to fully expand on its many forms, functions and applications in a comparative way. This volume aspires to

15 William N. Eskridge, Jr. & John Ferejohn, "Super Statutes" (2001), 50 Duke L.J. 1215.

16 ibid., 1265.

17 McDonnell, *supra* note 12.

18 Adam Perry & Farrah Ahmed, "The Quasi-Entrenchment of Constitutional Statutes" (2013) 73 Cambridge L.J. 414.

19 Adam Perry & Farrah Ahmed, "Constitutional Statutes" (2017) 37 Oxford J. Legal Stud. 461.

become a focal resource for scholars interested in quasi-constitutionality as a whole, from no single national perspective. This is the void we seek to fill.

## Contents in context

The seeds for this volume were planted in May 2016, when public law scholars from around the world gathered in New Zealand at Victoria University of Wellington for a two-day symposium on quasi-constitutionality and constitutional statutes. The purpose of the Symposium was to convene scholars engaged in the comparative study of quasi-constitutionality with a view to publishing a volume that would serve as the first point of reference on the subject. Here we are.

The book begins with a preface by The Rt. Hon. Sir Geoffrey Palmer QC, former Prime Minister of New Zealand, whose tenure as a public servant counts many achievements in public law, including the Constitution Act 1986 and the New Zealand Bill of Rights Act. He has now turned his efforts to codifying a constitution for New Zealand, moving the country away from its quasi-constitutional framework.

The volume is then divided in three main Parts, each of them preceded by a separate critical introduction in which a scholar contextualizes the chapters and offers reflections on the themes the chapters develop within that specific Part.

The first Part, titled "Forms", is composed of chapters that address, from a theoretical and comparative perspective, questions related to the recognition of constitutional statutes and quasi-constitutional legislation.

In Claudia Geiringer's introduction to Part I, "The comparative examination of (quasi-)Constitutional statutes – an unstable discourse", she introduces the three chapters, and explores some of the reasons for disagreements on the meaning of quasi-constitutionality itself. Ultimately, she concludes that the discourse on the subject provides scholars a tableau on which to explore what they are trying to signify when discussing the constitution itself.

In "The rise and recognition of constitutional statutes," Scott Stephenson studies the influence that constitutional statutes have on countries with "capital-C" constitutions, and those without. This chapter first argues that constitutional statutes have allowed both types of countries to circumvent traditional procedures in pursuing fundamental features of the lawmaking process through the second half of the twentieth century. In countries without a "capital-C" constitution, legislators use statutes as a substitute for a formal constitution; in those with a "capital-C" constitution, statutes can substitute the formal amendment process. However, the chapter goes on to argue that, despite the appearance of commonality, important distinctions remain. Namely, that in both systems the judiciary places different challenges in front of a legislature seeking to pursue change by means of constitutional statute.

In Sergio Verdugo's "How to identify quasi-constitutional legislation? An example from Chile", he offers a framework to identify quasi-constitutional legislation in countries that recognize a formal supreme constitution. After distinguishing five defining features and explaining how the sources of those features may impact on the stability of the particular legislation's quasi-constitutional status, the chapter explores the Chilean system for showing how the framework should be applied. Verdugo analyzes the evolution of two Chilean norms: the organic laws and the American Convention on Human Rights in the way it has been incorporated into the domestic legal regime. He also evaluates how the ongoing constitution-making process is engaging with these norms and impacting their quasi-constitutionality.

In the final chapter in this first Part of the volume, entitled "Exploring constitutional statutes in common law systems", Rivka Weill analyzes the dichotomy between regular statutes and constitutional provisions. She argues that constitutional statutes might mean different things to different political actors (including judges) and academics within the same legal system and across countries. Scholars should therefore analyze constitutional statutes along two vectors: what makes these statutes constitutional (identification) and what are the ramifications of such identification (consequences). It further argues that the answer to the first question affects the results of the second. Weill states that statutes are identified as constitutional based on either the process of their enactment or their content, which may itself be subdivided into two classifications: content in terms of importance and content in terms of entrenchment language. Constitutional statutes discussed in the literature and jurisprudence are often treated as though they are made of one cloth, when in fact they belong to different categories based on the justification for, as well as ramifications of, their constitutionality. Weill draws from the U.S., U.K., Canada, Israel, New Zealand and Australia.

The second Part is titled "Functions", and contains four chapters that explore the explanatory power of quasi-constitutionality in different institutional contexts.

In his critical introduction to this Part, Oran Doyle situates the chapters in the field, offers remarks that tie them together, and also pushes forward the inquiries they make. His introductory chapter is titled "Unearthing the 'constitutional' in quasi-constitutionality".

Mark Hickford's "Quasi-constitutionality and the Treaty of Waitangi: historicity and the political," begins by analyzing how one might theorize the political with regards to quasi-constitutionality, as well as broader constitutionalism as an organic concept. He goes on to argue that the dynamic, generative activity of constitutional materiality or reflection is political, and that this possesses a normative significance. Second, Hickford examines the Treaty of Waitangi as an object of deliberation in and through time, a "work-in-progress", which remains a relational and interpretative resource. Using this example, he reflects on how the Treaty might be placed in an analysis of "quasi-constitutionality", problematizing this concept as a putative tool.

In "Quasi-constitutionality in Canada and the weak-form model of constitutionalism and judicial review", John Helis demonstrates that the use of quasi-constitutional legislation by Canadian courts and tribunals goes the furthest within the Commonwealth towards a form of judicial review while also maintaining legislative supremacy. This approach fits within the Commonwealth model because fundamental rights are upheld through interpretation, although Canadian courts and tribunals have extended the interpretative approach to hold provisions of regular statutes inoperable, in contrast to invalid, when they conflict with certain quasi-constitutional statutes. Quasi-constitutionalism in Canada offers an option for jurisdictions seeking a stronger role for the courts in upholding fundamental rights while not uprooting the doctrine of legislative supremacy.

In the third chapter in this second Part of the volume, Richard Albert argues in "Quasi-constitutional amendments" that the difficulty of formal amendment in constitutional democracies has given rise to an increasingly common phenomenon: quasi-constitutional amendments. These are sub-constitutional changes that do not possess the same legal status as a constitutional amendment, that are formally susceptible to statutory repeal or revision, but that may achieve constitutional status over time as a result of their subject-matter. The impetus for a quasi-constitutional amendment is an intent to circumvent onerous rules of formal amendment in order to alter the operation of a set of existing norms in the constitution. Where constitutional actors determine, correctly or not, that the current political landscape would frustrate their plans for a constitutional amendment to entrench new policy preferences, they resort instead to sub-constitutional means whose successful execution requires less or perhaps even no cross-party or inter-institutional coordination. This strategy sometimes results in significant changes that have the functional effect though not the formal result of a constitutional amendment. In this chapter, he illustrates this phenomenon with reference to the Constitution of Canada, though he stresses at the outset that we can observe this phenomenon elsewhere in the world.

The fourth chapter in this second Part is written by Nikos Skoutaris. In "Reflecting and building asymmetries: The role of (sub-)constitutional statutes in Spain and the UK", he offers a comparative analysis of the role that (sub-) constitutional statutes play in Spain and the U.K. in reflecting political asymmetries and creating constitutional ones. He argues that the processes that led to the drafting of the relevant documents have taken into account those very different political aspirations that certain ethnic and political communities had in those countries. At the same time, he shows that the distribution of competences between the various tiers as regulated by those statutes has translated the de facto political asymmetries into de jure constitutional asymmetries.

In the final chapter in this Part, entitled "Quasi-constitutionality in armed conflict detention", Jonathan Hafetz applies theories of quasi-constitutionality to international law and, more specifically, to the law governing detention in armed conflict. Debate continues over the legal framework for detention in non-international armed conflict (NIAC), which includes conflicts between a state (or multiple states) and non-state actors, as opposed to international armed conflicts, which involve conflicts between states. This debate is typically resolved through a conflict-of-laws analysis that turns on the relationship between international humanitarian law, which applies to situations of armed conflict, and international human rights law, which governs outside such situations. The chapter offers a different perspective. It describes how the impulse among jurists, states and civil society to articulate baseline requirements on such questions as the authority to detain, the permissible scope of that authority and the accompanying procedural safeguards exhibits several features that might be deemed quasi-constitutional. While the emerging norms can be trumped or altered by the ordinary lawmaking process (treaties or the development of customary international law), they reflect an effort to entrench minimum safeguards in an area that implicates fundamental rights.

The third Part of this volume focuses on "Applications". The chapters in this Part consider the ways in which constitutional statutes and quasi-constitutionality operate in relation to particular tensions and debates present in various jurisdictions.

This third Part begins with a critical introduction by Dean Knight titled "Quais-constitutionality and the constitutional jigsaw puzzle". In his remarks, he comments on each of the chapters in this final Part of the volume.

In "Constitutionally obligatory legislation: a case study in legal constitutionalism", Lael K. Weis notes that there are important distinctions between legal and political constitutionalism, with regards to quasi-constitutionality. Moreover, that looking to political constitutionalism for guidance has limitations for an understanding of the gap between constitutional law and ordinary legislation within the domain of legal constitutionalism. In particular, it may result in overlooking phenomena within this conceptual space that are unique to legal constitutionalism, and the significance of which can only be understood in terms of a distinctively legal constitutionalist perspective, where constitutional law is identified primarily on the basis of its pedigree (i.e. whether it originates from, or is otherwise traceable to, the written constitution) rather than by its subject matter or its function. This chapter offers a case study in legal constitutionalism that concerns a phenomenon of this kind: legislation enacted to give effect to constitutional rights, both by defining the scope and content of the right and by determining how the right is implemented. Focusing on constitutional rights provisions that have increasingly been drafted in ways that not only contemplate legislation rather than direct judicial enforcement as the primary means of implementation, but that require it: creating constitutional obligations that require the state to enact legislation to give effect to fundamental social values – referred to as "constitutionally obligatory legislation". This chapter provides a single-jurisdiction case study that examines the phenomenon of constitutionally obligatory legislation in South Africa.

In the second chapter in this Part, entitled "Quasi-constitutionalism and informal legislative entrenchment: a case study", Sofia Ranchordás observes that the Affordable Care Act, widely known as Obamacare, has remained remarkably resistant to repeal, despite its opponents' best efforts. She builds a compelling case to explain why and how informal entrenchment forces have helped keep this law alive, while also offering a broader theory about how an ordinary statute becomes informally entrenched.

Franciska Coleman's "Quasi-entrenched living statutes: creating a multicultural rights regime" uses comparisons between the rights revolutions in Egypt and Tunisia and the civil rights revolution in the U.S. to argue that quasi-entrenched statutes are often better vehicles for articulating the rights aspirations of multicultural societies than more traditional approaches to constitutionalism. She seeks to identify the characteristics of quasi-entrenched living statutes that make them particularly well-suited for creating sustainable multicultural rights regimes and the implications of such quasi-entrenchment for rights jurisprudence in emerging democracies.

Finally, in "The quasi-Constitutionality of non-statutory law: executive constitutional interpretation in Japanese Law", James C. Fisher offers general reflections on the utility and application of the notion of quasi-constitutionality, concluding that it validly applies to legal norms reflected in conventions as well as those in statutes. Moreover, he argues that it applies solely to jurisdictions containing a "Master Text Constitution", since it necessarily concerns the relationship between that document and the constitutional legal order as whole. He goes on to demonstrate that Japanese constitutional law contains a norm awarding systemic legal validity to constitutional interpretations by the executive. Fisher goes on to show that this norm is subject to limits, and that it is justified by the particular institutional structures that have traditionally supported the issuing of executive constitutional interpretations.

## The study of quasi-constitutionality and constitutional statutes

Quasi-constitutionality and constitutional statutes form an interesting but so far largely shapeless area of research. The many chapters in this volume highlight areas of agreement and disagreement among scholars steeped in the subject. Our objective in this volume is not to offer definitive answers to the questions raised by quasi-constitutionality and constitutional statutes. Rather, it is to gather important voices in the field to outline the first major approximations of conceptual frameworks for identifying these phenomena and their implications. We hope that scholars will variously build on, critique and use the analyses in this volume to help us better understand what amounts to quasi-constitutionality and how we can recognize constitutional statutes as well as their origins and consequences.

# Part I
# Forms

# The comparative examination of (quasi-)constitutional statutes – an unstable discourse

*Claudia Geiringer**

What is a quasi-constitutional statute and how does it differ from an 'ordinary' statute (or, indeed, from an 'ordinary' constitution)? To get a sense of how unsettled these issues remain (even as a matter of domestic law but certainly as a question of comparative study), we need look no further than the fraught question of terminology. Why, we might ask, do we speak of '*quasi*-constitutional' statutes at all? What work, if any, is the 'quasi' doing here? Why do we not just use the more forthright epithet '*constitutional* statutes'?

This terminological question attracted such energetic debate at the symposium that preceded this volume that it is worth taking a moment to unpick the nature of the difficulty. For those who come from a jurisdiction operating under a 'capital-C' (formal, written or supreme law) Constitution,[1] the term 'quasi-constitutionality' has immediate appeal. It denotes a status resembling in one or more important respects, yet not quite the same as, the formal Constitution. Helpfully, too, it leaves room in the terminological hierarchy for true 'constitutional' statutes – those that are formally incorporated into, or perhaps that share all the formal attributes of, the 'capital-C' Constitution.[2]

The prefix 'quasi' is doing some heavy lifting here. Even so, let us not miss the irony. At least in United States discourse, the phenomenon of quasi-constitutionality is being used by scholars to challenge the dominant tradition of American constitutionalism (one that is fixated on the formal document) and to re-invigorate earlier, and broader, traditions that view the constitution as a complete description of the rules, principles and practices that regulate public power and/or as an embodiment of fundamental values to which the polity is committed.[3] The language of '*quasi*-constitutionality' undercuts this project,

* Chair in Public Law, Victoria University of Wellington Faculty of Law; Co-Director, New Zealand Centre for Public Law. My thanks to the editors for their helpful feedback on a draft.

1 These terms, too, attract debate – as reflected in the contributions to this Part. In this introductory chapter, I avoid entering into that debate and use the terms interchangeably.

2 See, e.g. V MacDonnell, 'A Theory of Quasi-Constitutional Legislation' (2016) 53 *Osgoode Hall Law Journal* 508, 525–526.

3 WN Eskridge Jr and J Ferejohn, 'Super-Statutes: The New American Constitutionalism' in RW Bauman and T Kahana (eds), *The Least Examined Branch: The Role of the Legislatures in*

just as the discourse on quasi-constitutionality seeks to advance it. A thing that is 'quasi', after all, simulates but is not the real thing.[4]

When one comes out, entirely, from under the shadow of the written Constitution, things get more complicated still. For countries that lack a 'capital-C' Constitution, the term 'quasi-constitutionality' is virtually unintelligible. In such jurisdictions, statutes have long been understood as an authoritative (perhaps even *the most* authoritative) source of constitutional law. Why, then, we might ask, have they suddenly become 'quasi'?

Unsurprisingly, then, in the United Kingdom and New Zealand literature, the simpler term 'constitutional statutes' is almost invariably preferred.[5] But this terminology embodies a conundrum of its own. According to the dominant tradition in these jurisdictions, the constitution is a broad stable that comprises all of 'the system or body of fundamental principles under which a nation is constituted or governed'.[6] A constitutional statute is that part of the constitution (so understood) that is found in statute law.[7] This is an expansive definition, and one that (at least in its traditional form) repudiates any claim to elevated legal status for such instruments.[8]

The puzzle is that, although this tradition endures, it now sits alongside of (and indeed sometimes intermingles with) a newer discourse; one that uses the epithet 'constitutional' to denote 'special' in some kind of legally cognisable sense.[9] In other words, within contemporary traditions of unwritten constitutionalism, the adjective 'constitutional' denotes both the common-or-garden and the special, depending on the circumstances and, indeed, sometimes simultaneously.[10] All statutes are equal but some, it turns out, are more equal than others.

*the Constitutional State* (Cambridge, Cambridge University Press, 2006); M Palmer, 'Using Constitutional Realism to Identify the *Complete* Constitution: Lessons from an Unwritten Constitution' (2006) 54 *American Journal of Comparative Law* 587.

4 See, e.g. Oxford English Dictionary Online: '1. Prefixed to a noun with the sense "resembling or simulating, but not really the same as, that properly so termed; having some but not all of the properties of a thing or substance; a kind of"'.

5 E.g. D Feldman, 'The Nature and Significance of "Constitutional" Legislation' (2013) 129 *Law Quarterly Review* 343; PA Joseph, *Constitutional and Administrative Law in New Zealand* (4th edn, Wellington, Brookers Ltd, 2014) 28.

6 G Palmer and M Palmer, *Bridled Power* (4th edn, Melbourne, Oxford University Press) 4.

7 See, e.g. Joseph (n 5) 28–29.

8 See AV Dicey, *Introduction to the Study of the Law of the Constitution* (8th edn, London, Macmillan, 1915) 37–38.

9 E.g. M Elliott, 'Embracing "Constitutional" Legislation: Towards Fundamental Law?' (2003) 54 *Northern Ireland Legal Quarterly* 25, 41 (discussing this tension, albeit in different terms); Feldman (n 5); P Craig, 'Constitutionalising Constitutional Law: HS2' [2014] *Public Law* 373.

10 See, e.g. C Geiringer, 'The Constitutional Role of the Courts under the NZ Bill of Rights: Three Narratives from Attorney-General v Taylor' (2017) 48 *Victoria University of Wellington Law Review* 547 at 569.

From the preceding discussion, it is apparent that terminological debates about how we should describe (quasi-)constitutional statutes do not rest on mere linguistic preference. Rather, they reveal fundamental ambivalences and instabilities in the nature of the enterprise in which we are engaged. Basic questions remain unsettled. What exactly *is* a quasi-constitutional (or constitutional) statute and how has it earned this status? What consequences flow from it having done so? And what function is served by a discourse on quasi-constitutionality, anyway?

This volume may well be the first concerted attempt to deal with these (and other related) questions from a comparative perspective, with the three illuminating chapters that make up this Part each offering a different lens onto them. In what follows, I begin with a brief introduction to each of the three chapters. I then use the space allotted to me to expand on the theme of instability. I explore some of the reasons why we find it so difficult to agree on the meaning of (quasi-)constitutionality (and on its legal ramifications), and I try to tease out both the challenges and the opportunities that this presents for comparative scholarship. Ultimately, I conclude that the great virtue of a discourse on (quasi-)constitutionality is that it provides us a tableau in which to explore what it is we are trying to signify when we talk of the constitution itself.

## 1. Scott Stephenson – the rise and recognition of constitutional statutes

The first chapter in this Part, by Scott Stephenson, uses the phenomenon of 'constitutional statutes' (*his* preferred terminology) as a lens onto the dichotomy between systems of written and unwritten constitutionalism in the common law world. For Stephenson, a 'constitutional statute' is one that regulates 'a fundamental feature of the lawmaking process' (defined broadly to include the basic structure and powers of the institutions of government, and any limitations on the exercise of those powers).

Stephenson makes two central points. The first is that, within both systems (albeit for different reasons) the post-War period has witnessed the increasing use of constitutional statutes in ways that have tested previously accepted understandings of the boundaries between statutory and formal (capital-C) constitutional change. So in countries that lack a capital-C Constitution, statutes have been used during this period to effect change of a kind that was previously considered to fall outside the regulatory competence of the unwritten constitution – most obviously, the regulation of a federal structure, and the enactment of bills of rights. And as well as extending into these (previously off-bounds) subject areas, these new-generation constitutional statutes have sometimes also possessed, or been found to possess, one or more of three 'typical attributes' of formal Constitutions: enactment by means of a special procedure, entrenchment, and/or normative superiority, enforced through judicial review.

Over the same period, in countries *with* a 'capital-C' Constitution, Stephenson points to a parallel development. Whereas previously, constitutional statutes were confined to the role of supplementing or substantiating the formal Constitution, during this period, they emerged as a means (perhaps even as the principal means) to pursue fundamental change. Thus substantial challenges to the role of the state – propelled, for example, by the emergence of the administrative state, the forces of internationalisation and globalisation, the civil rights revolution (in the United States) and the severance of ties with the United Kingdom (in the former dominions) – have been met not through constitutional amendment but, in the main, through legislative enactment.

In these parallel developments, Stephenson identifies a point of seeming commonality or convergence between systems of written and unwritten constitutionalism within the common law world. On the other hand, Stephenson's second point is that this apparent bridging of the divide is, at least to some extent, undermined by patterns of judicial recognition within the two systems. In systems that lack a capital-C Constitution, courts have generally recognised and given effect to constitutional statutes, so long as the legislature has made sufficiently clear its intention to change a fundamental feature of the law-making process. The danger within such systems, however, is that if the legislature enacts a constitutional statute that appears 'too ordinary', the courts may treat it in the same way as ordinary law, undermining its capacity to bring about intended changes.

On the other hand, in jurisdictions that *have* a capital-C Constitution, the danger is the converse. If legislatures enact statutes that appear 'too constitutional', the statute may be invalidated for inconsistency with the formal Constitution. This means that the scope for the use of constitutional statutes in systems with a formal Constitution is more constrained.

## 2. Sergio Verdugo – how to identify quasi-constitutional legislation

Although Stephenson speaks across the written/unwritten divide, he confines himself to addressing the phenomenon of constitutional statutes within common law systems. The second chapter, by Sergio Verdugo, addresses the phenomenon through a very different lens. Verdugo examines 'quasi-constitutional legislation' (*his* terminology) in Western legal systems that possess a formal Constitution. Although he does not exclude common law jurisdictions from his inquiry, his chapter is richly informed by civil law practice, in particular, in relation to the enactment of 'organic' laws – a self-consciously constitutional form of statutory law-making.

Verdugo's project is twofold: first, to develop a theoretical framework for identifying quasi-constitutional legislation (thus facilitating accurate comparative inquiry); second, to explore that framework by reference to the example of Chile.

For Verdugo, legislation is quasi-constitutional if it enjoys some or all of the key features of the formal Constitution – that is, the characteristics that make that particular Constitution distinguishable from the rest of the legal system. This approach is relative rather than absolute; what is quasi-constitutional depends on the particular qualities associated with the formal Constitution in each respective jurisdiction. Nevertheless, Verdugo is able to identity five characteristics which will *generally* render legislation quasi-constitutional. These are: the existence of substantial regulatory overlap with the subject matter controlled by the formal Constitution; some degree of protection of the quasi-constitutional instrument from ex-post facto judicial review on the grounds of unconstitutionality; supremacy (such that the quasi-constitutional instrument can be used to review ordinary legislation); rigidity (such that the quasi-constitutional instrument is harder to modify than ordinary legislation); and inclusion in the constitutional canon (such that the quasi-constitutional instrument is a privileged tool for interpreting the formal Constitution itself).

For Verdugo, quasi-constitutionality is a matter of degree. Quasi-constitutional statutes may exhibit one or more of these features, and may exhibit them more or less strongly. And they can also acquire these features formally (through a constitutional text) or informally (through political or judicial practice).

Verdugo then explores this framework by examining two different kinds of regulatory instrument that have been accorded quasi-constitutional effect within the Chilean legal system: the *leyes orgánicas constitucionales* (LOCs) – a form of constitutionally prescribed organic law – and the American Convention on Human Rights (ACHR), as implemented in Chile. Verdugo uses these contrasting examples to explore the mix of formal and informal elements by which regulatory instruments can come to possess quasi-constitutional effect. He also uses them as a window onto questions of political acceptance and legitimacy. Whereas the quasi-constitutional status of the ACHR has attracted relatively little controversy, the LOCs have remained contentious throughout their history. An obvious reason for this lies in the fact that the LOCs were established by the Pinochet Constitution of 1980. The constitutionally prescribed requirement of a legislative super-majority for their repeal or amendment thus effectively establishes a minority veto power for policies put in place by the military Junta.

Verdugo, however, suggests an additional reason for the contentiousness of the LOCs: the combination of constitutional rigidity with a regulatory regime that is both broad in scope and detailed in style. In the result, instead of constitutionalising broad framework rules that might have good reason to enjoy a degree of stability, the LOCs end up entrenching a significant part of the legislative agenda. In contrast, the ACHR is both more limited in scope and abstract enough to allow for evolving interpretations.

A second and related point of contrast is that, whereas the LOCs have acquired some of their quasi-constitutional features formally (though constitutional prescription), the ACHR has acquired its quasi-constitutional status informally, that is, through judicial and political practice. The quasi-constitutional status of the ACHR is thus more unstable but also more dynamic and adaptable, allowing for informal change to adapt to political pressures. Verdugo ends by suggesting that this analysis, derived from the Chilean experience, may offer insights into the reasons for the contentiousness of formal quasi-constitutional legislation in other jurisdictions, such as Hungary, Spain and Venezuela.

## 3. Rivka Weill – exploring constitutional statutes in common law systems

Whereas the first author prefers the epithet 'constitutional', and the second 'quasi-constitutional', the third author hedges her bets, professing an interest in '"constitutional statutes" and the related phenomenon of "quasi-constitutionality"'.

Rivka Weill's chapter shares Stephenson's focus on constitutional statutes within the common law world. Weill analyses such statutes along two vectors: first, what *makes* a statute 'constitutional' and second, what consequences flow from it. Weill sees these two questions as deeply connected in the sense that the former dictates the latter. The ramifications of constitutionality flow, she says, from the basis on which we have identified the statute as constitutional in the first place.

Weill identifies and contrasts three bases on which a statute might properly be regarded as constitutional. The first is where the statute has been enacted as a result of a process of constitutional, rather than ordinary, politics. Weill's point here is the Ackermanian one: that the legislature may, on occasion, enact statutes that reflect the outcome of momentous constitutional processes, involving resort (whether formal or informal) to the constitutive authority of the People. As is well known, Ackerman suggests (in the United States context) that this constitutive authority can manifest through an 'extended process of interaction between political elites and ordinary citizens'.[11] Weill agrees, and draws a parallel with certain United Kingdom practices, such as (in recent times) the use of referenda. For Weill, this process-based reason for recognising a statute as 'constitutional' must involve a resort to the People themselves. Legislative super-majorities will not do.

Weill accords the highest normative priority to this category of 'constitutional' statutes, arguing that they should be accorded the key attributes of constitutional law. They should, for example, be accorded primacy over regular statutes, and only be repealed through the same (constitutive) process by which they were adopted.

Weill then contrasts this process-derived reason for recognising a statute as constitutional with reasons that flow, instead, from the content of the statute itself. Weill divides these into two sub-categories. The first comprises statutes that the legislature has marked out expressly for special treatment – through the inclusion, for example, of primacy or entrenchment clauses. For Weill, statutory language of this kind does not, by itself, bestow constitutional status but, rather, sets in place a tool that may or may not be recognised (by political actors) in different ways.

The second content-based category comprises statutes that contain subject matter that we might regard in some way as fundamental. Again, Weill does not

11 B Ackerman, *We the People: Transformations* (Cambridge, MA, Harvard University Press, 1998) 187.

regard substantive content as, in itself, sufficient to justify recognising a statute as 'constitutional'. Rather, such a status may be attained over time, in an evolutionary fashion, because political actors acknowledge the special constitutional importance of the particular rule. This conception of constitutionality draws explicitly on Eskridge and Ferejohn's model (in the United States context) of 'super-statutes' – statutes that gain their special status because they 'successfully penetrate public normative and institutional culture in a deep way'.[12]

As will already be clear, Weill sees the consequences of all content-based claims to constitutionality as both contingent and negotiable. She identifies numerous examples of common law courts affirming the relative priority of such enactments – most commonly, through interpretive presumptions, declarations of incompatibility, or rejection (or narrowing) of the doctrine of implied repeal. But she suggests that strong claims of priority (for example, substantive or procedural entrenchment clauses) come into direct conflict with the doctrine of legislative supremacy and, for that reason, tend either to be ignored by the courts or down-graded to a requirement of express repeal. She stresses the revolutionary character of any decision by the courts to uphold such strong claims of priority (which would, she says, signal a unilateral intention to transform the underlying basis of the constitution).

## 4. What exactly is a (quasi-)constitutional statute? Variance, contingency and instability

These three thought-provoking examinations of the subject each, in their own way, illuminate what it is we mean when we call a statute (quasi-)constitutional, and each offer penetrating insights into the ways in which we might address the subject as a matter of comparative inquiry. On the other hand, they also illustrate how unsettled and contingent this basic question of definition remains.

Let us consider, first, the substantial differences between the definitions offered in each of the three chapters. At its bluntest, this is reflected in their respective width. Verdugo's is the broadest, recognising at least five distinct bases of quasi-constitutionality that mirror what he sees as the five typical attributes of a formal Constitution. Stephenson's definition focuses solely on function but is scarcely less wide, given the breadth of the constitutional subject matter it comprehends. Weill's definition, on the other hand, is far narrower, identifying three very specific, and comparatively limited, circumstances in which a statute might be regarded as constitutional.

If we compare the respective criteria in more detail, we see, first, that each author takes a very different approach to the relevance of the subject matter that the statute regulates. Stephenson regards constitutional subject matter (or function) as both a necessary and a sufficient condition of 'constitutionality'.

12 WN Eskridge Jr and J Ferejohn, 'Super-Statutes' (2001) 50 *Duke Law Journal* 1215, 1215. See further n 22 and associated text.

Verdugo regards it as sufficient (as long as there is substantial regulatory overlap), but not necessary. Further, Stephenson and Verdugo define 'constitutional' subject matter in different ways. While Stephenson's definition is fixed (the regulation of a fundamental feature of the law-making process), Verdugo's is relative (subject matter that involves substantial regulatory overlap with the written Constitution in the particular jurisdiction).

For Weill, the constitutional nature of the subject matter, though relevant, is *neither* necessary, *nor* sufficient. She agrees with Verdugo that it is for each state to choose for itself what subject matter it wishes to regulate as a matter of constitutional or fundamental law. But in any event, she considers substantive content an insufficient basis, on its own, to justify recognising a statute as constitutional.

The three authors take similarly varied approaches to the relevance of the process by which the statute was enacted. This is, for Weill, the *preeminent* means of achieving constitutional status. But it forms no part of Stephenson's formal definition, nor is it reflected in any of Verdugo's five criteria.

Finally, the three authors also take different approaches to the relevance, to this question of identification, of the extent to which a statute possesses – or claims to possess – typical 'attributes' of a formal Constitution (such as supremacy and entrenchment). This, again, forms no part of Stephenson's formal definition. On the other hand, Verdugo would categorise as quasi-constitutional any statute that possesses one of these attributes – whether formally or informally, and whether to greater or lesser extent. Weill, too, regards claims of this kind as highly relevant, but would only categorise a statute as 'constitutional' on this basis if a range of political actors have, in essence, acceded to any such claim.

This significant variation, as between the chapters, is also accompanied by a degree of internal instability – or at least, contingency – in the definitions employed by each author. Stephenson, as we have seen, starts out with an expansive, functional definition that includes all statutes that regulate fundamental aspects of the law-making process, broadly conceived. But, as Stephenson acknowledges, constitutional statutes in this broad sense are a longstanding feature of constitutional practice – both in systems with, and without, a capital-C Constitution. Stephenson's real interest is in a narrower subset – those statutes that blur the traditional distinction between these two systems. Thus, a second and more conditional definition emerges from his chapter – one that manifests somewhat differently within each of the two systems. In jurisdictions without a formal Constitution, it comprises statutes that regulate subject matters previously thought to be outside the ken of the unwritten constitution and/or that possess one or more of the 'typical attributes' of capital-C Constitutions. In jurisdictions *with* a capital-C Constitution, it comprises statutes that move beyond supplementation and substantiation of the formal document, while nevertheless *eschewing* these typical attributes.

Verdugo's definition is also contingent and unstable (self-consciously so). First, as we have seen, his concept of quasi-constitutionality is jurisdiction-specific: the characteristics of quasi-constitutionality shift to mirror the particular attributes of the formal Constitution within each respective jurisdiction.

Secondly, for him, quasi-constitutionality is not a question of yes or no, but of more or less. Particular statutes can exhibit more or fewer constitutional elements, and can exhibit them in stronger or weaker, and in more or less formal, fashion. Thus, as with Stephenson, the apparent breadth and simplicity of Verdugo's initial definition is no more than an entry point into a textured and contingent landscape.

Weill's definition, too, is something of a moving target. Even her process-related reason for constitutional recognition is dependent on a subjective assessment of whether the circumstances surrounding enactment manifest the voice of 'the People'. And her two content-based categories offer no more than a starting point for examination of the statute's post-enactment history, with constitutional status ultimately conferred (or not) by political actors.

## 5. Accounting for the variance – why are you asking?

In short, the answer to the question 'what exactly *is* a (quasi-)constitutional statute' is not only unsettled but contingent and unstable. Of course, some of this instability reflects principled disagreement (such as the authors' respective views on whether 'constitutional' subject matter necessarily involves the regulation of public power). But in the space remaining to me here, I want to suggest another factor that complicates and unsettles this definitional exercise: the presence of corresponding variation in the reasons for which such inquiry is being undertaken.

I mean 'reasons' here in two overlapping senses: first, the purpose of the scholarly undertaking; and, secondly, the doctrinal consequences (if any) that each author ascribes to the status of (quasi-)constitutionality.

### *a. The nature of the scholarly endeavour*

As to the first, let us begin by considering the broad (and overlapping) range of descriptive, analytical and normative tasks undertaken in the (quasi-)constitutionality scholarship. These include, but are not limited to:

- Identifying the content of the (small-c) constitution in a jurisdiction that lacks a formal document[13];
- Discussing the phenomenon by which, in certain jurisdictions, statutes have been formally accorded a form of enhanced constitutional status as part of an act of constitution-making[14];

13 E.g. M Palmer, 'What Is New Zealand's Constitution and Who Interprets It?' (2006) 17 *Public Law Review* 133.

14 E.g. Denis Baranger, 'The Language of Eternity: Judicial Review of the Amending Power in France (or the Absence Thereof)' (2011) 44 *Israel Law Review* 389, 415–416 (discussing French organic laws).

- Expounding a vision of legal or common law constitutionalism in a system without a capital-C Constitution (and, in doing so, putting pressure on the traditional hierarchy of laws in such jurisdictions)[15];
- Re-introducing alternative concepts of constitutionalism into jurisdictions *with* a capital-C Constitution (and, in doing so, putting pressure on the traditional hierarchy of laws in such jurisdictions)[16];
- Elucidating a theory of constitutional change that responds to the rigidity of formal amendment processes in certain capital-C Constitutions[17];
- Clarifying the circumstances in which (various) specific doctrinal consequences flow[18];
- Clarifying the circumstances in which (various) specific doctrinal consequences *should* flow[19].

My point here is twofold. First, this variance in purpose naturally impacts on what each scholar means by (quasi-)constitutional. In short, no one conception of (quasi-)constitutional could suit all these enterprises. Secondly, the fact that works of scholarship often seek to achieve more than one purpose helps to explain a degree of internal instability in the definitions proffered within each individual work.

Let us return to the three chapters to illustrate these points. Stephenson's project is (primarily) descriptive and analytical rather than normative; he makes no specific claims about what consequences *should* flow from the fact that a statute is 'constitutional'. Indeed, even as a descriptive matter, he is not particularly interested in tying down the precise ramifications of constitutionality (acknowledging, rather, that these vary both between and within the two types of constitutional system in which he is interested).

This indifference to the particular consequences that flow from (quasi-)constitutionality, whether as a matter of description or prescription, sustains Stephenson's expansive, subject matter-based definition. On the other hand, Stephenson's specific project is to identify patterns of continuity and change, as well as convergence and divergence, in systems with or without a capital-C Constitution. This focus ultimately puts some pressure on his broad criterion for identification which, on its own, is insufficiently revealing of such patterns (because constitutional statutes, in this broad sense, are a longstanding feature of constitutional practice in both systems). Thus, as we have seen, other (more specific, yet more contingent) definitions emerge.

15 E.g. Elliott (n 9).
16 E.g. Eskridge and Ferejohn (n 12).
17 E.g. B Ackerman, *We the People: The Civil Rights Revolution* (Cambridge, MA, Harvard University Press, 2014).
18 E.g. T Khaitan, '"Constitution" as a Statutory Term' (2013) 129 *Law Quarterly Review* 589.
19 E.g. F Ahmed and A Perry, 'The Quasi-Entrenchment of Constitutional Statutes' (2014) 73 *Cambridge Law Journal* 514.

Verdugo's ambitious project is to develop a universally applicable theoretical framework for identifying quasi-constitutional statutes in countries that have a supreme law Constitution. Such a project necessitates an encompassing framework – one that can comprehend within its girth substantial jurisdiction-by-jurisdiction variation. Verdugo's criteria for identification thus mark out broad outlines on which to hang jurisdiction-specific experience. The challenge for Verdugo (similarly to Stephenson) is that these very general criteria are, in themselves, unrevealing of questions of comparative strength, comparative reception or comparative legitimacy – matters with which Verdugo is ultimately concerned. Verdugo deals with this by emphasising the contingent nature of his criteria, with their application to specific cases being a matter, as we have seen, of more or less, rather than yes or no.

Far more than the two chapters that precede it, Weill's project is self-consciously normative. Her project is not simply to describe or categorise an emerging phenomenon but to identify when a statute *should* be regarded as constitutional. This explains why her criteria for identification are narrower than those deployed by the other two authors, and far more focused on questions of process (that is, on how constitutional status might be earned). On the other hand, Weill is also interested in the circumstances in which, and ways in which, political actors (including judges) themselves attribute legitimacy to constitutional statutes. This competing focus dictates a degree of instability in her definition as, viewed through this lens, the question of identification is a matter of political and judicial reception.

### *b. Does the tail wag the dog?*

To repeat, the first sense in which the 'reasons' for the inquiry impact on the question of definition is in the sense of the particular descriptive, analytical and/or normative focus of each work of scholarship. The second (overlapping) sense relates to the doctrinal consequences, if any, that each author ascribes to the status of (quasi-)constitutionality. This is the converse of the point made by Weill as to the relationship between questions of identification and ramifications. She suggests there is a deep connection between the two, with the latter flowing from the former. In other words, the doctrinal consequences of ascription of the status of (quasi-)constitutionality depend on what the particular statute did to deserve that status in the first place.

This is a useful and revealing point. But here, I want to turn it on its head and suggest that the opposite is also true; that one's view as to the specific doctrinal consequences of recognising a statute as (quasi-)constitutional may, in fact, dictate one's criteria for identification rather than the other way around. In this instance, the tail does, indeed, wag the dog.

Thus, the starting point for Weill is that a constitutional statute is one that generates doctrinal consequences that set it apart from ordinary statutes. More specifically, in the course of the chapter, she identifies the following relevant doctrinal consequences: interpretive priority, judicial enforcement of primacy or entrenchment clauses, immunity (or partial immunity) from the doctrine of implied repeal, and the issuance of non-binding declarations of legislative incompatibility. Just as much as the converse, Weill's criteria for identification reflect the circumstances in which she considers these specific consequences are justified and/or likely.

The interconnectedness between questions of identification and ramifications is thus even deeper than Weill suggests. Indeed, in some instances, the two inquiries may be virtually inseparable. For example, Verdugo's criteria for identification correspond to the key 'features' of the formal Constitution. These 'features' are, in large part, synonymous with Weill's 'consequences or ramifications' (including, for example, rigidity, supremacy and constitutional protection). So, then, on this account, the question of identification and ramifications is almost one and the same.

## 6. Expounding the constitutional

In short, we cannot reach agreement on what (quasi-)constitutional means because we do not agree on what (quasi-)constitutional looks like – that is, on what consequences it generates. Indeed, it seems from the three chapters that we do not even agree on whether a (quasi-)constitutional statute needs to generate any distinct consequences at all. Remember, both Stephenson and Verdugo suggest that a statute may be considered (quasi-)constitutional purely because of constitutional subject matter, and without displaying any other attributes that distinguish it from ordinary law.

Weill, it will be remembered, explicitly rejects this subject-matter based approach. Her interest is in statutes that can be distinguished from ordinary law because they generate distinct legal implications, rather than simply on the basis of their 'constitutional' subject matter. And, in truth, much of the detail of Stephenson's and Verdugo's analyses also concerns statutes that generate such consequences. On this basis, we might posit that a (quasi-)constitutional statute is one that generates doctrinal consequences that resemble (on some level) the typical consequences generated by a constitution, properly so-called.

But this very general statement poses more questions than it answers. What kind of constitution does the statute need to resemble – capital-C or small-c, or either? How close must the resemblance be? And what *are* the typical consequences generated by a constitution of either kind?

All these questions remain unsettled. In the remaining space, I want to focus briefly on the third, which I find the most interesting. It is worth noting in passing that each of the three authors in this Part articulate the typical attributes of a formal Constitution in slightly different ways. However, these differences are relatively minor. It is when we try to articulate the consequences or ramifications of small-c constitutionalism that things start to get really murky.

As we saw at the start of this chapter, the tradition of unwritten constitutionalism contains at least two competing narratives about the meaning of 'constitutional': one denoting ordinariness (at least as a matter of judicial doctrine); the other extraordinariness. Even if we accept Weill's advice and focus on the latter narrative ('constitutional' means special), we soon discover that it fractures into multiple understandings of what 'special' might look like.

We can illustrate this by reference to two particularly illuminating works of scholarship. The first is Tarunabh Khaitan's discussion of 'constitution' as a statutory term.[20] He uncovers at least five legal consequences of a finding that a statute (or statutory provision) is constitutional under current United Kingdom law: immunity (or partial immunity) from the doctrine of implied repeal; special interpretation (of the constitutional provision itself); elevation of the provision to a principle of legality (giving it interpretive priority vis-à-vis other statutes); protection from override by 'Henry VIII clauses' (that is, secondary instruments that are permitted to override primary legislation); and special treatment for certain appropriation-related purposes. The last two of these consequences are statutory; the other three arise as a result of judicial construction and thus draw on judicial conceptions of the attributes of 'constitutionality' in a common law context. Khaitan shares the view expressed above that our test for recognising a statute as 'constitutional' might differ depending on which of these consequences we have in mind (that is, that the tail wags the dog).[21]

The second is Eskridge and Ferejohn's elaboration (in the United States context) of the concept of 'super-statutes'. These are statutes that seek to establish a new normative or institutional framework and that, following an extended period of inter-institutional (and public) debate, exhibit a degree of 'stickiness', such that their underlying principles become foundational or axiomatic even while matters of detail remain controversial and subject to ongoing revision. Such statutes exhibit a 'gravitational pull' that bends and reshapes the surrounding landscape. But this is not a matter of formal (and consistently applied) doctrine but of pragmatic, hybrid application. Thus, super-statutes sometimes attract different rules of interpretation (but not always), sometimes trump ordinary laws (but not always), and sometimes reshape constitutional understandings (but not always). Eskridge and Ferejohn analogise this form of 'quasi-constitutionality' or 'fundamental law' to the gap-filling role played by the common law: a form of normative backdrop that influences the way other statutes are read and applied.[22] This is small-c constitutionalism pure and simple.

These two works of scholarship expose, but by no means exhaust, a huge variety of understandings of the legal (and other) consequences of small-c constitutionalism, and illustrate how these may impact, in turn, on how we understand the phenomenon of (quasi-)constitutionality and its doctrinal ramifications. In

20 Khaitan (n 18).
21 Ibid., 609.
22 Eskridge and Ferejohn (n 12). See also Eskridge and Ferejohn (n 3); WN Eskridge Jr and J Ferejohn, *A Republic of Statutes: The New American Constitution* (New Haven, CT, Yale University Press, 2010).

short, we do not agree on what is (quasi-)constitutional because we do not agree on the attributes of constitutionality itself.

## 7. Conclusion: exploring the hinterland

This introductory chapter has emphasised the considerable instability that characterises quasi-constitutionality discourse. We do not agree on what quasi-constitutionality is (or even what to call it), and we do not agree on the consequences or ramifications that flow from it. We do not agree on what the relationship is between 'quasi-constitutionality' and 'constitutionality', and we do not agree on the characteristics of the latter any more than we do on the characteristics of the former.

The foregoing analysis suggests a point of caution for endeavours to address the phenomenon of quasi-constitutionality from a comparative perspective. It suggests that one of the ever-present risks associated with comparative study – that of comparing apples and pears – may be particularly acute in this context. We need to be very careful (as, indeed, are the three authors in this Part) to expose the assumptions that we bring to the table, as well as those underlying particular works of domestic scholarship on which we rely.

On the other hand, the foregoing analysis also suggests how fruitful such comparative inquiry may be. This is for two related reasons. The first is that a comparative discourse on quasi-constitutionality challenges us to explore the spaces that lie between the Diceyan precept that all statutes are equal, and the hard-edged notions of supremacy and entrenchment that characterise standard expositions of the capital-C Constitution. This wide-open constitutional hinterland turns out to be far richer and more textured than we might at first suppose – a fact that the literature on quasi-constitutionality has perhaps only just begun to explore.

The second reason is that a conversation about quasi-constitutionality forces us to confront and question what it is we are trying to signify when we talk of the constitution itself. Ultimately, as we have seen, an argument about what it is we mean by (quasi-)constitutional is an argument about what it is we mean by constitutional.

Against that background, this volume of chapters provides a rich entry point into a relatively unexamined, and potentially fertile, area of comparative inquiry.

# 1 The rise and recognition of constitutional statutes

*Scott Stephenson*[*]

## I. Introduction

The common law world of constitutionalism is often divided and analysed according to the presence or absence of a 'capital-C constitution'.[1] On one side of the aisle sits countries such as Australia, Canada and the United States with a document called 'the Constitution' that has certain attributes (enactment by means of a special procedure, entrenchment against subsequent amendment or repeal and superiority over ordinary laws) and on the other side sits countries such as Israel,[2] New Zealand and the United Kingdom without such a document. While forms of government can be distinguished along a number of lines (e.g., federal versus unitary states, presidential versus parliamentary systems), the presence or absence of a capital-C constitution is an important characteristic that has historically served as an important and illuminating entry point for assessing issues such as the judiciary's role in the system of government, the process of constitutional change and the scope of legislative power. In this chapter, I study the influence that constitutional statutes have on this distinction.

The concept of a constitutional statute is, as the growing body of scholarship on the subject attests,[3] a slippery one. For the purposes of this chapter, I define

* Senior Lecturer, Melbourne Law School, The University of Melbourne. Thanks, in particular, to Or Bassok, Tarun Khaitan and Lael Weis as well as the other participants of the Global Symposium on Quasi-Constitutionality and Constitutional Statutes, Victoria University of Wellington, 19–20 May 2016 and the International Society of Public Law 2016 Conference, Humboldt University, 17–19 June 2016 for their excellent comments and suggestions.

1 The literature sometimes refers to the presence or absence of a 'written' or 'codified' constitution: Vernon Bogdanor, *The New British Constitution* (Hart, 2009) 8–10.

2 Israel's Basic Laws are enforced by judicial review, but are for the most part not entrenched against amendment and repeal through the ordinary lawmaking process. This state of affairs begs the question whether Israel has a de facto capital-C constitution: Ruth Gavison, 'Legislatures and the Quest for a Constitution: The Case of Israel' (2006) 11 Rev of Constitutional Studies 345.

3 In addition to the chapters in this volume, see, e.g., Bruce Ackerman, We the People: The Civil Rights Revolution (Harvard University Press 2014); Farrah Ahmed & Adam Perry, 'Constitutional Statutes' (2017) 37 OLJS 461; Paul Craig, 'Constitutionalising Constitutional Law:

constitutional statutes as statutes that share the principal *function* of a capital-C constitution, but not all its typical *attributes*. Their function is to regulate a fundamental feature of the lawmaking process such as the structure and powers of the three arms of government and, in a federation, the multiple levels of government, yet they lack at least one of the attributes mentioned above: enactment by special procedure, entrenchment and superiority. Part II discusses this definition in greater detail. Two arguments about constitutional statutes are made in this chapter.

First, legislatures in parts of the common law world increasingly turned to constitutional statutes to pursue changes to the fundamental features of the lawmaking process in the second half of the twentieth century and early part of the twenty-first century. In countries without capital-C constitutions, constitutional statutes rose to prominence as a substitute for the enactment of a capital-C constitution, allowing legislatures to attempt to bring about the types of changes to their systems of government that were once generally thought to require a capital-C constitution. In countries with capital-C constitutions that are especially difficult to amend, constitutional statutes rose to prominence as a substitute for amendment to their capital-C constitutions, allowing legislatures to attempt to bring about changes to their systems of government without having to face the considerable hurdles presented by the formal amendment procedure. The rise of constitutional statutes thus cuts across the traditional divide in the common law world, appearing to be a point of commonality and convergence.

Second, however, the appearance of commonality and convergence is potentially misleading because the presence or absence of a capital-C constitution affects the way in which and the extent to which the judiciary recognises constitutional statutes. In particular, the judiciary has placed different challenges in front of legislatures seeking to pursue change by means of constitutional statute. In systems without a capital-C constitution, legislatures must be alert to the risk of enacting constitutional statutes that appear *too ordinary*. If a constitutional statute appears to be too similar to ordinary law, the courts may treat it in the same way as ordinary law, which potentially undermines its capacity to bring about its intended changes to the system of government. In systems with a capital-C constitution, legislatures must be alert to the risk of enacting constitutional statutes that appear *too constitutional*. If a constitutional statute appears to supplant or modify the capital-C constitution, the courts may invalidate the statute for attempting to circumvent the formal amendment procedure.

The distinction between systems with and without a capital-C constitution thus takes on a new form. The rise of constitutional statutes breaks down the

HS2' (2014) PL 373; William N. Eskridge & John A. Ferejohn, *A Republic of Statutes: The New American Constitution* (Yale University Press 2010); David Feldman, 'The Nature and Significance of "Constitutional" Legislation' (2013) 129 LQR 343; Vanessa MacDonnell, 'A Theory of Quasi-Constitutional Legislation' (2016) 53 Osgoode Hall LJ 508.

divide insofar as it allows courts in systems without a capital-C constitution to undertake judicial review of ordinary laws in a similar manner to that which occurs in systems with a capital-C constitution. However, courts in a system with a capital-C constitution have the important and distinctive power to review constitutional statutes for compatibility with the capital-C constitution, which reduces the scope for legislatures in these systems to innovate by means of constitutional statute.

## II. Background

### *A. What is a constitutional statute?*

Before it is possible to chart the rise of constitutional statutes, it is first necessary to identify what they are. In this chapter, I distinguish constitutional statutes from ordinary law on the basis of their *functions* and distinguish them from capital-C constitutions on the basis of their *attributes.* A constitutional statute is defined as a statute that has the function of regulating a fundamental feature of the lawmaking process. By lawmaking process, I mean not only the enactment of law by the legislature, but also the application of law by the executive and the interpretation of law by the judiciary. By fundamental features,[4] I mean, at a minimum, the basic structures and powers of the institutions involved in that process. They include matters such as the way in which the legislature, executive and judiciary are constituted, the manner in which they exercise their powers and any limitations on the exercise of those powers that stem from, for example, a bill of rights and a federal division of powers. Constitutional statutes and capital-C constitutions share this principal function.[5]

What distinguishes a constitutional statute from a capital-C constitution is that the former does not share all of the latter's typical attributes. A capital-C constitution's typical attributes are that it (i) is enacted by means of a special procedure (e.g., a referendum, convention or supermajority vote in a legislature), (ii) is entrenched against amendment or repeal through the ordinary lawmaking process and (iii) is considered superior to ordinary law, which generally entails that a court has the power to invalidate or disapply ordinary laws that are found to be incompatible with the capital-C constitution.[6] As discussed in Parts III and IV, the most significant change to constitutional statutes over the second half of the twentieth

4 While fundamental is an imprecise term, it is a familiar concept in the study of constitutionalism. Jon Elster, for example, argues that 'some laws may be deemed "constitutional" because they regulate matters that are in some sense more fundamental than others': 'Forces and Mechanisms in the Constitution-Making Process' (1995) 45 Duke LJ 364, 366.

5 A capital-C constitution can perform *other* functions such as making statements relating to the identity and values of the polity. Further, it is not the *only* document that regulates the fundamental features of the lawmaking process, as Part II(B) discusses.

6 A capital-C constitution can have other attributes, for example, some capital-C constitutions have provisions that are unamendable. While unamendable constitutional provisions have

century is that they have come to acquire some of the attributes typically associated with capital-C constitutions. It is increasingly common to find constitutional statutes that are enacted by means of a special procedure and/or that are considered superior to ordinary laws. A constitutional statute can, by the definition adopted here, have some, but not all, of these attributes. If it has all of these attributes, it should be considered part of the capital-C constitution.[7]

## B. *The history of constitutional statutes*

Constitutional statutes are by no means new. Countries such as New Zealand and the UK have long existed without a capital-C constitution, thus relying exclusively on constitutional statutes to regulate the fundamental features of their lawmaking processes. Take, for example, the Acts of Union joining England and Scotland from the early eighteenth century.[8] They unquestionably concern a fundamental feature of the lawmaking process (the establishment of a single Parliament in Westminster) yet are not entrenched against subsequent amendment or repeal[9] and are not superior to ordinary law. While constitutional statutes have a long history, for most of that history they were generally not recognised as a special form of law and were often understood to have *none* of the typical attributes of a capital-C constitution. This view of constitutional statutes is most famously captured in AV Dicey's work from the nineteenth century where he stated that the UK's system of government recognises 'no marked or clear distinction between laws which are not fundamental or constitutional and laws which are fundamental or constitutional'.[10] To underscore the point, he set out a hypothetical conflict between two laws where one unquestionably regulates a fundamental feature of the lawmaking process (the Act of Union) and one that unquestionably does not (an Act regulating the dentistry profession)[11]:

> neither the Act of Union with Scotland nor the Dentists Act 1878, has more claim than the other to be considered a supreme law. … Should the Dentists Act 1878, unfortunately contravene the terms of the Act of Union, the Act of Union would be *pro tanto* repealed.

grown in popularity in recent decades, they are arguably not so common as to be a *typical* attribute.

7 On the definition adopted in this chapter, a capital-C constitution does not need to be contained in a single document.

8 Union with Scotland Act 1706; Union with England Act 1707.

9 As the Union with England Act 1707 dissolved the Scottish Parliament, repeal would have to occur by an Act of UK Parliament in Westminster. For some of the constitutional complications that surround this issue, see Vernon Bogdanor, *Devolution in the United Kingdom* (Oxford University Press 1999) chs 4, 7.

10 AV Dicey, *Introduction to the Study of the Law of the Constitution* (MacMillan & Co, 10th ed., 1959) 89.

11 ibid 145.

This long history of constitutional statutes is by no means confined to systems without capital-C constitutions. In many systems with a capital-C constitution, it is well established that the document does not regulate *all* the fundamental features of the lawmaking process. Capital-C constitutions can be terse, leaving considerable gaps and containing provisions lacking necessary details, and thus require supplementation and substantiation.[12] It is, for instance, not possible for the US Constitution's mere 7,762 words to regulate all the fundamental features of the US' lawmaking process.[13] Indeed, capital-C constitutions sometimes expressly provide for their supplementation and substantiation. The Australian Constitution, for example, contains a number of provisions that operate 'until the Parliament otherwise provides'.[14] Further, it permits Australia's state legislatures to refer additional topics of legislative power to the federal legislature.[15]

## III. The appearance of commonality and convergence

A number of important changes to the use of constitutional statutes occurred over the course of the second half of the twentieth century and early part of the twenty-first century. This Part discusses the legislative developments while Part IV discusses the judicial developments. During this period, legislatures in parts of the common law world increasingly sought to regulate the fundamental features of the lawmaking process by means of constitutional statute. Despite the long history of constitutional statutes outlined above, developments during this period are noteworthy for two reasons. First, in systems without a capital-C constitution, constitutional statutes emerge as an alternative – and, in many cases, the preferred – mode of pursuing the types of constitutional change that would have previously prompted legislators to pursue enactment of a capital-C constitution. Second, in systems with a capital-C constitution, constitutional statutes emerge as an alternative – and, in many cases, the preferred – mode of pursuing changes to the fundamental features of the lawmaking process established by their capital-C constitutions, going beyond supplementation and substantiation of these documents. In both systems, therefore, a point of commonality and convergence appears to emerge – the rise of constitutional statutes as a substitute for capital-C constitutional law.

### *A. Constitutional statutes in systems without a capital-C constitution*

Prior to the second half of the twentieth century, a number of functions were generally understood to require the enactment of a capital-C constitution. Two

12 Lael K. Weis, 'Constitutionally obligatory legislation: a case study in legal constitutionalism', this volume. MacDonnell (n 3).

13 Zachary Elkins, Tom Ginsburg & James Melton, *The Endurance of National Constitutions* (Cambridge University Press 2009) 105.

14 Australian Constitution 1901, ss 7, 10, 24, 30, 31, 65, 67, 96.

15 ibid s 51(xxxvii).

of the most prominent were the establishment of a federal system of government and the enactment of a judicially enforced bill of rights. As both functions impose limits on the lawmaking process,[16] they were thought to require inclusion in an entrenched document superior to ordinary laws that derived its authority from the fact that it was enacted by means of a special procedure. For example, in the second half of the nineteenth century, Australia and Canada adopted capital-C constitutions because the creation of a federal system was thought to require one.[17] Prior to the developments discussed below, a bill of rights was thought to require all the attributes of a capital-C constitution.[18] Innovative uses of constitutional statutes in the second half of the twentieth century challenged both assumptions.

Beginning in the 1970s, the UK undertook two major constitutional changes that were federal in character by means of constitutional statute. First, it joined the European Union (EU), giving another government (or governmental organisation) the power to enact laws that bind the UK and take priority over domestic law.[19] Second, it established legislatures in Northern Ireland, Scotland and Wales, and devolved power to them in respect of certain subjects.[20] These developments do not amount to the creation of a *full* federal system. UK Parliament retains, for example, the power to repeal the legislation granting EU law primacy over domestic law and the power to enact legislation on devolved matters using the ordinary lawmaking process. It would, however, be a mistake to underestimate the magnitude of these changes.

In its quotidian operation, the UK's relationship to the EU shares the most salient features of a full federal system – that is, the EU has power to make laws with respect to certain subjects, the UK is bound to comply with those laws, and the judiciary is empowered to enforce the UK's compliance with EU law. The principal point of distinction from a full federal system is its lack of entrenchment. However, even here it quickly came to be accepted that, as a matter of politics, UK Parliament could only withdraw the UK from the EU after first obtaining the people's assent at a referendum.[21] The legal regime thus came to enjoy a level of entrenchment beyond that of ordinary law albeit one that was enforced through the political rather than judicial process. Similarly,

16 A federation limits the levels of government by dividing power between them and a bill of rights generally limits the arms of government by restricting the positions on rights they can adopt.

17 If the Australian and Canadian colonies had not federated, they could have continued without a capital-C Constitution in line with the UK, which is what occurred in New Zealand.

18 Scott Stephenson, *From Dialogue to Disagreement in Comparative Rights Constitutionalism* (Federation Press 2016) 1, 34.

19 European Communities Act 1972.

20 Government of Wales Act 1998 (UK); Northern Ireland Act 1998 (UK); Scotland Act 1998 (UK).

21 Supporters of the UK's withdrawal from the EU did not call for UK Parliament to withdraw, but instead called for a referendum on the subject to be held.

devolution in Scotland has come to take on an increasing federal character following the emergence of a constitutional convention, recognised in law, to the effect that UK Parliament will not legislate in respect of matters devolved to Scotland without first obtaining the consent of Scottish Parliament (the Sewel Convention).[22] Steps continue to be taken that blur the boundary between devolution and federalism, including an amendment to the Scotland Act 1998 made in 2016 that recognises that '[t]he Scottish Parliament and the Scottish Government are a permanent part of the United Kingdom's constitutional arrangements'.[23]

A similar level of innovation by means of constitutional statute occurred in respect of bills of rights. The first example is the New Zealand Bill of Rights Act 1990 ('NZ BoRA'), which empowers courts to undertake rights-based judicial review, and requires the executive to review each proposed law for compatibility with rights and notify Parliament of any inconsistencies with rights. These changes to the lawmaking process were made without entrenching the NZ BoRA or establishing it as superior to ordinary law.[24] Less than a decade later the UK followed suit with an even more extensive set of changes. In addition to the features found in the NZ BoRA, the UK Human Rights Act 1998 ('UK HRA') establishes a new parliamentary committee with extensive human rights functions, including review of proposed laws for compatibility with rights, and vests courts with the power to declare statutes incompatible with rights in circumstances where a declaration does not affect the operation, status or validity of the impugned statute.[25] The instrument is not entrenched against subsequent amendment or repeal. The idea of enacting bills of rights by means of constitutional statute then spread to Australia's subnational jurisdictions, which do not have capital-C constitutions.[26] The Australian Capital Territory and the State of Victoria enacted bills of rights modelled on the UK HRA, and included an additional imposition on the executive to respond publicly to each declaration of incompatibility issued by a court.

An even more thoroughgoing example of the rise of the constitutional statute is arguably found in Israel. In contrast to the abovementioned examples that relate to discrete subjects (i.e. federalism, bills of rights), Israel has almost an entire constitutional system established by means of constitutional statute.

22 Scotland Act 1998 (UK), s 28(8).

23 ibid s 63A(1).

24 Bill of Rights Act 1990 (NZ), s 4.

25 The new parliamentary committee, the Joint Committee on Human Rights, was established in connection with, but not directly by, the Act.

26 Some of Australia's states and territories have, however, entrenched individual provisions that concern fundamental features of the lawmaking process: see, e.g., the legislation considered in *Attorney-General (NSW) v Trethowan* (1931) 44 CLR 394. They are also bound by the Australian Constitution, but it generally exerts only a limited degree of influence over them. As discussed in Part IV, however, that influence has proven to be significant in the context of rights protection.

Drafted and enacted over the course of the second half of the twentieth century, its set of Basic Laws perform all the functions that are associated with a capital-C constitution – indeed, they were created as draft chapters of a proposed capital-C constitution – but are, for the most part, not entrenched and do not make a prima facie claim to take priority over ordinary law.[27] Constitutional statutes, in short, play a pivotal role in regulating large parts of its lawmaking process.

During this same period, legislators increasingly sought to imbue constitutional statutes with one of the attributes of a capital-C constitution – enactment by means of a special procedure. In particular, the referendum arose as a popular means of asking the people to decide on fundamental features of the lawmaking process. In the UK, referendums have been held on the country's membership of the EU in 1975 and 2016, as well as on the voting system in 2011. In New Zealand, referendums have been held on the term of Parliament in 1967 and 1990, as well as on the voting system in 1992, 1993 and 2011.

Not every common law country turned its back on capital-C constitutional law in the second half of the twentieth century. India and South Africa are two prominent examples of countries that enacted capital-C constitutions during this period. Constitutional statutes did not, therefore, wholly replace capital-C constitutional law, but instead emerged as a popular substitute for capital-C constitutional law.

### *B. Constitutional statutes in systems with a capital-C constitution*

During the same period, constitutional statutes also rose to prominence in several countries with capital-C constitutions. While the second half of the *nineteenth* century saw major acts of capital-C constitutional lawmaking in Australia, Canada and the US,[28] with one exception – the 1982 amendments to the Canadian Constitution – they saw no such acts during the second half of the *twentieth* century. Amendments to their capital-C constitutions were predominantly minor in character, for example, codifying existing constitutional conventions that had been, or were at risk of being, violated.[29] Yet the period following the end of World War II saw many developments that prompted these countries to reconsider fundamental features of their lawmaking process, including the emergence of the administrative state, the rise of the global human rights movement,

27 Some provisions are entrenched and two Basic Laws arguably make a claim to priority over ordinary law: Basic Law of Israel: Human Dignity and Liberty (1992), s 8; Basic Law of Israel: Freedom of Occupation (1994), s 4.

28 Australia and Canada drafted and enacted their original capital-C constitutions. The US introduced significant changes to its capital-C constitution, namely the Thirteenth, Fourteenth and Fifteenth Amendments.

29 See, e.g., the 1977 amendment in Australia codifying the convention on the procedure for filling casual Senate vacancies and the Twenty-Second Amendment in the US codifying the convention on presidential term limits.

the civil rights revolution in the US and the establishment of full economic, legal and political independence from the UK in Australia and Canada. The responses to these developments typically occurred by means of constitutional statute.[30]

Significant alterations to the review of executive action in response to the rise of the administrative state were implemented through, for example, the Administrative Procedures Act of 1946 in the US and the Administrative Decisions (Judicial Review) Act 1976 in Australia. The removal of UK Parliament's power to legislate for Australia occurred through a series of Acts adopted in 1942[31] and 1986.[32] Canada enacted the Official Languages Act in 1969, which declared French and English to be Canada's official languages and gave persons the right to receive government services in either language. The achievements of the US civil rights movement were captured in a series of statutes including the Civil Rights Act of 1964, the Voting Rights Act of 1965 and the Fair Housing Act of 1968. The Canadian Bill of Rights 1960 attempted to enact an entire bill of rights by means of constitutional rather than by means of an amendment to the country's capital-C constitution. Furthermore, major statutes were enacted in Australia and Canada to provide for the protection of human rights, especially in the field of non-discrimination, including the establishment of new oversight bodies and the conferral of new enforcement powers on courts.[33] In the 1980s, Australia's federal and state legislatures sought to integrate Australia's judicial system through a system of 'cross-vesting' legislation that granted federal courts jurisdiction to hear cases involving state matters and granted state courts jurisdiction to hear cases involving federal matters.[34] Another possible, albeit contestable, example from the 2000s was the Canadian government's attempts to reform the Canadian Senate.[35] Although the government sought to rely on the formal amendment procedure set out in the Canadian Constitution, it was that part of the procedure (s 44) that allows amendment using the ordinary lawmaking process (i.e. no supermajority in Parliament or agreement of the provinces is required). The result, therefore, would have been an amendment by means of a constitutional statute (i.e. an unentrenched law).

30 There are, of course, some exceptions: see, e.g., the 1946 amendment in Australia expanding the federal government's power over social security and the Nineteenth Amendment in the US prohibiting denial of the right to vote based on sex.

31 Statute of Westminster Adoption Act 1942 (Aus).

32 Australia Act 1986 (Aus); Australia Act 1986 (UK).

33 Racial Discrimination Act 1975 (Aus); Sex Discrimination Act 1984 (Aus); Australian Human Rights Commission Act 1986 (Aus); Disability Discrimination Act 1992 (Aus); Age Discrimination Act 2004 (Aus); Canadian Human Rights Act 1977 (Can).

34 In each jurisdiction, the short title of the Act was Jurisdiction of Courts (Cross-Vesting) Act 1987.

35 Bill S-4 (30 May 2006), C-43 (13 December 2006). These bills lapsed at the end of the first session of Parliament, but were reintroduced in the second session as C-19 and C-20 respectively. Bill C-19 was reintroduced again in 2009 as Bill S-7.

As even this small set of examples illustrates, the fundamental features of the law-making process in Australia, Canada and the US did not remain fixed during over the course of the second half of the twentieth century even though the text of their capital-C constitutions mostly did. Part of the explanation for the shift to constitutional statutes as the principal driver of constitutional change is the rigidity of the capital-C constitutions in these countries. The documents that they adopted in the eighteenth and nineteenth centuries included amendment procedures that, in practice, turned out to impose significant barriers to reform. The Australian Constitution requires amendments to be approved by the federal legislature, by a majority of voters nationally and by a majority of voters in a majority of states. Prior to 1982, UK Parliament was responsible for amending the Canadian Constitution. That power was exercised at the request of Canada and a practice – if not also a constitutional convention – existed whereby the Canadian federal government would not submit a request to the UK without first obtaining the consent of the provinces if the proposed amendment affected the provinces.[36] The US Constitution requires an amendment to be proposed either by a joint resolution of two-thirds of the House and Senate or by a national convention called by Congress at the request of two-thirds of the states that is then ratified by three-fourths of the states either through their legislatures or ratifying conventions.[37]

The federal character of these three countries helps explain their onerous amendment procedures. Each procedure is designed to protect the subnational polities from the central government. While the central government generally takes the lead in proposing constitutional amendments, approval is also required from, in Australia, the states' voters, in Canada, the provincial governments and, in the US, state legislatures or state ratifying conventions. This hurdle arguably became increasingly difficult to surmount over the course of the twentieth century as most major constitutional changes were directed towards empowering the centre over the periphery. In particular, World Wars I and II prompted a consolidation of power in national governments to conduct military operations and engendered the idea that each country was a single nation rather than a collection of states or provinces. As Bruce Ackerman put it in the US context, the Constitution's amendment procedure

> made sense for [the Founders], but it no longer makes sense for us. … We understand ourselves today as Americans first and Californians second. But the Founders wrote Article V for a people who thought of themselves primarily as New Yorkers or Georgians. We have become a nation-centered people stuck with a state-centered system of formal revision.[38]

36 There was some uncertainty as to the precise scope and content of the convention, especially whether it required the consent of all provinces or only a substantial majority. These questions were addressed in *Reference Re Resolution to Amend the Constitution* [1981] 1 SCR 753.

37 US Constitution 1788, Art V.

38 Ackerman (n 3) 28.

This trend towards centralisation only accelerated with the proliferation of international law instruments, which are generally ratified and implemented at the national level, and globalisation, which often requires nationwide responses.[39] These centripetal forces pushed up against the centrifugal features of the amendment procedures, decreasing the attractiveness and feasibility of pursuing constitutional change through amendment of the capital-C constitution.

The origins of many of the constitutional statutes mentioned above can be understood as responses to the rigidities of each country's capital-C constitution. Canada's Bill of Rights 1960, for example, emerged after Prime Minister John Diefenbaker initially sought to insert a bill of rights into the Canadian Constitution, but abandoned the plan after it became clear he would be unable to secure provincial approval.[40] Prime Minister Stephen Harper's efforts to reform the Canadian Senate by means of s 44 came against a background of repeated failures to reform the Senate with the approval of the provinces. There had been at least twenty-eight major proposals for Senate reform since the early 1970s, all of which were unsuccessful.[41] The failure of the First Reconstruction to end racial discrimination in the US led the key protagonists of the Second Reconstruction – that is, the civil rights movement – to adopt a different approach of using statutes, which would allow for more comprehensive regulation so that less room for manoeuvre from recalcitrant parties was left as well as more flexibility so that those regulations could be updated as circumstances changed.[42] In Australia, the preference for statutory forms of rights protection emerged after a number of failed attempts to amend the Constitution to include new, or expanding existing, rights provisions.[43] In 2008, for example, Prime Minister Kevin Rudd rejected constitutional rights reform in favour of statutory rights reform, establishing a committee to investigate the possibility of enacting a bill of rights that was explicitly prohibited from considering options that involved constitutional amendment.[44]

## C. *Transcending the divide*

The rise of constitutional statutes across parts of the common law world during the second half of the twentieth century cuts across the traditional divide between countries with and without a capital-C constitution, often in a striking

39 This is not to deny that there were also important developments in the other direction such as the Quiet Revolution in Quebec.

40 Stephenson (n 18) 17–18.

41 Serge Joyal, *Protecting Canadian Democracy: The Senate You Never Knew* (McGill-Queen's Press 2003) ch 2.

42 Ackerman (n 3) ch 1.

43 For details, see Scott Stephenson, 'Rights Protection in Australia' in Adrienne Stone & Cheryl Saunders (eds), *Oxford Handbook of the Australian Constitution* (Oxford University Press 2018).

44 ibid. Even this less ambitious agenda failed to produce a bill of rights: Human Rights (Parliamentary Scrutiny) Act 2011 (Aus).

fashion. For example, the bills of rights enacted as constitutional statutes are the product of constitutional designers reaching across the divide on multiple occasions. In drafting their instruments, New Zealand and the UK drew on experiences from Canada, and Australia drew on experiences from New Zealand and the UK (as well as Canada). The points of overlap among the bills of rights are so extensive that it is possible to speak of developments in these four countries – two with a capital-C constitution and two without – as forming a single approach to rights protection.[45]

Constitutional statutes thus appear to be a point of commonality and convergence between the two common law constitutional traditions. It represents a step away from the tradition of capital-C constitutional law, allowing legislatures to pursue major reforms to government without worrying about the constraining effects of entrenchment on future generations. And it represents a step away from the traditions in systems without a capital-C constitution, allowing legislatures to engage in comprehensive constitutional reform on issues such as federalism and rights protection that were previously thought to require capital-C constitutional law. The constitutional statute, in short, appears to occupy a middle ground between the two traditions that countries from both sides of the aisle have embraced.

## IV. Points of judicial difference and divergence

Appearances can, however, be misleading. Once we turn to examine how courts have responded to the rise of the constitutional statute, an important distinction between systems with and systems without a capital-C constitution emerges. While there continues to be points of commonality and convergence insofar as judges have at different times embraced and resisted constitutional statutes in both systems, the trend of judicial decision-making reveals distinctive challenges for legislatures in each system.

### *A. Constitutional statutes in systems without a capital-C constitution*

In systems without a capital-C constitution, legislatures have not encountered much difficulty in securing significant constitutional change by means of constitutional statute. Courts have shown a willingness to embrace constitutional statutes, modifying and even abandoning longstanding constitutional principles in order to recognise and distinguish them from ordinary law. Indeed,

45 Mark Tushnet, *Weak Courts, Strong Rights: Judicial Review and Social Welfare Rights in Comparative Constitutional Law* (Princeton University Press 2008); Stephen Gardbaum, *The New Commonwealth Model of Constitutionalism: Theory and Practice* (Cambridge University Press 2013); Janet L. Hiebert and James B. Kelly, *Parliamentary Bills of Rights: The Experiences of New Zealand and the United Kingdom* (Cambridge University Press 2015); Stephenson (n 18). That is not to say that the presence or absence of a capital-C constitution has no effect on the instruments: see Stephenson (n 18) ch 9.

constitutional statutes have come to be understood as a distinctive form of law in large part due to the judicial decisions in these countries mapping their contours and consequences. The judiciary has, in short, played a pivotal part in contributing to the rise of constitutional statutes in systems without a capital-C constitution.

The UK provides the most prominent example of a judiciary coming to recognise constitutional statutes as a distinct form of law. The process began in the early 1990s with the *Factortame* cases,[46] which significantly modified, if not outright abolished,[47] the keystone of the UK constitution, the principle of parliamentary sovereignty. Contrary to the traditional understanding of that principle, the House of Lords disapplied a *later* statue, the Merchant Shipping Act 1988, for non-compliance with an *earlier* statute, the European Communities Act 1972 ('ECA'). While academics were quick to acknowledge the constitutional significance of this development,[48] judges were not. There was little discussion in *Factortame* about the broader implications of the judgement.

Then came the judgement of Laws LJ in *Thoburn*,[49] a decision of an intermediate appellate court that recognised the significance of *Factortame* and sought to situate the ECA within a general category of constitutional statutes. He said:

> We should recognise a hierarchy of Acts of Parliament: as it were 'ordinary' statutes and 'constitutional' statutes. The two categories must be distinguished on a principled basis. ... Ordinary statutes may be impliedly repealed. Constitutional statutes may not.[50]

He suggested that constitutional statutes should be identified as those laws that alter relations between government and individual 'in some general, overarching manner' or alter the scope of fundamental rights – in other words, statutes that affect the fundamental features of government.[51] His non-exhaustive list of constitutional statutes covered laws on a range of subjects – fundamental rights (the Magna Carta 1297, the Bill of Rights 1689 and the UK HRA), the composition of the state (the Union with Scotland Act 1706), representation (the Representation of the People Acts 1832, 1867 and 1884), EU membership (the ECA) and devolution (the Scotland Act 1998 and the Government of Wales Act 1998).

About a decade later, the UK Supreme Court began to follow suit. In 2012, Lord Hope in *H v Lord Advocate* observed that the Scotland Act 1998 is likely

46 *R v Secretary of State for Transport; Ex parte Factortame Ltd (No 1)* [1990] 2 AC 85; *R v Secretary of State for Transport; Ex parte Factortame Ltd (No 2)* [1991] 1 AC 603.

47 N. W. Barber, 'The Afterlife of Parliamentary Sovereignty' (2011) 9 International J of Constitutional L 144.

48 See, e.g., HWR Wade, 'Sovereignty – Revolution or Evolution?' (1996) 112 LQR 568.

49 *Thoburn v Sunderland City Council* [2003] QB 151.

50 ibid [62]–[63].

51 ibid [62].

immune from implied repeal 'because of the fundamental constitutional nature of the settlement that was achieved by the Scotland Act.'[52] In 2014, Lords Neuberger and Mance in *R (HS2 Action Alliance Ltd) v Secretary of State for Transport* noted that the UK has a number of constitutional instruments, citing a slightly expanded set of statutes to those mentioned by Laws LJ in *Thoburn*.[53]

The judiciary has also recognised another change to a fundamental feature of the lawmaking process that has occurred by means of constitutional statute. Section 3 of the UK HRA requires courts to interpret statutes in a manner that is compatible with rights. The courts have construed this provision to include the ability to rewrite a statute by adding or removing words contrary to the intention of Parliament in certain circumstances.[54] This broad understanding of s 3 is a significant alteration to the respective roles of Parliament and the judiciary because it allows courts to exercise a power that is in some situations arguably *more* disruptive than the power associated with a system of capital-C constitutional law – that is, the power to invalidate statutes for incompatibility with the capital-C constitution. A power to rewrite statutes not only allows the judiciary to invalidate the legislature's position on rights as expressed in statute, but also allows the judiciary to install its position on rights into law by rewriting the statute. By contrast, a power of invalidation allows the judiciary to invalidate the legislature's position on rights as expressed in statute, but does not allow it to install an alternative position.[55]

In Israel, the Supreme Court has taken even greater steps to recognise its set of constitutional statutes. In 1995, the Court declared in the *Bank Mizrahi* case[56] that the enactment of two Basic Laws in 1992 containing supremacy clauses signified the elevation of *all* Basic Laws to a position of supremacy vis-à-vis other laws, and, consequently, the conferral of a power on the judiciary to invalidate ordinary laws for incompatibility with them. Barak CJ did not shy away from recognising the significance of this development, comparing the judgement to that of Marshall J in the US case of *Marbury v Madison*.[57]

Not all constitutional statutes have been embraced in all systems without a capital-C constitution. They have been greeted with greater equivocation in New Zealand where courts have, in general, refused to go as far as their counterparts in the UK in recognising a distinction between constitutional statutes

52 [2013] 1 AC 413, [30].

53 [2014] 1 WLR 324, [207].

54 See, e.g., *Ghaidan v Godin-Mendoza* [2004] 2 AC 557.

55 Stephenson (n 18) 156–7; Aileen Kavanagh, 'What's So Weak about 'Weak-Form Judicial Review?' The Case of the UK Human Rights Act 1998' (2015) 13 International J of Constitutional L 1008, 1019.

56 *United Mizrahi Bank Ltd v Migdal Collective Vill* [1995] 49 (4) PD 221.

57 5 US 137 (1803). For a discussion of the Court invocation of *Marbury v Madison*, see Rivka Weill, 'Hybrid Constitutionalism: The Israeli Case for Judicial Review and Why We Should Care' (2012) 30 Berkeley J of International L 349, 374.

and ordinary statutes.[58] With respect to the Bill of Rights Act 1990, they have construed its interpretive provision in line with pre-existing principles of statutory interpretation rather than, as in the UK, adopting a construction that confers new powers on the judiciary.[59] The lack of special judicial recognition in respect of the Act is not, however, entirely surprising. Courts are not only prohibited from disapplying statutes enacted after the Act for incompatibility with rights, but also statutes enacted *before* the Act.[60] This position differs from the position of other ordinary laws where a later statute generally prevails over an incompatible earlier statute.[61] New Zealand's experience thus demonstrates that it is possible for courts to treat constitutional statutes in broadly the same manner as ordinary law if they are not prompted to recognise their constitutional status. This point is considered in more detail below.

### B. *Constitutional statutes in systems with a capital-C constitution*

As in systems without a capital-C constitution, there is a mixture of judicial embrace and ambivalence towards constitutional statutes in systems with a capital-C constitution. On the one hand, in the mid-1980s the Supreme Court of Canada declared provincial human rights legislation to be a form of 'fundamental law' to which the doctrine of implied repeal does not apply.[62] In 1996, the Court described such legislation as enjoying '*quasi*-constitutional status'.[63] In 2002, Iacobucci and Bastarache JJ suggested that 'this Court has repeatedly reiterated the view that human rights legislation has a unique quasi-constitutional nature and ought to be interpreted in a liberal and purposive manner in order to advance the broad policy considerations underlying it'.[64] On the other hand, the Court adopted narrow constructions of the rights contained in the Bill of Rights 1960, having found only one statute to be incompatible with rights since its enactment.[65] Australia's bills of rights have met a similar fate, with the courts

58 Rebecca Prebble, 'Constitutional Statutes and Implied Repeal: The Thoburn Decision and the Consequences for New Zealand' (2005) 36 Victoria University of Wellington LR 291.

59 *Hansen v R* [2007] 3 NZLR 1. An intermediate court of appeal has, however, implied a new power to issue non-binding declarations of incompatibility into the Act, describing the statute as 'ordinary legislation only in the sense that it is not entrenched. Its substance is of constitutional importance': *Attorney-General v Taylor* [2017] NZCA 215, [79].

60 Bill of Rights Act 1990 (NZ), s 4.

61 *Ellen Street Estates Ltd v Minister of Health* [1934] 1 KB 590, 597; *Pickin v British Railways Board* [1974] AC 765, 789.

62 *Insurance Corporation of British Columbia v Heerspink* [1982] 2 SCR 145, 158; *Winnipeg School Division No 1 v Craton* [1985] 2 SCR 150, [4].

63 *Newfoundland Association of Public Employees v Newfoundland (Green Bay Health Care Centre)* [1996] 2 SCR 3, [20] (emphasis in original).

64 *B v Ontario (Human Rights Commission)* [2002] 3 SCR 403, [44].

65 *R v Drybones* [1970] SCR 282.

adopting narrow constructions of the rights[66] and construing the operative provisions in line with pre-existing principles of statutory interpretation.[67]

There is, however, a significant point of distinction between the judicial recognition of constitutional statutes in systems with and in systems without a capital-C constitution. Courts in systems with a capital-C constitution have the power to review constitutional statutes for compatibility with the capital-C constitution and, importantly, have not hesitated in using this power to reject legislative attempts to use constitutional statutes to change fundamental features of the lawmaking process – that is, to resist the rise of the constitutional statute. These rejections have occurred even where the constitutional statute would have generated significant benefits to the polity and even where it would not have conflicted with the express terms of the capital-C constitution. In Australia, the High Court in *Re Wakim; Ex parte McNally*[68] invalidated a central element of the cross-vesting scheme introduced above, holding that federal courts could not be invested with state jurisdiction. This prohibition was not expressly set out in the Constitution, but rather inferred from the absence of a reference to state jurisdiction in the provisions relating to the conferral of jurisdiction on federal courts. The Court maintained this view even though the legislation sought to introduce a scheme that would 'be very convenient and usually less expensive and time-consuming for litigants'.[69] In *Momcilovic v The Queen*,[70] the Court indicated that it would not be constitutionally permissible for the federal legislature to enact a bill of rights similar to that found in the Australian Capital Territory, State of Victoria and the UK because a crucial element – the non-binding declaration of incompatibility – would violate the Australian Constitution's separation of powers doctrine. Again, there is nothing in the terms of the Constitution that prohibit federal courts from issuing non-binding remedies, with the finding following from the narrow definition of judicial power that the Court has adopted in its separation-of-powers jurisprudence.

In Canada, in addition to its underenforcement of the Bill of Rights 1960, the Supreme Court repudiated Prime Minister Harper's proposal to reform the Senate using s 44 of the Constitution, holding that the proposed changes would require compliance with the more onerous amendment procedure.[71] The Court maintained this position by relying on a number of unwritten features of the Constitution, including it 'basic structure'.[72]

Finally, in the US, the Supreme Court began to unravel the Voting Rights Act of 1965 in 2013 in *Shelby County v Holder* by invalidating the requirement for certain jurisdictions to require federal preclearance before implementing any changes to

66 See, e.g., *Bare v Small* [2013] VSC 129.
67 *Momcilovic v The Queen* (2011) 245 CLR 1.
68 (1999) 198 CLR 511.
69 ibid [34] (McHugh J).
70 (2011) 245 CLR 1.
71 *Reference re Senate Reform* [2014] 1 SCR 704.
72 ibid [27].

their voting laws or practices.[73] The Court held that the formula for determining affected jurisdictions was no longer responsive to currents needs even though Congress had revisited the issue and specifically reauthorised the provision in 2006.[74]

## C. A new point of distinction

A new point of distinction between systems with and without capital-C constitutions emerges from these patterns of judicial recognition. From the experiences of Israel and the UK, it appears that it is possible for a legislature to change fundamental features of the lawmaking process, and in particular the judiciary's role in that process, in a system without a capital-C constitution by means of constitutional statute. However, as New Zealand's experience demonstrates, legislatures must be alert to the possibility of enacting constitutional statutes that appear *too ordinary*. Courts will treat constitutional statutes no differently from ordinary law – for example, applying the ordinary principles of statutory interpretation – if they make no explicit or implicit claim to constitutional status, thus warranting different treatment from ordinary law. While this scenario is also a possibility in systems with a capital-C constitution, it presents, at least in one respect, a more intractable problem in systems without a capital-C constitution. In systems with a capital-C constitution, there is a clear benchmark that a legislature can aim to meet if it wants to change a fundamental feature of the lawmaking process – the capital-C constitution's formal amendment procedure. In systems without a capital-C constitution, no such benchmark exists. As a result, legislatures do not know what they must include in, or how emphatically they must word, a constitutional statute to ensure it receives the appropriate form of judicial recognition. For instance, would the UK's judiciary have construed s 3 of the UK HRA (the interpretive provision) in line with the ordinary principles of statutory interpretation if that provision had been worded differently? If so, which word or combination of words tipped the balance? If not, which feature(s) of the UK HRA make the explicit or implicit claim to warrant different treatment from ordinary law?

By contrast, in systems with a capital-C constitution, legislatures must be alert to the possibility of enacting constitutional statutes that appear *too constitutional*. If a legislature enacts constitutional statutes that appear to modify or supplant the capital-C constitution, the judiciary is likely to invalidate them for attempting to amend the capital-C constitution without use of the formal amendment procedure – that is, for attempting to circumvent the capital-C constitution. As the experiences of Australia and Canada suggest, legislatures must be especially careful because courts are prepared to invalidate constitutional statutes even if they do not violate the express terms of the Constitution, but instead violate an implication, principle or structure. As the experience of

73 570 US 2 (2013).

74 There were other dimensions to the Court's reasoning, including that the provisions imposed an impermissible burden on state sovereignty.

Australia suggests, courts are prepared to invalidate constitutional statutes even if they serve a useful purpose and the position set out in the capital-C constitution is only productive of delay and cost. And as the experience of the US suggests, courts are prepared to invalidate constitutional statutes even if they concern a matter of great social importance and were, prior to enactment, accompanied by a period of extraordinary popular deliberation and support.[75]

The rise of constitutional statutes thus alters rather than eliminates the divide between systems with and without a capital-C constitution. As Israel and the UK's experience suggests, courts in systems without a capital-C constitution now exercise strong powers to review ordinary laws for compatibility with a set of higher legal norms. Thus, one traditional point of distinction between the two systems – the presence or absence of judicial review of statutes – is significantly eroded. However, as the experiences of Australia, Canada and the US suggest, courts in systems with a capital-C constitution have the power to review constitutional statutes for compatibility with the capital-C constitution. Not only does this maintain a point of distinction between the roles of the judiciary in the two systems, but it also maintains a point of distinction between the roles of the legislature. While legislatures in systems without a capital-C constitution appear to have broad discretion to change the fundamental features of the lawmaking process by means of constitutional statute, there appears to be an upper limit to what legislatures can achieve in systems with a capital-C constitution.

## V. Conclusion

The rise of constitutional statutes across parts of the common law world in the second half of the twentieth century is arguably a product of the perceived rigidity of some capital-C constitutions. For systems without one, constitutional statutes developed as a means of achieving the same constitutional goals while leaving future legislatures free to amend and repeal the resulting laws as they see fit. For systems with one, constitutional statutes developed as an alternative means of pursuing constitutional change. Yet the constitutional statute has not proven to be a wholly effective method of escaping one's constitutional history. The traditional divide lives on albeit in a new form. Patterns of judicial recognition differ because courts in systems with a capital-C constitution have sought to stop legislatures from using constitutional statutes to circumvent the formal amendment procedure. As a result, while there appears to be ample scope for constitutional statutes to continue to rise in systems without capital-C constitutions, it appears that a more constrained future may lie ahead for constitutional statutes in systems with capital-C constitutions.

75 For an overview of the activities that preceded the enactment of the civil rights laws, see Ackerman (n 3).

# 2 How to identify quasi-constitutional legislation?

## An example from Chile

*Sergio Verdugo*[*]

### 1. Introduction

Judges and scholars from different jurisdictions have identified legislation that seems superior from the rest of the legal system, but not superior to the constitution, and discussed whether that legislation is a sort *quasi-constitutional* legislation (QCL). Some constitutions explicitly regulate a sort of QCL. For instance, the French 1958 Constitution defined a category of 'organic laws' as a particular type of legislation whose enactment and modification requires, among other conditions, the approval of the *Conseil Constitutionnel.*[1] Countries like Spain, Chile, and Hungary have implemented (and modified) the French 'organic law' model. Although other constitutions do not explicitly regulate QCL, political, or judicial practices sometimes assign a special value to legislation enacted by ordinary legislative procedures. In the US, for instance, scholars discuss whether there is a sort of 'small-c constitution' because, among other reasons, of existing statutes that are particularly difficult to modify.[2] Although legal scholars are discussing the phenomenon of QCL, attempts to provide a comparative law approach are still scarce. Scholars tend to focus on specific issues like entrenchment,[3] and most scholarship focuses on common law systems.[4]

QCL could arguably only exist in countries that possess a supreme constitution in the context of a jurisdiction that recognizes legal hierarchy among sources of law. The problem of quasi-constitutionality in countries like Britain and New Zealand is complicated. Because those jurisdictions do not have

* Professor of Constitutional Law, Universidad del Desarrollo (Chile). I thank Wojciech Sadurski and John Ferejohn for valuable conversations. I also thank Farrah Ahmed, José Díaz-de-Vald és, Daniel Francis, Felipe Jiménez, Monaliza da Silva, and Emily White, for useful comments. I benefited from the feedback received in the 'Symposium on Quasi-Constitutionality,' Victoria University of Wellington (May 2016).

1 See, e.g., Hubert Amiel, 'Les Lois Organiques' [1984] RDP 405. For a critical account, Jean-Pierre Camby, 'La Loi Organique Dans a Constitution de 1958' [1989] RDP 1401.

2 W Eskridge and J Ferejohn, *A Republic of Statutes. The New American Constitution* (Yale University Press 2010).

3 Nicholas Barber, 'Why Entrench?' (2016) 14 ICON 325.

4 Weill (Chapter 3) and Stephenson (Chapter 1) address common law countries.

a formal constitution that could be recognized as hierarchically superior to ordinary legislation, their statutes cannot resemble any higher norm. Therefore, they cannot be *quasi*-constitutional. If statutes in these countries regulate matters that are traditionally regulated by constitutions (e.g., a bill of rights or the regulation of a Parliament), then it could be argued that those statutes be part of the constitution. However, because there is no hierarchically superior constitution in these countries, it would be hard to determine whether assigning a constitutional status to a particular piece of legislation will have a practical legal effect. Perhaps for this reason, scholars that have written about this topic in these jurisdictions typically prefer to speak about *constitutional statutes*.[5]

In this article, I offer a theoretical framework or method that aims to identify quasi-constitutional legislation in Western countries that recognize hierarchically superior constitutions, such as France, Spain, and the US. Since these countries recognize a constitution that is *supreme* over the entire legal system, non-constitutional legislation can hardly be considered to have a formal constitutional status. However, sometimes lawmakers or judges enact or recognize norms that resemble specific key characteristics from the big-c Constitution, creating a realm of *quasi*-constitutional norms. After identifying those key characteristics, I contend that these legal systems have complicated (sometimes explicitly, other times implicitly) the organization of their sources of law by incorporating another type of norm: the QCL. To illustrate my argument, I use two examples from the Chilean constitutional system: the organic laws and the American Convention on Human Rights (as implemented in Chile). Although I mainly focus on these examples to show how to operationalize the QCL framework, I believe that this framework can be used to identify QCL in countries that possess a formally superior constitution. I will make some brief comparative remarks that make this claim plausible.

I use a formal perspective to define what a constitution is: it is the single written legal text called 'constitution' that possesses a higher value compared to the rest of the legal system's norms. Because this formal approach does not need to develop a substantive criterion to identify which matters are constitutional and which ones are not, sometimes important matters are left outside of this perspective. For instance, if the formal constitution does not define how to appoint or elect a prime minister, then the rules regulating the prime minister's nomination do not have a constitutional status. This approach differs from material perspectives that focus on the content of the rules.[6] Under this material

5 Farrah Ahmed and Adam Perry, 'Constitutional Statutes' (2017) 37 OJLS 461; F Ahmed and A Perry, 'The Quasi-Entrenchment of Constitutional Statutes' (2014) 73 C.L.J. 514; Rebecca Prebble, 'Constitutional Statutes and Implied Repeal: The Thoburn Decision and the Consequences for New Zealand' (2005) 36 V.U.W.L.R. 291.

6 The most prominent example is probably Carl Schmitt's conceptual approach to the constitution. For Schmitt, the constitution is the 'decision over the type and form of the political unity.' Carl Schmitt, *Constitutional Theory* (first published 1928, Duke University Press 2008) 75–82.

approach, the regulation on how to appoint or elect the prime minister would be constitutional even if the constitutional text remains silent on the topic.

My formal approach is useful for two reasons: first, it helps to identify the set of principles and norms that constitutional-drafters wanted to include as supreme legal norms. For instance, consumer protection rules can be *constitutional* in some constitutions (e.g., Article 60 of the Portuguese Constitution) and not in others (e.g., the US Constitution). Second, the formal approach contributes to producing certainty about the norms that judges are supposed to enforce against inferior legal rules.

## 2. A framework for recognizing QCL

The method for identifying QCL consists of, first, determining the key *features* of the formal constitution. These features are the characteristics or elements that make the constitution distinguishable from the rest of the legal system. The second part of the method consists in identifying the pieces of non-constitutional legislation that enjoy some or all of those characteristics.

The QCL's characteristics can originate explicitly from a constitutional provision (I call this type of origin as 'formal'), or from political or judicial practices ('informal'). For example, a constitutional provision can require an exceptional supermajority for modifying a non-constitutional statute (the origin is formal), or a court decision can use a non-constitutional statute for reviewing a piece of ordinary legislation (the origin is informal). In both cases, the non-constitutional norm acquires a quasi-constitutional status, but the source of that status is different. The QCL could be formal, informal, or mixed, depending on whether the origin of its constitutional features is formal or not.

The formal QCL possesses a static hierarchy because its legal status could only change if the constitution is modified. Thus, if the constitution is not modified, we can expect the QCL' characteristics to be stable. On the contrary, the stability of informal QCL will depend on how settled the political or judicial practices that created the quasi-constitutional features are. For instance, if a court overrules a prior judicial decision that assigned a quasi-constitutional status to a specific piece of legislation, that status would be contested.

What are the distinctive key features that a constitution or a political or judicial practice can transmit to a piece of legislation? Below I identify five possible features. A supreme constitution usually possesses most of these five features, in weaker or stronger senses, whereas ordinary legislation does not typically enjoy any of these characteristics. However, sometimes non-constitutional legislation has one or more of these features, acquiring a quasi-constitutional status. QCL does not need to have all these features to be quasi-constitutional. It needs at least one. The more of these features a QCL has, and the stronger they are, the more the QCL will resemble the constitution itself.

The first feature is *Constitutional Subject-Matter*: a QCL may regulate matters that are also controlled by the constitution, whatever the content of the constitution is. Although there are constitutional provisions that are common to numerous constitutions, other arrangements are rare (e.g., the right to bear arms). What is relevant, for the limited purpose of this paper, is that: 1) the constitution-designers wanted to entrench a particular rule by including it in the constitution, and 2) the legislator enacted a piece of legislation on that same topic, affecting or developing the will of the original constitution-designers.

To some degree, all norms have subject-matters connected to the constitution.[7] However, the subject-matter feature is limited because it only operates when there is a substantial regulatory overlap (e.g., a human rights treaty with the constitutional bill of rights) or when a QCL elaborates in detail something that is already regulated by the constitution in a general way (e.g., a statute developing the details of the legislative procedure established in the Constitution). A non-constitutional designer intervenes the constitution without formally reforming it, affecting or developing the will of the original constitution-makers further.

The second feature is *Constitutional Protection*. Judges cannot challenge a constitutionally protected QCL on the ground that it is unconstitutional, in particular by an ex-post judicial review mechanism. This is a common characteristic that exists in most supreme constitutions,[8] and sometimes this feature can be transmitted to a non-constitutional norm. If the QCL is informal, the stability of this feature depends on how settled are the founding judicial doctrines. If the QCL is formal, its quasi-constitutional status depends on the limitations that the constitution establishes to challenge the QCL. For instance, the constitution may establish a deadline for judges to challenge the QCL, or require a judicial supermajority for declaring its unconstitutionality.

The third feature that a QCL may have, is *Constitutional Supremacy*. Judges may use or invoke the QCL to review ordinary legislation that is considered to be incompatible with the QCL. This feature may be weak or strong. Judges use a strong supreme QCL to invalidate ordinary legislation, while they apply weak supreme QCL to specific cases with preference over ordinary legislation without invalidating that ordinary legislation. The supremacy feature also means that the *lex-posterior-derogate-legi-priori* principle does not apply to ordinary legislation enacted after a QCL.

The fourth feature is *Constitutional Rigidity*, and it exists when a QCL is harder to modify than ordinary legislation. Diverse mechanisms can make a QCL rigid, such as a legislative supermajority requirement, or the approval of an additional institution (e.g., a court). According to the *Constitute Project* database, 60 constitutions require a legislative supermajority rule for modifying

7 After all, under a Kelsenian approach all legal rules acquire their validity from the basic norm. Hans Kelsen, *Pure Theory of Law* (first published 1934, University of California Press 1967) 198–199.

8 Scholars have been fascinated with the exceptions. On the possibility of an unconstitutional constitution, see Richard Albert 'Four Unconstitutional Constitutions and Their Democratic Foundations' [2017] 50 Cornell Int'l L.J. 169. On the unconstitutionality of constitutional amendments, see Yaniv Roznai, *Unconstitutional Constitutional Amendments: The Limits of Amendment Powers* (Oxford University Press 2017).

certain kinds of non-constitutional legislation,[9] and 41 constitutions include 'organic laws.'[10] An example is the French organic laws, which require absolute majority and ex-ante judicial compulsory approval.

The French organic laws are rigid,[11] but they also have a quasi-constitutional status because of other features: they engage with specific constitutional subject-matters,[12] and once approved, they enjoy constitutional protection,[13] and arguably supremacy.[14] Similar organic laws exist in countries like Colombia. The Colombian *leyes estatutarias* are rigid (their modification requires absolute majority and compulsory ex-ante control) and enjoy constitutional protection,[15] although their supremacy feature seems unstable due to the Colombian Court jurisprudence.[16]

Although the rigidity is usually a formal feature (i.e., it is explicitly created by the constitution), it can also be informal. For instance, American scholars have discussed whether the creation of a legislative supermajority to protect specific legislation is constitutionally allowed, or not.[17] Eskridge and Ferejohn provide another example: specific statutes are 'super-statutes' because, among other reasons, their modifications are rare[18] and they should 'be considered something more than ordinary lawmaking.'[19] Also, these super-statutes arguably enjoy a degree of supremacy, and judges can include them in the constitutional canon.[20]

9 Constitute, 'Supermajority Required for Legislation' <www.constituteproject.org/search?lang=en&key=legsupr> accessed 30 March 2016.
10 Constitute, 'Organic Laws' <www.constituteproject.org/search?lang=en&key=orglaw> accessed 30 March 2016.
11 They are easier to modify than constitutional provisions, but harder to reform than ordinary laws. Olivier Duhamel, *Droit Constitutionnel. Le Pouvoir Politique En France* (Éditions du Seuil 1999) 341.
12 G Burdeau and others, *Manuel Droit Constitutionnel* (Librairie Général de Droit et de Jurisprudence 1993) 61. Dominique Rousseau, *Droit Du Contentieux Constitutionnel* (Montchrestien 1992) 98.
13 A 'decision of the French constitutional court extends to an entire statute and provides it with a label of constitutionality.' Otto Pfersmann, 'Concrete Review as Indirect Constitutional Complaint in French Constitutional Law. A Comparative Perspective' (2010) 6 EuConst 223, 225.
14 John Bell, *French Constitutional Law* (Oxford University Press 1992) 31.
15 Humberto Nogueira, 'Los Tribunales Constitucionales de América Del Sur y Sus Competencias' (2005) Provincia 27, 47.
16 Mónica Arango, 'El Bloque de Constitucionalidad En La Jurisprudencia de La Corte Constitucional Colombiana' (2004) Anu. Jur. Precedente 79.
17 See the debate about a 3/5ths majority rule required for increasing a tax rate: J McGinnis and M Rappaport, 'The Constitutionality of Legislative Supermajority Requirements: A Defense' (1995) 105 Yale L. J. 483; Robert Leach, 'House Rule XXI and an Argument against Constitutional Requirement for Majority Rule in Congress' (1997) 44 UCLA L.R. 1253.
18 W Eskridge and J Ferejohn, 'Super-Statutes' (2001) 50 Duke L. J. 1215, 1217.
19 ibid., 1266.
20 The super-statutes 'tend to trump ordinary legislation when there are clashes or inconsistencies' and sometimes the 'super-statutes can reshape constitutional understandings.' ibid., 1216.

The *Constitutional Canon* is the fifth feature. It exists when judges use the QCL as a privileged tool for interpreting (and even changing the meaning of) the constitution. Bruce Ackerman, for instance, contends that 'landmark statutes' like the 1964 Civil Rights Act have amended the US Constitution.[21] However, judges cannot use those landmark statutes to review ordinary legislation; they can theoretically declare the unconstitutionality of those statutes, and (although unlikely) the ordinary legislative process can modify them.[22] In other words, even though landmark statutes do not necessarily enjoy supremacy, constitutional-protection or rigidity, they are QCL because they become part of the constitutional canon.

It is important to acknowledge that also international treaties can be treated as QCL when considered from a domestic perspective. From this perspective, the value of supra-national law typically derives from the national constitution.[23] After the treaty is incorporated into the legal system, treaties can be legally invoked and domestic judges need to use them to solve cases. If domestic judges find a contradiction between the treaty and a domestic piece of legislation, the question of which norm should be preferred becomes inevitable. The domestic legal hierarchy of international treaties varies according to the legal system in which the treaty is going to be applied. Some constitutions (but not all) assign a superior legal value to treaties.[24] If the treaties are considered to be part of the Constitution, they will have a constitutional status. If the treaties are deemed to be under the supremacy of the constitution, but above the ordinary laws, then they can be quasi-constitutional. They can also be equivalent to ordinary legislation. Sometimes, the same international treaty can have a different legal status in two different countries. For example, while the Argentinian Constitution explicitly gives a constitutional status to the American Convention on Human Rights (ACHR) (Article 75, N°22),[25] the Chilean Constitution remains silent. In both countries, domestic judges have complicated the issue.[26]

21 Ackerman explicitly rejects the term 'quasi,' and gives the Civil Rights Act a 'full constitutional status.' Bruce Ackerman, *We the People: The Civil Rights Revolution*, vol 3 (Harvard University Press 2014) 34. Sometimes, QCL that change the meaning of the constitution also come from administrative regulations or executive. An interesting example is the interpretation of Article 9 of the Japanese Constitution. See Fisher (Chapter 12).

22 Rivka Weill, 'Constitutional Statutes or Overriding the Court' (2016) 13 Jerusalem Rev. Leg. Stud. 1, 12.

23 Yaniv Roznai, 'The Theory and Practice of Supra-National Limits on Constitutional Amendments' (2013) 62 ICLQ 557.

24 Consider, e.g., the discussion about whether EU law is supreme. P Craig and G de Búrca, *EU Law* (5th edn, Oxford University Press 2011) 256-301.

25 This provision has given room for broadening the *constitutional-canon* and *supreme* features of the ACHR. Víctor Bazán, 'El Derecho Internacional de Los Derechos Humanos Desde La Óptica de La Corte Suprema Argentina' (2010) 8 Est. Const. 359.

26 I will explain the Chilean case in Section 5. Regarding the Argentinian case, see Sergio Verdugo, 'La Corte Suprema Argentina y la (Pérdida de) Autoridad en la Corte Interamericana de

## 3. Brief introduction to the Chilean constitutional system

After a military coup in 1973, the Pinochet dictatorship established the 1980 Constitution, which included a Kelsenian-type Constitutional Court that had the power of judicial review over legislation.[27] The appointment mechanisms of the Court were controlled directly or indirectly by the military. After the dictatorship finished due to a plebiscite that the opposition won, the leaders of the military regime and the opposition agreed on a transition to democracy that included not replacing the 1980 Constitution, but only introducing modifications to it.[28] The leaders of the dictatorship also benefited from this agreement.[29] Thus, the 1980 Constitution remained, and a consensual democracy type of regime started. Although electoral democracy was restored, and the opposition won the Presidential elections many times in a row, during the 90s and the early 2000s many authoritarian enclaves still shaped the political dynamic of the country. That way, the non-elected Senators, Pinochet's position as a commander of the army and as a Senator, and the powers of the National Security Council, to name a few enclaves, were key for understanding the politics of that time. Legislators tried to eliminate the authoritarian enclaves, but the opposition only agreed to modify them gradually. Finally, in 2005 a bipartisan agreement eliminated most of the authoritarian enclaves.[30] They removed the National Security Council's powers, all Senators were required to be elected, the appointment mechanisms of the Constitutional Court were modified (and the Court's powers were expanded), and the appointment mechanisms of the military commanders were changed. President Lagos symbolically replaced Pinochet's signature by his own and endorsed the new constitutional text as a fully democratic Constitution.[31]

However, some scholars contended that the 2005 reform was insufficient for democratizing the Constitution, as some provisions were still limiting majority rule.[32] During the 2011 student protests, a new demand for a significant constitutional replacement started to grow, and politicians (mainly from the left) started to discuss the possible mechanisms for enacting a new constitution.

Derecho Humanos en el Caso Menem' [2017] 36 Act. Jurídica 467. It seems that the domestic application of the ACHR is heterogeneous. See, e.g., Miriam Henríquez, 'La Polisemia Del Control de Convencionalidad Interno' (2014) 24 Rev. Colombiana Der. Intern. 113.

27 In general, see Robert Barros, *Constitutionalism and Dictatorship: Pinochet, the Junta, and the 1980 Constitution* (Cambridge University Press 2002).

28 In general, see Carlos Andrade, *Reforma de La Constitución Política de La República de Chile de 1980* (Ed. Jurídica Chile 1991).

29 C Heiss and P Navia, 'You Win, You Lose Some: Constitutional Reform in Chile's Transition to Democracy' 49 [2007] 49 Latin American Politics and Society 163.

30 In general, see Emilio Pfeffer, *Reformas Constitucionales 2005* (Ed. Jurídica Chile 2005); Claudio Fuentes, *El Pacto* (Universidad Diego Portales 2012).

31 Ricardo Lagos, 'Prólogo' in Francisco Zúñiga (ed.), *Reforma Constitucional* (LexisNexis 2005).

32 J Couso and A Coddou, 'Las Asignaturas Pendientes de La Reforma Constitucional Chilena' in Claudio Fuentes (ed.), *En el Nombre del Pueblo: Debate Sobre el Cambio Constitucional en Chile* (Universidad Diego Portales – Fundación Boll 2010).

President Bachelet' administration endorsed this constitutional demand, and strongly promoted a constitution-making process. Despite the fact that the country ranks well in relevant political and economic indicators,[33] the social demand for replacing the Constitution has increased substantially.[34] Among other reasons, current promoters of constitutional change argue that 1980 Constitution lacks legitimacy because it can still be connected to the dictatorship, that it does not protect social rights sufficiently, and that some institutional arrangements prevent the expression of majorities by, for example, requiring supermajorities to approve key legislative modifications.[35] Among the matters that are currently under discussion, as I will show, are the organic laws (LOCs) and the Constitutional Court's power to review the constitutionality of the LOCs through an ex-ante mandatory judicial review mechanism.

It should be noted that the constitutional regulation of international treaties is not one of the major themes of the public discussion connected to the demand for constitutional replacement. However, scholars and politicians have still discussed the status of international treaties in the context of the constitution-making debate. The 1980 Constitution said little about international treaties, but the 1989 reform introduced a rule establishing that human rights recognized by international treaties 'limit national sovereignty' (Article 5). Later, the 2005 reform added procedural rules for the approval of international treaties. Both the 1989 and 2005 reforms triggered a debate about the hierarchy of international human rights law in Chile.

## 4. The Chilean LOCs

Among the instructions Pinochet gave to the constitutional drafting commission (CENC), he suggested not to include some of his ideas in the final constitutional text but, instead, in other rules he called 'constitutional laws.' Those laws were going to have an 'intermediate hierarchy between the Constitution and the statutes.'[36] The CENC members were already familiar with the French model of organic laws,[37] and Bertelsen (one of the key CENC members) argued that the organic laws are useful because they supplement the Constitution, which should

33 Chile ranks seventh in the index of economic freedom, and twenty-sixth out of 102 in the Rule of Law Index. See The Heritage Foundation, 'Index of Economic Freedom'. World Justice Project, 'Rule of Law Index'.

34 See a compilation of the relevant polls in PNUD, *Opinión Ciudadana y Cambio Constitucional. Análisis Desde La Opinión Pública* (PNUD 2015).

35 Among many articles stating more or less the same arguments, see, e.g., Claudia Heiss, 'Legitimacy Crisis and the Constitutional Problem in Chile: A Legacy of Authoritarianism' [2017] 24 Constellations 470. For a skeptical approach, see, e.g., Andrew Arato, 'Beyond the Alternative Reform or Revolution: Postsovereign Constitution-Making and Latin America' 40 Wake Forest L. Rev. 891.

36 Augusto Pinochet, 'Normas Para La Nueva Constitución' 142.

37 See Jorge Guzmán Dinator's presentation in CENC, 'Sesión 22'.

only provide a general institutional framework and avoid in-depth regulations.[38] Other CENC members argued that the LOCs should be subjected to an ex-ante judicial review procedure and that only an absolute legislative majority should be able to modify them. They believed that unstable Congressional majorities should not modify the LOCs. Some CENC members suggested that the LOCs were superior to the ordinary laws because their purpose was to regulate public institutions,[39] that they were an 'extension of the Constitution,' and that their consistency with the Constitution should be indisputable.[40] The LOCs were supposed to regulate a limited set of matters, such as the organization of Congress, legislative procedure, and the powers of the Judiciary. Thus, the LOCs possessed the following formal features: constitutional subject-matter, rigidity, and, arguably, constitutional protection.

In revising the CENC's proposal, the Junta enhanced the LOC's legislative majority requirement to a 3/5th majority rule[41] and broadened the subject-matters that the LOCs were going to regulate, including the regulation of the Constitutional Court, political parties, and electoral laws.[42]

During the dictatorship years, the Junta had the power to enact the LOCs by unanimity (since there was no Congress, the Junta was the legislator). Because modifying the Constitution during the dictatorship was costly (the process required a plebiscite), the Junta found that the LOCs were an attractive regulatory tool. After the dictatorship finished, the 1989 constitutional reform lowered the legislative quorum for modifying the LOCs from a 3/5th rule to a 4/7th rule.[43] It was hard for the new elected Congress to achieve the necessary majorities to reform the LOCs enacted by the Junta.[44] Nevertheless, the Congress still managed to create new LOCs that were not considered by the original text of the 1980 Constitution: the criminal prosecutors' statute, the regulation of certain non-continental territories, and the electoral primaries.[45]

The Constitutional Court's ex-ante judicial review power over the LOCs developed some problems, including the impossibility to review the LOCs when the Congress decides not to submit the bills to the Court, and the creation of complex criterions to determine when a legislative provision is actually 'organic.'[46] Also, scholars argue that the ex-ante judicial review system does not

38 CENC, 'Sesión 344'.

39 CENC, 'Sesión 358'.

40 CENC, 'Sesión 409'.

41 Luz Bulnes, *La Constitución Política de La República de Chile. Concordancias, Anotaciones y Fuentes* (Ed. Jurídica Chile 1981) 91–92.

42 Luz Bulnes, 'La Ley Orgánica Constitucional' (1984) Rev. Chil. Der. 227, 229.

43 Andrade (n 28) 229.

44 John B. Londregan, *Legislative Institutions and Ideology in Chile* (Cambridge University Press 2000) 64.

45 Ley 19,519 (1997), Ley 20,193 (2007), and Ley 20,414 (2010).

46 Emilio Pfeffer, 'Algunos Problemas Que Se Derivan Del Control Obligatorio de Constitucionalidad Que Ejerce El Tribunal Constitucional Sobre Las Leyes Orgánicas Constitucionales' (1998) 4 Ius Et Praxis 259; A Buchheister and S Soto, 'Criterios Para La Calificación de

protect the Constitution effectively,[47] and that the Court has expanded the subject matters regulated by LOCs, broadening the matters that require a legislative supermajority.[48] Although Chilean scholars seem to agree that the ex-ante control system is flawed, sometimes the Court has enacted important (but rare) decisions. The paradigmatic example is a set of decisions from the 80s when the Court helped to frame fair electoral conditions for the plebiscite that was going to decide whether Pinochet was going to remain as the chief of the Executive branch.[49]

What is the hierarchy of the LOCs in the Chilean system? An early Constitutional Court decision stated that the LOCs have an intermediate status between the Constitution and ordinary legislation.[50] Some scholars elaborated similar arguments (e.g., 'they are less *law* than the Constitution but more *law* than statutes'),[51] and even suggested that the LOC's possess 'super-legality' or even a constitutional status.[52] Even though some believe that constitutional judges can theoretically declare the unconstitutionality of a LOC,[53] a constitutional challenge against a LOC is highly unlikely because all the LOCs are previously (ex-ante) approved by the Constitutional Court before their enactment. After the Court's approval (ex-post), the only way to challenge a LOCs is by demonstrating that the LOC produces an unconstitutional result during an ordinary court proceeding, affecting the Constitution in a way the Court did not previously consider in its ex-ante ruling.[54] Because ex-post judicial review challenges to the LOCs are rare,[55] it could be argued that, after they are enacted, the LOCs possess an informal constitutional protection feature.

Normas Orgánico Constitucionales En La Jurisprudencia Del Tribunal Constitucional' (2005) 32 Rev. Chil. Der. 253; Andrés Bordalí, 'Análisis Crítico Del Control Preventivo y Represivo de Constitucionalidad de Las Normas Jurídicas Por Los Tribunales Constitucionales' in Humberto Nogueira (ed.), *Jurisdicción Constitucional en Chile y América Latina* (LexisNexis 2005).

47 Martin Shapiro argued that the ex-ante review system was unable to predict the practical operation of the law under review. Martin Shapiro, 'Revisión Judicial a Priori y a Posteriori. Los Modelos Norteamericano y Europeo' (1993) 20 Rev. Chil. Der. 475.

48 Patricio Zapata, *Justicia Constitucional* (Ed. Jurídica Chile 2008) 442–448; Lucas Sierra, 'La Supramayoría En La Potestad Legislativa Chilena Como Anomalía Democrática' in L Sierra and L Mac-Clure, *Frente a la Mayoría* (CEP – PNUD 2011) 39–42.

49 One of these decisions obliged the Junta to establish an electoral court before the plebiscite (STC 33/1985).

50 STC 7/1981.

51 Lautaro Ríos, 'Las Leyes Orgánicas Constitucionales' (1983) 10 Rev. Chil. Der. 39.

52 See, for example, Zapata (n 48) 401, and Jorge Correa's intervention in Lucas Sierra (ed.), *Diálogos Constitucionales* (CEP 2015) 368.

53 Bulnes (n 42) 231–232.

54 Sergio Verdugo, 'El Sello de Constitucionalidad de Los Preceptos Legales Declarados Constitucionales En El Control Preventivo' (2009) 13 RD y Ciencias Penales 57.

55 Even the ex-ante judicial review challenges are rare. See Sergio Verdugo, 'Control Preventivo Obligatorio. Auge y Caída de La Toma de Razón Al Legislador' (2010) Año 8, N° 1 Est. Const. 201. However, nowadays the Tribunal seems to be using more its ex-ante judicial review powers: STC 2857/2015, 2831/2015, 2779/2015, 2910/2015.

Even though the LOCs supplement the Constitution by detailing and complementing constitutional rules, the LOCs are not considered to be part of the constitutional canon, and judges cannot use them to review inferior legislation (ordinary legislation cannot contradict the LOCs because they regulate different subject-matters).[56]

### *The debate about the LOCs*

In the early 80s, the *Grupo de los 24* (a group of scholars that opposed the dictatorship) accused the LOCs of trying to perpetuate the dictatorship's policies.[57] Scholars still use this argument to show how the LOCs (or at least some LOCs) protect the dictatorship's legacy against the will of elected majorities,[58] and 'deceiving' the democratic political process,[59] by 'excessively subsidizing the parties that lose elections.'[60] These kinds of arguments usually include an attack against the electoral system (already replaced in 2015), the ex-ante review power of the Constitutional Court, and the entrenched constitutional reform procedure.[61]

To justify their arguments against the LOCs, some Chilean scholars quote Dahl's arguments for majoritarian democracy,[62] Böckenforde's essay on democracy,[63] Waldron's arguments against judicial review,[64] and Sadurski's rationale for political equality.[65] They say that a deviation from majority rule can violate political equality by giving too much weight to the minority's

56 Miriam Henríquez, *Las Fuentes Formales Del Derecho* (LegalPublishing 2009); Sebastián Soto, *Congreso Nacional y Proceso Legislativo* (Thomson Reuters – UC 2015) 332–334. See, also STC 260/1997.

57 Grupo de los 24, 'Las Críticas Del Grupo de Los 24' 10. Also, Francisco Cumplido, *¿Estado de Derecho En Chile?* (Instituto Chileno Estudios Humanísticos 1983) 71–72.

58 For example, see Fernando Muñoz, 'Leyes Orgánico-Constitucionales: Insatisfactoria Rigidización de La Democracia' [2006] Anuario de Derecho Constitucional Iberoamericano 115.

59 Fernando Atria claims that the both the LOCs and the constitutional reform procedure are 'tricks' (*trampas*) to unbalance the legislative arena in favor of the dictatorship's heirs. Fernando Atria, *La Constitución Tramposa* (LOM 2013) 44–54.

60 Zapata (n 48) 403. See similar criticisms in Carlos Huneeus, *La Democracia Semisoberana. Chile Después de Pinochet* (Taurus 2014) 166–170; Christian Suárez, 'La Constitución Celda o "Straightjacket Constitution" y La Dogmática Constitucional' (2009) 24 Universum 248; Julia Urquieta, 'Una Nueva Constitución Para Un Nuevo Chile' in Francisco Zúñiga (ed.), *Nueva Constitución y Momento Constitucional* (LegalPublishing – Thomson Reuters 2014) 57–59.

61 Before the 2005 reform, criticisms against the LOCs also targeted the non-elected Senators and the powers of the National Security Council. K Cazor and M Fernández, 'Constitución, Principio Democrático y Reformas Constitucionales' (2002) XIII RD (Valdivia) 147; Marc Carrillo, 'Las Hipotecas de La Constitución de Chile' (2002) 115 Rev. Estud. Polit. 81.

62 Robert Dahl, *Democracy and Its Critics* (Yale University Press 1991).

63 Ernst W. Böckenforde, 'Democracia Como Principio Constitucional', *Estudios sobre el Estado de Derecho y la Democracia* (Trotta 2000).

64 Jeremy Waldron, 'The Core of the Case against Judicial Review' (2006) 115 Yale L. J. 1346.

65 Wojciech Sadurski, *Equality and Legitimacy* (Oxford University Press 2008).

capacity to veto legislation.[66] As a response, others claim that the justification of the LOCs relies on arguments that can defeat the majority rule as the default position.[67] An example is the need to entrench the electoral system for avoiding the manipulation of an incumbent majority that can violate electoral equality (e.g., by gerrymandering districts). Another example is the defense of the institutions that control political power (e.g., the *Contraloría*, an agency that reviews the legality of administrative regulations) against elected majorities that have incentives to threaten the independence of those institutions.[68]

Since the LOC regulation prevents simple majorities from completely controlling the legislative procedure, legislators from the majority typically promote the elimination of the LOCs. Thus, it is logical to expect that they will use the Chilean constitution-making debate as an opportunity to advance this agenda.

Since 1990 and 2016 (I did not consider the 2017 Presidential platforms) Chilean political parties have been organized into two stable coalitions: a right-wing coalition named *Chile-Vamos* (former *Alianza*), and the center-left *Nueva-Mayoría* (old *Concertación*). *Chile-Vamos* has two parties and some minor organizations. *Nueva-Mayoría* has a diverse number of parties and organizations, ranging from a Catholic center-left party (PDC) to a couple of socialist parties, and the Communist Party (since 2014). The *Nueva-Mayoría* rules the country today (2014–2018), and ruled the country in the past (1990–2010). Although the *Alianza* ruled the country for a brief period (2010–2014), the *Nueva-Mayoría* usually has a simple majority in Congress.

The first political (non-scholarly) attack against the LOCs came during the 1989 reform when the *Concertación* and some centre-right politicians advocated lowering their legislative supermajority requirement. Later, *Concertación* legislators promoted eliminating or modifying the LOC's supermajority requirement, including a proposal by President Lagos during the debates of the 2005 reform.[69] Then, President Frei (*Concertación*), who was running to be President again, promised to replace the Constitution and to eliminate the LOCs.[70] During the 2013 presidential campaign, Bachelet (who was going to be elected

66 Sierra, Busch and Quezada rely on Böckenforde's work, while Jiménez and others use the arguments by Dahl, Waldron and Sadurski. Sierra (n 48) 16; T Busch and F Quezada, 'Regla de La Mayoría e Instituciones Contramayoritarias. Una Perspectiva Para La Discusión Sobre Un Cambio Constitucional En Chile' (2013) 78 Rev. Der. Publ. (Santiago) 139, 147; G Jiménez and others, 'La Debilidad de Las Súper-Mayorías' (2013) 41 RD (Valparaíso) 359, 362–365.

67 Soto (n 56) 328–332.

68 I have elaborated these arguments before. See Sergio Verdugo, 'Las Justificaciones de La Regla de Quórum Supra-Mayoritaria de Las Leyes Orgánicas Constitucionales' (2012) 39 RD (Valparaíso) 395; Sergio Verdugo, 'Las Debilidades de La Crítica a Las Súper-Mayorías' (2014) 42 RD (Valparaíso) 355.

69 Zaldívar and Moreno, 'Moción'. For the 2005 proposal, see Pfeffer, *Reformas Constitucionales 2005* (n 30) 629–630.

70 Comisión Oceanos Azules, 'Una Constitución Para El Bicentenario (Propuesta Eduardo Frei)' 5.

again) offered a constitutional agenda that included eliminating the LOCs.[71] During that year, one of the *Alianza* presidential candidates offered to revise the LOC system.[72] Several other proposals were discussed that year, including some left party proposals advocating the elimination of the LOCs.[73]

Nowadays, the mainstream position is to reduce the LOC's supermajority requirement or (at least), to limit their scope.[74] Even a *ChileVamos* proposal promoted reducing the number of matters to be regulated by the LOCs,[75] despite the existence of conservative positions within *ChileVamos.*[76] For many politicians, the LOCs' rigid regulations cover too many topics in an over-detailed way. Thus, instead of constitutionalizing substantial rules that have good reasons to enjoy a degree of stability and entrenchment, the LOCs ended up constitutionalizing a significant part of the legislative agenda.[77] An example is the reform of the LOC that regulates the parliamentary electoral system. Since the 1990s, centre-left politicians have advocated and failed, to replace the electoral regime. That electoral system was initially designed by the dictatorship to help the right coalition to elect more legislators.[78] Even though the left coalition usually has a simple majority in Congress, it was only after 25 years that they convinced some right legislators to help them achieve the supermajority they needed to replace the electoral system.[79]

If the promoters of constitutional replacement succeed and a new constitution is enacted, it seems likely that they will eliminate the LOCs or, at least, that they will modify them.

## 5. The Chilean application of the ACHR

The 1980 Constitution's original text said little about international treaties. The 1980 Constitution only established that international treaties require the

71 Chile de Todos, 'Programa de Gobierno de Michelle Bachelet 2014–2018' 34 <http://michellebachelet.cl/programa/> accessed 7 April 2016. 20 constitutional scholars supporting Bachelet developed the idea in Appendix F of Francisco Zúñiga (ed.), *Nueva Constitución y Momento Constitucional* (LegalPublishing – Thomson Reuters 2014) 298.

72 See proposal: José García (ed.), *¿Nueva Constitución o Reforma? Nuestra Propuesta: Evolución Constitucional* (LegalPublishing – Thomson Reuters 2014) 532.

73 Appendixes C and D of Zúñiga (n 71).

74 See García, Zapata, Sierra, Correa and Navarro, in a debate reproduced by Sierra (n 52) 347, 358–359, 368, 381, 485.

75 ChileVamos, 'Propuesta Constitucional de Chile Vamos' 16.

76 See UDI, 'Nuestra Visión Del Proceso Constituyente: Chile No Necesita Una Nueva Constitución' 13–14.

77 An influential PDC scholar and the PDC proposal argue that there is no relevant reform that can be made without modifying at least one LOC provision. Zapata in Sierra (n 52) 358–359. See the PDC proposal in Patricio Zapata, *La Casa de Todos* (Ediciones UC 2015) 160.

78 G Rahat and M Sznajder, 'Electoral Engineering in Chile: The Electoral System and Limited Democracy' (1998) 17 Electoral Studies 429.

79 Ley 20,840 (2015).

approval of the Congress following the ordinary lawmaking process. However, treaties in the Chilean system (as in many countries) have informal rigidity because countries rarely denounce, invalidate, unilaterally revoke or agree to revoke treaties. In Chile, the primary challenge against the quasi-constitutional status of the treaties is the possibility that the Constitutional Court will review them. Are treaties in Chile protected against challenges of constitutionality?

During the 80s and 90s, many Chilean scholars said yes,[80] even though the 1989 constitutional reform established that the 'essential rights streaming from human nature,' such as the ones recognized by the Constitution 'and by international treaties,' limit sovereignty (Article 5). Some scholars understood that under the 1989 reform human rights treaties (i.e., the ACHR) cannot be constitutionally challenged because they acquired a constitutional or quasi-constitutional status,[81] and the Constitutional Court rarely discussed the constitutionality of a treaty.[82] Moreover, some decisions of the Inter-American Court of Human Rights (IACtHR) have become constitutionally relevant in Chile. A famous example is a decision that instructed Chile to change its freedom of speech regulation regarding films, after the censorship of a controversial movie that supposedly harmed Catholic beliefs.[83] Chilean legislators amended the 1980 Constitution to adjust it to the IACtHR's standard, explicitly prohibiting censorship (Ley 19, 742, 2001).

The 2005 constitutional reform established, among other modifications, that the Constitutional Court could review treaties using its ex-ante judicial review power, but said nothing regarding the possibility of an ex-post review. The reform also prohibited the treaties to be 'derogated, modified or suspended' by other means than the ones of international law. The rule prohibits the Congress to reform a treaty unilaterally, and many scholars argue that it also forbids the Court to strike down a treaty provision using its ex-post judicial review powers.[84] In a divided decision, the Court made stated that although it has the limited authority to declare that the application of an international treaty violates

80 Miguel Fernández, 'La Reforma Al Artículo 5° de La Constitución' (1989) 16 Rev. Chil. Der. 809; Fernando Saenger, 'Consideraciones Para Estimar Que Los Tratados En Materia de Derechos Humanos No Forman Parte de La Constitución' (1993) 20 Rev. Chil. Der. 647.

81 C Troncoso and T Vial, 'Sobre Los Derechos Humanos Reconocidos En Tratados Internacionales y En La Constitución' (1993) 20 Rev. Chil. Der. 695; Humberto Nogueira, 'Constitución y Derecho Internacional de Los Derechos Humanos' (1993) 20 Rev. Chil. Der. 881. About the Supreme Court decisions, see Miriam Henríquez, 'Jerarquía de Los Tratados de Derechos Humanos' (2008) 6 Est. Const. 73.

82 See, e.g., an exceptional decision declaring the unconstitutionality of the treaty establishing the International Criminal Court (STC 346/2002). Later, the Tribunal did not question the constitutionality of a constitutional reform that authorized the approval of the treaty (STC 1415/2009).

83 *The Last Temptation of Christ* case IACtHR Series C No 73 (5 February 2001).

84 Marisol Peña, 'Control de Constitucionalidad de Los Tratados Internacionales. La Experiencia Chilena a Un Año Después de La Reforma' (2006) XXXVI Jornadas Chilenas Der. Públ.

the Constitution for a specific case, it lacks the power to void a treaty.[85] Thus, if the Court has any power over the treaties, it is a weak power. In any case, Court has never struck down an ACHR provision using its ex-post review powers, and it is unlikely that it will do so.[86] The ACHR seems to be constitutionally protected against judicial challenges.

Is the ACHR part of the constitutional canon? The Constitutional Court has used the ACHR to justify its decisions,[87] and it has elaborated an unstable jurisprudence defending the view that the ACHR rights are incorporated into the Constitution via Article 5.[88] The *Bloque de Constitucionalidad* doctrine (BDC, stating that the ACHR and the Constitution integrate a single abstract bill of rights)[89] seems to be increasingly accepted, primarily by the Supreme Court.[90]

Has the ACHR acquired supremacy? The Congress's practices tend to promote the ACHR's supremacy, at least in the legislative realm, by rejecting bills on the ground that Chilean lawmakers do not have the authority to enact laws that violate the ACHR. For instance, the Congress has rejected at least three bills intended to reestablish the death penalty, partly arguing that the capital punishment violate the ACHR.[91]

Although the IACtHR promotes the *control de convencionalidad* doctrine (CDC), through which all domestic judges must prefer the application of the ACHR over local legislation that violates the ACHR,[92] the CDC has divided Chilean scholars, and its reception by domestic judges is complicated.[93] The

85 STC 1288/2008.

86 Miriam Henríquez, 'Improcedencia Del Control Represivo de Constitucionalidad de Los Tratados Internacionales' (2007) 5 Est. Const. 119. Scholars advocating for an ex-post review against treaties are nowadays rare. An exception is Teodoro Ribera, 'Los Tratados Internacionales y Su Control a Posteriori Por El Tribunal Constitucional' (2007) 5 Est. Const. 89.

87 Juan Beca, 'De La Discusión Sobre La Jerarquía de Los Tratados Internacionales a La Idea de Pluralismo Constitucional' (2014) 5 RD y Ciencia Política 22.

88 The Constitutional Tribunal incorporated the right to personal identity to the constitutional canon, claiming that the right is protected by Article 5 and the 'dignity clause' (STC 1340/2009). Other rulings avoid to endorse the incorporation doctrine (STC 1537/2011, 1563/2011, 1656/2011). Also, see a divided decision where five (out of ten) Justices followed the incorporation doctrine (STC 2408/2014).

89 Pablo Ruiz-Tagle, 'Una Visión Democrática y Liberal de Los Derechos Fundamentales Para La Constitución Del Bicentenario' in Andrés Bordalí (ed.), *Justicia Constitucional y Derechos Fundamentales* (LexisNexis 2006) 108–110.

90 Gonzalo Aguilar, 'La Corte Suprema y La Aplicación Del Derecho Internacional. Un Proceso Esperanzador' (2009) 7 Est. Const. 91.

91 Claudio Troncoso, *Parlamento y Política Exterior de Chile. Un Balance de Veinte Años (1990–2010)* (Konrad Adenauer Stiftung 2011) 61–65.

92 The landmark case is *Almonacid-Arellano et al v. Chile* IACtHR Series C No 154 (26 September 2006). About the IACtHR's CDC evolution, see, e.g., Juan Hitters, 'Control de Convencionalidad (Adelantos y Retrocesos)' (2015) 13 Est. Const. 123.

93 Some criticize the IACtHR rulings that incorporate implicit rights. Álvaro Ferrer and others, 'Corte Interamericana de Derechos Humanos En El Caso Atala Riffo y Niñas v. Chile' (2012) 1 Der. Públ. Iberoamericano 201; Gonzalo Candia, 'Derechos Implícitos y Corte

Chilean Supreme Court lacks the power to invalidate legislation, and some scholars argue that that the Constitutional Court used the CDC implicitly,[94] though the Court has never explicitly promoted the CDC in a majority decision. Criminal judges invoked CDC for not applying some Military Code provisions to specific cases,[95] but those decisions lack stare decisis power, and they are still binding for other cases. If the ACHR is supreme, it is in a weak and unstable sense. The feature is informal.

The following facts are undisputed in Chile today: 1) Nobody claims that ordinary legislation can derogate treaty provisions; 2) The Court sometimes invokes the ACHR to justify its decisions; 3) The ACHR and the IACtHR's jurisprudence play a contested role in understanding the Chilean bill of rights; and 4) Most scholars claim that the human rights treaty provisions are hierarchically higher than ordinary legislation.[96] Even scholars that disagree with the CDC acknowledge the importance of human rights treaties complementing the constitutional bill of rights.[97]

Although the ACHR is a QCL, most of its quasi-constitutional features are unstable.

### *The ACHR and the constituent debate*

The Chilean constitution-making public debate has rarely focused on the status of the ACHR, but scholars and some politicians have nevertheless briefly addressed the issue.

For instance, a key Bachelet advisor argued that the application of the ACHR rights should have preference over domestic legislation,[98] and others proposed to establish a compulsory ex-ante judicial review system for international treaties

Interamericana de Derechos Humanos' (2015) 42 Rev. Chil. Der. 873; Sergio Fuenzalida, 'La Jurisprudencia de La Corte Interamericana de Derechos Humanos Como Fuente Del Derecho' (2015) XXVIII RD (Valdivia) 171. See a defense of the IACtHR, e.g., in Humberto Nogueira, 'Diálogo Interjurisdiccional, Control de Convencionalidad y Jurisprudencia Del Tribunal Constitucional En Período 2006–2011' (2012) 10 Est. Const. 57.

94 Gonzalo Aguilar, 'El Tribunal Constitucional Chileno Frente a La Jurisdicción Militar' (2015) 22 RD (Coquimbo) 23.

95 Núñez in Sierra (n 52) 403.

96 See, e.g., Raúl Bertelsen, 'Rango Jurídico de Los Tratados Internacionales En El Derecho Chileno' (1996) 23 Rev. Chil. Der. 211.

97 Emilio Pfeffer, 'Breves Reflexiones y Algunas Propuestas En Torno a Los Derechos, Garantías y Deberes Constitucionales' in José García (ed.), *¿Nueva Constitución o Reforma? Nuestra Propuesta: Evolución Constitucional* (LegalPublishing – Thomson Reuters 2014) 174–175; José Díaz-de-Valdés, 'Bases de La Institucionalidad: Una Revisión Propositiva' in José García (ed.), *¿Nueva Constitución o Reforma? Nuestra Propuesta: Evolución Constitucional* (LegalPublishing – Thomson Reuters 2014) 109–110.

98 Francisco Zúñiga, 'Nueva Constitución Para Chile. Las "Bases" y Las Nuevas Ideas Político-Constitucionales' (2014) Rev. Der. Publ. (Santiago) 27, 30–32. See a similar proposal by 20 constitutional scholars helping to build Bachelet's platform. Zúñiga (n 71) 276.

for avoiding a possible unconstitutionality decision on an ex-post basis.[99] Others promoted using the constitution-making process to make the treaties hierarchically superior to domestic legislation.[100]

Although not all the constitutional proposals deal with the ACHR,[101] the ones that do so advocate for using international human rights law as a basis for enacting a new bill of rights. Bachelet's program stated that the Constitution 'must recognize the maximum value to the principles and international conventions regarding human rights,'[102] and the PDC proposal stated that the new constitution should 'explicitly adhere to international human rights law,' which must be 'completely binding for all branches of government.'[103] A conservative proposal acknowledged the importance of human rights treaties recognizing 'essential rights' despite the skepticism against the IACtHR's activism.[104]

Because Chilean politicians widely acknowledge the importance of following the ACHR, it seems likely that the new constitution will deepen the influence of the ACHR.

If a new constitution is not enacted, and criticisms against the ACHR or the IACtHR grow, they may threaten the quasi-constitutional status of the ACHR because the Constitution does not strongly protect its features. The quasi-constitutional status of the ACHR is mostly informal.

## 6. Concluding remarks

As illustrated in Table 2.1, both the LOCs and the ACHR have quasi-constitutional status. Both regulate constitutional subject-matters, and they both enjoy a degree of rigidity, although in diverse ways. Also, they both possess some level of constitutional protection and judicial challenges against them are unlikely. They also have differences. While the LOCs are not part of the constitutional canon and do not enjoy supremacy, the ACHR is arguably part of the constitutional canon and enjoys an unstable and weak supremacy over domestic legislation.

99 See Pfeffer and Avilés interventions in Sierra (n 52) 384–385, 404.

100 Miriam Henríquez, 'Tratados Internacionales. Reflexiones En Torno a Una Nueva Constitución' in E Chia and F Quezada (eds.), *Propuestas para una Nueva Constitución* (Instituto Igualdad – UCH 2015). Some promote to regulate a clearer system for incorporating international law, distinguishing constitutional treaties from non-constitutional treaties. Ximena Fuentes, 'Una Nueva Constitución Para Chile y El Diseño de Un Esquema de Incorporación Del Derecho Internacional Al Sistema Jurídico Chileno' in E Chia and F Quezada (eds.), *Propuestas para una Nueva Constitución* (Instituto Igualdad – UCH 2015).

101 See the right-wing and communist proposals in García (n 72) 529–541 and Zúñiga (n 71) 235–250.

102 Chile de Todos (n 71) 30.

103 See the proposal in Zapata (n 77) 146.

104 UDI, *Nuestra Visión del Proceso Constituyente: Chile No Necesita una Nueva Constitución* (2015) 14–16.

*Table 2.1* LOCs and ACHR as QCL

| *Feature* | *LOCs* | *ACHR* |
|---|---|---|
| Constitutional Subject-matter | Yes. Formal | Yes. Informal |
| Constitutional Protection | Limited | Yes. Informal |
| Supremacy | No | Arguably yes in the weak version. Informal |
| Rigidity | Yes. Formal | Yes. Formal |
| Constitutional Canon | Arguably no | Yes. Informal |

The legitimacy of the ACHR has benefited from a human rights discourse, while the LOCs' connection to the dictatorship makes them vulnerable to political criticisms. LOCs frequently obstruct legal change because of their broad scope and too detailed regulations, while the ACHR's scope is abstract enough to allow diverse interpretations. The informal quasi-constitutional status of the ACHR seems to be flexible and unstable.

When politicians try to modify or eliminate the LOCs, they need to change the LOCs' constitutional features by a *formal* legal change that requires a supermajority that is particularly hard to achieve. On the contrary, when some reject the ACHR (for instance, imagine a conservative group criticizing a progressive IACtHR jurisprudence), an *informal* change of its quasi-constitutional status might be sufficient to calm down the criticisms. A repeal of the BDC and CDC doctrines (which provide for the ACHR' constitutional canon and supremacy features) is a feasible strategy that does not trigger the same political costs associated with an ACHR denunciation or straight derogation. If the ACHR loses its supremacy feature and it is no longer considered to be part of the constitutional canon, the ACHR would still be a QCL because it is rigid and it is protected against possible judicial challenges.

The Chilean example supports the idea that, in countries that have a supreme constitution, informal QCL can be unstable and it is easier to adapt to political pressures compared to formal QCL. Because formal QCL can only be modified by a formal constitutional reform, their stability depends on how easy it is to reform the constitution.

The criticisms against formal QCL in Hungary and Spain may provide similar lessons. Scholars and international organizations criticized the Hungarian cardinal laws because of their extensive scope preventing majorities to make relevant changes.[105] The Spanish organic laws (that require an absolute majority)

105 M Bánkuti and others, 'From Separation of Powers to a Government without Checks: Hungary's Old and New Constitutions', *On Hungary's 2011 Fundamental Law* (Central European University Press 2012). A Jakab and P Sonnevend, 'Continuity with Deficiencies: The New Basic Law of Hungary' (2013) 9 EuConst 102.

have received criticisms based on the extensive and unclear subject-matters they regulate, since the early 80s.[106] Another example is the 1999 Venezuelan Constitution, whose organic laws require a 2/3rd majority and necessary ex-ante judicial approval for their modification.[107] On the other side, the French organic laws (which require absolute majority and necessary ex-ante judicial approval) seem to be less controversial.[108]

The framework offered in this paper, including the five features and the distinction between formal and informal QCL, can be used to examine these organic laws or other types of QCL when countries recognize a formal supreme constitution. If successful, this framework will be useful for providing conceptual clarity in comparative research.

106 Angel Garroena Morales, 'Acerca de Las Leyes Orgánicas y de Su Espuria Naturaleza Jurídica' (1980) 13 Rev. Estud. Polit. 169. Before 1985, the Spanish organic laws used to be subject to a mandatory ex-ante judicial review. Louis Favoreu, *Los Tribunales Constitucionales* (Editorial Ariel 1994) 121.

107 They were created by the 1961 Constitution with a different legal structure. See Allan Brewer-Carías, *El Sistema de Justicia Constitucional En La Constitución de 1999* (Ed. Jurídica Venezolana 2000) 90, 96–97.

108 Some French scholars acknowledge the importance of the need for stability, and for avoiding the existence of unconstitutional regulation in key matters. Rousseau (n 12) 99; Burdeau and others (n 12) 651, 678.

# 3 Exploring constitutional statutes in common law systems

*Rivka Weill*[*]

A vibrant discussion currently underway in common law systems explores the notion of "constitutional statutes" and the related phenomenon of "quasi-constitutionality." The phenomenon of "constitutional statutes" poses an interesting conceptual challenge when such statutes enjoy the characteristics typical of the *formal* constitution. Bundling together the idea of a "constitution" with the idea of a "statute" seems paradoxical. The constitution with a big-C (or the *formal* constitution) came to be identified with the following three characteristics: identification, supremacy, and entrenchment. *Identification* means that it is relatively easy to identify the various parts of the constitution. There is a commonly accepted document or set of documents that citizens and elites alike refer to as the country's constitution. *Supremacy* means that the legal system includes a hierarchy of norms that defines the constitution as supreme over regular law, particularly statutes. Thus, a statute should not infringe on a constitutional provision, and, if it does, the courts are typically authorized to exercise judicial review to protect the supremacy of the constitution. Lesser remedies than invalidation may also be the result of the supremacy of the constitution. *Entrenchment* means that the constitutional amendment process is typically more arduous than is the process of amendment of regular statutes. Obviously, different countries offer a spectrum of these characteristics and the fulfilment of the requirements is often a matter of degree. Nonetheless, all three characteristics are intended to distinguish between statutes and the constitution.

This chapter focuses on "constitutional statutes" that enjoy the characteristics normally associated with the formal constitution alone. To conceive of statutes as tantamount to constitutional provisions seems to undermine the very *raison d'etre* of a constitution. If statutes enacted by the regular legislature may be treated as constitutional, then there seems to be no easy identification, supremacy, or entrenchment.

* Professor Rivka Weill is a Senior Research Scholar at Yale Law School (2018–2019) and a faculty member of the Harry Radzyner Law School, IDC. I thank Richard Albert and Joel Colón-Ríos for inviting me to present this paper at a Global Symposium on Quasi-Constitutionality and Constitutional Statutes at Victoria University of Wellington on May 19–20, 2016. Special thanks are due to Claudia Geiringer for her penetrating and thoughtful comments at the symposium that challenged me to improve this essay.

Some commentators may use the term "constitutional statutes" to depict the *material* constitution without ascribing any of the *legal* implications that set such constitutional statutes apart from regular statutes. This latter phenomenon is beyond the purview of this essay.

It should further be clarified that the essay uses the terms "formal" versus "material" constitutions while others may use the terms "written" versus "unwritten" constitutions. What they mean to say is that these *unwritten* constitutional norms do not enjoy the characteristics of the formal constitution. Constitutional statutes are interesting for being relevant both to countries traditionally characterized as having only a material constitution, as well as to countries enjoying a formal constitution.

Although the chapter takes interest in constitutional statutes that matter legally as such, it by no means intends to focus on the implications of these statutes for the work of the courts alone. Rather the aim of the chapter is to portray how constitutional statutes may affect the dialogue between the different branches of government.

The phenomenon of "constitutional statutes" is spread throughout common law countries. In the UK, the *Thoburn* decision of Laws L.J. from 2002 and the more recent *H v. Lord Advocate* as well as *HS2* decisions of the Supreme Court from 2012 and 2014 respectively all recognize the notion of constitutional statutes.[1] Bruce Ackerman's *We the People* from the 1990s, as well as William Eskridge and John Ferejohn's work a decade later on *Super-Statutes*, laid the groundwork for this discussion in the U.S.[2] In New Zealand, the Court of Appeal's 2001 *Pora* decision and the High Court's 2015 *Taylor* decision may arguably be viewed as the New Zealand version of *Thoburn*.[3] In Israel, the constitutional revolution of the mid-1990s crystallized the recognition that Basic Laws enacted by the legislature using regular legislative procedures may be treated as constitutional.[4] In Canada, an examination of the concept of quasi-constitutionality arose as part of the attempt to understand the Canadian Bill of Rights Act 1960 (CBRA) as well as the Charter's override power.[5] In Australia, the mid-1990s High Court decision in *Coco v. The*

1 Thoburn *v.* Sunderland City Council, [2003] Q.B. 151 (2002); BH (AP) (Appellant) and another *v* The Lord Advocate and another (Respondents) (Scotland)—KAS or H (AP) (Appellant) *v* The Lord Advocate and another (Respondents) (Scotland) [2012] UKSC 24; R. (on the application of Buckinghamshire CC) *v* Secretary of State of Transport [2014] UKSC 3, [2014] 1 W.L.R. 324 (also known as: HS2 Action Alliance Ltd).

2 Bruce Ackerman, *We the People: Foundations* (1991); Bruce Ackerman, *We the People: Transformations* (1998); Bruce Ackerman, *We the People: The Civil Rights Revolution* (2014); William N. Eskridge, Jr. & John Ferejohn, *Super-Statutes*, 50 Duke L. J. 1215 (2001); William N. Eskridge, Jr. & John Ferejohn, *A Republic of Statutes: The New American Constitution* (2010).

3 Taylor *v.* Attorney General, [2015] NZHC 1706; R *v* Pora, [2001] 2 NZLR 37 (CA). An appeal against the decision in *Taylor* was recently dismissed by the Supreme Court of New Zealand. Attorney General v. Taylor, [2018] NZSC 104.

4 CA 6821/93 United Mizrahi Bank Ltd. *v.* Migdal Collective Vill., 49 (4) PD 221 [1995] (Isr.). Rivka Weill, *Hybrid Constitutionalism: The Israeli Case for Judicial Review and Why We Should Care*, 30 Berkeley J. Int'l L. 349 (2012).

5 Peter W. Hogg, *Constitutional Law of Canada §12.3(b)* (5th ed., vol. 1); Rivka Weill, *Juxtaposing Constitution-Making and Constitutional-infringement Mechanisms in Israel and*

*Queen*, and the recent extra-judicial writings of NSW Chief Justice James Spigelman suggest that the topic continues to be relevant in legal circles around the world.[6]

While the discussion of constitutional statutes proliferates in these different countries, there is not much cross-fertilization in the way these hybrids are analyzed. Some of these countries grapple with "constitutional statutes" as though they are the only ones confronting the dilemmas raised by them. This is especially evident in U.K. and U.S. scholarship.[7] Yet in different countries, the phenomenon of quasi-constitutionality might mean different things to different political actors and academics. The sticking point is how to identify constitutional statutes (*canon construction*) and why bother identifying them (*ramifications*). The answers vary within and across countries.

Not all countries are positioned alike with regard to the ramifications of constitutional statutes. Two archetypal constitutional models define a country's position: constitutional supremacy, typified by the U.S., and legislative supremacy, exemplified in the U.K. system. American constitutional supremacy is based on a two-tier system: higher constitutional law and lower regular statutes.[8] British legislative supremacy traditionally equated constitutional law with regular law.[9] Thus, recognizing the existence of constitutional statutes in the U.S. aligns its model more closely with legislative supremacy than traditionally perceived. When the U.K. develops the notion of constitutional statutes, it shifts away from a model of legislative supremacy toward one of constitutional supremacy. Thus, the two models do not contrast, but share a continuum.

Identifying where a country stands along that continuum and how it came to be positioned there is crucial to understanding what a country might gain or lose from these developments. For each country, the incentives for utilizing constitutional statutes differ. Thus, for example, the U.S. may lose some of the advantages associated with the formal constitution by recognizing the phenomenon of constitutional statutes. It may primarily sacrifice easy identification of constitutional norms, clear supremacy of these norms as well as a defined track for their amendment. The U.K. may gain some of the advantages of the formal constitution by recognizing constitutional statutes, otherwise not available to it under the traditional understanding of legislative sovereignty.

The phenomenon of constitutional statutes is not unique to common law systems. In fact, civil law systems may appear to be more natural "habitats" for constitutional statutes. In civil law systems, "organic statutes" enjoy an intermediate status between

*Canada: On the Interplay between Common Law Override and Sunset Override*, 49 Isr. L. Rev. 103 (2016).

6 Coco *v* The Queen (1994) 179 CLR 427; James Spigelman, *Statutory Interpretation and Human Rights* (2008).

7 Ackerman Foundations, *supra* note 2 at 4, 252; Scott Stephenson, *The Supreme Court's Renewed Interest in Autochthonous Constitutionalism*, P.L. 2015 394; Tarunabh Khaitan, "Constitution" as a Statutory Term, 129 L.Q.R. 589 (2013).

8 Bernard Bailyn, *The Ideological Origins of the American Revolution*, 160–229 (1992).

9 Albert V. Dicey, *Introduction to the Study of the Law of the Constitution*, 39 (8th ed. 1915).

constitutional and regular law. The legislature may enact these organic statutes yet they override regular law, which must then be aligned with them.[10] The French constitutional system, for example, recognizes "organic statutes" to which regular statutes must conform or be treated as unconstitutional (*supremacy* feature).[11] In some systems, organic statutes require the support of legislative super-majorities for their enactment or amendment (*entrenchment* feature).[12]

This essay focuses on constitutional statutes in common law countries alone because they share unique characteristics. Statutes are historically younger than common law, and they are blunter in their influence on the development of law.[13] Parliaments were initially established as gatekeepers of monarchy's power of taxation.[14] Only later did they become principally engaged in legislation. In the meantime, courts were developing common law, case-by-case, in an evolutionary fashion. While some of us treat all judicial decisions as "common law," the term uniquely describes situations in which the courts make new law, as distinguished from interpreting legal norms or filling gaps.[15]

With this background in mind, the concept of a constitutional statute raises particular questions in the common law context. Does the emergence of "constitutional statutes" attempt to credit certain statutes with the status once belonging to some parts of the common law alone? Are constitutional statutes a common law phenomenon in the sense that the very notion of constitutional statutes depends on recognition by the courts? Do statutes become "constitutional statutes" only by their integration into the common law? To answer these intertwined questions, it is best to focus on constitutional statutes in common law systems. This chapter will further discuss western common law countries alone that share a common cultural background though constitutional statutes exist in other countries as well.

This essay argues that we should analyze constitutional statutes along two deeply connected vectors: what makes these statutes constitutional (*identification*) and what are the ramifications of such identification (*consequences*). It further argues that the answer to the first question affects the results of the second. The essay argues that statutes are identified as constitutional based on either the *process* of their enactment or their *content*, which may itself be subdivided into two classifications: content in terms of importance and content in terms of entrenchment language. Of course, a statute may be deemed constitutional based on *both* process and content, but the essay suggests that a constitutional statute that owes its status to process stands

10 Charles M. Fombad, "The Evolution of Modern African Constitutions: A Retrospective Perspective", in *The Separation of Powers in African Constitutionalism* at 48 fn. 157 (Charles M. Fombad ed. 2016).

11 John Bell, French Constitutional Law 63 (1992).

12 *See e.g.* Spain's Constitution (1978), §81; Dominican Republic's Constitution (2010), §112.

13 Guido Calabresi, *A Common Law for the Age of Statutes* (1982).

14 Carl J. Friedrich, *Constitutional Government and Democracy: Theory and Practice in Europe and America*, 271 (Revised ed. 1949).

15 Aharon Barak, *Purposive Interpretation in Law* (2005).

higher in the hierarchy of norms than a constitutional statute that owes its standing to content alone.

The essay does not treat content as a *necessary* condition for identifying constitutional statutes. Although we typically define constitutional law as dealing with the distribution of state power and individual rights, this is descriptive rather than prescriptive for the purpose of this essay. Defining constitutional law by its content is characteristic of countries with a material constitution alone. As constitutional law and regular law stand on par in these systems, the only distinguishing feature is their content. In contrast, requiring constitutional statutes that have formal legal implications—which are the focus of this essay—to conform to a predefined content would put the courts or some other institution as the guardian of what the constitution is about. The courts in some systems exercise such powers by applying the "unconstitutional constitutional amendment" doctrine. While this is a possible choice of a constitutional system, it is by no means universal.[16] It would further take away from the political branches and the polity at large the power to define over time what their unique constitutional law is about.

Constitutional statutes are often treated as though they are made of one cloth, when in fact they belong to different categories based on the justification for, as well as ramifications of, their constitutionality. *Thoburn* may serve as an example. In that decision, Laws L.J. enumerated the following statutes as constitutional: Magna Carta 1297, the Bill of Rights 1689, the Union with Scotland Act 1706, the Reform Acts 1832, 1867, and 1884, which distributed and enlarged the franchise, the Human Rights Act 1998, the Scotland Act 1998, and the Government of Wales Act 1998.[17] Yet, as will be discussed below, some of these constitutional statutes owe their status to process and some to their content, and there are different ramifications for each. Moreover, within the same country, different lists of constitutional statutes may be composed by different authorities since a country may lack consensus regarding the basic question of identification.

Part I discusses constitutional statutes that should be accorded their special status because of the process of their enactment. Part II discusses constitutional statutes that are the result of the legislature bestowing on them special status by using entrenchment language. Part III deals with constitutional statutes that gain their status in an evolutionary way over time because of the importance of their content to their society. Part IV tackles the special category of statutes that require supermajorities or referenda for their repeal. It suggests that some of these statutes should be accorded their special status based on process while others based on content, with different ramifications for each. Part V concludes by showing why it is so important to distinguish between these different types of constitutional statutes.

16 Rivka Weill, *The New Commonwealth Model of Constitutionalism Notwithstanding: On Judicial Review and Constitution-Making*, 62 Am. J. Comp. L. 127 (2014).

17 Thoburn, *supra* note 1, at para 62. The Supreme Court proposed a somewhat different list in the HS2 decision, *supra* note 1, at 382.

## I. Process-based constitutional statutes

The statutes discussed in this part bear the title "statutes" but their process of enactment differentiates them from other statutes. While regular statutes are enacted by the legislature alone, these constitutional statutes are the product of a higher authority than the legislature—typically the People. That means they are the result of an "extended process of interaction between political elites [especially the various branches of government] and ordinary citizens."[18] As they are the product of a higher authority, they deserve the superior status of a constitution.

### *A. Constitutional politics*

Because it is the legislature that codifies the text, the idea of a statute embodying constitutional text seems objectionable on its face. Granting the legislature the power to make both legislative and constitutional law would undermine the very hierarchical nature of law. Nonetheless, rejecting the idea that the legislature can codify constitutional law would be a grave misread of comparative experience. Legislative assemblies are often permitted or even required to adopt constitutional documents at the inception of the state. It is preferable at the founding moment to see two separate assemblies formulating laws—a constituent assembly in charge of adopting the constitution and a regular legislature in charge of enacting regular law. Separating the two tasks enables the constituent assembly to consider the long-term benefit to society at large, disconnected from daily political considerations. It would have further enabled that body to garner a separate mandate from the People for the enactment of constitutional law. But this model may not be affordable to new states. Often, the pool of people one would find in the legislature is the same as that which could populate a constituent assembly.

Participants in the first legislature of a newly established state often play dual legislative and constitutive roles.[19] This legislature enjoys a special mandate by the People to adopt a constitution as the Founding Fathers and Mothers of the state. This founding moment harnesses the People's energy to define their constitutional identity. There may be greater social willingness to reach compromises during the celebratory moment of the birth of the new state. As the mechanism for this self-definition, the first legislature may be treated as a better proxy for the People than a regular legislature operating during regular times. Constitutional documents adopted by the legislature at the founding moment are usually called "Constitutions" rather than "constitutional statutes."

What we might fail to comprehend as a society is that this unique process may repeat itself beyond the founding moment, during less revolutionary times. That is, the legislature may enact statutes that reflect the outcome of

18 Ackerman, Transformations, *supra* note 2, at 162.

19 Jon Elster, "Legislatures as Constituent Assemblies", in *The Least Examined Branch: The Role of the Legislatures in the Constitutional State* 181 (Richard W. Bauman & Tsvi Kahana eds. 2006).

momentous constitutional processes. The political actors involved are aware that these constitutional statutes were enacted by the People and only codified by the legislature. Thus, dissenters accept the legitimacy of these enactments even when they reject their content.[20]

Since, in the life of the matured state, the legislature is treated as the composer of regular law, yet we sense that some rare statutes have been enacted as a result of constitutional politics, we label them "constitutional statutes." They are perpetuated as "androgynous"—merely *quasi*-constitutional—while in fact they should be accorded full constitutional status based on the process of their enactment.

## *B. American constitutional statutes*

Bruce Ackerman's *We the People* trilogy has contributed greatly to our understanding of the phenomenon of constitutional statutes. Ackerman argues that the American People have revolutionized their constitutional law through extra-Article V mechanisms. Ackerman developed criteria for identifying when the People's voice results in constitutional law, whether it is codified in formal constitutional amendments, statutes or Court decisions. He suggests, for example, that the Civil Rights Act 1964, the Voting Rights Act 1965, and the Fair Housing Act 1968 should all be treated as constitutional statutes.[21]

Ackerman suggests that, in addition to the formal Article V mechanism for constitutional amendments, there is the living Constitution which is developed in a common law fashion through a six-stage process, recurring every decade or three: (i) one of the national institutions *signals* change; (ii) it then *proposes* the content of that change in statutes or judicial decisions; (iii) subsequent *triggering elections* give the People an opportunity to elect presidential and legislative candidates who belong to one or the other side of the constitutional debate; (iv) if reformers win the elections, they earn a mandate to *elaborate* the constitutional change; (v) later, *ratifying elections* determine the fate of the reform; and (vi) *consolidating* occurs when even the opponents of the constitutional reform "switch in time" and accept its finality. The constitutional change should gain bipartisan support if it is to be binding constitutionally.[22]

The American incentives for supplementing formal constitutional amendments with constitutional statutes are manifold: *First*, true commitment to popular sovereignty suggests that Article V constrains constituted bodies but the People

20 Rivka Weill, *Evolution vs. Revolution: Dueling Models of Dualism*, 54 Am. J. Comp. L. 429 (2006).

21 Ackerman, The Civil Rights Revolution, *supra* note 2.

22 The Australian procedure of double dissolution in case of persistent disagreement between the two houses over fundamental issues does not necessarily replicate Ackermanian politics. It is about replacing the identity of the body in charge of deciding the change (joint sitting instead of the separate consent of each of the two houses) because of lack of ability to overcome the resistant branch. It is not about the resistant branch switching in time to accept that the people have spoken regarding the constitutional issue.

may express their sovereignty in other ways as well. Thus, statutes should be identified as "constitutional" when they express the sustained, deep, and deliberative decision of the People.

*Second*, Article V is too rigid to be treated as the sole mechanism for making constitutional law. While it is difficult to produce false positives using Article V, this mechanism might easily lead to false negatives. Failing to recognize and validate these extra-Article V mechanisms might mean the death of popular sovereignty in America.

*Third*, Article V does not reflect America's current national identity. Consent under Article V relies on the importance of federalism, in which the dual players are the national legislative assembly and state legislatures. But, after the Civil War, Americans came to identify themselves first as a national rather than federal people. This shift prompted the need to supplement Article V with a higher-law -making mechanism that relies on national institutions, and the interplay between Congress, the Court, and the President.

### *C. U.K. constitutional statutes*

Ackerman intended to describe a uniquely American process of higher lawmaking by analyzing the unique American constitutional history. In fact, similar higher lawmaking processes are manifested in other countries. Most surprising of all is their operation in the U.K., where scholars have long assumed there is no special process for the enactment of constitutional law.[23] The British frequently cite Dicey for the proposition that in Britain: "[N]either the Act of Union with Scotland nor the Dentists Act, 1878, has more claim than the other to be considered a supreme law."[24]

However, during the height of Dicey's writings on parliamentary sovereignty, British constitutional law was enacted using a different process than regular law. Between 1832 and 1911, the British constitutional system operated *de facto* under a unique "referendal model" of popular sovereignty. The First Reform Act in 1832 started the British democratization process by extending the franchise to the middle class. The democratization brought great pressure on the Upper House, and it led the Lords to recharacterize their veto from aristocratic to the instrument of a democratic-referendal power. By vetoing constitutional legislation initiated by the Commons, the Lords allowed the People to pronounce their judgment on it. Following the Lords' veto, the Commons would typically dissolve and the election would function like a semi-referendum on the topic. If the election returned the reformers to power, the Lords would accept that the People had spoken and allow the constitutional legislation to pass. The Lords would not consent to the content of the reform but recognize that it was

23 David Feldman, *The Nature and Significance of "Constitutional" Legislation*, 129 L.Q.R. 343 (2013).

24 Dicey, *supra* note 9, at 78.

the product of constitutional politics. Otherwise, the election would affirm that the Lords had accurately represented the People on that issue and had been justified in exercising their veto.[25]

Major political actors and scholars of the period recognized this to be the practice. The most important constitutional enactments of the period—the three Reform Acts of 1832, 1867 and 1884 democratizing British elections, the Irish Church Act 1869 amending the Union Act and the Parliament Act 1911 redefining the two Houses' power—passed through this special constitutional process. Even Dicey acknowledged that the Lords had to yield to the Commons when the latter represented the People's will, since the People were the true sovereign in Britain.[26] Some of these enactments found their way to the "list" suggested by Laws L.J.—principally the three reform acts—although Judge Laws did not assign them to the list because of their process of enactment.

This referendal model came to an end in 1911, when the Parliament Act 1911 transformed the Lords' veto power from absolute to suspensory. Even after 1911, the suspensory veto had the potential to enable constitutional politics but to a more limited extent. Further diminution of the Lords' veto power in the Parliament Act 1949 led Britain to adopt the referendum as a replacement of the Lords' veto.[27]

What is notable is that some of the constitutional statutes identified by Laws L.J. as constitutional were endorsed by the People in referenda. In 1975, Britain conducted a national referendum on continuing British membership in the European Union. Although the referendum was declared consultative, the government committed to abide by its results.[28] This referendum may be seen as ratification of the European Communities Act 1972. The government also held referenda on Scotland's and Wales' devolution in 1979 and repealed the devolution Acts following their defeat in the referenda. It eventually enacted devolution Acts, after the public endorsed devolution in referenda held in 1997 in both Scotland and Wales.[29] These referenda may be seen as ratifying the Scotland Act 1998 and the Government of Wales Act 1998 appearing in Laws' list.

### *D. American and British constitutional statutes compared*

The incentives that lead the British to resort to constitutional statutes must be differentiated from those influencing the Americans. The British developed their

25 Rivka Weill, *We the British People*, Public law 380 (2004).

26 Dicey, *supra* note 9, at 287; Rivka Weill, *Dicey Was Not Diceyan*, 62 Cambridge L.J. 474 (2003).

27 Rivka Weill, *The Anglo-American Constitutional Model: Why the British and American Constitutional Systems Are Not as Different as Most Think* (JSD Thesis, Yale Law School, 2002) (available at the Yale Law School Library).

28 A. Chander, *Sovereignty, Referenda, and the Entrenchment of a United Kingdom Bill of Rights*, 101 Yale L.J. 457 (1991).

29 D. Denver et al., *Scotland Decides: The Devolution Issue and the Scottish Referendum* (2000); L. Andrews, *Wales Says Yes* (1999).

popular sovereignty model against the backdrop of parliamentary sovereignty. The British transformation to popular sovereignty was influenced by two opposite but equally powerful desires: On one hand, Parliament wanted to enable the People to voice their opinions and grant a *specific* mandate as pre-condition for constitutional change. On the other, Parliament wanted to avoid a break with the past—which historically has often entailed violence[30]—even as it launched a new British constitutional system.

Thus, the British, in a common law evolutionary fashion, developed a new higher lawmaking track in which they *supplemented* existing constitutional mechanisms (primarily Parliament) with additional players (the People) through referendal elections in the nineteenth century or referenda in the twentieth century. This need to gain the consent of both Parliament and the People to enact constitutional law stands at the center of Brexit politics in the twenty-first century.[31]

This development is markedly different than the American approach. American constitutional statutes are designed to change the identity of the political actors whose consent is needed to achieve constitutional change. Instead of garnering supermajorities in Congress and seeking consensus among the various state legislatures, the American approach to constitutional statutes is satisfied by aligning all national political institutions in favor of constitutional change. Recognizing constitutional statutes in America would require breaching the Article V amendment process (or at least reading it as a nonexclusive mechanism), while no similar "price" is paid to recognize such statutes in Britain.

Ideally, all political actors should recognize that these "statutes" are the product of "We the People," and as such should be accorded all three attributes of constitutional law—easy identification, supremacy and entrenchment. Thus, the various political actors, including the courts, should treat regular statutes conflicting with these constitutional statutes as invalid or at least inoperative. Changing the content of the constitutional statutes would require resorting to the People.

However, these constitutional statutes do not enjoy the status of formal constitutional enactments in America or in Britain. Even Ackerman himself, fell short of treating the very statutes he identified as full constitutional amendments.[32] Rather, these statutes are treated like the constitutional statutes that gained their status because of their content rather than process, as further discussed below.

## II. Language-based constitutional statutes

This part discusses statutes that the legislature chose to mark as worthy of special constitutional treatment by requiring either explicit repeal or meeting

30 Hannah Arendt, *On Revolution* (1977).

31 R (on the Application of Miller and another) *v* Secretary of State for Exiting the European Union, [2017] UKSC 5.

32 Rivka Weill, *Constitutional Statutes or Overriding the Court-On Bruce Ackerman's We the People: The Civil Rights Revolution*, 13(1) Jerus. Rev. Leg. Stud. 1 (2016).

substantive criteria, as prerequisites for their repeal. These constitutional statutes are the product of normal politics and thus challenge traditional understanding of legislative sovereignty.

### *A. Explicit repeal or override*

Another type of constitutional statutes is one in which the legislature used entrenchment language. The Canadian federal legislature, for example, enacted the CBRA through regular legislative processes, and its repeal requires simple legislative majorities.[33] Nonetheless, the CBRA requires any statute infringing on its provisions to use an explicit language of override:

> Every law of Canada shall, unless it is expressly declared by an Act of the Parliament of Canada that it shall operate notwithstanding the Canadian Bill of Rights, be so construed and applied as not to abrogate, abridge or infringe ... [34]

This is a deviation from the standard parliamentary sovereignty doctrine which permits the legislature to implicitly repeal statutes.[35] The CBRA could have led the courts to treat it as merely an *interpretive* (but not overriding) bill of rights, requiring courts to make reasonable efforts to interpret other statutes to align with the CBRA. This in itself deviates from standards of interpretation under parliamentary sovereignty.[36]

The CBRA does not explicitly answer the dilemma of what courts should do in a case of irresolvable conflict and absent explicit notwithstanding language in the later conflicting regular statute. The Canadian Supreme Court ultimately held that, in such a case it will declare the later conflicting statute inoperative.[37] It interpreted the CBRA as an overriding document.

Explicit repeal is a procedural requirement; the legislature must use certain "magic words" to affect repeal. Requirements of explicit repeal or override are supposedly not aimed at entrenchment. There is nothing truly counter-majoritarian about them. A legislative majority can get its way, but it must be clear about it. The requirement allows society to give special treatment to fundamental values, by insisting that repeal comes after clear deliberation with the legislature taking public responsibility for its actions. Explicit repeal or override requirements are further intended to deter a legislature from deviating from the quasi-entrenched constitutional statute.

33 Peter W. Hogg, Constitutional Law of Canada §35.1 (5th ed., vol. 2).

34 Canadian Bill of Rights Act, 1960 S.C., ch. 44, § 2 (Can.).

35 Karen Petroski, *Retheorizing the Presumption Against Implied Repeals*, 92 Cal. L. Rev. 487 (2004).

36 J.W.F. Allison, *The English Historical Constitution: Continuity, Change and European Effects*, 221–236 (2007).

37 Regina *v.* Drybones, [1970] 3 S.C.R. 282 (Can.).

Nonetheless, the effects of this quasi-entrenchment tool are hotly debated in the U.K. and New Zealand. When common law courts interpret statutes, they generally assume that, if the legislature desired to abolish an earlier statute, it would have done so explicitly. Thus, courts would interpret a statute to imply the repeal of an earlier statute only when the two cannot be otherwise reconciled. Implied repeal is a last resort tool. When statutes are quasi-entrenched through language requiring explicit repeal, the courts might not resort to implicit repeal at all, which might thus frustrate the most recent will of the legislature.[38] This seems to negate parliamentary sovereignty.

Besides deterring the legislature from breaching the constitutional statute, the main effect of explicit repeal or override requirements is to alter a court's understanding of its choices when interpreting a statute. Courts would be reluctant to usurp the legislature's role by invalidating statutes. Even in Canada, the *Drybones* decision stands out as exceptional in invalidating a statute based on the CBRA in the pre-Charter era. As an interpretive technique, explicit repeal or override requirements thus enable the legal system to maintain the appearance that it is faithful to legislative sovereignty.

What should courts do when a later statute cannot be interpreted to align with a quasi-entrenched constitutional statute and this later conflicting statute contains no explicit repeal or override language? Cynics might say that this situation would never happen; that courts are experts at creative interpretation and can always find a way to dissolve the conflict that would make the later statute inoperative. The facts on the ground may suggest that the cynics are not so off the mark.

Jurists have suggested that the later inconsistent statute should prevail if the "necessary implication" is that it repeals the earlier semi-entrenched one.[39] This is a fair reading of Laws' *Thoburn* opinion.[40] It is not, however, the opinion of the UK Supreme Court which requires explicit repeal.[41] If you are not cynical and you do not abide by the necessary implication solution, then you might need to accept the *Drybones* solution in such cases of irresolvable conflict.

Alternatively, a constitutional system may decide that despite the legislature's attempt to bestow semi-constitutionality on a statute by requiring explicit repeal or override, this requirement should not be respected. Instead, the courts should recognize even an implicit repeal of the semi-entrenched statute. In such a case, the legislature's attempt to bestow semi-constitutionality on the statute would fail. Thus, how later legislatures and courts respond to semi-constitutionality

38 Farrah Ahmed and Adam Perry, *The Quasi-Entrenchment of Constitutional Statutes*, 73 Cambridge L.J. 514 (2014).

39 *Id.*

40 Thoburn, *supra* note 1, at para 63.

41 *H v Lord Advocate, supra* note 1, at para 30 of Lord Hope's opinion with whom Lady Hale and Lord Kerr agreed.

language is determinative of whether a statute may gain or maintain semi-"constitutional" status over time or not.

### *B. Substantive entrenchment*

In the comparative context, it is not common to find legislatures using statutory language that requires explicit repeal or override.[42] More typical is substantive entrenchment language, mandating that subsequent legislatures abide by a certain substantive standard set by an earlier legislature.

One would think that substantive entrenchment would fare differently than the procedural requirement of explicit repeal. The main task of parliament is to legislate with respect to others, not to govern its own legislative procedures. If parliament is able to create an effective substantive entrenchment, it is relinquishing its legislative power to a previous majority, which is entirely beyond its democratic authority. This distinction between forbidding substantive entrenchment but allowing procedural entrenchment is at the crux of the "manner and form" theory.[43]

This is why courts' translation of substantive entrenchment into a procedural explicit repeal or override mechanism makes sense. By treating substantive entrenchments as procedural, "manner and form," requirements demanding *explicit* repeal or override by simple majorities, parliament's sovereignty is supposedly maintained. Under this theory, every constitutional statute that is substantively entrenched must be read to contain an implicit "notwithstanding clause," which enables the legislature to either abide by substantive entrenchment or explicitly override it when enacting later statutes. Parliament remains free to enact for others, it must only be clear about expressing its will.

The British 1934 case of *Ellen Street* is often brought up as an example that substantive entrenchment has no effect in parliamentary sovereignty systems.[44] The case dealt with section 7(1) of the Acquisition of Land (Assessment of Compensation), Act, 1919, which provided:[45]

> The provisions of the Act or order by which the land is authorised to be acquired, or of any Act incorporated therewith, shall, in relation to the matters dealt with in this Act, have effect subject to this Act, and so far as inconsistent with this Act these provisions shall cease to have or shall not have effect.

42 For Israel's experience with override: Rivka Weill, *Reconciling Parliamentary Sovereignty and Judicial Review: On the Theoretical and Historical Origins of the Israeli Legislative Override Power*, 39 Hastings Const. L. Q. 457 (2012).

43 Sir W. Ivor Jennings, The Law and the Constitution, 139–45 (3rd ed., 1943); Robin Elliot, *Rethinking Manner and Form: From Parliamentary Sovereignty to Constitutional Values*, 29 Osgoode Hall L. J. 215 (1991).

44 Ellen Street Estates, Ltd *v* Minister of Health, [1934] All ER Rep 385.

45 Id. at 387 (citing the Act).

The appellants argued that this substantive entrenchment provision can be amended via explicit repeal alone and otherwise the statute prevails over later conflicting statutes. Appellants lost the case but the judges found that the 1919 statute was repealed in "the plainest and most unambiguous terms"[46] and that the later statutes were "clearly inconsistent"[47] with the 1919 Act. Thus, even if the judges did not require explicit repeal of substantive entrenchment, the circumstances of the case came very near to it.

The logic that substantive entrenchment is an explicit repeal requirement arose already in *Ellen Street*. It definitely resonates in later treatment of constitutional statutes in common law countries.

The 1998 UK Human Rights Act (HRA) offers another telling example.[48] Section 3(1) of the HRA states: "So far as it is possible to do so, primary legislation and subordinate legislation must be read and given effect in a way which is compatible with the Convention rights."[49] Section 4 further provides that, if the court reaches the conclusion that primary legislation "is incompatible with a Convention right, it may make a declaration of that incompatibility."[50] It further clarifies that a declaration of incompatibility "does not affect the validity, continuing operation or enforcement of the provision in respect of which it is given."[51] Furthermore, such declaration "is not binding on the parties to the proceedings in which it is made."[52]

The HRA rejects a *Drybones* solution. Instead of forcing the legislature to explicitly repeal the HRA, the courts explicitly declare the existence of repeal [incompatibility] in a particular context. The mechanism of making the legislature pay an explicit public political price for violating a constitutional statute is also present under the HRA. Therefore, it is no surprise that *Thoburn* included the HRA in the list of constitutional statutes requiring explicit repeal.

New Zealand Bill of Rights Act (NZBRA) 1990 provides a more complex example. It was enacted as regular legislation that may be repealed by simple majorities. The parliament explicitly rejected a stronger version modeled after the American constitution.

On the one hand, Section 6, like Section 3 of the HRA, states: "Whenever an enactment can be given a meaning that is consistent with the rights and freedoms contained in this Bill of Rights, that meaning shall be preferred to any other meaning."[53] It thus orders the courts to use robust interpretation in favor of the protection of rights. It also includes substantive entrenchment language in Section 5, which reads: "Subject to Section 4, the rights and freedoms contained in this

46 Id., Maugham L.J. opinion.
47 Id., Scrutton L.J. opinion.
48 Cf. Weill, *The New Commonwealth Model, supra* note 16.
49 Human Rights Act, 1998, §3(1).
50 Id. §4(2).
51 Id. §4(6)(a).
52 Id. §4(6)(b).
53 New Zealand Bill of Rights Act, 1990, §6.

Bill of Rights may be subject only to such reasonable limits prescribed by law as can be demonstrably justified in a free and democratic society."[54] This language is identical to Section 1 of the Canadian Charter of Rights and Freedoms from 1982, which operates as a full formal constitution.[55] Based on this language, proportionality review became the standard in Canada and later in New Zealand.

On the other hand, the NZBRA seems to reject the possibility that a later conflicting statute must explicitly repeal it. Quite the opposite. Section 4, which supersedes the proportionality requirement, provides:

> No court shall, in relation to any enactment (whether passed or made before or after the commencement of this Bill of Rights)–
>
> (a) hold any provision of the enactment to be impliedly repealed or revoked, or to be in any way invalid or ineffective; or
> (b) decline to apply any provision of the enactment— by reason only that the provision is inconsistent with any provision of this Bill of Rights.[56]

Thus, when courts are unable to reconcile statutes in an interpretation that favors the NZBRA, both earlier and later statutes seem to prevail over the NZBRA. However, if the courts rigorously interpret a conflicting statute in a way that aligns it with the NZBRA, then the legislature is forced to use explicit language to overcome the courts' interpretation. In addition, the New Zealand Supreme Court in a majority opinion in 2018 held that the courts enjoy an implied power to declare a statute incompatible with the NZBRA, thus replacing the legislature as the entity making an explicit override.[57]

### C. *The constitutionality of these entrenched statutes*

By entrenching a statute, the legislative branch sets a tool that may affect the dynamics between the different political branches of government. In the above examples discussed, entrenched legislation led to the following semi-constitutional characteristics: easy identification of the semi-constitutional statutes based on entrenchment language (*identification*); favorable treatment of entrenched statutes by the courts through interpretation or at least declarations of incompatibility of conflicting statutes (*semi-superiority*); special processes for amending the entrenched statute to the extent that political actors accepted and enforced the demand for explicit repeal or override (*semi-entrenchment*).

These constitutional statutes differentiate between interpretation and invalidity. Entrenchment language leads to robust interpretation, and courts are discouraged

54 Id. §5.
55 Constitution Act 1982, Part I, §1.
56 New Zealand Bill of Rights Act 1990, §4.
57 *Taylor, supra* note 3.

and oftentimes even prohibited from declaring later conflicting statutes inoperative. The preference for rigorous interpretation over inoperability supposedly maintains legislative sovereignty.

But it is arguable that the power to interpret statutes creatively allows the courts to intervene in legislative sovereignty more readily then declaring a statute inoperable. The reasons are as follows:

*First*, the courts can frustrate the legislature's intentions by robust interpretation. Let's take an illustrative example. If I commit to meet you at 14:00 today and you interpret "today" to mean any day, then you might take advantage of that flexibility. You would have better respected my will if you declared that today cannot happen and thus the meeting is inoperative.

*Second*, the court's decision may materially affect the remedies of the parties to the case. If the court interprets the statute in a robust way that aligns with the petitioners' rights, then the petitioners receive the remedies they petitioned for immediately. If, on the other hand, the court finds such interpretation impossible and declares the statute inoperative, then the litigants might have to wait for the legislature to act in order to address their grievances.

*Third*, the court's decision might hinder the legislature's ability to respond to the judicial ruling. When a court declares a statute inoperative, the void might spur the legislature to gather majorities needed to draft a different legislative scheme. But the forces of inertia and "veto-gates" operate differently when a statutory arrangement remains intact, and the legislature desires merely to amend that arrangement in response to judicial interpretation.

*Fourth*, when the courts invalidate a statute, their decision resonates throughout the political arena and is thoroughly discussed. The courts thus weigh carefully whether to embark on such a costly course. Too many judicial decisions to invalidate statutes may result in structural changes to the courts' jurisdiction and power. In contrast, no similar constraints operate to restrain the courts from adopting robust interpretation of statutes. Frustrating the legislative will through interpretation would always be a matter of judgment.

This discussion thus suggests that robust interpretation, typically resulting from the desire to protect constitutional statutes, is a mark of the semi-superiority of the constitutional statute. It might be no less intrusive on parliamentary sovereignty than declarations of invalidity.

## III. Content-based constitutional statutes

A third type of constitutional statutes are those that attain their special status over time, in an evolutionary fashion, because they were later legally acknowledged as having special constitutional importance.

Commentators often define constitutions by the topics they regulate—primarily the division of power among branches of government and individual rights. Laws' definition in *Thoburn* is a classic example:

> In my opinion a constitutional statute is one which (a) conditions the legal relationship between citizen and state in some general, overarching manner, or (b) enlarges or diminishes the scope of what we would now regard as fundamental constitutional rights. (a) and (b) are of necessity closely related: it is difficult to think of an instance of (a) that is not also an instance of (b). The special status of constitutional statutes follows the special status of constitutional rights.[58]

The problem with such a content-based definition is that it is both over- and under-inclusive. The definition is over-inclusive in the sense that content alone should not be enough to warrant special status; rather it should be one of several factors weighing on such a decision. It is under-inclusive in the sense that it grants political actors the power to exclude topics as not worthy of constitutional status because they do not "fit" an expected content, even if the body polity decided otherwise.

The constitutional statutes that fit this third category are not about a predefined content. Rather, one could use Eskridge and Ferejohn's work on superstatutes to draw some typical characteristics of statutes that attain constitutional importance over time because of their content. It should be noted that scholars tend to conflate Ackerman's and Eskridge and Ferejohn's work on constitutional statutes. This conflation is understood in light of the fact that some statutes make it to both Ackerman's and Eskridge and Ferejohn's lists. The most prominent examples are the Civil Rights Acts of the 1960s. However, this essay suggests that their work elaborates different categories of constitutional statutes—Ackerman deals with process-based constitutional statutes while Eskridge and Ferejohn deal with content-based constitutional statutes.

Eskridge and Ferejohn define a constitutional statute as follows:

> A super-statute is a law or series of laws that (1) seeks to establish a new normative or institutional framework for state policy and (2) over time does "stick" in the public culture such that (3) the super-statute and its institutional or normative principles have a broad effect on the law—including an effect beyond the four corners of the statute.[59]

Eskridge and Ferejohn write that constitutional statutes "successfully penetrate public normative and institutional culture in a deep way."[60] Constitutional statutes "aspire toward changing the common law baseline, and they actually have that effect over time … [and they enjoy] expansive, imperial interpretation."[61] "The key to super-statutedom is acceptance in public culture."[62] Eskridge and Ferejohn

58 Thoburn, *supra* note 1, at para 62.
59 Eskridge and Ferejohn, *Super-Statutes, supra* note 2, at 1216.
60 *Id.* at 1215.
61 *Id.* at 1219.
62 *Id.* at 1230.

emphasize that superstatutes' post-enactment history is often more important than their enactment history.[63] Their emphasis is legitimation achieved through "evolution rather than revolution."[64] The historical perspective is essential to the determination. It is easier in hindsight to decide which statutes enjoy such gravitational force in the legal system that they deserve to be treated as constitutional statutes. The Magna Carta, enumerated in the *Thoburn* decision, comes to mind as one rising to this level of constitutionality.[65]

The criteria suggested by Eskridge and Ferejohn for identifying these statutes seem elusive. Even if we concede that there are statutes that match their criteria, we may disagree about which statutes should make the "list." This is where the courts' role becomes essential. Whereas the legislature may mark statutes as constitutional using language, courts may assist to identify constitutional statutes that are content-based by reading into them a requirement of explicit repeal or override. The content of the statutes then amounts to substantive entrenchment, and this may be overcome only by the legislature's explicit repeal or override. Of course, the courts do not read a requirement of explicit repeal or override in vacuum. They may do so only if in their judgment the way different political actors have treated these statutes raises them to the status of content-based constitutional statutes.

This phenomenon owes its birth to the common law. Through common law development, statutory derogation of common law rights must be explicit.[66] Rights and values that have gravitational force are protected under common law no less simply because the rights and values had their birth in statute. Common law thus incorporates statutory contributions to the development of fundamental rights and values. In this light, *Thoburn* does "for *statutory* constitutional guarantees," as Laws suggested, "what the law already does for *common law* constitutional guarantees."[67]

By requiring explicit language, various constitutional systems, including Israel during its pre-constitutional revolution era, developed common law bills of rights.[68] How are those common law rights and values provided for? One idea is that those rights and values are protected through statutory interpretation. In the absence of explicit legislative authorization to the executive branch, the administration may not infringe on individual rights and values (*ultra-vires*). Everything turns on the interpretation of the authorizing statute, which is usually interpreted narrowly. A different idea is that this common law bill of rights exists even when there is no statute to expound. Under the common law principle of legality, it requires explicit statutory authorization to be infringed upon.

63 *Id.* at 1231.
64 *Id.* at 1271.
65 Tom Bingham, The Rule of Law 210–213 (2010).
66 Calabresi, *supra* note 13.
67 John Laws, *Constitutional Guarantees*, 29 Statute L. Rev. 1 (2008).
68 Weill, *Juxtaposing, supra* note 5.

The same two ideas may be offered by extension to explain constitutional statutes that owe their status to the common law based on their content. The courts either require explicit language to override the constitutional statute or they incorporate the statute's content into the common law so that its content enjoys protection as part of the common law constitutional rights and values.

## IV. Going beyond explicit repeal or override: supermajorities and referenda requirements

Sometimes legislatures use entrenchment language to require supermajorities or even the consent of the people in a referendum, as a prerequisite for amending the constitutional statute. Is such a statute "constitutional" because of process or entrenchment language?

To qualify as a constitutional statute based on the process of enactment, it is not enough that the statute requires a special process for its repeal. It is necessary that the statute itself was enacted via a special process. Also, the special enactment process must involve the People or some higher external authority, as was typical in the Dominions of the British Commonwealth.

The typical examples of "manner and form" restrictions in the literature do not fit the template; they were instances of an imperial legislature binding the lower authority of the Dominion, not examples of a legislature binding itself to certain procedures, as the "manner and form" theory originally conceived.[69] Thus, for example, in the famous *Trethowan* case—the precedential holding on the validity of manner and form requirements—the High Court and the Privy Council required the New South Wales Parliament to comply with Section 7A of the Constitution Act 1902 (NSW) and hold a referendum as a prerequisite for abolishing the Upper House (the Council).[70] They issued injunctions preventing the presentation of the bills affecting such change to the Governor for royal assent until approved by a referendum, as provided in Section 7A. However, the various courts upholding the requirement to hold a referendum as a binding "manner and form" requirement emphasized that this was possible because the NSW was an inferior Dominion legislature. The Imperial British legislature required Dominion legislatures to abide by manner and form under the Colonial Laws Validity Act 1865.[71]

The People may serve as a different source of higher authority. But even the enactment of a statute with the support of supermajorities in the legislature cannot be equated with the People's support. Empirical evidence demonstrates

69 *Cf.* Jennings, *supra* note 43, at 139–45; Geoffrey Marshall, Constitutional Theory 41–53 (1971).

70 Attorney-General for New South Wales *v.* Trethowan, 44 CLR 394 (1931) (High Court); 47 CLR 97 (Privy Council).

71 See also: Carmel McLure, *Key Judicial Decisions on the Constitution Act 1889 (WA) and the Constitution Acts Amendment Act 1899 (WA)*, 36 U. W. Austl. L. Rev. 234, 235 (2012–2013).

that, even when legislation is supported by an overwhelming majority of the representatives, it may not enjoy similarly enthusiastic support of the People. Citizens' electoral votes are usually too far removed from a representative's vote to equate the will of the representatives with the will of the citizenry.[72] Brexit may serve as reminder of the truth of this distinction.

When constitutional statutes attain their status because of process, a constitutional system is expected to give full force to the requirements for supermajorities and referenda as prerequisites for the amendment of these statutes. Otherwise, these higher authorities lose their hierarchical status and have worked in vain.

If, on the other hand, the statutes are "constitutional" based on legislative entrenchment language alone, then in some jurisprudences the courts may treat the requirements for supermajorities or referenda as themselves subject to direct explicit repeal. This way parliamentary sovereignty is retained. Support for this approach may be drawn from jurisprudence discussing the difference between singly and doubly entrenched provisions. Singly, as distinguished from doubly, entrenched provisions refer to provisions requiring super-majorities or referenda that are not themselves entrenched. Section 189 (2) of the New Zealand Electoral Act 1956, which is now found in Section 268 of the Electoral Act 1993, provides a ready example:

> No reserved provision shall be repealed or amended unless the proposal for the amendment or repeal-
>
> (a) Is passed by a majority of seventy-five per cent of all the members of the House of Representatives; or
> (b) Has been carried by a majority of the valid votes cast at a poll of the electors of the European and Maori electoral districts …[73]

When enacting the statute, the Attorney General explained in the parliamentary debates that the government intended single-entrenchment: "Under our Constitution, Parliament cannot bind successive Parliaments, and each successive Parliament may amend any law passed by the previous Parliament."[74] This means that the New Zealand Parliament understood Section 189(2) to allow, by simple majorities, the legislative body to directly abolish the entrenching requirement for supermajorities or referenda.

The courts could also interpret "supermajorities" as requiring an absolute majority. Absolute majority requirements are not truly entrenching provisions but are merely quorum or attendance requirements. If all MPs are present and voting, an absolute majority is the regular majority required. Like explicit repeal, the

72 Weill, Dicey, *supra* note 26.

73 Electoral Act 1956 §189 (2) (New Zealand).

74 Philip A. Joseph, *Constitutional Entrenchment and the MMP Referendum*, 16 N. Z. U. L. Rev. 67, 73 (1994) (citing NZPD vol. 310 (1956) at 2839).

restriction is aimed at ensuring the amendment is not undertaken absent-mindedly or without full accountability.[75] Under this interpretation, legislatures may tighten the requirements for repeal while remaining faithful to majority rule.

Alternatively, the courts could treat these supermajorities or referenda requirements as binding despite the fact that they were enacted by the legislature alone. This interpretation would have systemic consequences, transforming the constitutional system over time from parliamentary sovereignty to "self-embracing" sovereignty (*supermajorities requirements*) or even popular sovereignty (*referenda requirements*).[76] Still, this transformation would require more than action by the courts to treat these requirements as binding; the legislature would have to comply with this transformation. A self-embracing sovereignty is especially problematic for numerous reasons,[77] not least because one would want to locate the locus of sovereignty in some kind of political body capable of action. Granting the minority of legislatures the power to decide the fate of society does not seem democratically prudent.

Of course, the political actors may *de facto* comply with supermajorities or referenda requirements. The constitutional statutes may effectively emulate the effects of a supreme binding constitution. For example, the entrenchment found in the New Zealand Electoral Act discussed above has enjoyed compliance from parliaments and governments since its enactment.[78] Since there was no test case of a legislature breaching the entrenchment, and no judicial response to such breach, it cannot be ascertained whether the New Zealand system remained a full-fledged parliamentary sovereignty system.

It may be that the status of the entrenched provisions of the New Zealand Electoral Act transformed over time so that it is not a matter of political expediency alone to abide by them but they became also legally binding. Further, their breach might risk the wrath of the entire constitutional system and be no less than revolutionary. In this light one may understand the words of the Hon. J.R. Marshall, the then New Zealand Attorney General, introducing the entrenched provisions to the House of Representatives:

> What we are doing has a moral sanction rather than a legal one, but to the extent that these provisions are unanimously supported by both sides of the House, and to the extent that they will be universally accepted by the people, they acquire a force which subsequent Parliaments will, I believe, respect and which subsequent Parliaments will attempt to repeal or amend at their peril against the will of the people.[79]

75 This was Justice Cheshin's minority opinion regarding Israel's Basic Laws in *United MiIzrahi Bank, supra* note 4.

76 Obviously, not every referendum amounts to expressing the People's will. It has to fulfill the requirements that guarantee that the People's broad, deep, and decisive consent was granted.

77 Weill, *The New Commonwealth Model, supra* note 16.

78 Joseph, *supra* note 74.

79 J. B. Robertson, *The Reserved Provisions of the Electoral Act*, 1 Otago L. Rev. 222 (1965–1968).

## V. Epilogue

Understanding why a statute deserves "constitutional" status has far-reaching implications that shape the constitutional dialogue between the political actors. Depending on the reason a statute is viewed as constitutional, the clauses regarding override, proportionality, or entrenchment will be treated differently by the political actors. If a statute is deemed constitutional because of its process of enactment, then we should expect that a similar process would be needed to repeal the statute (*strong entrenchment feature*). Absent that type of repeal, we should not expect that override may be used to circumvent judicial (proportionality) scrutiny. Otherwise, the stringent process would have no purpose, and the higher authority would be effectively placed on par with the regular legislature (*superiority feature*).

If, however, the legislature or the courts attributed semi-constitutionality to the statute based on an entrenchment language or content alone, then we should expect that at least in some traditions entrenchment might be overcome by explicit language. Proportionality scrutiny might be overcome by explicit language as well. In such cases, the constitutional statute might not achieve true supremacy or lasting entrenchment. The constitutional system might collapse again to full parliamentary sovereignty.

There is probably no court in the world that better understood this logic than the Israeli Supreme Court deciding the status of the Basic Laws. The Israeli Basic Laws were enacted by the legislature using the same process of enactment as any other statute. They were not endorsed by large majorities, and their provisions generally permit the legislature to repeal them by simple majorities.[80] The Court in the famous *United Mizrahi Bank* decision could not agree on the theory that may explain why these Basic Laws should be treated as Israel's formal constitution.[81] While President Barak in a plurality opinion opted for the strong theory that their process of enactment was different (regardless of reality), it was Justice Cheshin in a minority opinion who suggested that they may be subject to explicit repeal or override. The other plurality opinion, written by the then retiring President Shamgar, suggested that "Basic Laws" are the mechanism by which the Knesset successfully limits its own sovereignty. The Court understood how much was at stake in choosing a theory to explain the Basic Laws' constitutional nature, and the theoretical quagmire meant they could not reach a *Marbury*-like unanimous consent.[82] They had to settle for a divided Court that achieved more than could possibly be imagined with so few tools, in light of the real constitutional facts of Israel's development.

80 Weill, *Reconciling, supra* note 42.
81 *United Mizrahi Bank, supra* note 4. Weill, Hybrid Constitutionalism, supra note 4.
82 Marbury *v.* Madison, 5 U.S. (1 Cranch) 137 (1803).

Constitutional statutes thus present fascinating tools whose ultimate status depends on how they are treated by the various branches of government within a given system. While some of us deny the existence of constitutional statutes, it seems that they pervade constitutional law of the various western common law countries to such a degree that not tackling with the subject is ignoring large chunks of what constitutional law is all about.

# Part II
# Functions

# Unearthing the 'constitutional' in quasi-constitutionality

*Oran Doyle*[*]

The chapters in this part weave a rich tapestry of quasi-constitutional practices, including but not limited to constitutional statutes. They allow us to explore both the function that quasi-constitutional practices can play in legal systems and, more broadly, the function that the concept of quasi-constitutionality can play in comparative constitutional law and theory. In both cases, our understanding of quasi-constitutionality is parasitic on prior understandings of 'constitutional'. Here we run into some difficulties, however, because comparative constitutional law (itself a rather nebulous term) lacks a unitary understanding of the word 'constitutional' and its cognates. Sometimes, we use 'constitutional' to connote a moral value, that of constrained government. Other times, we use 'constitutional' in a neutral and descriptive way simply to identify the laws and practices that relate to governance. This double usage arguably reflects a fundamental difference in our understanding of law: is it purely a positive fact or does it necessarily involve moral aspiration?

Even within the descriptive use of 'constitutional', however, comparative constitutional lawyers operate with two different understandings. On the one hand, there is the political constitution: the set of practices and laws that constitute the governance function of the state, including the imposition of constraints on government and legislative powers. The political constitution is paradigmatically associated with the United Kingdom and a small number of former British colonies. Its distinguishing feature is content and function: laws and practices that have a particular content or function are *constitutional.* On the other hand, there is the legal constitution: a master-text document interpreted by the courts that stipulates the validity criteria for all other laws and practices in the legal system.[1] The legal constitution is so prevalent that it lacks a paradigm, although the US Constitution occupies a disproportionately large space in the collective consciousness of comparative constitutional lawyers. The distinguishing feature of the legal constitution is status: laws that hold a superordinate status within

* Associate Professor, Trinity College Dublin.

1 The terminology reflects a debate in UK constitutional theory between political and legal constitutionalism.

a legal system are *constitutional.* This in turn makes the scope of the legal constitution relatively precise: interpretative approaches may broaden the meaning of particular provisions but it is clear what provisions are constitutional. In contrast, the political constitution is amorphous. Because legal consequences do not necessarily follow from being a component of the political constitution, its boundary lines are not so carefully policed.

Few if any comparative constitutional lawyers could subscribe entirely to one understanding of 'constitutional' to the exclusion of the other. The content of the legal constitution depends on contingent decisions in particular states about the laws to which they wish to accord this superordinate status. But comparative studies are drawn to consider laws of a similar content or function, rather than just laws of a contingently similar status. One example. In Japan, the Diet amended the Public Offices Election Act to change from a multi-seat constituency system to one of single-seat constituencies combined with proportional representation. The Supreme Court upheld the constitutionality of this change on the basis that the Diet was free to design the electoral system, within some broad limits.[2] In contrast, in Ireland the Constitution mandates a multi-seat PR electoral system for the lower House.[3] Constitutional amendments were required to change this system, the people twice rejecting referendum proposals to that end. If a comparison of the Japanese and Irish approaches to this issue falls within comparative constitutional law, it does so on the basis of a shared understanding of the content or functions of laws rather than their legal status. Whether or not they are included in the master-text constitution, electoral laws are constitutional because of the role they play in constituting the governance function of the state. Even those working within constitutional systems dominated by a legal constitution employ some understanding of a political constitution. Conversely, even within the paradigmatic case of the political constitution, the United Kingdom, legal-constitutional understandings permeate, whether because of the influence of the ECHR and EU law or the migration of constitutional theory developed in systems dominated by a legal constitution. This is reflected in doctrines of implied repeal, with which some of the following chapters engage.

The chapters in this part employ understandings of quasi-constitutionality that reflect the competing usages of the word constitutionality. Mark Hickford theorises about the political in approaching not only quasi-constitutionality but constitutionalism more generally.[4] He explores the Treaty of Waitangi, agreed in 1840 between representatives of the Crown and Māori chieftains in the North Island of New Zealand. Hickford offers a subtle and nuanced account of how the Treaty figured in the negotiation and subsequent interpretation of Section 9 of the State-Owned Enterprises Act 1986, which provided 'Nothing in

2 Supreme Court, grand bench, November 10, 1999, *Minshu* Vol. 53, No. 8, 1704. I am grateful to Satoshi Yokodaido for this point.

3 Article 16.

4 Mark Hickford, 'Quasi-Constitutionality and the Treaty of Waitangi: Historicity and the Political'.

this Act shall permit the Crown to act in a manner that is inconsistent with the principles of the Treaty of Waitangi'.[5] In his conceptualisation of these practices, Hickford deploys a broad understanding of the political constitution. This leaves little need or scope for a concept of quasi-constitutionality and Hickford unsurprisingly concludes that quasi-constitutionality is a narrow conceptual aid in this context. As a concept, quasi-constitutionality is more functional in systems dominated by a legal constitution where there is a (notionally, at least) bright line between what is in the constitution and what is not. Given the open-endedness of the political constitution, there is less, if indeed any, analytical work to be done by the concept of quasi-constitutionality.

For those in a system dominated by a legal constitution, therefore, quasi-constitutionality could connote laws (and practices) that are part of the political constitution but not the legal constitution. In this vein, Nikos Skoutaris presents those statutes in Spain and the United Kingdom that provide for the devolution or assignment of power to regions.[6] In both countries, statutes provide differing levels of autonomy to different regions, reflecting both historical divergence and political preference. Skoutaris argues that these (sub-)constitutional statutes translate political asymmetries into constitutional ones, creating a vicious circle that crystallises and possibly exacerbates the political asymmetries.[7] On an optimistic reading, he suggests, an advantage of (sub-)constitutional statutes may be that their open and flexible character allows them adapt better to the changing political necessities of a multi-national state.[8] The statutes are an example of quasi-constitutionality in Spain: political-constitutional in character but not formally part of the legal constitution. In the UK, however, this categorisation is superfluous: they are simply constitutional statutes, part of the political constitution as I have defined it above. Again, we see how the concept of quasi-constitutionality has a greater analytical function in explaining legal systems dominated by a legal constitution.

Another way of understanding quasi-constitutional statutes is provided by John Helis.[9] Rights-based statutes found in Canada, the United Kingdom, Australia and New Zealand instantiate weak-form judicial review, because they are based solely on interpretation rather than allowing for judicial invalidation. However, in Canada, the courts have granted an intermediate status to some such statutes. They are not subject to implied repeal: human rights legislation can render conflicting provisions in other statutes inoperable.[10] Even without declaring a statute inoperable (a remedy so far only recognised for the Canadian Bill of Rights and human rights legislation), a court can apply quasi-constitutional statutes in priority

5 Hickford, at Ibid., 106.
6 Nikos Skoutaris, 'Reflecting and Building Asymmetries: The Role of (Sub-)Constitutional Statutes in Spain and the UK'.
7 Skoutaris, at Ibid., 174.
8 Skoutaris, at Ibid., 175.
9 John Helis, 'Quasi-Constitutionality in Canada and the Weak-Form Model of Constitutionalism and Judicial Review'.
10 Helis, at Ibid., 117–118.

sequence over other legislation, achieving much the same effect.[11] Helis adverts to how a similar practice applies in the United Kingdom, for instance in respect of the European Communities Act 1972.[12] However, Canada operates in the very different context of a legal constitution, which Helis considers an instance of strong-form judicial review. As such, quasi-constitutionality refers to an intermediate legal status, higher than an ordinary statute but lower than the constitution. This provides a different function for the concept of quasi-constitutionality, namely the delineation of a semi-constitutional status. In this context, quasi-constitutional is an apt label for a doctrinal artefact that is difficult to explain in other terms. In contrast, in the United Kingdom the treatment of the European Communities Act 1972 imports into a predominantly political constitution an understanding of legal status more normally associated with a legal constitution.

Quasi-constitutional amendment is Richard Albert's proposal for how we should theorise a prominent puzzle in comparative constitutional law: the extent to which sub-constitutional law and practice may appear to supplement and change the legal standards contained in the master-text written constitution.[13] Albert argues that a quasi-constitutional amendment is a sub-constitutional alteration to the operation of a set of existing norms in the constitution. It does not possess the same legal status as a constitutional amendment but it may achieve the function though not the formal status of constitutional law over time as a result of its subject-matter and importance.[14] Albert offers three Canadian examples of quasi-constitutional amendments, the most compelling of which is the Regional Veto Law 1996, which requires a Cabinet minister to first obtain the consent of each of the five major regions as well as a majority of all provinces before introducing a major amendment proposal under the multilateral default amendment procedure.[15] The substantive effect (if not the form) of the Regional Veto Law, therefore, is to introduce a statutory requirement that must be satisfied in addition to the requirements contained in the master-text constitution. This makes amendment more difficult by granting an effective veto power to constitutional actors who otherwise would not have such a power. It is arguable, however, that it would be simpler to characterise this phenomenon as quasi-amendment rather than quasi-constitutional: it shifts the way in which the constitution operates without actually amending the constitution itself.[16]

Finally, Jonathan Hafetz employs the concept of quasi-constitutionality to international law and the regulation of detention in non-international armed conflict.[17] Hafetz identifies three broad approaches to the legal authority, grounds and

11 Helis, at Ibid., 117.

12 Helis, at Ibid., 175.

13 Richard Albert, 'Quasi-Constitutional Amendments'.

14 Albert, at Ibid., 136.

15 Albert, at Ibid., 139–141.

16 I explore these issues further in Oran Doyle, 'Informal Constitutional Change' (2017) 65 Buff. L. Rev. 739.

17 Jonathan Hafetz, 'Quasi-constitutionality in armed conflict detention'.

procedures for non-international armed conflict detention. One relies on international humanitarian law, which tends to give the state significant power. The other relies on international human rights law, which tends to constrain state power significantly. Between these two extremes, there are convergence-based approaches that seek to integrate the requirements of international humanitarian law and international human rights law.[18] Responding to other international law scholarship, Hafetz characterises these convergence-based approaches as the elaboration of quasi-constitutional norms, identified by their matter, elevated status and degree of importance, but subject to over-ride by the regular international law-making process.[19] They seek to fill perceived gaps within the existing legal framework by balancing competing demands of liberty and security, in a manner similar to domestic constitutional balancing processes.[20] For Hafetz, therefore, quasi-constitutionality performs the analytical function of linking the development of international law, by way of analogy, to domestic constitutional processes that seek to constrain but not eliminate state power.

Each of the chapters in this part provides a compelling analysis of important political and legal phenomena. The label of quasi-constitutionality links them together as examples of practices on the periphery of legal constitutionality. For Helis, Skoutaris and Hafetz, the label performs a dignifying function: the laws and practices in question gain credibility from their association with established constitutionality. For Albert, its effect is the opposite: quasi-constitutional amendments offend constitutionally prescribed amendment procedures. For Hickford, it is an irrelevance: the broad political constitution leaves little need or scope for a concept of quasi-constitutionality.

As we have seen, the different chapters deploy different understandings of quasi-constitutionality. For Skoutaris, it captures laws with constitutional content but not constitutional status. For Helis, it captures laws with an intermediate constitutional status. For Albert, it captures effective constitutional amendments made otherwise than through prescribed procedures. For Hafetz, it captures an analogy with domestic constitutional procedures. While the language of quasi-constitutionality enables cross-jurisdictional conversation, it also creates a risk of talking past one another. Future scholarship may establish a common core of quasi-constitutionality, allowing for more direct cross-jurisdictional comparison. In the meantime, however, quasi-constitutionality focuses our attention on the nuances and tensions within our prior understanding of constitutionality, while directing our attention to important laws and practices on the constitutional periphery, as the following chapters ably demonstrate.

18 Hafetz, at Ibid., 176–177.
19 Hafetz, at Ibid., 177–178.
20 Hafetz, at Ibid., 191.

# 4 Quasi-constitutionality and the Treaty of Waitangi

## Historicity and the political[1]

*Mark Hickford*

This chapter has two aims. First, it sets out my own thoughts as to how one might theorize about the political in approaching questions not only of 'quasi-constitutionality' but also broader constitutionalism as an organic concept. In presenting this argument, I start from the standpoint that New Zealand's constitutional framing, similarly to the United Kingdom, is pre-eminently historical-political with its own peculiar accent or idiosyncrasies. It is vitally legalistic in various aspects such that it is improper to regard the legal and the political as divided in mutually exclusive realms.[2] By so doing, I wish to demonstrate that the grounding of dynamic, generative activity of constitutional materiality or reflection, whether, say, institutional or that of clusters of actors, is *political* and this possesses a neglected normative significance. As with K. D. Ewing or Martin Loughlin, I consider the analytical departure point to be political as opposed to juristic or jurisprudential in a narrow, legally-focused sense.[3] It is inaccurate to claim that law is constitutive of politics. The protean actualities are much more complex and intriguing. Historicity, appreciated

1 I am grateful for the comments of Joel Colón-Ríos, Roberto Gargarella, Graham Gee, Colin Keating, the Rt Hon Sir Geoffrey Palmer, Richard Clarke, the Rt Hon Sir Kenneth Keith and Matthew Palmer. I am also very appreciative of the permission of Sir Geoffrey Palmer, the former Prime Minister at the time of writing (the Rt Hon John Key), the Leader of the Opposition, the Cabinet Office and relevant departments for access to the New Zealand archival papers referred to in this chapter.

2 Mark Hickford, 'The Historical, Political Constitution – Some Reflections on Political Constitutionalism in New Zealand's History and Its Possible Normative Qualities' (2013) New Zealand Law Rev 585, 586–587, 622. The vital role of legalism interweaving with political constitutionalism is still recognized in such an account but the concern is with the neglect and forgetfulness a focus on judicial processes and jurisprudence gives rise to if historical-political factors and behaviours are not accorded considerable analysis (ibid., 622–623). Also see Mark Hickford, 'Historicity and the Political Constitution' (2019) King's Law Journal (forthcoming) and Mark Hickford, 'Reflecting on the Treaty of Waitangi and its Constitutional Dimensions: A Case for a Research Agenda' in Mark Hickford and Carwyn Jones eds., *Indigenous Peoples and the State: International Perspectives on the Treaty of Waitangi* (Routledge, 2018) 140–165.

3 K. D. Ewing, 'The Resilience of the Political Constitution' (2013) German Law Journal 2111; Martin Loughlin, *Foundations of Public Law* (Oxford University Press, 2010) 10–13. See also, David Feldman, 'The Distinctiveness of Public Law' in Mark Elliott and David Feldman eds., *The Cambridge Companion to Public Law* (Cambridge University Press, 2015) 17, 21–25.

with subtlety, perseverance and patience, permits us to unveil and illuminate dynamic interactions between and among state and non-state actors.[4]

Second, it examines a treaty initially marked at Waitangi on 6 February 1840 in the northern peninsula of what became colonial New Zealand. An undoubtedly legal instrument within *ius gentium* or law of nations, as well as a political compact, it poses intriguing challenges for how one might interpret 'quasi-constitutionality'. It is an object of deliberation in and through time.[5] It speaks to the dynamism and flexibilities of historical-political constitutionalism, allowing plural indigenous polities to harbour or reserve spaces for negotiating the terms of politics *and* law in conversations without end, as a work-in-progress. Notwithstanding the complex co-existence of such polities throughout the territorial space claimed by the *arriviste* crown since 1840, these reserved points are not necessarily located *within* the introduced anglophone legal system although they might be perceived as such (and therefore consistent with its not uncontested claims to jurisdictional pre-eminence).

Furthermore, whilst this treaty remains a *relational* and *interpretative* resource, it cannot be regarded as exhaustively expressing crown-indigenous interactions. In the wake of contemporary treaty settlement politics and policies for addressing legally-defined 'historical claims',[6] power relations relative to the landscape, to the crown-state, localized communities and municipal government, are being incrementally recalibrated or adjusted through legislation expressing previously negotiated agreements.[7] Within the strict confines of this chapter, I will venture some reflections on how the arresting example of

4 In saying this, I recognize the conceptual technique or tactic of certain commentators, such as Mark Walters, in claiming that all non-positivistic constitutional principles are imbricated with legalism or may be construed as law as opposed to non-legal political or conventional norms (Walters, 'The Unwritten Constitution as a Legal Concept' in David Dyzenhaus and Malcolm Thorburn eds., *Philosophical Foundations of Constitutional Law* (Oxford University Press, 2016) 33–52). But this is an analytical reconstruction of pasts in circumstances where the relevant governmental actors or cohorts of such actors were unaware of these considerably subsequent renditions or interpretations of their acts, certainly in relation to aspects this chapter is examining let alone those regarding complex constitutional thought or narratives in, say, the mid-nineteenth century (see Hickford [n 2] and the sources cited therein).

5 Mark Hickford, 'Looking Back in Anxiety: Reflecting on Colonial New Zealand's Historical-Political Constitution and Laws' Histories in the Mid-Nineteenth Century' (2014) 48 New Zealand Journal of History 1, 21.

6 In policy settings, 'historical claims' are defined as those arising before 21 September 1992. With Section 2 of the Treaty of Waitangi Act 1975, we have the following statutory definition for 'historical Treaty claim', inserted on 13 December 2006: 'a claim made under Section 6(1) that arises from or relates to an enactment referred to in Section 6(1)(a) or (b) enacted, or to a policy or practice adopted or an act done or omitted by or on behalf of the Crown, before 21 September 1992'. Settlement legislation will contain specific provisions on their definition to be understood through reference to the preceding, relevant deed of settlement.

7 See the text accompanying notes 93–96 in this chapter.

a presence such as the Treaty of Waitangi (and those pre-existing polities it recognized) might be placed in any analysis situating 'quasi-constitutionality', problematizing it as a putative tool.

## Placing politics

Accessing the value of politics, notwithstanding its seeming ordinariness, appears undeniably important to me albeit philosophically elusive in many ways. Yet Bernard Williams, Raymond Geuss, Michael Oakeshott, Hannah Arendt, William Connolly and Duncan Ivison have endeavoured to capture something of it as plausibly as possible.[8] Ivison observes the ineradicable uncertainties at work where politics engages different sociabilities or modes of interaction with developing issues.[9] 'Politics', Oakeshott noted, 'is a conversation between diverse interests, in which activities that circumstantially limit one another are saved from violent collision'.[10] Much of my own effort has been directed towards venturing accounts of it not only in a historicized, operational sense but also from a constitutional standpoint, considering the design, shaping and configuring of relative powers as well as their refinement or adjustment. In this vein, it proves trying to ascertain the work that 'quasi-constitutionality' might perform, except in limited interpretative terms, as Adam Perry and F. Ahmed already identify. It then makes sense to use the term '*constitutional*' rather than qualifying such a term; that is, they have suggested explicit legislative language within an ordinary enactment would be required to repeal a constitutional statute (or provision) in the variety of ways they have outlined.[11] Scott Stephenson's definition of 'quasi-constitutionality' may be considered broadly plausible although what he characterizes as 'quasi-constitutional' might generally be construed as 'constitutional' in a regime where the arrangements comprise a bricolage of customary, non-codified elements or norms along with specific enactments.[12] These attributes enjoy a long-standing pedigree. Edward Augustus Freeman in 1864 observed how the

> doctrine of ministerial responsibility, … the duty of a whole Ministry to stand together in Parliament, the consequent duty of a dissentient Minister

8 For those not cited elsewhere in this essay: Bernard Williams, *In the Beginning Was the Deed: Realism and Moralism in Political Argument* (Princeton University Press, 2005); Michael Oakeshott, *Rationalism in Politics and Other Essays* (Liberty Fund, 1991); Hannah Arendt, *The Human Condition* (2nd edn, Chicago University Press, 1998); William Connolly, *The Terms of Political Discourse* (3rd edn, Blackwell, 1993).

9 Duncan Ivison, *Postcolonial Liberalism* (Cambridge University Press, 2002) 91.

10 Michael Oakeshott, *The Politics of Faith and the Politics of Scepticism*, Timothy Fuller ed. (Yale University Press, 1996) 130.

11 Adam Perry and F. Ahmed, 'The Quasi-Entrenchment of Constitutional Statutes' (2014) 73 CLJ 514.

12 Stephenson in this volume.

> to compromise or conceal his differences with his colleague, or else to resign his office – all these doctrines … are mere customs which have gradually, and some of them very recently, grown up, and of which the law of England knows nothing.[13]

Yet these were facets of 'what is commonly called constitutional or parliamentary government'.[14] Thomas Babington Macaulay commented in 1849 that two jurists, Jean-Louis De Lolme and William Blackstone, had even failed to acknowledge the existence or significance of cabinet.[15]

There is much to be said for deeply grounding our theoretical assumptions or intuitions in complicated lived practices, acknowledging the idiosyncrasies or accents peculiar to varied histories in particular jurisdictions, whether the constructs known as 'New Zealand', 'Canada', the 'United Kingdom' or otherwise. Some of this must engage examining contemporary practices not only of the courts but also the interior lives (interiority) of legislative and executive branches together with their untidily complex interactions with others. To approach these behaviours with acute sensitivity is undeniably exacting methodologically.[16] For one thing, the interior lives of politics are as ephemeral as gossamer and dew. Mere traces are left scattered in fragments, in archival deposits. '[P]olitics is historically located: it has to do with humans interacting in institutional contexts that change over time',[17] requiring finely-grained, temporally-minded excavations of contextual richness through a variety of manuscript, oral memorialization and other unpublished sources. Too much effort is expended on the readily observable, accessible outputs or outcrops of legislative and judicial processes, such as statutes or court decisions or high-level treatises, without engaging with the threads of messy interdependencies of action and deliberation beyond the simplicities of dialogical models or tropes in jurisprudential thought. At the very least, this misplaced effort is apt to misdirect understanding and analysis through narrowing one's gaze.

'Quasi-constitutionality', to the extent it performs any function, ought to be understood against such a complex, jostling background. As William Eskridge junior and John Ferejohn remarked in 2001, '[n]ot all statutes are created equal'.[18] Likewise, not all clauses or provisions within legislation are equal in their legal interpretative significance. 'Creation' as a concept though is slightly misleading or points in a direction not necessarily conducive to meaningful analysis except in the narrowest of circumstances or senses, as both Eskridge and

13 Edward A. Freeman, 'Presidential Government' in *Historical Essays* (Macmillan, 1871) 384.
14 Ibid.
15 T. B. Macaulay, *The History of England from the Accession of James II, Volume IV* (Longman, Brown, Green and Longmans, 1855) 435 (in this passage, he uses the term 'ministry' as an alternative to 'cabinet').
16 Hickford (n 2) 593–623.
17 Raymond Geuss, *Philosophy and Real Politics* (Princeton University Press, 2008) 13.
18 William N. Eskridge Jr. and John Ferejohn, 'Super-Statutes' (2001) Duke LJ 1215.

Ferejohn recognize themselves in their important article on quasi-constitutionality. Their own focus tended to be on legalistic assumptions of value, particularly super-statutes, not necessarily at a point of inception but across time. These moments of variable materiality or significance – whether constitutional or *quasi*-constitutional (if that term is to be used at all) – are perhaps seen most elusively albeit critically in the non-legal aspects of constitutional settings, what we may characterize as 'political'. It is this facet which intrigues this essay. To adapt a term of Roberto Gargarella the constitutional-political 'engine-room' within an indigenous or an anglophone-settler New Zealand context remains untouched through narrowly legally-driven or focused analyses.[19] Notwithstanding the desires of certain commentators to see everything political as having a legal form of pre-act authorization (or preferably so),[20] the engine of activity is indeed political although legal expressions are resorted to give additional heft in relation to affecting third parties and their relative status or conduct throughout given communities. In short, as opposed to contractual arrangements, statutes *tend* to aspire to regulating or constraining the behaviours of broad classes of person subject to the enacted instrument. So-called 'super-statutes' are 'adopted by the legislature but implemented by agencies and judges'.[21] As with several philosophers, I see the political as having a normative value all too readily neglected or dismissed, not only concerning its discursive or philosophical features but also relative to institutional design and inter-personal behaviours within and across institutional frameworks. The political is invariably a principal site for coordinating differences between logics of at least conflicting value propositions and, occasionally, even ostensibly incommensurable ones. In sorting out how to get things done (or to refrain from doing things), politics permits options to be presented and choices made in circumstances of contestation and human finitude.

But there is more than that in play. Nicholas Barber has identified 'political entrenchment' as a concept that can emerge through a 'non-legal constitutional rule' or, I would suggest, a custom or relatively settled, regularized practice that carries with it extensive negotiation or bargaining costs, if one is to achieve any change or adjustment to such a practice or customary norm.[22] These elements are tricky to identify in advance. Often, they are discussed or experienced either afresh or with

19 For Roberto Gargarella's concept of an 'engine room' see his *Latin American Constitutionalism, 1810–2010: The Engine Room of the Constitution* (Oxford University Press, 2013). His own meaning of it is that it embraces the 'organic' part of the constitution, not the part dedicated to the declaration of rights but the one that organizes the division of powers, checks and balances.

20 See David Howarth, 'The Politics of Public Law' in Elliott and Feldman eds., (n 3), 37 at 43–46.

21 Eskridge and Ferejohn (n 18) 1265.

22 N. W. Barber, *The Constitutional State* (Oxford University Press, 2010) 89–103. Also, David Feldman, 'Constitutional Conventions' in Matt Qvortrup ed., *The British Constitution: Continuity and Change – A Festschrift for Vernon Bogdanor* (Bloomsbury, 2015) 93–119.

some novelty through crossing a hitherto less-than-visible tripwire or one that might have been forgotten or neglected through a lack of substantive stress-testing in the recent past, leading to what is euphemistically known as 'noise' in the political realms of activity. What politics engages is indeed a desire for influencing relations in contest.[23] Acampora adds that 'one might prudently strive to compete well as a means [towards] greater success[es]'.[24] The exhausting reality is that a so-called triumph is never so complete – the actors in question simply have *a* win but the challenges of contest and bargaining persist tirelessly even in the sense of converting a momentary win into implementing policies agreed to with one's political peers or a coalition of supporters (or at least those not opposing or perhaps even those refraining from benign alignment – for now). Self-interested moves in political activity, even if seemingly unseemly or unpleasant, may yield normative value behaviourally, whether advertently or not, through various outputs that subsequently discipline conduct or open up new possibilities for political negotiation or legal action. There are undoubted moments of unpleasantness and difficulty, as any individual who interacts with others to secure a certain direction in the face of disagreement can testify. The configuration of forces on the ground might be such that the actor's tactical moves in the rich messiness of getting something agreed to give rise to such consequences.

## The importance of historicity or a 'historical turn' in constitutional analysis

Within this context, *historicity* plays an influential role in the way I see constitutionality and how one ought to theorize about it. For a start, this is largely because what may appear less than visible to legal scholars or jurists – that is, phenomena beyond, or of a different sort to, disclosed court decisions or positive law such as primary legislation – influences much of constitutional materiality or significance. As I have noted elsewhere, its role is certainly not determinative nor can it be regarded as deterministic; it ought not to be angled towards teleological enterprises, whether through endeavouring to retrieve some moment of 'original intent', as certain jurists are wont to do, or deploying its insights in an abridged or foreshortened fashion for contemporary policy issues in any controlling sense.[25] The invaluable methodological contributions of

23 Christa D. Acampora, 'Demos Agonistes Redux: Reflections on the *Streit* of Political Agonism' (2003) 32 *Nietzsche-Studien* 374, 379.

24 Ibid.

25 Hickford (n 2) 586, 588, 622. Also, Hickford (n 5), 1–3. On the interpretative sensitivities required: J. G. A. Pocock, 'The Treaty between Histories', in Andrew Sharp and P. G. McHugh ed., *Histories, Power and Loss: Uses of the Past – A New Zealand Commentary* (Bridget Williams, 2001) 75–95, 76–83, 86–95. 'Original intent' is problematic for historical analysis, as Gordon Wood and J. N. Rakove have observed: J. N. Rakove, 'Parchment Barriers and the Politics of Rights', in Michael Lacey and Knud Haakonssen eds., *A Culture of Rights: The Bill of Rights in Philosophy, Politics and Law – 1791 and 1991* (Cambridge University

J. G. A. Pocock and Quentin Skinner remain apposite to the stance this chapter assumes.[26] Ascertaining myriad pasts and their contested influences on episodes or moments that produce, say, practices, specific logics of political economy, policy pronouncements, legislative activities or enactments in and through time, requires one to recover or to unveil the underlying or informing practices or intellectual thought. Perhaps this can reveal possibilities or ways of seeing and speaking otherwise recreated, adjusted, dismissed or foregone.[27] Recently, Vernon Bogdanor has contended that the 'historic constitution' is at an end in the United Kingdom or, more modestly, that it is undergoing a process of being replaced.[28] I would disagree, especially so in relation to New Zealand. Yet, as Edmund Burke himself cautioned long ago,[29] *historicity* neither determines nor compels behaviours. But it can illuminate many of the changeable or adaptive tissues of understanding and deliberation, oftentimes seemingly ephemeral or elusive until an issue emerges, shepherded or stewarded by particular servants of the crown or legislators. Historicity mainly exerts influence through supplying at least preliminary understandings of apparently plausible options for action or inaction on a case-by-case basis – what has been pursued before or not; why have these courses of activity or understanding been pursued in the past and not departed from. Skinner has expressed this observation well in saying, 'What you can hope to legitimise, however, depends [*may* depend, I would suggest] on what courses of action you can plausibly range under existing normative principles'.[30] He continued: 'But this implies that, even if your professed principles never operate as your motives, but only as rationalisations of your behaviour, they will nevertheless help to shape and limit what lines of

Press, 1991) 98–143, 100–101 (n 6, citing Wood: 'When confronted with these contrasting meanings of the Constitution, historians … are not supposed to decide which was more "correct" or more "true". Our task is rather to explain the reason for these contrasting meanings and why each side should have given to the Constitution the meaning it did').

26 J. G. A. Pocock, 'Quentin Skinner: The History of Politics and the Politics of History' (2004) 10 Common Knowledge 532; Holly Hamilton-Bleakley, 'Linguistic Philosophy and *The Foundations*', in Annabel Brett, James Tully and Holly Hamilton-Bleakley eds., *Rethinking the Foundations of Modern Political Thought* (Cambridge University Press, 2006) 20–33, 24–33; J. G. A. Pocock, *Political Thought and History: Essays on Theory and Method* (Cambridge University Press, 2009).

27 As ventured in Mark Hickford, *Lords of the Land: Indigenous Property Rights and the Jurisprudence of Empire* (Oxford University Press, 2011) 458–460; Hickford, 'John Salmond and Native Title in New Zealand: Developing a Crown Theory on the Treaty of Waitangi, 1910–1920' (2008) 38 Victoria University of Wellington Law Review 853.

28 Vernon Bogdanor, 'Constitutional Reform in Britain: The Quiet Revolution' (2005) 8 Annual Political Science Review 73, 73–77; id, *The New British Constitution* (Hart, 2009) xi, 3–21.

29 See the excellent account in Richard Bourke, *Empire & Revolution: The Political Life of Edmund Burke* (Princeton University Press, 2015) 774: 'Properly understood, therefore, the past did not bind legislative authority in the present: it simply guided it'.

30 Quentin Skinner, *Liberty before Liberalism* (Cambridge University Press, 1998) 105.

action you can successfully pursue'.[31] Certainly, novel sources can be brought to bear, whether these might be exogenous and introduced from beyond the archipelago of New Zealand, or adapted endogenously or otherwise through an intermingling or ensemble of voices. Nothing precludes those possibilities. Elsewhere, I have commented that Geoffrey Palmer's previous proposals to introduce an entrenched or codified legal-constitutional framework to New Zealand – a Palmeresque trope – might yet become part of the overall juristic-political architecture.[32] The inherent flexibility of an introduced ancient constitution imported with an *arriviste* crown albeit undeniably imperial brought with it opportunities, very much unrealized potential at a number of points. Vitally, however, it also conveyed undeniably real risks and fragilities, as majoritarian settler communities increasingly exerted a demographic sway.[33]

The introduced anglophone constitution within New Zealand is a fabric descended from antiquity. It is layered with many histories of lived experiences and practices. Such an imaginary differs from a bare lawyerly constitution, divined or distilled with reference to the officially identifiable pronouncements of legislative assemblies or courts. Rather, it gives us ones that are inhabited and lived, contested and critiqued, adjusted iteratively as well as sustained. Here lies its strengths and opportunities, its very weaknesses and frailties. Edmund Burke contemplated a genealogical descent.[34] Oakeshott once noted how, '[o]ur task is to find some means of being at home in the complexity we have inherited, and cannot now avoid, without indulging ourselves in the false hope of discovering a market in which we can exchange it for simplicity'.[35] These flexible characteristics in times of flux occasioned much analytical reflection in nineteenth-century British accounts.[36] Seemingly ordinary steps at a distance might obtain constitutional or quasi-constitutional significance incrementally or cumulatively. That is a central feature of these inherited 'ancient' or historical-political constitutional settings. Henry Sumner Maine, for one, worried about the ease with which legislation of constitutional significance might be enacted through an ordinary process: orientations towards extending the electoral franchise had subverted the constitutional settings in his view whilst the inherent flexibility of the framework had enabled such subversion.[37] Yet these organic, jurisgenerative qualities attributable to a historical-political constitution align with

31 Ibid.

32 Geoffrey Palmer, *Reform: A Memoir* (Victoria University Press, 2013), 727–732; Hickford (n 2) 622–623 (and note 138).

33 Well documented in the standard texts regarding colonial New Zealand. Hanna Wilberg has suggested that the shift towards responsible and representative government constituted an original breach of the Treaty of Waitangi: Wilberg, 'Judicial Remedies for the Original Breach?' [2007] New Zealand Law Rev 713, 714–15.

34 Edmund Burke, *Reflections on the Revolution in France* (J. Dodsley, 1790) 47–49.

35 Oakeshott (n 10) 120.

36 For instance, Henry S. Maine, *Popular Government: Four Essays* (John Murray, 1885) 54.

37 Ibid., 240.

certain understandings of treaty-based and indigenous legal discourses.[38] Each may be seen as expressing an organic picture of shared, inter-societal norms having been made through treaties or other forms of indigenous interaction with state officials or representatives (and continuing to be so formed).

There is another reason to grasp the importance of historicity when dealing with matters of constitutional or quasi-constitutional significance. If pursued with a deep, searching awareness of the archival record, it requires the contingency of twenty-first century vanities, understandings or assumptions to be approached with scepticism and non-schematically. Rigorous historicity alerts one to the frailties of assumptions as to law associated with a colonial inheritance and other discourses or understandings neither readily imbricated nor accommodated within the conventional introduced legal system. *Mana* is one such conceptual discourse.[39] As a concept, *mana* connotes an other-worldly, sacred or immaterial quality, such as 'authority stemming from the indwelling of spiritual power'.[40] In February 2008, for instance, before the repeal of the Foreshore and Seabed Act 2004, a heads of agreement between the *hapū* ('clans') of Te Whānau a Āpanui and the crown declared that it aimed to 'recognise the unbroken, inalienable and enduring mana of the hapu of Te Whanau a Apanui in relation to the public foreshore and seabed in their rohe (region), which is held and exercised as a collective right'. Those eight nominated instruments to assist such recognition were undeniably limited, however, in that they were a subject to agreement 'consistent with the object of the Foreshore and Seabed Act'.[41] In such a vein, they would be less than adequate expressions of the full sensitivities of *mana* as a concept – appropriately, there would always be a withholding from a legal regime not well adapted to non-colonial inheritances. Likewise when one speaks of *mana motuhake, rangatiratanga* or *manaakitanga*: their historicity, let alone their varying dimensions or elasticity in applying to differing circumstances, cannot be fully expressed through positive legal concepts in the introduced anglophone legal settings. Nor should it be in my view, although there are jurists who claim the introduced law's capacity to assemble all within its imperialistic embrace. There is something to be said for not ensnaring all the world in totalizing legalism, as if a singular way of reflecting on constitutions is indeed helpful or respectful given the myriad ways in which those who compose communities of interpretation may wish to use other conceptual

38 Jeremy Webber, 'Relations of Force and Relations of Justice: The Emergence of Normative Community between Colonists and Aboriginal Peoples' (1995) 33 Osgoode Hall Law Journal 623. Janna Promislow, 'Treaties in History and Law' (2014) 47 UBC L Rev 1085, 1104.

39 Also Carwyn Jones, 'Whakeke i Ngā Ngaru – Riding the Waves: Māori Legal Traditions in New Zealand Public Life', in Lisa Ford and Tim Rowse eds., *Between Indigenous and Settler Governance* (Routledge, 2013) 174, 178–179.

40 Joan Metge, *Tuamaka: The Challenge of Difference in Aotearoa New Zealand* (Auckland University Press, 2010) 126.

41 Extracted from attachment to 'Te Whanau a Apanui foreshore and seabed agreement', 28 February 2008, www.scoop.co.nz/stories/PA0802/S00461.htm (accessed 12 March 2016).

registers or vocabularies. Moves might yet be established in politics that give rise to adjustments in legal forms of recognition. Politics might yet garner a better conditionality in indigenous-crown relations law and practice through negotiating iterative or incremental steps often expressed in positive legal enactments. But these possibilities for, and of, change need not be stabilized, fossilized or fixed through reference to an overriding unitary text.

Our analytical repertoire is impoverished. It is insufficiently attuned to contested histories and customs in and through time let alone the significance of the political, as unattractive or unappealing as it might appear. I say this openly as one who is a historian and one who has been a legal-public policy practitioner within the interior of the executive wing of central government. One ought to consider and factor into accounts of constitutionalism, the cluttered machinations of democratic or representative politics building often momentary coalitions amongst or within collections of peers or rivals. Rivalrous contest is understood to be endemic, seemingly unattractive or tarnished to certain commentators (even though undeniably frail and human) but to acknowledge its presence humbly is to appreciate the limitations and vagaries of inter-personal or communal existence. Scepticism concerning the detached generalities of jurisprudence and its overall narrowness as a discipline remains appropriate on all fronts. As Jürgen Habermas recognizes, technocratic governance, whether that of courts or of international organizations, is problematic if the contextual role of various, 'out-of-doors' communities, pressing interests or publics do not leaven it. He adverts to the legitimacy acquired through political activity mustering or eliciting support from the *dēmos* ('will-formation') or deliberating on the risks of squandering such support or seeking to adjust it.[42] 'In contrast to the decisions of national cabinets that cover all policy fields', he says, 'the agenda of functionally specialized organizations is confined to particular areas of responsibility, so that this narrow focus does not allow [or incentivize] the undesirable external effects of decisions to be taken into account'.[43] Alexis de Tocqueville characterized the judiciary within the United States as playing an élite, aristocratic role in a mixed constitutional setting combining legislative, executive and adjudicative functions.[44]

## Examining an indigenous-crown treaty compact: how it puzzles the performative or functional role of 'quasi-constitutionality'

Exploring the functionality that 'quasi-constitutionality' might possess is difficult in a broader, historicized context. For abstract legal or doctrinal analysis,

42 He has also argued how in the contemporary European Union setting, political parties may be unready to 'engage in processes of opinion- and will-formation that shape mentalities and deviate from established routines' (Jürgen Habermas, *The Lure of Technocracy*, translated Ciaran Cronin [Polity, 2015] 20). See also the difficulties noted in Peter Mair, *Ruling the Void: The Hollowing of Western Democracy* (Verso, 2013).

43 Habermas (n 42) 56.

44 Alexis de Tocqueville, *Democracy in America: De la démocratie en Amérique*, ed. Eduardo Nolla (Liberty Fund, 2010) II, 431, 433.

speaking to what, say, the appellate judiciary might entertain in interpreting statutory provisions is one thing. Quite another, however, is getting at how to situate constitutionality more accurately across bureaucratic and legislative behaviour. This is why theorizing about politics in a constitutional sense remains critical. Does 'quasi' as a qualifier supply a useful analytical tool for evaluating what is happening when statutory or other legal instruments are enacted and when interpretations, whether judicial or non-judicial (on the part of political actors, legislators or officials), might invest those instruments with (or divest those instruments of) constitutional status at one moment in time or another?

The treaty initially marked at Waitangi in February 1840 is appropriately seen as an exemplar of an instrument of historical-political constitutional significance, interacting with legal-constitutional litigation and legislative activity. It is peculiarly challenging to scholarly commentary. Its status is dynamic, changeable and contested: positive legal reflections of it in municipal law are merely fragments, exhibiting fragility although they may possess potency in their legal interpretative qualities or status for a time. Underneath all these fragments lies two texts of a treaty, one in English; another rendered in Māori on the part of, say, Henry Williams containing terms constructed with a comparatively recent missionary heritage (*kāwanatanga* or 'governorship'), which was the one predominantly signed (except at Waikato heads).[45] In very simplistic terms, the treaty ceded at least 'governorship' to the crown whilst the indigenous signatories and their communities received certain guarantees, including the complete chieftainship (*tino rangatiratanga*) or 'full, exclusive, and undisturbed possession of their lands and estates, forests, fisheries, and other properties, so long as it is their wish and desire to retain the same in their possession' under the second article.[46] Whether conceptions of *kāwanatanga* correspond with the implications of 'sovereignty' or the extent to which *tino rangatiratanga* approximates with legal and political autonomy persist as subjects of historical and jurisprudential dispute.[47] These treaty texts, contestable as they might be, are the constant. This treaty comprising more than a single text engenders an analytical and theoretical challenge. It is currently treated as an instrument that is not necessarily

45 Atholl Anderson, Judith Binney and Aroha Harris, *Tangata Whenua: An Illustrated History* (Bridget Williams Books, 2014) 227; P. Parkinson, '"Preserved in the Archives of the Colony": The English Drafts of the Treaty of Waitangi' (2005) 11 Revue Juridique Polynésienne 1.

46 There is an extensive literature and debate on these terms: for instance, Waitangi Tribunal, *He Whakaputanga me te Tiriti the Declaration and the Treaty: The Report on Stage 1 of the Te Paparahi o Te Raki Inquiry* (Wai 1040, 2014).

47 The commentary is extensive and cannot be traversed here in sufficient detail. Richard Hill, *Maori and the State: Crown-Maori Relations in New Zealand / Aotearoa, 1950–2000* (Victoria University Press, 2009) 221–223, 275–293; *He Tirohanga ō Kawa ki te Tiriti o Waitangi* (Te Puni Kōkiri, 2002).

inherently enforceable through the ordinary domestic courts[48] but influences executive governmental conduct (changeably and variably), and has been reflected in statutes with a consequence that those provisions might be treated as constitutionally material or at least as having quasi-constitutional status interpretatively. Along with other sources and tropes (including theological ones), it bridges, associates or threads several historical communities in narratives of on-going entanglement. Relatively soon after its signing, it came to be referred to as '*the* Treaty of Waitangi' featuring a definite article, even though certain hapū communities or actors within them might not have seen it as deserving an unqualified centrality as to how relations with the incoming crown might be narrated or thought about. Oral conditions or understandings remain challenging to recover, as D. F. McKenzie once wrote, and Judith Binney noted in reciting Hōne Mohi Tāwhai's use of a simile in February 1840 at the Hokianga signing site for the treaty as to how the textual expressions of European settlers would 'float light, like the wood of the w[h]a[u] tree, and always remain to be seen', whereas the utterances of Māori would 'sink like a stone'.[49] Institutional and constitutional design wrestled with the political pluralities of crown-indigenous interaction in New Zealand. These aspects still lie beneath the surface, although anglophone vocabularies of 'sovereignty' or 'subsidiarity' may conceal the aspirations of hapū politics as having had or possessing more autonomous status than otherwise suggested textually.[50]

The Treaty supplies a normative canvas, volunteered by the crown's representatives in 1840 as a possible source of discipline or constraint as much for their own conduct and that of settlers, far from complete or exhaustive in its coverage of crown or state-iwi-hapū relations law and practice. The Treaty's interest for us in reflecting on pluralities of political-constitutional thought is that it poses as an *aide-mémoire*, a source of normative evaluation and critique regarding governmental behaviours – expressed in certain positive legal outputs but lying beyond them. Certainly, however, it has been adverted to in legislative enactments, most intensively since 1975. Eskridge and Ferejohn usefully suggest that 'super-statutes' are grounded in 'popular sovereignty' in any democratically shaped setting or one that is predicated on representative

48 This may change, hence my intentional use of the phrase 'not necessarily'. See also, Dame Sian Elias, 'The Meaning and Purpose of the Treaty of Waitangi', October 2015, *Māori Law Review*, http://maorilawreview.co.nz/2015/10/the-meaning-and-purpose-of-the-treaty-of-waitangi-dame-sian-elias/#_edn15 (last accessed, 6 March 2016).

49 Tāwhai, *Great Britain Parliamentary Papers* ('GBPP'), 1845, xxxiii (108), 10. D. F. McKenzie, *Oral Culture, Literacy & Print in Early New Zealand: The Treaty of Waitangi* (Victoria University Press, 1985); J. Binney, 'History and Memory: The Wood of the Whau Tree, 1766–2005' in Giselle Byrnes ed., *The New Oxford History of New Zealand* (Oxford University Press, 2009) 73.

50 Hickford (n 27); Richard Hill, 'Maori and State Policy' in Giselle Byrnes ed., *The New Oxford History of New Zealand*, 113, 113–114.

assemblies.[51] These statutory measures are 'adopted by the legislature but implemented by agencies and judges'.[52] One might justifiably cavil at the unproblematic use of a term such as 'popular sovereignty' given its contingent, historical dimensions.[53] But the central point is that legislative enactments can have the general effect of aligning any putative quasi-constitutional qualities with represented opinion. Legislators and politicians in the executive will usually have better connections and access to diverse constituencies – the *dēmos* – than jurists.[54] Theorists have identified these forms of representation and connectivity as sources for refreshing legal norms as conditions change.[55] In addition, political actors, such as certain legislators, may initiate policy moves or proposals on a broad array of issues invoking or requiring eclectic or catholic resort to analytical registers of a non-legal quality, including economic or sociological forms of reasoning. By contrast, courts are invariably constrained through the legalistic frames of analytical reference they conventionally deploy and do not ignite activities *ab initio* of their own accord with a view to policy formulation.

Momentary tactical decisions arising out of bargaining or negotiating in political activity can be of constitutional significance and yield material with constitutional signification in the form of legislative enactments, which have an after-life in how they exert influences in subsequent years. One instance is Section 9 of the State-Owned Enterprises Act 1986 (sponsored by Geoffrey Palmer, then deputy prime minister in the fourth Labour government). Its curial interpretation is well traversed.[56] Section 9 provided: 'Nothing in this Act shall permit the Crown to act in a manner that is inconsistent with the principles of the Treaty of Waitangi'. Elsewhere Matthew Palmer explores this clause's appearance although without having cited the relevant caucus, legislative drafting or policy files.[57] Its emergence as a provision was pressing and curious, evidencing the relevance of the contingent, as the policy to which it was annexed belatedly – the proposed establishment of state-owned enterprises whereby trading operations of state departments were separated from the ministerial policy formulation or advisory arms – was already well advanced, with a bill having already proceeded through select committee

51 Eskridge and Ferejohn, 1267.
52 Ibid., 1265.
53 Richard Bourke and Quentin Skinner eds., *Popular Sovereignty in Historical Perspective* (Cambridge University Press, 2016).
54 Eskridge and Ferejohn, 1266.
55 Jeremy Waldron, 'The Rule of Law in Public Law', in Mark Elliot and David Feldman eds., *The Cambridge Companion to Public Law* (Cambridge University Press, 2015) 56, 65–66.
56 Jacinta Ruru ed., *'In Good Faith': Symposium Proceedings Marking the 20th Anniversary of the Lands Case* (New Zealand Law Foundation and Faculty of Law, University of Otago, 2008).
57 Matthew Palmer, *The Treaty of Waitangi in New Zealand's Law and Constitution* (Victoria University Press, 2008) 93–94, 137–138 and 400–401 (note 19, which sets out the communications from Colin Keating and Richard Clarke that Matthew Palmer received).

(reported back on 11 December 1986). This policy was perceived on Geoffrey Palmer's part to be of constitutional significance, an observation noted in the Court of Appeal.[58] Strong Māori reservations to the policy emerged and indigenous leaders, particularly Hepi Te Heuheu of Ngāti Tuwharetoa, were engaged in a serious negotiation with key ministers as the deadline approached for incorporation into the bill of a large number of amendments to clarify the state-owned enterprises policy and better effect its implementation. These amendments were to be presented to parliament in a supplementary order chapter or SOP. Playing an influentially timely role was a brief interim *Muriwhenua* report of the Waitangi Tribunal on the State-Owned Enterprises Bill, with counsel and Te Tai Tokerau indigenous interests pursuing avenues of pressure through that forum.[59] This report advised:

> The honour of the Crown is at stake. We think it inconsistent with the principles of the Treaty of Waitangi that that particular relationship of the Maori and the Crown should in any way be diminished, or even threatened with compromise. We do not think in particular that the Crown should dispose of lands that are the subject of claims and risk thereby some prejudice to the claimants' position.[60]

Operating as a standing commission of inquiry, this tribunal's then solely recommendatory jurisdiction enabled it to critique contemporaneous policy developments (or omissions) with express reference to the 'principles of the Treaty of Waitangi' under Section 6 of its statute, the Treaty of Waitangi Act 1975.[61]

As drafted by Richard Clarke in December 1986 and reviewed by then chief parliamentary counsel, Walter Iles, the treaty provision for the proposed state-owned enterprises enactment was expressed initially in typescript in the following terms as clause 8A of what would be a supplementary order paper: 'Nothing in this Act shall permit the Crown to *transfer or divest itself of any of its obligations under* the Treaty of Waitangi [emphasis added]'.[62] Preliminary executive wing efforts to find a compromise that would be acceptable to Māori were

58 *New Zealand Māori Council v Attorney-General* [1987] 1 NZLR 641, 669 per Richardson J.

59 Waitangi Tribunal to Minister of Māori Affairs, 8 December 1986, Wai 22: 'The policy proposed in the State-Owned Enterprises Bill involves a transfer of Crown land to the Forestry Corporation, the Land Corporation and other corporations. It will then cease to be Crown land. Although it appears Ministers will retain a power of direction to the proposed corporations, that power, it seems to us, is likely to be limited and insufficiently wide to enable the return of Crown land pursuant to a recommendation of this Tribunal, or might otherwise involve claimants in an additional adversary'.

60 Ibid.

61 Section 6(1), Treaty of Waitangi Act 1975.

62 Iles and Clarke, 11 December 1986, ABRC W5612 6860/764/2, Archives New Zealand, Wellington ('ANZ(W)").

reflected in language recommended by officials and eventually prepared in Clarke's hand. Keating, a senior official and experienced negotiator seconded to the Treasury from the then Ministry of Foreign Affairs (where he was chief legal advisor), developed the words 'act in a manner inconsistent with the principles of' on the late evening of 10 December 1986 with the approval of Palmer and the prime minister, David Lange. These terms were subsequently inserted in Clarke's handwriting in place of the phrase italicized above on the early morning of 11 December 1986. The late adjustment of the draft wording was accompanied by Iles' penned request that it be printed in typescript form by 9.00 am that morning coupled with a clause prescribing the treatment of Māori claims to land transferred to state enterprises with a view to readying those clauses as a supplementary order paper in advance of caucus.[63] As Iles wrote on 22 October 1986, the principal bill itself was 'unusual' in that it had been 'drafted by a former Parliamentary Counsel, Mr Richard Clarke, who is now a partner in Messrs Chapman Tripp Sheffield Young', evidencing the bespoke aspects of the policy preparation and the legislative measure in draft.[64] Clarke and Iles were instructed to insert the treaty provision, with content advice coming from Palmer and Keating. Clarke also recalls labouring with Iles on the precise words (which Keating had written).[65] This belated change's backstory is particularly revealing because it is an example of a political bargaining process which ultimately resulted in a constitutionally significant outcome. Keating remembers it becoming clear around 10 December that Māori leaders were not satisfied with oral representations to the effect that Treaty obligations residing with the crown would not be divested but would remain intact and effective in the execution of the state-owned enterprises policy. At a meeting that evening in the prime ministerial office (attended by Prime Minister Lange, Palmer and himself) it was revealed that ministers had received an ultimatum. Māori leaders remained anxious that the proposed legislation could result in an infringement to the principles of the Treaty. Keating asked whether Ministers were really willing to back these oral assurances and, if so, why not align the statutory language accordingly. It was on the basis of affirmative answers that Keating developed the wording that Clarke and Iles inserted the following day and which ultimately became Section 9 of the Act (Keating took the proposed wording to Clarke and Iles with the approval of Lange and Palmer).[66]

63 'The Government Printer. Please set up and supply 12 pulls by 9 a.m. W Iles Chief Parl[iamen]t[ar]y Counsel 11/12/86'. The handwriting in relation to what became Section 9 was identified by Clarke himself.

64 Iles to G. D. S. Taylor, 22 October 1986, ABRC W5612 6860/764/2, ANZ(W).

65 Clarke to Sir Geoffrey Palmer, 11 May 2016.

66 Keating to author, 22 April 2016 and 4 May 2016. Keating cannot recall seeing the draft itself cited at note 63 above. Clarke to Palmer, 22 May 2016 (on file with author): 'Late in the afternoon/early evening of 10 December 1986 I was working at Treasury on matters relating to the Bill when Colin arrived unexpectedly to say that, following discussions held by the [Prime Minister] and/or [Palmer], something had to go in the Bill regarding the Treaty,

Later on the morning of 11 December 1986, the Labour Party caucus approved Palmer's rather narrowly expressed proposal to amend the bill in order to 'preserve the rights of claims before the Waitangi Tribunal', without any explicit references to the 'principles of the Treaty' at least in the caucus minutes.[67] In accordance with orthodox practice, copies of the supplementary order paper were not distributed to caucus members. Having said that, Palmer recollects that an oral reference to 'principles of the Treaty' would have been made although it was not captured in the contemporaneous caucus record.[68] Cabinet approval was not able to be sought in view of time pressures. The phraseology of 'principles of the Treaty of Waitangi' was already located, in a path-dependent sense, in that Waitangi Tribunal's instituting statute from 1975, supplying a readily accessible terminology for the drafter to draw upon at a pressing moment in late 1986. Clarke recalls Iles had suggested referring to the principles of the Treaty as this expression had been used in the Conservation Bill which was then in Parliament (but not enacted until 1987). Keating's recollection is that the observation that those words were in that Bill already and had cabinet and caucus approval almost certainly created in Lange and Palmer's minds a sense of internal 'political cover'.[69] Moreover, the executive had embarked on studied engagement with the Treaty. A number of cabinet papers mused on its implications for policy in 1986 although the overall variety and richness of the general situation pressing upon and informing the fourth Labour government's stances on Treaty of Waitangi-related policies, including the drafting of Section 9, cannot be addressed here.[70] Several idiosyncratic things came together. Prepared late in the legislative process following the select committee phase, Section 9 prompted litigation in the High Court and the Court of Appeal upon the passage of the State-Owned Enterprises Bill and its assent on 18 December 1986.[71]

via an SOP as the Bill was then in Parliament and had already been considered by the Select Committee. The matter had to be attended to immediately as the Bill was on the verge of being enacted'.

67 'Minutes of the 98th meeting of the Labour Government caucus held in the Government caucus room, on Thursday 11 December 1986 commencing at 10.05 am', MB267-102,726, 2, Palmer papers, Macmillan Brown Library, Christchurch ('Palmer papers').

68 Palmer to author, 4 May 2016.

69 Clarke to Sir Geoffrey Palmer, 22 May 2016; Keating to author, 13 July 2016 (on file with author).

70 Palmer (n 57) 135–139, 371–372; Andrew Sharp, *Justice and the Māori: The Philosophy and Practice of Māori Claims in New Zealand since the 1970s* (2nd edn., Oxford University Press, 1997) 87–98; Andrew Sharp, 'The Problem of Māori Affairs, 1984–1989', in Martin Holland and Jonathan Boston eds., *The Fourth Labour Government: Politics and Policy in New Zealand* (2nd ed., Oxford University Press, 1990) 251–269.

71 The parties negotiated the details of an agreement to set out a process for addressing Māori claims in relation to land that was to be transferred to state-owned enterprises. This agreement was reflected in legislation. In the wake of that agreement, the Court of Appeal in *New Zealand Māori Council v Attorney-General* [1987] 1 NZLR 641, 719 issued a minute reserving leave to the parties to resort to the court 'in case anything unforeseen should arise'.

A ministerial committee had been established to oversee not only the state-owned enterprises policy but also its legislative expression, with Palmer chairing. As the bill approached enactment, public relations communications on the policy were to be cleared by Palmer and coordinated through his office.[72] In his second reading address on the bill, Palmer referred to reassurances having been given to the Federation of Māori Authorities that the government would not take any steps to prejudice the interests of Māori under the Treaty or to subvert the Waitangi Tribunal process.[73] Despite such focus Palmer considered the import of Section 9 as minimal or non-existent even given the 'land claims' provisions proposed complementarily *via* the supplementary order paper.[74] Something of this sentiment is reflected in Palmer's memorandum for the ministerial coordinating committee on state-owned enterprises that he chaired in June 1987. It reported how the Treaty principles provision signalled a 'commitment to *honour* the Treaty' whereas 'Section 27 establishes a mechanism for implementing the principles of the Treaty in the context of the transfer of land'.[75] Indeed, notwithstanding the use of the indefinite article in that memorandum, these clauses were surmised to have exhaustively operationalized the extent of what Section 9 could contribute, a view held to be incorrect in the courts.

Keating has also disclosed that, after the bill was enacted and before the team of seconded officials was disbanded, he raised concerns with ministers that the policy enshrined in Section 9 might be difficult to sustain in the absence of prescribed safeguards or an oversight mechanism to ensure that the practical implementation of the new state-owned enterprises machinery would indeed remain consistent with the principles of the Treaty. Palmer was very supportive of this. For a time, under his leadership, certain seconded officials acted informally in that capacity. But it appears that the notion lapsed after policy responsibility shifted back to line ministers and departments. Māori disenchantment with the state-owned enterprises policy seems to have intensified, as they perceived no evidence that the executive was committed to the Section 9 policy in practice. Ultimately, in the aftermath of the Court of Appeal ruling, the crown did move to implement a statutory safeguard policy in amending legislation, a critical legal development.[76]

Specific clauses obtained the not uncontested (episodically variable) status of being treated as constitutionally material or even super-statutory provisions *within* the interior lives of the executive wing. It need not acquire this 'normative force through a series of public confrontations and debate

72 Memorandum to Special Ministerial Coordinating Committee on State Owned Enterprises (1986), MB930-119,316, Palmer papers.

73 SOE Legislation – Bills etc, (1986), (MB267-102,880), Palmer papers.

74 Palmer (n 32) 406–407.

75 Palmer to Ministerial Coordinating Committee on the State-Owned Enterprises Bill, 16 June 1987, MB267-102,814 (emphasis added), Palmer papers.

76 Refer to *New Zealand Māori Council v Attorney-General* [1987] 1 NZLR 641.

over time'.[77] Rather, such status might emerge or re-emerge with such a quality (or lose it) through less than public contexts; through tactical missteps or mis-memory, through re-configurations of political support, through a lack of regular stress-testing or litigation. With the Contact Energy selldown of shares in 1999, the absence of Section 9 of the State-Owned Enterprises Act in that corporate's subsequent incarnation did not occasion, at that time, any difficulty from the perspective of the executive branch. But, even though seen as a precedent, it proved an unreliable predictor of subsequent behaviour, as in 2012 the then John Key-led government felt compelled to ensure that a comparable version of Section 9 applied to mixed-ownership model entities where the crown shareholding was to be reduced to no less than 51 percent of any class of issued shares or of voting securities in the company.[78] In February 2012, the initial proposal for consultation had raised the possibility of not extending Section 9 to such entities as one option amongst three.[79] An erroneous disclosure of the consultation document with marginalia on the part of usually anonymized officials within the treasury, including references to whether Section 9 conferred any benefit, exacerbated concerns already harboured by some as to policy-formulators' intentions to jettison New Zealand Māori Council or broader iwi-hapū concerns around asset transfers where the operations of the entities (hydro-electric power generators, for instance) touched natural resources subject to claims (freshwater and geothermal resources). Thus, a deleted passage revealed in the draft included the following: 'Given the limited powers that Ministers will exercise, the continued application of Section 9, or a Section 9-like provision, would have no practical effect and is therefore not necessary'.[80] It added that, 'Investors will also look to the precedent of other sales of Crown assets, particularly Air New Zealand and observe that no Section 9 obligation applies'.[81]

This inadvertent publication occurred a mere three days before the prime minister attended Waitangi events with various cabinet colleagues, including an annual iwi chairs forum meeting in neighbouring Paihia on 5 February with a policy-driven agenda. Anxieties around Section 9's possible absence also afforded a leverage point for legal counsel of the New Zealand Māori Council to use apprehended litigation as a way of dramatizing indigenous rights and interests in water in circumstances where the initial public offers of shares were to be in entities that generated hydro-electric power. Political-public policy

77 *Contra*, Eskridge and Ferejohn, 1270.

78 Public Finance (Mixed Ownership Model) Amendment Act 2012, s 45Q.

79 'Asset sale draft plan blunder', *New Zealand Herald*, 2 February 2012 (www.nzherald.co.nz/business/news/article.cfm?c_id=3&objectid=10782863, accessed 30 March 2016).

80 *Extension of the Mixed Ownership Model: A Proposal to Change Legislation in Relation to: Genesis Power, Meridian Energy, Mighty River Power, Solid Energy New Zealand – Consultation with Māori*, February 2012, 24 (comments deleted by Andrew Craig on 31 January 2012).

81 Ibid.

strategic motivations influenced the retention of a Section 9-like clause relative to mixed-ownership model entities through what eventually became Section 45Q,[82] in parallel with on-going negotiations with iwi advisory group members supporting the freshwater iwi leaders' group. Section 45Q(1) of the amended Public Finance Act 1989 broadly followed the drafting stance of Section 9 in stating that, 'Nothing in this Part shall permit the Crown to act in a manner that is inconsistent with the principles of the Treaty of Waitangi (Te Tiriti o Waitangi)'. Interaction between iwi leaders, their advisors and denizens of the executive wing continued, with sophisticated documentation and interplay.[83] In these circumstances Section 9 enjoyed a constitutional materiality irrespective of transactional precedents to the contrary. Particular configurations of relationship with the executive – iwi leaders; Māori Party – and timing (leading up to and around the scheduled events at Waitangi) prompted proposals to retain a Section 9-like clause for the mixed-ownership model. It was drawn upon to ameliorate the possibilities of political and legal contest relative to a policy on 'mixed ownership' that had been taken to the electorate as a campaign manifesto point in November 2011. By that stage, the iwi chairs forum had already become a regularized part of the calendar of cabinet government-iwi engagement. At the plenary annual meeting on 5 February 2016, 13 ministers supported by some 30 officials attended while approximately 60 chairs and their advisors spoke to a carefully crafted policy agenda. In 2007 this iwi chairs forum was in its embryonic phase of organization, having been convened in 2005 at Takahanga marae in Kaikōura, with its first substantial correspondence to ministers in the Helen Clark government addressing freshwater resources. Ultimately, the mixed-ownership model policy and the insertion of Section 45Q of the Public Finance Act led to an unsuccessful judicial review of the proposal to sell-down government shares in Mighty River Power Limited on the application of the New Zealand Māori Council in the Supreme Court.[84]

Strategically, senior levels within the executive branch appreciated from the very outset in February 2012 that the contentiousness concerning the Treaty provision would end in court. There was, therefore, every incentive to expedite the process to a conclusion, with the government proving willing to test its

82 Moves to retain and extend a Section 9-like provision were already afoot late on the evening of 5 February 2012. Māori Party discussions with relevant senior Ministers in early February were also an influencing factor given the confidence and supply arrangements with the Key-led government. As I was staffing for the prime minister at Waitangi, I recall receiving a copy of the impending proceedings challenging the mixed ownership model proposals from Donna Hall, solicitor for the New Zealand Māori Council, on 5 February at the Copthorne Hotel entrance in Waitangi.

83 For instance, the document entitled Te Rūnanga o Ngāi Tahu, *Summary Report: Te Wai Pounamu – Te Mana o Te Wai Case Study Report* (June 2015), http://iwichairs.maori.nz/wp-content/uploads/2015/06/Case-Study-Te-Waipounamu-Te-Mana-o-Te-Wai-June-2015.pdf (accessed 31 July 2016); *Ngāti Tuwharetoa's Relationship with Our Ancestral Waters: Supplementary Document for the Deputy Prime Minister*, June 2012.

84 *New Zealand Māori Council v Attorney-General* [2013] 3 NZLR 157.

policy preferences against the Treaty principles through the Tribunal, High Court and Supreme Court.[85] On 27 February 2013, the Supreme Court determined as a matter of jurisdiction that,

> the proposed sale of the shares (on which the claim of material prejudice is based) is reviewable for consistency with the principles of the Treaty [under Section 9 of the State-Owned Enterprises Act and Section 45Q of the Public Finance Act 1989].[86]

In dismissing the appeal of the New Zealand Māori Council and the Waikato Rivers and Dams Claim Trust, however, the court concluded that the partial sell-down would not impair, to a material extent, the crown's ability to remedy any Treaty breach relating to indigenous interests in the Waikato River. Ministerial affidavit evidence proved critical in persuading the court, detailing the various policy and negotiations processes underway. Now, such work is continuing with considerable challenge, as the mix of interests engaged across New Zealand, the regional variability in community approaches, and water demand relative to resources, signifies the value of politics in sorting ways through. Importantly, though, the Supreme Court read 'Parliament's enactment of s 45Q [as demonstrating] a concern that there is potential Crown action under Part 5A which might, but for the restraint imposed by s 45Q, be inconsistent with the principles of the Treaty'.[87] At the time of writing, a discussion document has been issued to engage consultation although threats of a return to the courts predicated on the affidavit evidence of ministers referenced in the February 2013 decision remain ever-present.[88] These public law consequences emerged from tactical decision-making attempting to further an already determined policy objective. Not for the last time, let alone the first, such efforts, the calculations of support required, led to adjustments in policy and law with constitutional implications relative to the exertion of influence on discrete outcomes.

## A treaty reflecting constitutionally material presences elsewhere – concluding reflections

These otherwise ordinary legislative provisions reflect a constitutionally material presence lying elsewhere. The treaty represents a form of shorthand for clusters or thickets of politically and legally dense state-indigenous relations

85 Leave to appeal directly from the High Court to the Supreme Court was given on 18 December 2012: *New Zealand Māori Council v Attorney-General* [2012] NZSC 115.

86 *New Zealand Māori Council v Attorney-General* [2013] 3 NZLR 157, [7].

87 Ibid., [61].

88 Ministry for the Environment, *Next Steps for Fresh Water: Consultation Document* (February 2016) 9–10, 27–32.

that are dynamic and exert interpretative effects upon legislative, judicial and executive behaviours. These plural, multi-directional relations are not insulated from change. How these relations are expressed at given moments is historically dynamic and contingent; that is, unexpected phenomena or contexts might emerge pressing for tactical (occasionally strategic), behavioural responses or even non-responsiveness. But it is the specific prompts or conditions, historically-located, which yield analytical insights. Statutory sections pertaining to these treaty relations – often with express mention of the 'principles of the Treaty of Waitangi' and particular forms of official conduct or deliberation required relative to these, such as 'give effect to' or 'have particular regard to'[89] – effectively perform what could be construed as an *aide-mémoire* function, reminding institutions or actors to deliberate or consider the Treaty's pertinence in given circumstances.[90] It gains an interpretative foothold, one that is iterative. As Eskridge and Ferejohn state, '[t]he tension between the desirability of normative updating and the need for it to be legitimate along lines of popular sovereignty is a pervasive problem for modern representative democracies'.[91]

Even less visible, however, are those seemingly banal or ordinary provisions, which partly reflect and partly conceal points of constitutional interpretative difference that are located in politics but seldom find clear expression in statutes. Jurists and scholars may be unaware of these subtle points (or not even trouble to locate them) and the statute may not supply any obvious interpretative footholds for courts to understand the constitutional materiality of any clauses. Here, the contextual or background normative status of the Treaty might assist in argument but it is far from evident that it always can if those engaging with the text are not privy to its richer, underlying points of reference. Hence, 'accommodated activities' in clause 9 of the Ngā Rohe Moana o Ngā Hapū o Ngāti Porou Bill, reflect an agreement to disagree as to whose authority – hapū or crown – authorized the presence of such activities historically, such as seawalls or certain jetties. Considerable research, thoughtfulness and memory is required if such conditionalities are to be appreciated in juristic or academic analysis.

Problematically, treaty relations between an incoming crown and indigenous populations assume a colonial trope, paternalistically 'protective' in its orientations notwithstanding the much more symmetrical or indeed asymmetrical relations (favouring indigenous influence) upon the ground where initial coastal settlements were established. Ballantyne recognizes this point as to the assumptions of 'protection', as have others.[92] A shared territorial space in an

89 Amongst recent legislative drafting formulations, Section 5 of the Public Records Act 2005 stands out in referring expressly to the 'Treaty of Waitangi' and not to 'principles'.

90 I have adapted this *aide-mémoire* concept from Nicholas Barber in 'Why Entrench?' (2016) 14 International Journal of Constitutional Law 325–350.

91 Eskridge and Ferejohn (n 18), 1272.

92 Tony Ballantyne, *Entanglements of Empire: Missionaries, Māori, and the Question of the Body* (Auckland University Press, 2014) 248–249.

archipelago, from 1840 encouraging notions of a shared, imagined polity and community in places of entanglement or intermingling, also required deliberate thought concerning designing government and constitutional settings and the possibilities of evaluation and critique. Here, then, lies the risk with a treaty instrument like that starting its formal journey at Waitangi: its assumptions of asymmetrical relations, even if this imbalance was only realized across time – and the challenge to decolonize its constitutional implications or, at the very least, to recalibrate those power relations in situations where hapū admitted strangers (settlers) onto territories, often subject to terms.

This recalibration is occurring subtly in ways that permit the crown to sustain the view that it remains jurisdictionally pre-eminent within New Zealand. For example, through processes of settling historical Treaty-related claims resulting settlement legislation, such as Te Awa Tupua (Whanganui River Claims Settlement) Act 2017,[93] Te Arawa Lakes Settlement Act 2006, or site-specific statutes emerging out of settlement negotiations, like Te Urewera Act 2014. Voices hitherto neglected or minimized are now being re-factored into public decision-making processes relative to natural resources or to particular sites, such as waterways or areas once classified as national parks. With Te Urewera, for instance, it ceased to be defined as a national park under the National Parks Act 1980 while Section 11(1) declared it to be 'a legal entity, [with] all the rights, powers, duties, and liabilities of a legal person' (the fee simple estate that resided with the crown is now vested in that new person identified as 'Te Urewera'). Clause 4.20.1 of the deed of settlement is clear that 'Te Urewera land will no longer be vested in the Crown'. Because Te Urewera is no longer a national park, the otherwise potent form of a Treaty of Waitangi provision in the Conservation Act 1987[94] no longer applies, is effectively replaced by Section 20 of Te Urewera Act, which is headed '[d]ecision making affecting the relationship of iwi and hapū with Te Urewera'. In short, a bespoke or expressly designed understanding of how a treaty context might be expressed in a particularized setting or arena has replaced it. To elaborate, Section 20 is envisaged as partly expressing how those relations are to be given tangible recognition through the activities of the administering authority for Te Urewera (namely Te Urewera Board), including, for instance, the requirement to grant an activity permit or concession in relation to the area. The stated purpose of such actions is to 'recognise and reflect' both Tūhoetanga and 'the Crown's responsibility under the Treaty of Waitangi (Te Tiriti o Waitangi)' (Section 20(2) of Te Urewera Act). Section 18(3) of Te Urewera Act, setting out the functions of the board, refers to aspects of Tūhoe understanding specific to that community, '*mana me*

93 For the deed of settlement: Ruruku Whakatupua – Te Mana o Te Awa Tupua (5 August 2014), http://nz01.terabyte.co.nz/ots/DocumentLibrary/140805RurukuWhakatupua-TeManaOTeAwaTupua.pdf.

94 Section 4 of the Conservation Act provides: 'This Act shall so be interpreted and administered as to give effect to the principles of the Treaty of Waitangi'.

*mauri*' being one such example and defined as conveying 'a sense of the sensitive perception of a living and spiritual force in a place'. It is critical to understand the underlying significance of such measures. A 'concession' represents a statutory proxy for certain powers associated with, or attributable to, proprietorship of land in the conservation regulatory regime. That is, under the National Parks Act, a concession is defined through reference to the Conservation Act 1987, where a 'concession or concession document means', among other things, a lease or an easement, as well as a permit or licence.[95] A landscape of relations and power is being crafted in a bespoke fashion, with a constitutional and governmental significance despite, at one level, the apparent ordinariness of the legal terms and concepts being deployed. These instances reveal the incremental steps in political re-negotiation and the resetting of relations, at least for a time, in a constitutional setting not dominated by a codified, entrenched form of constitutional text, perhaps suggesting the conceptual limitations of 'quasi-constitutionality' beyond the constrained interpretative arena Perry and Ahmed already set out. Those institutions and actors pertinent to the analysis of constitutionalism and its historicity in this chapter include those other than a legislature or the courts. As demonstrated in this chapter, a range of officials, indigenous polities and those acting for aspects of such communities, non-governmental organizations and coteries of advisors must also be considered in examining the phenomena of constitutional norms.[96] Drawing these diverse threads together illustrates the narrowness of 'quasi-constitutionality' as an aid, especially if one is concerned with recovering and analysing the materialities of constitutional norms across state-indigenous relations in an array of settings.

95 Conservation Act 1987, s 2(1).
96 Hickford (n 27).

# 5 Quasi-constitutionality in Canada and the weak-form model of constitutionalism and judicial review

*John Helis*

The new Commonwealth, parliamentary, or weak-form model of constitutionalism and judicial review has been receiving increased attention for its ability to uphold fundamental rights in a seemingly middle-ground approach between legislative and judicial supremacy. In this emerging approach, statutory instruments protecting fundamental rights in a number of Commonwealth countries are being used to interpret and review other laws. The *Canadian Charter of Rights and Freedoms* is often referred to as the Canadian example of this model, but its constitutional status brings the *Charter* closer to judicial and constitutional supremacy compared to the statutory rights instruments in other Commonwealth jurisdictions.[1] Far more equivalent to the weak-form model are the federal and provincial statutes that have been declared quasi-constitutional by the Supreme Court of Canada. These statutes have an increasingly significant effect on the interpretation and review of other legislation. In this respect, Canada is unique within the Commonwealth for maintaining both strong and weak-form models of judicial review.

This article will consider the characteristics of quasi-constitutionality in Canada within the context of the weak-form model of judicial review, and will demonstrate that it provides the most developed form of judicial review among the rights-based statutes found in the United Kingdom, Australia, and New Zealand, which are collectively viewed as the weak-form model. Canadian quasi-constitutional legislation fits within the weak-form model because the role of the judiciary in scrutinizing legislation for compliance with fundamental rights is based on interpretation rather than invalidation. In this approach, legislation is interpreted consistently with fundamental rights, even if this at times involves a strained interpretation of a regular statute. Unlike other Commonwealth jurisdictions, however, courts and tribunals in Canada have gone a step further and apply quasi-constitutional statutes in priority sequence over regular statutes when a conflict between the two cannot be reconciled through interpretation. Most notably, under some categories of quasi-constitutional statutes the

1 *Canadian Charter of Rights and Freedoms*, Part I of the *Constitution Act*, 1982, being Schedule B to the *Canada Act* 1982 (UK), 1982, c 11.

conflicting provision can be declared inoperable. The inoperability of a provision displays some of the practical characteristics of invalidation that result when a statute is inconsistent with the *Charter*, particularly for the individual litigant whose rights have been infringed, although it remains an extension of the interpretative mandate as the impugned provision merely temporarily yields to prioritize a fundamental right contained in a quasi-constitutional statute in that particular instance. The notion that quasi-constitutional statutes have an elevated legal status over all other statutes in the interpretative exercise has been accepted in Canada with limited controversy, even when it involves the courts recognizing certain principles as fundamental without an explicit basis in legislative intent.

This article will begin in Part I by reviewing the attributes of the interpretative mandate in the weak-form model of judicial review, and will reveal how quasi-constitutional statutes in Canada fit within this model. Part II will consider how courts address circumstances of irreconcilable conflict, and the extent of the remedies available under quasi-constitutional legislation. Lastly, Part III will examine the evolving theoretical basis of quasi-constitutionality, which displays a partial reliance on the concept of fundamental law alongside legislative supremacy.

## I. The weak-form model of judicial review and the interpretative mandate

The statutory rights instruments in a number of Commonwealth jurisdictions, including the *Human Rights Act* in the UK, the *New Zealand Bill of Rights Act*, the *Human Rights Act* of the Australian Capital Territory, and the *Charter of Human Rights and Responsibilities Act* of the state of Victoria, are often collectively referred to as the new Commonwealth model of constitutionalism and judicial review.[2] These statutes do not provide a strong-form model of rights protection and judicial review as under the American Bill of Rights, but they do influence the compliance of other legislation with fundamental rights far beyond that found in the common law approach to rights protections traditionally followed in the Commonwealth. The term "new Commonwealth model," first coined by Stephen Gardbaum,[3] is commonly used to describe this approach, although others have employed alternate terms such as "parliamentary bill of rights model,"[4] "weak-form" model of judicial review,[5] and "the model of

2 *Human Rights Act*, 1998 c 42 (UK)*; New Zealand Bill of Rights Act*, 1990/109; *Human Rights Act*, 2004 A2004-5 (Austrian Capital Territory); the *Charter of Human Rights and Responsibilities Act*, 2006, Act No. 43/2006 (State of Victoria).

3 Stephen Gardbaum, "The New Commonwealth Model of Constitutionalism" (2001) 49 American Journal of Comparative Law 707.

4 Janet Hiebert, "Parliamentary Bill of Rights: An Alternative Model?" (2006) 69 Modern Law Review 7.

5 Mark Tushnet, "Alternative Forms of Judicial Review" (2003) 101 Michigan Law Review 2781; or just "weak judicial review" by Jeremy Waldron, "The Core of the Case against Judicial Review" (2006) 115 Yale Law Journal 1346.

democratic dialogue."[6] These terms are generally used synonymously, although the terms new Commonwealth model and parliamentary bill of rights model capture what Gardbaum refers to the "twin mechanisms of judicial and political rights review of legislation."[7] It is the first of these two functions that this article is most concerned with since it is comparable to the form of judicial review which occurs under Canadian quasi-constitutional statutes. This article will therefore refer to the weak-form model of judicial review for its distinctiveness from the strong-form model which is based on judicial and constitutional supremacy.

Unlike the strong-form model, where the courts can strike down or invalidate statutes that violate fundamental rights, the primary characteristic of the weak-form model of judicial review is the interpretation of other statutes in accordance with the rights-protecting statute, what Mark Tushnet calls the "interpretative mandate."[8] Central to this is therefore the adoption of a form of judicial review which is not conflated to judicial supremacy.[9] The rights statutes in the UK, New Zealand, and Australia explicitly recognize the interpretative mandate.[10] Section 3 of the UK's *Human Rights Act*, for instance, provides that "So far as it is possible to do so, primary legislation and subordinate legislation must be read and given effect in a way which is compatible with the Convention rights."

Tushnet argues that the interpretative mandate as a form of judicial review is most clearly revealed in situations where the interpretation of a statute in accordance with rights appears to be a radical departure from the face-value wording of the statute.[11] This is similar to Trevor Allan's observation that the difference between interpreting a statute in accordance with rights and invalidating a statute for its violation of rights is a distinction of degree and not of kind.[12] In other words, while it is uncontroversial to interpret a statute in accordance with fundamental rights when its wording is open to either a rights-restrictive or rights-protective reading, since the rights-based statute simply acts as a tiebreaker, it is more contentious and possibly even as controversial as striking down another statute when an interpretation results in a radical departure

6 Alison Young, *Parliamentary Sovereignty and the Human Rights Act* (Oxford: Hart Publishing 2009) ch 5. Kent Roach also refers to "dialogic judicial review." Kent Roach, "Dialogic Judicial Review and Its Critics" (2004) 23 Supreme Court Law Review 49.

7 Stephen Gardbaum, *The New Commonwealth Model of Constitutionalism: Theory and Practice* (Cambridge University Press 2013) 2.

8 Mark Tushnet, *Weak Courts, Strong Rights: Judicial Review and Social Welfare Rights in Comparative Constitutional Law* (Princeton University Press 2008) 25–26.

9 Janet Hiebert, "New Constitutional Ideas. But Can New Parliamentary Models Resist Judicial Dominance When Interpreting Rights?" (2004) 82 Texas Law Review 1963, 1965.

10 UK *Human Rights Act*, (n 2) s 3; *New Zealand Bill of Rights Act*, (n 2) s 6, Austrian Capital Territory *Human Rights Act*, (n 2) s 30; State of Victoria *Charter of Human Rights and Responsibilities Act* (n 2) s 32.

11 Tushnet, *Weak Courts, Strong Rights* (n 8) 25.

12 T. R. S. Allan, *The Sovereignty of Law* (Oxford University Press 2013) 41.

from the interpretation that would result from the traditional methods of statutory interpretation.

The rights statutes in the UK, Australia, and New Zealand, and the courts that interpret and apply them, differ in their application of the interpretative mandate. The New Zealand courts have generally taken a restrained approach to the interpretative mandate when compared to other jurisdictions.[13] In contrast, the courts in the UK have moved away from a textual method of interpretation to a teleological or purposive approach which undertakes to fulfill the spirit of the legislation.[14] Lord Nicholls in *Ghaidan v Mendoza* described the extent of the interpretative mandate under the UK *Human Rights Act* in quite expansive terms:

> Section 3 enables language to be interpreted restrictively or expansively. But Section 3 goes further than this. It is also apt to require a court to read in words which change the meaning of the enacted legislation, so as to make it Convention-compliant. In other words, the intention of Parliament in enacting Section 3 was that, to an extent bounded only by what is "possible", a court can modify the meaning, and hence the effect, of primary and secondary legislation.[15]

Lord Millett went as far as referring to the interpretative mandate as allowing a court to "read in and read down … supply missing words, so long as they are consistent with the fundamental features of the legislative scheme," even if it involves stretching the interpretation to "almost (but not quite) to breaking point."[16]

The *Charter* has been referred to as the Canadian example of the weak-form model because the judicial authority to review legislation can be overridden by Parliament through the Section 33 notwithstanding clause.[17] The important distinction is that the *Charter* is a constitutionally entrenched law compared to the statutory form of the rights regimes that constitute the weak-form model in the other Commonwealth jurisdictions. This has resulted in some disagreement over whether the *Charter* properly fits within the weak or strong-form model of judicial review. Jeremy Waldron, for example, views the *Charter* as falling more squarely

13 Gardbaum, *The New Commonwealth Model of Constitutionalism: Theory and Practice* (n 7) 145. See especially: *Quilter v Attorney-General*, [1997] NZCA 207. The Court of Appeal subsequently applied the *New Zealand Bill of Rights Act* with more vigor in the 2000 case of *R v Poumako*, [2000] NZCA 69.

14 Christopher Jenkins, "The Institutional and Substantive Effects of the Human Rights Act in the United Kingdom" (2001) 24 Dalhousie Law Journal 218.

15 [2004] UKHL 30 [32].

16 Ibid [67].

17 See for example: Tushnet, *Weak Courts, Strong Rights* (n 8) 31; Jeffrey Goldsworthy, "Homogenizing Constitutions" (2003) 23 Oxford Journal of Legal Studies 483, 483; Jeffrey Goldsworthy, "Judicial Review, Legislative Override, and Democracy" (2003) 38 Wake Forest Law Review 451, 454–59; Gardbaum, *New Commonwealth Model of Constitutionalism: Theory and Practice* (n 7) 27; Hiebert "New Constitutional Ideas" (n 9) 1965.

within the strong-form model because of the infrequent use of the notwithstanding clause.[18] The frequency that the notwithstanding clause is invoked, however, is a practical consideration related to political culture and does not speak to the theoretical question of whether the *Charter* can be properly classified as an example of the weak-form model. More important than the frequency that the notwithstanding clause is used is the fact that the *Charter* embodies a form of judicial supremacy which is balanced with what Janet Hiebert refers to as "temporary but renewable" political dissent.[19] Others view it as balancing judicial supremacy with legislative supremacy.[20] As such, the *Charter* can be more appropriately described as being based on the doctrine of judicial supremacy with a mechanism which allows for incursions of legislative supremacy. While this represents a compromise of sorts between the two purer forms of parliamentary and judicial supremacy, it differs from the weak-form model which seeks a form of a judicial review that does not outright adopt judicial and constitutional supremacy. For this reason, quasi-constitutional statutes in Canada can more properly be characterized as the Canadian example of the weak-form model because of their statutory form.

Quasi-constitutional laws in Canada are comprised mostly of federal and provincial statutes, but a common law principle has also received this designation. The common thread among quasi-constitutional laws is that they are all rights-based regimes, and they can be grouped into six categories that correspond to the type of rights they uphold. The first is the *Canadian Bill of Rights*, which reflects the initial legislative attempt to protect civil liberties in Canada, and which served as a precursor to the constitutionally entrenched *Charter*. This statute is now of limited use, although it was the first to be called quasi-constitutional by a Supreme Court Justice who described it as "a half-way house between a purely common law regime and a constitutional one."[21] Accordingly, some of the important elements of quasi-constitutionality were first developed under the *Canadian Bill of Rights* and are now more frequently applied under other quasi-constitutional statutes. The second category consists of federal, provincial, and territorial human rights statutes, which protect the individual against discrimination from both government and private actors.[22] The third and fourth categories of quasi-constitutional laws are statutes that protect personal privacy

18 Waldron (n 5) 1356–57.

19 Janet Hiebert, "Rights-Vetting in New Zealand and Canada" (2005) 3 New Zealand Journal of Public and International Law 63, 64; Janet Hiebert, "Bills of Rights: How Different Is the Commonwealth Alternative?" (Paper presented at the 2006 Annual Meeting of the American Political Science Association, 30 August–3 September, 2006).

20 Barbara Billingsley, "Section 33: The Charter's Sleeping Giant" (2002) 21 Windsor Yearbook of Access to Justice 331; Richard Albert, "Advisory Review: The Reincarnation of the Notwithstanding Clause" (2008) 45 Alberta Law Review 1037 [1], [6].

21 *Canadian Bill of Rights*, SC 1960, c 44; *R v Hogan*, [1975] 2 SCR 574, 597. See also: *Alberta Bill of Rights*, RSA 2000, c A-14.

22 See especially: *Battlefords and District Co-operative Ltd. v Gibbs*, [1996] 3 SCR 566 [18]; *B. v Ontario (Human Rights Commission)*, [2002] 3 SCR 403 [44]; *Gould v Yukon Order of Pioneers*, [1996] 1 SCR 571 [120].

and those that provide access to information held by government.[23] Statutes which designate English and French as official languages, or which expand the right to government services in one of these languages, are the fifth category of quasi-constitutional statutes.[24] Finally, the common law protection of a person's good reputation has been referred to as quasi-constitutional by the Supreme Court of Canada.[25]

Judicial review under quasi-constitutional legislation begins with an approach similar to the interpretative mandate found in the Commonwealth. The difference is that the Commonwealth statutes refer to "interpreting" or "reading" other legislation to make it compatible with human rights, while many quasi-constitutional statutes in Canada contain primacy provisions which provide that they prevail when in conflict with other legislation.[26] The interpretative strategies traditionally developed to avoid conflict between statutes therefore have little to no application when a potential conflict involves a quasi-constitutional statute, where the court must adopt an interpretation that is consistent with the quasi-constitutional one.

The Supreme Court of Canada first established that the doctrine of *generalia specialibus non derogant*, which ensures that specific legislation is prioritized over general legislation, does not apply to quasi-constitutional human rights legislation in the 1982 decision of *Insurance Corporation of British Columbia v Heerspink*.[27] Rather, quasi-constitutional legislation applies in priority sequence even over more specific statutes. In *Winnipeg School Division No 1 v Craton*, decided three years after *Heerspink*, the Court also declared that the doctrine *leges posteriores priores contrarias abrogant*, which results in the implied repeal of an earlier statute by a latter one when two statutes are in conflict, similarly does not apply to quasi-constitutional human rights legislation. Instead, the Court held that human rights legislation "may not

23 See especially: *Lavigne v Canada (Office of the Commissioner of Official Languages)*, 2002 SCC 53 [24]; *Canada (Information Commissioner) v Canada (Commissioner of the Royal Canadian Mounted Police)*, 2003 SCC 8 [26]; *Canada (Information Commissioner) v Canada (Minister of National Defence)*, 2011 SCC 25 [40], [79]; *Alberta (Information and Privacy Commissioner) v United Food and Commercial Workers, Local 401*, 2013 SCC 62.

24 *Lavigne*, ibid. [23]; *Canada (Attorney General) v Viola*, [1991] 1 FC 373 (CA), 386.

25 See *Éditions Écosociété Inc. v Banro Corp*, 2012 SCC 18 [57], in which the Court relied on its early statement in *Hill v Church of Scientology of Toronto*, [1995] 2 SCR 1130 [120].

26 Different terminology is used in quasi-constitutional human rights statutes, including primacy, paramountcy, precedence, supersedes, and "[n]o provision of any Act … may derogate." The jurisprudence has not placed much weight on these differences, which suggests that these terms are largely interchangeable. In *Newfoundland (Human Rights Commission) v Newfoundland (Workplace Health, Safety and Compensation Commission)*, 2005 NLCA 61 (CA) [17], [42], both the majority and dissenting Justices of the Newfoundland Court of Appeal agreed that there was no legal significance to the distinctions between the terms "takes precedence over," as found in Newfoundland's legislation, and "are paramount over," contained in Manitoba's *Human Rights Code*.

27 [1982] 2 SCR 145, 148.

be altered, amended or repealed, nor may exceptions be created to its provisions, save by clear legislative pronouncement."[28]

As with the other rights-protecting statutes in the Commonwealth, the primacy of quasi-constitutional legislation has a significant effect on the interpretation of other legislation. The *Heerspink* decision involved an insurance company that terminated a client's fire insurance policy because it considered him to be a "moral hazard" after he was charged with the offence of trafficking marijuana. The *Insurance Act* provided that a policy can be terminated by an insurance company with fifteen days' notice. Justice Ritchie of the Supreme Court of Canada found that a conflict between the *Insurance Act* and the *Human Rights Code* could be avoided when the provision of the *Insurance Act* was interpreted to require "reasonable cause" for termination of the policy. Reasonable cause is not explicitly found in the *Insurance Act*, although this ensures that a policy cannot be cancelled for discriminatory reasons and thus brings the interpretation of the *Insurance Act* in line with the *Human Rights Code*.

## II. Judicial review and the extent of the interpretative mandate

Despite the influence of the interpretative mandate, there are instances when even a strained interpretation cannot result in the interpretation of a statute in accordance with a right-protecting one. The method by which this is addressed reveals the most significant differences between quasi-constitutional legislation in Canada and the various rights statutes in the Commonwealth. Two approaches have developed on how to address conflicts between a rights-protecting statute and a regular one that cannot be reconciled through interpretation. The first method involves a declaratory statement from a court that a statutory provision is "inconsistent" with a rights-protecting statute. This is what Mark Tushnet refers to as the "augmented interpretative mandate."[29] Such orders do not affect the validity, operation, or enforcement of the law, but rather serve as an avenue for the courts to identify rights infringements in other statutes while Parliament retains the exclusive authority to address such infringements. The second involves a recognition that a rights-protecting statute prevails when it conflicts with another statute in a manner that cannot be reconciled through interpretation, and requires the court to prioritize the application of the rights-protecting statute. In some instances, this may involve the conflicting statute being declared inoperable or inapplicable in the circumstances.

Provisions in the UK *Human Rights Act*, the *Human Rights Act* of the Australian Capital Territory, and the State of Victoria *Charter*, explicitly allow courts to declare provisions in other statutes incompatible when they cannot be

28 [1985] 2 SCR 150 [1985] 2 SCR 150, 156.
29 Tushnet, *Weak Courts, Strong Rights* (n 8) 27.

interpreted consistent with the rights statute.[30] Such authority is not explicitly found in the *New Zealand Bill of Rights Act*, although the Court of Appeal in the 2017 decision of *Attorney General v Taylor* upheld a declaration issued by the High Court that a statute prohibiting prisoners from voting is inconsistent with the right to vote in the *New Zealand Bill of Rights Act*.[31]

Declarations of incompatibility provide a relatively uncontroversial role for the courts in protecting rights. The courts apply the legislation that cannot be interpreted in accordance with the right-protecting statute, point out the discordance in a declaratory statement, and leave it to the legislature to take any corrective action. Jeffrey Goldsworthy explains that any moral or political considerations which constrain a majority in parliament from acting a certain way do not affect the doctrine of legislative supremacy, whose purpose is to ensure that no other institution "has legal authority to invalidate or override statutes."[32]

While the consistency of this method with legislative supremacy makes declarations of incompatibility an attractive form of rights protection in the Commonwealth, the obvious limitation is that it leaves the individual litigant by the wayside in a way that defies the legal maxim *ubi jus ibi remedium* – where there is a right, there must be a remedy. This was recognized in the 2008 case of *Burden and Burden v The United Kingdom*, where the European Court of Human Rights found that the *Human Rights Act* failed to provide an effective remedy because a declaration of incompatibility is not binding but rather dependent on the discretion of the executive.[33] The Court acknowledged that the development of a constitutional convention requiring the Minister to give effect to declarations of incompatibility may eventually convince the Court of the effectiveness of this procedure, although this has not yet occurred.

In contrast, declarations of inoperability under quasi-constitutional legislation in Canada provide a full remedy to the litigant whose rights have been infringed. When a statutory provision conflicts with one of two categories of quasi-constitutional legislation, namely the *Canadian Bill of Rights* and human rights legislation, a court or tribunal can proceed to declare the impugned provision inoperable. This is one of the most significant attributes of quasi-constitutional legislation, and is seemingly the most advanced form of judicial review within the weak-form model. This remedy was first endorsed by the Supreme Court of Canada under the *Canadian Bill of Rights* in the 1970 decision of *R v Drybones* after a decade of "conflicting judicial opinions" over the question of the extent of its impact over conflicting legislation.[34] The *Drybones* case presented a clear example of

30 UK *Human Rights Act* (n 2) s 4; Australian Capital Territory *Human Rights Act*, (n 2) s 32(2); State of Victoria *Charter* (n 2) s 36. In the State of Victoria *Charter* it is referred to as a "declaration of inconsistent interpretation."

31 [2015] NZHC 1706 [109].

32 Jeffrey Goldsworthy, "Is Parliament Sovereign? Recent Challenges to the Doctrine of Parliamentary Sovereignty" (2005) 3 New Zealand Journal of Public and International Law 7, 31.

33 [2008] ECHR 357 [40]–[41].

34 [1970] SCR 297; Peter Hogg, *Constitutional Law of Canada* (5th edn, Carswell 2007) 35.5.

a conflict with the *Canadian Bill of Rights* which could not be reconciled through interpretation, because the *Indian Act* imposed a much harsher penalty against an Indigenous person for being intoxicated in public compared to the penalty imposed against a non-Indigenous person under the local liquor ordinance. Since this violation of the guarantee of equality before the law in the *Canadian Bill of Rights* could not be reconciled through interpretation, the Court held that the impugned provision of the *Indian Act* was inoperative.

Despite the significance of this remedy its use was not as widespread as hoped, due to the Court's restrictive interpretation of the *Canadian Bill of Rights* that viewed the rights it protects as being frozen in time as they existed when it was enacted in 1960.[35] This resulted in a shift in focus from the *Canadian Bill of Rights* to federal and provincial human rights statutes in the 1970s.[36] The explicit recognition from the Supreme Court of Canada that human rights legislation can render conflicting provisions in other statutes inoperable came in the 1985 *Craton* decision. That case was a challenge to the authorization of mandatory retirement policies under Manitoba's *Public School's Act* as discrimination on the basis of age contrary to the province's *Human Rights Act*. A unanimous Court found that the authorization of such policies constituted a clear conflict with the *Human Rights Act* which could not be reconciled through interpretation. Accordingly, the Supreme Court dismissed the appeal from the Court of Appeal's decision finding the provision inoperable.[37]

A comparable remedy was developed in the UK for irreconcilable conflicts with the *European Communities Act* 1972. The European Court of Justice has long held that Community law holds primacy over national law, which is supported by Section 2 of the ECA.[38] The courts have viewed the priority of Community law as a rule of statutory construction, whereby national legislation is to be interpreted in accordance with Community law.[39] The real controversy arose

35 Walter Tarnopolsky, "A New Bill of Rights in the Light of the Interpretation of the Present One by the Supreme Court of Canada" in Law Society of Upper Canada (ed), *The Constitution and the Future of Canada* (R DeBoo 1978) 181–91. The frozen concept of rights was applied by the Supreme Court of Canada in the following decisions: *Robertson and Rosetanni v R*, [1963] SCR 651, 654; *R v Burnshine*, [1975] 1 SCR 693 R v Burnshine, [1975] 1 SCR 693, 702; *Smythe v The Queen*, [1971] SCR 680 [683], [686]. See also: Justice Pigeon's dissent in *R v Drybones* (n 34); *Authorson v Canada (Attorney General)*, [2003] SCR 40 [51]–[52].

36 Claire Mummé, "At the Crossroads in Discrimination Law: How the Human Rights Codes Overtook the Charter in Canadian Government Services Cases" (2012) 9 Journal of Law & Equality 103 [15].

37 *Craton* (n 28) [153]–[154], [157].

38 See especially: *Van Gend en Loos v Nederlandse Administratie der Belastingen*, [1963] ECR 1; *Flaminio Costa v ENEL*, [1964] ECR 585; *Amministrazione della Finanze dello Stato v Simenthal SpA*, [1978] ECR 628.

39 Jay Arangonés, "Regina v Secretary of State for Transport Ex Parte Factortame Ltd.: The Limits of Parliamentary Sovereignty and the Rule of Community Law" (1990) 14 Fordham International Law Journal 777, 778. See: *Garland v British Rail Engineering Ltd* (No 2), [1982] UKHL 2.

in the *Factortame* litigation, where nationality requirements for registration of fishing vessels under a domestic statute in the UK conflicted with Community law and were irreconcilable through interpretation. In that instance the House of Lords "disapplied" the domestic law to uphold Community law which has priority.[40] Few reasons were provided in *Factorame* for the special status of the ECA, and it was not until the 2002 decision of *Thoburn v Sunderland City Council* that Laws LJ attributed it to its constitutional status.[41] Among the various statutes shortlisted as constitutional is the *Human Rights Act*, which by some accounts is the "cornerstone" of the new British constitution.[42] Not surprising, the suggestion has been made that this remedy should be extended to other constitutional statutes.[43] In the case of the *Human Rights Act* this would require legislative amendment as the interpretative mandate in Section 3 explicitly provides that it "does not affect the validity, continuing operation or enforcement of any incompatible primary legislation."

The accessibility of orders of inoperability under quasi-constitutional legislation is as significant as their scope, as the remedy is not limited to the courts but can also be issued by administrative tribunals. The Supreme Court of Canada confirmed in the 2006 decision of *Tranchemontagne v Ontario (Director, Disability Support Program)* that administrative tribunals, including those that are not specifically created to administer human rights legislation, have the duty to apply human rights statutes in the course of deciding a case properly before them.[44] Challenging a statute under human rights legislation is not as direct as a *Charter* challenge, but rather requires discrimination in the provision of a government service created by a statute. In these types of cases claims are brought under human rights legislation against publicly funded programs established by legislation. In *Hendershott v Ontario (Ministry of Community and Social Services)*, for example, the Human Rights Tribunal of Ontario found that providing the applicant fewer benefits under social assistance legislation for the support of her children because she lives and is dependent on her parents constitutes a breach of the *Human Rights Code*, and the respondent was ordered to "cease to consider the fact that a minor parent is living with her or his own parents in the calculation of benefits for the minor parent's children."[45] Similarly, in *Ivancicevic v Ontario (Minister of Consumer Services)*, the same Tribunal found that a ban on holding marijuana while at a restaurant discriminated against the applicant, who held a prescription to use marijuana to alleviate chronic

40 *R v Secretary of State for Transport, Ex p Factortame Ltd (No 2)*, [1991] 1 AC 603.

41 [2002] EWHC 195 (Admin), [2003] QB 151.

42 Vernon Bogdanor, *The New British Constitution* (Hart Publishing 2009) xiii. The *Human Rights Act* was described by Lord Irvine of Lairg as occupying "a special place in our programme of reform." Lord Irvine of Lairg, *Human Rights, Constitutional Law and the Development of the English Legal System: Selective Essays* (Hart Publishing 2003) 97.

43 Bogdanor, ibid 80.

44 2006 SCC 14.

45 2011 HRTO 482 [134].

pain, and it ordered that the impugned provision "should not be applied."[46] According to one account, these claims are surpassing similar constitutional challenges before the superior courts because tribunals are more accessible and cost effective.[47]

A similar result can occur without a court issuing an explicit declaration of inoperability, which remains the preferred approach since declarations of inoperability have only been endorsed by the courts under the *Canadian Bill of Rights* and human rights legislation. As a result of how some of the other categories of quasi-constitutional statutes operate, declarations of inoperability are not required to apply them in priority sequence over other legislation. For instance, in *Ontario (Community Safety and Correctional Services) v Ontario (Information and Privacy Commissioner)*, the Supreme Court of Canada found that the general right to access government information is to be applied over a conflicting statute that contains a confidentiality provision, unless the conflicting statute contains a clear override provision.[48] There was no need to declare the conflicting statute inoperable given the nature of the right to access government information. The Court instead applied the quasi-constitutional statute and abstained from applying the conflicting one.

## III. Theoretical basis of quasi-constitutionality

The implicit repeal of an earlier statute by a later one has been called a "logical consequence" of legislative supremacy because it prevents one legislature from binding a subsequent one, and has been recognized as an important constitutional principle since at least the 1930s.[49] Both quasi-constitutional statutes in Canada and constitutional statutes in the UK have been referred as "quasi-entrenched" because they are exempt from the doctrine of implied repeal.[50] Whether it is an indirect result of the Canadian experience with the *Charter*, or because the "new view" of legislative supremacy has influenced Canadian thinking on the subject, the idea that quasi-constitutional statutes cannot be implicitly repealed, that they apply in priority sequence even over more specific legislation, and that they can result in the inoperability of conflicting statutes, has not stirred considerable controversy or even much of a theoretical discussion. Consequently, as one

46 *Ivancicevic v Ontario (Minister of Consumer Services)*, 2011 HRTO 1714 [218].

47 Mummé (n 36) [2].

48 2014 SCC 31 [32]–[34].

49 Bogdanor (n 42) 60; *Vauxhall Estates v Liverpool Corporation*, [1932] 1 KB 723; *Ellen Street Estates Ltd. v Minister of Health*, [1934] 1 KB 590.

50 Farrah Ahmed and Adam Perry "The Quasi-entrenchment of Constitutional Statutes" (2014) 73 Oxford Journal of Legal Studies 514; Ruth Sullivan, *Sullivan on the Construction of Statutes* (5th edn, LexisNexis 2008) 497; Vanessa MacDonnell, "A Theory of Quasi-constitutionality" (2016) 53 Osgoode Hall Law Journal 508, 527.

commentator points out, the primacy of Canadian quasi-constitutional legislation and declarations of inoperability remain "relatively unexplored."[51]

Courts have attempted to justify declarations of inoperability as a remedy which is consistent with legislative supremacy. The most direct comments were made by Justice Bastarache, who wrote on behalf of the majority in the 2006 *Tranchemontagne* decision:

> This primacy provision has both similarities and differences with s. 52 of the *Constitution Act*, 1982, which announces the supremacy of the Constitution. In terms of similarities, both provisions function to eliminate the effects of inconsistent legislation. At the end of the day, whether there is a conflict with the Code or the Constitution, the ultimate effect is that the other provision is not followed and, for the purposes of that particular application, it is as if the legislation was never enacted. But in my view, the differences between the two provisions are far more important. A provision declared invalid pursuant to s. 52 of the *Constitution Act*, 1982 was never validly enacted to begin with. It never existed as valid law because the legislature enacting it never had the authority to pass it. But when a provision is inapplicable pursuant to s. 47 of the Code, there is no statement being made as to its validity. The legislature had the power to enact the conflicting provision; it just so happens that the legislature also enacted another law that takes precedence.[52]

The proposition that a legislature can include a primacy provision in a statute which displaces the doctrine of implied repeal and gives it an elevated legal status vis-à-vis other legislation has not been particularly controversial in Canada.[53] Most of the literature on declarations of inoperability has largely focused on the appropriate analytical framework when human rights legislation is used to challenge a statute creating a government service.[54] In contrast, questions surrounding the importance of constitutional statutes and their relationship

51 Mummé (n 36) [5].

52 (n 44) [35].

53 Peter Hogg asserts that the "theory under which primacy clauses are effective has never been articulated by the Court, but it must rest on the principle that a legislative body may bind itself as to manner and form" (n 34) 12.18.

54 See especially: Leslie Reaume, "Postcards from O'Malley: Reinvigorating Statutory Human Rights Jurisprudence in the Age of the Charter" in Fay Faraday, Margaret Denike and M. Kate Stephenson (eds.), *Making Equality Rights Real: Securing Substantive Equality Under the Charter* (Irwin Law 2006); Mummé (n 36); Lesli Bisgould, "Twists and Turns and Seventeen Volumes of Evidence, or How Procedural Developments Might Have Influenced Substantive Human Rights Law" (2012) 9 Journal of Law & Equality 1; Benjamin Oliphant, "Prima Facie Discrimination: Is Tranchemontagne Consistent with the Supreme Court of Canada's Human Rights Code Jurisprudence?" (2012) 9 Journal of Law & Equality 33; Wayne MacKay, "The Marriage of Human Rights Codes and Section 15 of the Charter in Pursuit of Equality: A Case for Greater Separation in Both Theory and Practice" (2013) 64 University of New Brunswick Law Journal 54.

with other statutes have been more controversial in the UK, where the traditional conception of parliamentary sovereignty and Dicey's declaration that "fundamental or so-called constitutional laws are under our constitution changed by the same body and in the same manner as other laws," have held more sway. Even though Lord Bridge in *Factortame* attributed the primacy of community law to a voluntary act of Parliament through the enactment of the ECA, some viewed this decision as revolutionary and contrary to the doctrine of parliamentary supremacy.[55]

Justice Bastarache was able to justify a declaration of inoperability on the basis of legislative intent in *Tranchemontagne* since Ontario's *Human Rights Code* contains a primacy provision, but the remedy has also been endorsed under human rights statutes that do not contain a primacy provision.[56] Following in the footsteps of *Heerspink*, where the Supreme Court of Canada first referred to human rights legislation as "fundamental law," these decisions recognize that the special status of quasi-constitutional statutes is not only due to their primacy provisions but also to the significance of the rights they uphold.[57] Most of the literature simply notes the fundamental nature of human rights legislation, although there has been some limited criticism which questions the use of this remedy in the absence of clear legislative intent through a primacy provision.[58]

55 H. W. R. Wade, "Sovereignty – Evolution or Revolution?" (1996) 112 LQR 568, 574; H. W. R. Wade, *Administrative Law* (Oxford University Press 2000) 28; Elizabeth Wicks, *The Evolution of Constitution: Eight Key Moments in British Constitutional History* (Hart Publishing 2006) 156.

56 See especially the Federal Court of Appeal in *Canada (Attorney General) v Druken*, [1989] 2 FCR 24. The Supreme Court of Canada denied leave to appeal in *Canada (Attorney General) v Druken*, [1988] SCCA 433 [1988] SCCA 433, and therefore endorsed the Federal Court of Appeal's decision. Mummé (n 36) [34]. See also the dissenting reasons of Dickson CJ and Lamer J in *Bhinder and Canadian Human Rights Commission v Canadian National Railway Co.*, [1985] 2 SCR 561 [18]–[19], and the dissenting reasons of McLachlin J and L'Heureux-Dubé J in *Cooper v Canada (Human Rights Commission)*, [1996] 3 SCR 854 [100].

57 Similar conclusions have also been reached about the primacy of quasi-constitutional statutes other than human rights legislation which do not contain a primacy provision. The following has been said about Ontario's *French Language Services Act*: "Unlike the Code, the FLSA does not contain a clause that gives it primacy over other legislation. However, given that the Court of Appeal has clearly stated that 'language rights are to be treated as fundamental human rights,' it logically follows that if an administrative tribunal's enabling legislation does not grant it the authority to decline applying the FLSA, it must consider the FLSA in the appeals before it." *Re: Workplace Safety and Insurance Board*, [2008] OIPC No 144 [71].

58 See: Maxime St-Hilaire, "The Codification of Human Rights in Canada" (2012) 42 Revue de Droit de l'Université de Sherbrooke 505 [83]; Ruth Sullivan, *Sullivan on the Construction of Statutes* (5th edn, LexisNexis 2008) 340; Shirish Pundit Chotalia, *The 2000 Annotated Canadian Human Rights Act* (Caswell 1999) 4. Peter Hogg, as a notable critic, acknowledged the case law holding that human rights legislation takes precedence over inconsistent statutes even in the complete absence of a primacy clause, and asserted "[t]his reasoning is

While the temporary disapplication of legislation in the UK is a remedy only made available under the ECA, the courts have begun to modify the traditional interpretative approaches in cases involving other constitutional statutes. Laws LJ in *Thoburn* was the first to reason that the special treatment of the ECA stems from its constitutional status, and that constitutional statutes are not subject to implied repeal but rather require express words. The Supreme Court agreed in *H v Lord Advocate*, and held that the *Scotland Act 1998* is "incapable of being altered otherwise than by an express enactment."[59] In *HS2 Action Alliance Ltd v Secretary of State for Transport*, the Court referred to conflict between constitutional statutes requiring "further considerations," which raises the possibility that the ECA does not automatically trump other constitutional statutes.[60] Lastly, the 2011 decision of *R (Governors of Brynmawr Foundational School) v The Welsh Ministers (Brynmawr)*, established that constitutional statutes are not subject to the maxim of *generalia specialibus non derogant*.[61] Farrah Ahmed and Adam Perry refer to these four decisions as collectively challenging "the Diceyan orthodoxy that a statute's constitutionality is irrelevant in law."[62]

In the absence of an explicit primacy provision the courts have turned to the pre-Diceyan concept of fundamental law. Laws LJ in *Thoburn* found that constitutional legislation "enlarges or diminishes what we would now regard as fundamental constitutional rights,"[63] and Lord Hope in *H v Lord Advocate* referred to the *Scotland Act 1998* as a "fundamental constitutional" statute in support of the conclusion that it can only be altered through express language.[64] The Supreme Court of Canada has similarly held that all quasi-constitutional statutes are fundamental law. The Court has gone as far as calling the fundamental nature of human rights legislation its "most important characteristic."[65] Accordingly, it has been suggested that this limits Parliament's authority to make legal changes to some statutes by implication and assigns to them a special meaning based on the desire to uphold fundamental rights, rather than remaining faithful

dubious," and that "in the absence of a primacy clause, the Court is in no position to create priorities between public policies." (n 34) 12.17, footnote 67.

59 [2012] UKSC 24 [30].

60 [2014] UKSC 3 [208]. See: Mark Elliott, "Constitutional Legislation, European Union Law and the Nature of the United Kingdom's Contemporary Constitution" (2014) 10 European Constitutional Law Review 379.

61 [2011] EWHC 519 [77].

62 Farrah Ahmed and Adam Perry, "Constitutional Statutes" (2017) 37 Oxford Journal of Legal Studies 461, 464.

63 *Thoburn* (n 40) [62].

64 (n 59) [30].

65 *Tranchemontagne* (n 44) [33]. For the other categories of quasi-constitutional statutes see especially: *Law society of Upper Canada v Skapinker*, [1984] 1 SCR 357 [10] (*Canadian Bill of Rights*); *Macdonell v Quebec (Commission d'accès à l'information)*, [2002] 3 SCR 661 [62] (access to information); *Lavigne* (n 23) [23]–[24] (privacy and language rights); *Hill* (n 25) [72] (the common law protection of the good reputation of an individual).

to legislative intent.[66] Mark Elliott, however, has argued that the recognition of a hierarchy between constitutional and non-constitutional statutes through the interpretative mandate provides a method for fundamental norms to be upheld without undermining legislative supremacy.[67]

Reliance on the seventeenth century legal concept of fundamental law largely associated with Sir Edward Coke and English customary or immemorial law is not an insignificant development. When J. W. Gough wrote about fundamental law in the 1960s, he was able to unequivocally assert that:

> English constitutional and legal historians nowadays are generally inclined to belittle the idea of fundamentals, and to suggest that it arose in the past from a misunderstanding of the true character of English law and the true omnipresence of the legislature. They emphasize the impossibility of attaching any precise meaning to the fundamental laws or fundamental rights which used to be invoked in England, and are therefore inclined to dismiss them as errors and confusions which we have outgrown.[68]

While the theoretical soundness of the concept and its relationship with legislative supremacy can be debated, it can no longer be summarily dismissed given the degree to which it is now being invoked by the courts in support of the augmented legal status of quasi-constitutional statutes in Canada and constitutional statutes in the UK. Regardless of where one stands in the debate, the use of the concept to define what the courts are actually doing is fitting. This is because a noticeable trend in modern accounts of fundamental law is its association with constitutional theory, particularly the inability to amend or repeal fundamental law through the regular legislative process, and the use of fundamental law to judicially review other laws.[69]

Determining which principles are fundamental is not as straightforward. The modern understanding of fundamental law and its association with constitutionality is viewed as having evolved from seventeenth century English roots and what Gough referred to as the "normal usage" of the term.[70] Even in the seventeenth century, however, during the height of fundamental law in English legal discourse, the understanding of the concept varied considerably, and Coke's perspective of fundamental law as English immemorial law was disputed by

66 Ahmed and Perry, "Constitutional Statutes" (n 62) 474.

67 Mark Elliott, "Embracing 'Constitutional' Legislation: Towards Fundamental Law?" (2003) 54 Northern Ireland Legal Quarterly 25, 31.

68 J. W. Gough, *Fundamental Law in English History* (Oxford University Press 1961) v.

69 Gough, ibid; J. G. A. Pocock, *The Ancient Constitution and the Feudal Law: A Study of English Historical Thought in the Seventeenth Century* (2nd edn, Cambridge University Press 1987) 48, footnote 2; Martyn Thompson, "The History of Fundamental Law in Political Thought from the French Wars of Religion to the American Revolution" (1986) 91 *The American Historical Review* 1103, 1103.

70 Gough (n 68) 160.

a number of other seventeenth century authors.[71] Gough tells us that the term was "vague and ill-defined,"[72] while Pocock referred to fundamental law as the "most important and elusive of seventeenth-century concepts."[73]

In the contemporary discourse David Jenkins has argued that the normative significance of some statutes means "that they themselves embody or generate higher-order principles that weave into a common law constitutional fabric."[74] Jenkin asserts that the core principles of such statutes transcend their text even if some of their provisions are amended over time. This suggests that over and above the degree to which Parliament has to be explicit when amending constitutional statutes, they possess an enduring character because of the nature of the rights they protect. In Canada Luc Tremblay is similarly in favour of looking at the content of statutes and their importance, and refers to the view that the status of quasi-constitutionality is based entirely upon the presence of a primacy provision as "orthodox."[75] Ahmed and Perry raise a number of difficulties with Jenkin's approach, including that it is not obvious which principles are part of the constitution, and they offer an approach that considers how a statute makes a substantial difference to "the things norms are about, namely, requirements, permissions and powers."[76] Despite the challenges, identifying fundamental principles is a role courts must necessarily fulfill to prevent the "casual or incidental erosion" of these principles.[77]

The difficulty in identifying constitutional principles in the UK does not exist in Canada to the same degree since such principles can more readily be drawn from the written Constitution. Indeed the term quasi-constitutional on its face suggests a relationship with the written Constitution. The most recent scholarship has therefore focused on the role of quasi-constitutional legislation in the implementation of constitutional obligations, which have been labelled "constitutional imperatives."[78]

In addition to this practical link with the written Constitution, quasi-constitutionality is also related to the normative elements of the Canadian Constitution that have been recognized by the courts. In *Reference re Secession of Quebec* the Supreme Court of Canada set out a non-exhaustive list of "four fundamental and organizing principles of the Constitution," which include

71 Richard Tuck, *Natural Rights Theories: Their Origin and Development* (Cambridge University Press 1979) 82–139.

72 Gough, (n 68) 2.

73 Pocock (n 69) 48.

74 David Jenkins, "Common Law Declarations of Unconstitutionality" (2009) 7 International Journal of Constitutional Law 183, 201.

75 Luc Tremblay, *The Rule of Law, Justice and Interpretation* (Queen's University Press 1997) 88, footnote 189.

76 Ahmed and Perry, "Constitutional Statutes" (n 62) 469.

77 Elliott, "Embracing 'Constitutional' Legislation" (n 66) 32.

78 MacDonnell (n 50) 511.

democracy, the protection of minorities, federalism, constitutionalism, and the rule of law.[79] Since the Court referred to these principles as informing and sustaining the constitutional text, it has been suggested that the specific provisions of the Constitution implement or actualize them.[80] It can also be argued that quasi-constitutional laws embody these constitutional principles and similarly help to implement and actualize them.

The courts have said the most about the relationship between quasi-constitutional laws and the principle of democracy. Most recently, three justices of the Supreme Court of Canada in the 2017 decision of *Douez v Facebook* held that quasi-constitutional rights "play an essential role in a free and democratic society and embody key Canadian values."[81] The relationship is due to the importance of equality and inclusion to democracy, and Federal Court of Appeal in *Vilven v Air Canada* stated: "[t]he *Canadian Human Rights Act* is quasi-constitutional legislation, which has been enacted to give effect to the fundamental Canadian value of equality, a value which has been described as lying at the very heart of a free and democratic society."[82] A unanimous Supreme Court of Canada in *Lavigne v Canada (Office of the Commissioner of Official Languages)* held that the federal *Privacy Act* serves as "a reminder of the extent to which the protection of privacy is necessary to the preservation of a free and democratic society."[83] On the flip side privacy is access to information legislation which has been called "fundamental to our democracy,"[84] as it is able to "increase transparency in government, contribute to an informed public, and enhance an open and democratic society."[85] The Supreme Court of Canada in *Hill v Church of Scientology of Toronto* found that "the protection of the good reputation of an individual is of fundamental importance to our democratic society," because "[d]emocracy has always recognized and cherished the fundamental importance of an individual. That importance must, in turn, be based upon the good repute of a person."[86]

Statutes protecting language rights help promote the principle of democracy largely through their close association with the freedom of expression and their symbiosis with the foundational constitutional principle of the protection of

79 [1998] 2 SCR 217 [32].

80 Sujit Choudhry and Robert Howse, "Constitutional Theory and the Quebec Secession Reference" (2000) 13 Canadian Journal of Law and Jurisprudence 143 [28].

81 2017 SCC 33 [58].

82 [2010] 2009 FC 367 [76].

83 *Lavigne* (n 23) [25].

84 *Canada (Information Commissioner) v Canada (Minister of National Defence)* (n 23) [79].

85 *(Ontario (Public Safety and Security) v Criminal Lawyers' Association*, 2010 SCC 23 [1]. See also: *Bronskill v Canada (Canadian Heritage)*, 2011 FC 983 [4]; *Dagg v Canada (Minister of Finance)*, [1997] 2 SCR 403 [65]–[66]; *Lavigne*, (n 23) [25]; Vincent Kazmierski, "Something to Talk about: Is There a Charter Right to Access Government Information?" (2008) 31 Dalhousie Law Journal 351.

86 *Hill* (n 25) [120].

minorities.[87] Likewise, language statutes advance the principle of federalism since the protection of language rights provided much of the impetus for Canada's federal structure.[88]

The Supreme Court has referred to the rule of law at its most basic level as protecting a sense of a "stable, predictable and ordered society."[89] Accordingly, when a court is asked to enforce a foreign judgment in Canada it is to take into account whether it would violate constitutional and quasi-constitutional rights.[90] In *Pro Swing Inc. v Elta Golf Inc.*, the Supreme Court of Canada was concerned that the enforcement of a foreign judgment in Ontario requiring the release of sensitive personal information, including credit card receipts, accounts receivable, and contracts, would run afoul of the quasi-constitutional right to privacy.[91] In *Douez v Facebook*, the Court also held that the public good of having Canadian courts adjudicate claims involving constitutional or constitutional rights should be taken into account when determining whether to enforce a forum selection clause in a contract.[92]

The limited attention given to Canadian quasi-constitutional statutes in the literature is surprising given the important role that these statutes fulfill in upholding fundamental rights. Some of the neglect can be attributed to the fact that attention has been diverted away from these statutes in favour of the more authoritative *Charter*. Nonetheless, these statutes offer significant and accessible remedies to rights claimants in a manner that prioritizes fundamental rights over regular legislation while not outright adopting a model of judicial and constitutional supremacy. In so doing they account for the most developed form of judicial review within the Commonwealth weak-form model. They also most clearly display a judiciary that does not shy away from recognizing and assigning augmented legal significance to legislation recognized as fundamental, even in the absence of explicit legislative intent.

87 *R v Beaulac*, [1999] 1 SCR 768 [17].
88 *Lalonde v Ontario (Commission de restructuration des services de santé)*, [2001] OJ No 4767 [86].
89 *Reference re Secession of Quebec* (n 78) [70].
90 *Pro Swing Inc. v Elta Golf Inc.*, 2006 SCC 52 [60].
91 Ibid [60]–[61].
92 (n 81) [58]–[59]. See also: *Demers c Yahoo! Inc.*, 2017 QCCS 4154.

# 6 Quasi-constitutional amendments

*Richard Albert*†

## I. Introduction—a phenomenon and its features

Defining what counts as a constitutional amendment has proven difficult for scholars of constitutional change.[1] In master-text constitutional democracies like the United States, some constitutional amendments may change the constitutional text but not its meaning; others may change its meaning but not its text; and still others may change both the text and its meaning.[2] The same definitional challenge confronts Canada. Its inherited traditions of unwritten constitutional norms combine sometimes uneasily with the modern vanguard of writtenness to complicate how we identify a constitutional change that amounts to a constitutional amendment.

These definitional challenges have grown even more complicated in recent years as both master-text and partially codified constitutional democracies have seen the rise of a curious phenomenon resulting from the marriage of constitutional law and politics: quasi-constitutional amendments. A quasi-constitutional amendment is a sub-constitutional alteration to the operation of a set of existing norms in the constitution. It is a change that does not possess the same legal status as a constitutional amendment, that is formally susceptible to statutory repeal or revision, but that may achieve the function though not the formal

† William Stamps Farish Professor of Law, The University of Texas at Austin. Email: richard.albert@law.utexas.edu. For helpful comments on an earlier draft, I am grateful to Dennis Baker, John Helis and Adam Perry. I have also benefitted from presenting an earlier draft at the Second Beetz-Laskin Conference on Canadian Constitutional Law, organized by Noura Karazivan, Jean Leclair and Patrick Macklem at the University of Montreal, and at the Policy Impact conference, hosted by Emmett Macfarlane at the University of Waterloo. This first appeared in 65 Buffalo L Rev 739–70 (2017).

1 See e.g., Zachary Elkins et al., *The Endurance of National Constitutions* (Cambridge University Press 2009) 55–59; Sanford Levinson, 'How Many Times Has the United States Constitution Been Amended? (A) < 26; (B) 26; (C) 27; (D) > 27: Accounting for Constitutional Change' in Sanford Levinson (ed.), *Responding to Imperfection: The Theory and Practice of Constitutional Amendment* (Oxford University Press 1995) 13, 25–32.

2 See David A Strauss, 'The Irrelevance of Constitutional Amendments' (2001) 114 Harv L Rev 1457, 1459.

status of constitutional law over time as a result of its subject-matter and importance—making it just as durable as a constitutional amendment.

## *A. The Canadian Bill of Rights*

The Canadian Bill of Rights of 1960 was a quasi-constitutional amendment. Passed as a simple statute in Parliament, the government of the day had high ambitions for it.[3] The Justice Minister compared it to the Magna Carta, declaring that the government was 'not enacting legislation for today only, or for this generation only, but that we are placing on our statute books legislation which we hope will have validity and effect in future generations'.[4] He insisted that the Bill of Rights would

> become part of our constitution just as the Senate and House of Commons Act, the Supreme Court Act of 1875, the Yukon Territories Act, and Northwest Territories Act became part of our constitution just as soon as they were passed by parliament.[5]

The Minister added that 'this bill of rights, although a statute of the parliament of Canada and not an amendment to the British North America Act, will be of equal force and effect as part of the Constitution of Canada'.[6] In short, the Bill of Rights would not be an ordinary law despite its legal status as just that.

Even more revealing was the admission from the government that it would have been 'impossible' to enact the Bill of Rights as a constitutional amendment binding on both federal and provincial actors.[7] The government conceded that 'the indications are clear that it would not be possible to get early agreement with the provinces for an amendment of the nature suggested'[8] when it was confronted with the criticism that there had been no provincial consultation and that the Bill of Rights should have introduced protections for rights and freedoms beyond only federal jurisdiction. Soon after the Bill of Rights was enacted, Bora Laskin suggested that although the Bill of Rights was a mere statute subject to ordinary repeal, it could over time become the beneficiary of 'such reinforcement as may come from its public character and from public

3 The Bill of Rights was rooted in what Janet Hiebert calls 'a novel (if not naïve) idea: creating a rights culture in governing that did not depend, exclusively, on judicial review'. Janet L Hiebert, 'Parliamentary Bills of Rights: An Alternative Model?' (2006) 69 Mod L Rev 7, 12. It created a duty on the Justice Minister to review every government bill for consistency with the list of recognized rights and freedoms, and to report any inconsistency to the House of Commons. SC 1960, Pt I, § 3(1).

4 House of Commons Debates, July 7, 1960, 3d Sess, 24th Parl, v VI 8–9, at 5885 (Can).

5 Ibid., 5886.

6 Ibid.

7 Ibid., 5887.

8 Ibid.

vigilance'.[9] Laskin recognized that the Bill of Rights could conceivably acquire special salience in law because of its significance in society.[10]

## *B. Origins, advantages and risks*

All quasi-constitutional amendments share one common point of origin, three distinct advantages, as well as three serious risks. As to their origins, quasi-constitutional amendments are the result of a self-conscious circumvention of onerous rules of formal amendment in order to alter the operation of a set of existing norms in the constitution. We are likely to see quasi-constitutional amendments in states whose constitutions are difficult to amend formally, often federal countries. Where constitutional actors determine, correctly or not, that the current political landscape would frustrate their plans for a constitutional amendment to entrench new policy preferences, they resort instead to sub-constitutional means—for instance, legislation or political practice—whose success requires less or perhaps even no cross-party and inter-institutional coordination.

Quasi-constitutional amendments entail three advantages for dominant constitutional actors. First, resort to quasi-constitutional amendment allows constitutional actors to secure the functional equivalent of a constitutional amendment at a much lower political cost. Second, quasi-constitutional amendment has near-certain likelihood of success in light of the fewer veto opportunities standing in the way. Third, under the right conditions, a quasi-constitutional amendment may ultimately become as functionally durable as a formal amendment even though it may be formally subject to ordinary legislative repeal.

Yet even as quasi-constitutional amendments offer these important advantages to dominant constitutional actors, they nonetheless expose the constitution to three nontrivial risks. First, they blur the line separating the constitutional from the non-constitutional, and risk obscuring the ordinary hierarchy of authority in a constitutional democracy. Second, recourse to these sub-constitutional strategies for constitution-level changes may reveal and moreover reinforce a mismatch between constitutional design and political practice that constitutional actors can in turn exploit for politically expedient purposes. Third, circumventing the rules of formal amendment undermines the constitution itself and the very purpose of codification. I develop each of these critiques later in the text.

In this chapter, I illustrate the phenomenon of quasi-constitutional amendment with reference to the Constitution of Canada—perhaps the world's most difficult to amend. I begin by identifying two additional quasi-constitutional amendments in Canada, both created after Patriation. I separate them into two

9 Bora Laskin, 'Canada's Bill of Rights: A Dilemma for the Courts?' (1962) 11 Int'l & Comp L Q 519, 533.
10 Ibid.

major categories according to their form: one quasi-constitutional amendment made by ordinary law, and another made extra-legally outside the ordinary process of lawmaking. I then trace the phenomenon of a quasi-constitutional amendment in Canada to the difficulty of formal amendment. I subsequently explain how the legacy of formal amendment failure in Canada has made it politically attractive if not necessary for constitutional actors to innovate quasi-constitutional amendment as a new path to institutional reform. I close with reflections on the forms and limits of constitutional change in Canada and what quasi-constitutional amendment teaches us about the constitutional text and its context.

I stress at the outset, however, that this phenomenon of quasi-constitutional amendment is not limited to Canada. For instance, scholars have observed what I define as quasi-constitutional amendments in the United States and Australia, two rigid constitutional democracies,[11] both rooted in a master-text constitution. William Eskridge and John Ferejohn have identified in the United States what they call a super-statute, which is a law or cluster of laws that 'seeks to establish a new normative or institutional framework for state policy' and 'stick[s]' over time in the 'public culture' in a way that it and its principles 'have a broad effect on the law—including an effect beyond the four corners of the statute'.[12] The laws they identify as super-statutes, for instance the Sherman Act of 1890 and the Civil Rights Act of 1964,[13] have acquired a special 'normative force' gradually over time.[14] Eskridge and Ferejohn understand super-statutes as mediating the difficulty of constitutional amendment with the core principle of popular sovereignty in the United States.[15]

In Australia, Scott Stephenson has observed constitution-level changes resulting from what he identifies as 'constitutional statutes', defined as laws that have 'the function of regulating a fundamental feature of the lawmaking process',[16] where '[t]he lawmaking process is broadly understood to include not only the enactment of law by the legislature, but also the application of law by the executive and the interpretation of law by the judiciary'.[17] Examples of constitutional statutes in Australia, which I might well understand as quasi-constitutional amendments, include statutes governing the administrative state, like the Administrative Decisions (Judicial Review) Act 1976 as well as rights-protecting statutes, both passed, Stephenson suggests, at least partly as a result of constitutional amendment difficulty.[18]

11 See Donald S Lutz, *Principles of Constitutional Design* (Cambridge University Press 2006) 170 tbl 5.7 (ranking the United States and Australia as two of the most rigid constitutions in his sample of study).
12 William N Eskridge, Jr & John Ferejohn, 'Super-Statutes' (2001) 50 Duke LJ 1215, 1216.
13 Ibid., 1231–42.
14 Ibid., 1270.
15 See ibid., 1267–71.
16 Scott Stephenson, 'The Rise and Recognition of Constitutional Statutes' (this volume).
17 Ibid., 2–3.
18 Ibid., 6–8.

In the British tradition, Adam Perry and Farrah Ahmed have also theorized the concept of a 'constitutional statute', which they define as a law that is 'about state institutions and which substantially influences, directly or indirectly, what those institutions can and may do'.[19] For them, the Scotland Act of 1998, the European Communities Act 1972 and the Human Rights Act 1998 are all examples of constitutional statutes.[20] Although the British Constitution is disaggregated over many texts and conventions, the judicial and political recognition of constitutional statutes may have the effect of creating what Perry and Farrah describe as a 'graduated legal system' that distinguishes the constitutional from the non-constitutional.[21] It is in the interstices of constitutionality and sub-constitutionality that we find quasi-constitutional amendments. It is therefore possible that we might find quasi-constitutional amendments also in the few constitutional democracies like Britain with uncodified and disaggregated constitutions.

## II. One statute and a committee

Quasi-constitutional amendments are not all created in the same way.[22] They may arise in the course of the normal legislative process, using the same institutions and rules commonly used to pass an ordinarily-entrenched statute, and may at that time or later be identified as a quasi-constitutional amendment. Constitutional actors may also make a quasi-constitutional amendment extra-legally—that is, without at all engaging the formal legislative process. In this Part, I illustrate how each of these routes has been used to produce a quasi-constitutional amendment in Canada.

### *A. Ordinary lawmaking*

Consider first the Regional Veto Law. It is an ordinary statute passed by Parliament in 1996 shortly after the 1995 Quebec referendum.[23] The Regional Veto Law fulfilled the federal government's promise to give Quebec a veto over future constitutional amendments, a pledge made as an inducement to encourage Quebec voters to reject secession.[24]

19 Farrah Ahmed & Adam Perry, 'Constitutional Statutes' (2016) 37 Oxford J Legal Stud 461, 471.

20 Ibid., 465, 471–72.

21 Ibid., 464.

22 This is an important distinction from quasi-constitutional statutes in Canada, which are enacted just as other laws are, only 'they are interpreted in the broad and generous manner usually reserved for constitutional rights' and they 'trump later, conflicting ordinary laws unless those laws provide otherwise.' Vanessa MacDonnell, 'A Theory of Quasi-Constitutional Legislation' (2016) 53 Osgoode Hall LJ 508, 510.

23 See An Act Respecting Constitutional Amendments, SC 1996, c 1 (Can).

24 See Robert A Young, 'Jean Chrétien's Québec Legacy: Coasting then Stickhandling Hard' (2004) 9 Rev Const Stud 31, 38.

The Regional Veto Law does for Quebec the same thing it does for the other regions of Canada, with the exception of the North.[25] It gives them each a veto in constitutional amendment.[26] The veto may be exercised by Ontario, Quebec, British Columbia and at least two provinces from each of the Atlantic and Prairie regions where the two represent at least half of the regional population.[27] The Regional Veto Law gives the veto to these regions indirectly through the federal government.[28] It requires a Cabinet minister to first obtain the consent of each of the five major regions as well as a majority of all provinces *before* introducing a major amendment proposal under the multilateral default amendment procedure.[29] The Regional Veto Law therefore confers a functional veto, not a formal one.

The Regional Veto Law has two important consequences. For one, it transforms the formal equality of the provinces under the Constitution's amendment rules into a deep formal inequality, giving special status to Ontario, Quebec and British Columbia and diminishing the power of the other seven provinces.[30] As Andrew Heard and Tim Swartz explain, the multilateral default amendment procedure has never really treated provinces as functional equals; populous provinces could always exercise more power than the others when they stood together.[31] The Regional Veto Law now formalizes and exacerbates what had before been only an implicit provincial inequality.

Second, the Regional Veto Law adds a new hurdle to what is already a difficult amendment process. It imposes a prior restraint on the power of Cabinet ministers to propose an amendment—something not contemplated by the constitutional amendment rules themselves.[32] It also complicates amendment under the multilateral default procedure by changing the sequence for a successful Parliament-initiated amendment: the Constitution requires federal proposal then provincial ratification but the Regional Veto Law now requires provincial consent then federal proposal and finally provincial ratification.[33] This has the potential to exacerbate amendment difficulty because the provincial

25 An Act Respecting Constitutional Amendments (n 23) § 1(1).
26 Ibid.
27 Ibid.
28 Ibid.
29 Ibid. Canada's Constitution codifies five amendment procedures. Three of them already give each of the affected provinces a veto over an amendment: the unilateral provincial procedure, the regional amendment procedure and the unanimity procedure. The fourth—the unilateral federal procedure—authorizes Parliament to amend its own internal constitution, and therefore makes no provision for provincial involvement. It is the fifth procedure—the multilateral default amendment procedure—that the Regional Veto Law was intended to address. See notes 56–67 and accompanying text.
30 Andrew Heard & Tim Swartz, 'The Regional Veto Formula and its Effects on Canada's Constitutional Amendment Process' (1997) 30 Can J Pol Sci 339, 340–41.
31 Ibid., 341.
32 See notes 56–67 and accompanying text.
33 See An Act Respecting Constitutional Amendments (n 23).

government that would grant its consent prior to the federal proposal might differ from the one that controls the assembly when the time later comes to formally ratify the amendment. The Regional Veto Law, passed as a simple statute, therefore now constrains the federal government and indeed all constitutional actors contemplating major constitutional change.

### B. *Extra-legal change*

Turn now to what one prominent scholar has called the 'frustrating puzzle' of Senate reform,[34] a subject of enduring debate since Confederation.[35] It took nearly 150 years for constitutional actors to change the Senate in any material way.[36] On January 19, 2016, the Minister of Democratic Institutions and the Government Leader in the House of Commons announced an Independent Advisory Board for Senate Appointments.[37] The Advisory Board is not formalized in a law. Its stated purpose is to create a 'new, non-partisan, merit-based process to advise on Senate appointments'.[38] Its larger purpose is to create an 'independent appointments process' that will 'contribute to creating a less partisan and more effective institution to serve Canadians'.[39]

According to the official release, the Advisory Board was 'established to provide advice to the Prime Minister on candidates for the Senate' and will be 'guided by public, merit-based criteria, in order to identify Canadians who would make a significant contribution to the work of the Senate'.[40] The Government moved expeditiously on Senate reform to secure the Senate's 'fundamental role in the representation of regional and minority interests in the legislative process'.[41]

The Government established six categories of merit-based criteria.[42] The first relates to gender, indigenous and minority status, with a view to gender balance in the Senate.[43] Non-partisanship and personal qualities of integrity and ethical conduct are also important, as is knowledge of the legislative process and the Constitution.[44]

34 CES Franks, 'The Senate and Its Reform' (1987) 12 Queen's LJ 454, 454.

35 Robert A MacKay, *The Unreformed Senate of Canada* (Oxford University Press 1926) 1.

36 One important change, effective as of 1965, requires Senators to retire by age 75. Constitution Act, 1965, c 4, § 29(2) (Can).

37 For a comprehensive catalogue of official announcements related to the new appointment process, see Senate Appointment Resources (June 23, 2017), www.canada.ca/en/democratic-institutions/services/senate-appointment-process.html.

38 Press Release, Gov't of Can, Government Announces Immediate Senate Reform (December 3, 2015), www.marketwired.com/press-release/government-announces-immediate-senate-reform-2079118.

39 Ibid.

40 Ibid.

41 Ibid.

42 Huguette LaBelle, Report of the Independent Advisory Board for Senate Appointments Permanent Process (July to November 2016) (2016) [*Independent Advisory Board*].

43 Ibid., 7–8.

44 See ibid., 14.

The Advisory Board will also look favourably on bilingual candidates and on nominees who have a record of leadership or achievement in public or community service, or in service to their profession or field of expertise.[45]

The new Senate appointments process has unfolded in two phases.[46] During the first phase, called the 'transitional process', the Advisory Board made appointment recommendations to the Prime Minister in early 2016 to fill Senate vacancies in Manitoba, Ontario and Quebec.[47] For each vacancy—five in total were identified—the Advisory Board prepared a list of five individuals who, in its estimation, deserve consideration for appointment to the Senate, and who 'meet the constitutional eligibility requirements at the time of the appointment to the Senate'.[48] The Advisory Board is said to have consulted broadly to ensure that a 'diverse slate of individuals with a variety of backgrounds, skills, knowledge and experience' required for a well-functioning Senate were nominated for the Board's consideration.[49] The Prime Minister ultimately nominated seven women and men to the Senate, three from Ontario and two each from Manitoba and Quebec.[50]

The second phase in the new process was launched in July 2016.[51] It is described as 'the permanent phase of the independent Senate appointments process', a process that now 'features an application process that is open to all Canadians'.[52] The first round of the application process was open for a four-week period ending on August 4, 2016.[53] In this permanent phase, the Advisory Board will be guided by the same criteria as the first 'with the end goal of ensuring a high standard of integrity, collaboration, and non-partisanship in the Senate'.[54]

## III. Formal amendment difficulty in Canada

Neither the Regional Veto Law nor the new Senate appointments process could have been formalized in a constitutional amendment. The Constitution is just too rigid, and the constitutional politics of amendment are just too fraught with

45 Ibid.
46 Ibid., 4.
47 Ibid.
48 Ibid., 13–50. The constitutional requirements relate to age (between 30 and 75), citizenship, real and personal property, and residency. Ibid.
49 Ibid., 10.
50 Prime Minister Announces Intention to Recommend the Appointment of Seven New Senators, Gov't Can (March 18, 2016) http://pm.gc.ca/eng/news/2016/03/18/prime-minister-announces-intention-recommend-appointment-seven-new-senators.
51 Minister of Democratic Institutions Announces Launch of the Permanent Phase of the Independent Senate Appointments Process, Gov't Can (July 7, 2016), http://news.gc.ca/web/article-en.do?nid=1095799&tp=1&_ga=1.62793134.328809842.1468471660.
52 Ibid.
53 Ibid.
54 Independent Advisory Board (n 42).

the risk of failure. A leading authority on the Canadian Constitution quite rightly identifies constitutional design as a key source of Canada's challenges:

> Successful constitutions divide into two main groups: those that are short, contain statements of abstract principles, and are difficult to amend; and those that are long, contain detailed provisions, and are relatively easy to amend. … Canada has a constitution that is difficult to amend yet includes many details. Not surprising, this approach has proven unsuccessful. We have the worst of both worlds.[55]

The Constitution of Canada codifies an escalating structure of five procedures of formal amendment.[56] Each may be used to amend specifically designated provisions and principles, and each rises in difficulty according to the importance of its associated provisions or principles.[57] Although some of the five amendment procedures are relatively easy and others are not, the complexity of the entire package of formal amendment rules may make the Constitution of Canada the most difficult in the democratic world to amend—not necessarily a badge of honour.[58]

### A. *The rules of constitutional amendment*

The lowest amendment threshold is the unilateral provincial procedure. It authorizes a provincial assembly to unilaterally amend the provincial constitution.[59] The next-lowest threshold—the unilateral federal procedure—confers an analogous power upon the Parliament of Canada: the power to unilaterally amend what Ian Greene has described as Parliament's internal constitution,[60] and matters relating exclusively 'to the executive government of Canada or the Senate and House of Commons'.[61] The third amendment route—the regional amendment procedure—incorporates the major feature of the unilateral federal amendment procedure: it applies to amendments affecting 'one or more, but not all, provinces' and requires

55 CES Franks, 'Representation and Policy-Making in Canada' in CES Franks et al. (eds), *Canada's Century: Governance in a Maturing Society* (McGill-Queen's University Press 1995) 68, 81.

56 Richard Albert, 'The Structure of Constitutional Amendment Rules' (2014) 49 Wake Forest L Rev 913, 944–45.

57 See ibid.

58 See Richard Albert, 'The Difficulty of Constitutional Amendment in Canada' (2015) 53 Alta L Rev 85, 105–06. Canada's Constitution may be the most difficult to amend only as relates to its basic structure. See ibid., 96.

59 Constitution Act, 1982, *being* Schedule B to the Canada Act, 1982, c 11, § 45 (UK) [Constitution Act, 1982].

60 Ian Greene, 'Constitutional Amendment in Canada and the United States' in Stephen L Newman (ed.), *Constitutional Politics in Canada and the United States* (SUNY Press 2004) 249, 251.

61 Constitution Act, 1982 (n 59) § 44.

the consent of the House of Commons and of the Senate, and also the approval of the legislative assemblies of the affected provinces.[62] This procedure must be used for amendments that have a provincial-federal interest in relation to at least one province and at most have regional, not national, scope.[63]

The two remaining amendment procedures are the most difficult. The multilateral default procedure applies to all subjects not otherwise assigned to a specific amendment procedure. It applies also exclusively to a specially designated class of subjects including proportional representation in the House of Commons, the powers and membership of the Senate (as well as the method of senatorial selection), the Supreme Court of Canada for all items except its composition, the creation of new provinces, and the boundaries between provinces and territories.[64] A successful amendment under this procedure requires approval from both federal and provincial actors: the House of Commons and the Senate, as well the provincial legislative assemblies of at least two-thirds of the provinces whose aggregate population amounts to at least half of the national total.[65] This is an onerous threshold by any measure.

The unanimity procedure is even more difficult than the multilateral default procedure. It requires the approval of both houses of Parliament and each provincial legislative assembly.[66] This procedure must be used for amendments involving the monarchy, the right to provincial representation in the House of Commons relative to the Senate, Canada's official languages beyond their provincial or regional use, the composition of the Supreme Court of Canada and Canada's formal amendment rules themselves.[67] Each of these five procedures, then, requires a greater quantum of agreement than the former, from a simple unicameral majority to successfully pass an amendment using the unilateral provincial procedure all the way up to the agreement of all federal and provincial legislatures, under the unanimity rule. In this escalating structure of amendment, the difficulty of amendment rises according to the importance of the amendable matter, the variable being the degree of provincial consent required for ratification.

### *B. The constitution in comparative perspective*

By comparison with other democratic constitutions, the Constitution of Canada may well be the most rigid, but only as to matters that Peter Russell has identified as involving 'mega constitutional politics'. The term refers to amendments that 'address the very nature of the political community on which the

62 Ibid., § 43.
63 Ibid.
64 Ibid., § 42.
65 Ibid., § 38(1).
66 Ibid., § 41.
67 Ibid.

constitution is based',[68] that have a 'tendency to touch citizens' sense of identity and self-worth',[69] and those that are 'concerned with reaching agreement on the identity and fundamental principles of the body politic'.[70] The escalating structure of amendment identifies which matters trigger mega constitutional politics: the ones amenable by either the default multilateral amendment procedure, or the unanimity procedure. Both authorize major reforms to the basic structure of the Constitution, for instance to the framework of government, to the polity, to Canadian identity or to federal-provincial relations.

We cannot know for certain whether these amendment procedures do in fact make the Canadian Constitution the most difficult to amend because the leading comparative study of constitutional rigidity has excluded Canada from the study sample.[71] The reason why is telling: Donald Lutz, the political scientist who created the index, admitted that he could not reliably determine what has constitutional status in Canada, and therefore what counts as an amendment to its Constitution.[72] Had he measured these two onerous amendment procedures in Canada, however, he might have found that they rank the country ahead of the difficulty score Lutz had calculated for the United States (5.10), the most rigid constitution in his 36-country sample.[73]

Using Lutz's own methodology—which quantifies every possible step in a formal amendment process and then aggregates the scores of each discrete step in a given amendment procedure to generate its index of difficulty—we arrive at an index of 4.50 for the multilateral default procedure, and 5.00 for the unanimity procedure.[74] Yet, as I have shown elsewhere in detail, Canada's formal amendment rules have been informally amended by judicial interpretation, parliamentary and provincial laws, and perhaps also by constitutional convention such that their outer measure of formal amendment difficulty under Lutz's scale may be upwards of 8.00.[75]

It is telling that Lutz could not determine what has constitutional status in Canada. This problem of identification—what the constitution is, and precisely *where* it is—has made it possible for constitutional actors to exploit the blurred distinction between constitutional and ordinary law to create quasi-

68 See Peter H Russell, *Constitutional Odyssey: Can Canadians Become a Sovereign People?* (University of Toronto Press 1992) 75.

69 Ibid.

70 Ibid.

71 Lutz (n 11) 170 tbl. 5.7. It is moreover difficult to quantify what scholars have referred to as 'amendment culture,' which may be more determinative of formal amendment difficulty than the amendment procedures themselves. See generally Tom Ginsburg & James Melton, 'Does the Constitutional Amendment Rule Matter at All? Amendment Cultures and the Challenges of Measuring Amendment Difficulty' (2015) 13 Int'l J Const L 686 (explaining theory of 'amendment culture').

72 See Lutz (n 11) 179 n16.

73 See ibid., 170 tbl. 5.7.

74 See Albert (n 58) 94, 99–100.

75 Ibid at 99–100.

constitutional amendments that may later mature into constitution-level changes. As I will suggest below, quasi-constitutional amendments are not fated to achieve constitutional status, though in some circumstances, they may well become as durable as formal constitutional amendments.

## IV. The consequence of formal amendment difficulty

Equally telling is that many of the most formally rigid constitutional democracies have generated the phenomenon of quasi-constitutional amendment. It is no coincidence that constitutional actors in Canada, the United States, and Australia have had recourse to sub-constitutional means to make constitution-level changes. These constitutions are extraordinarily difficult to amend,[76] perhaps even constructively unamendable for all but the most routine matters of governance.[77] The impetus behind quasi-constitutional amendment, then, is the difficulty of formal amendment.

### *A. The legacies of formal amendment failure*

Where constitutional actors determine, correctly or not, that the current political landscape would frustrate their plans for a constitutional amendment to entrench new policy preferences, they resort instead to sub-constitutional means whose successful execution requires less or perhaps even no cross-party or inter-institutional coordination. Their resort to sub-constitutional procedures reflects a strategic choice to circumvent the onerous rules of formal amendment in order to alter the operation of a set of existing norms in the constitution. In Canada, the political choice to chart a sub-constitutional path to constitutional change has been informed, if not compelled, by the modern legacies of formal amendment failure.

The 1987 Meech Lake and 1992 Charlottetown Accords promised transformative constitutional changes on the scale of Patriation. Meech Lake would have recognized the distinctiveness of Quebec within Canada, changed how senators are selected, constitutionalized the Supreme Court, and granted provinces new powers over immigration and constitutional amendment.[78] Charlottetown would have gone even further, for instance, introducing a 'Canada Clause' to express national values, redefining the federal distribution of powers, recognizing Aboriginal rights, reforming national institutions including the House of Commons, the Senate and the Supreme Court, and moreover, amending the rules of constitutional amendment.[79] Yet both major packages of amendments

76 See Lutz (n 11) 170 tbl. 5.7.

77 See Richard Albert, 'Constructive Unamendability in Canada and the United States' (2014) 67 Sup Ct L Rev (2d) 181, 182–83.

78 1987 Constitutional Accord, Ottawa, Ontario, June 3, 1987 [Meech Lake Accord].

79 Gov't Can, Consensus Report on the Constitution: Charlottetown, Final Text 417–18, 420–21, 423, 435 (1992) [Charlottetown Accord].

were defeated, the Meech Lake Accord as a result of an elapsed ratification deadline,[80] and the Charlottetown Accord at the hands of the people in an extra-constitutional referendum.[81]

These failures have not been without consequence. Writing in 1994, Edward McWhinney observed that 'Canadians as a whole are tired of the seemingly unending constitutional debate of the last three and half decades which has pre-empted consideration by Ottawa of other, deemed more pressing, economic problems'.[82] Beyond just constitutional fatigue, however, Warren Newman has more recently suggested that formal amendment failure has had an 'incalculable impact on our national psyche and on the way in which our political actors approach the question of constitutional reform'[83] Newman described the effect of our formal amendment failure as a 'trauma', and concluded that '[i]t may not yet be a propitious time for Canada's political leaders to "reopen" the Constitution in a broad and concerted way'.[84] The time may yet never come.

For constitutional actors, the prime directive is self-preservation. If indeed Canadians have grown tired of constitutional debates, elected constitutional actors will heed that caution and remember well that the Conservative government was routed at the polls not coincidentally the year after Charlottetown's defeat.[85] Whether Canadians would be open to a new round of major constitutional change is an empirical question in need of fresh data drawn from generations since Meech Lake and Charlottetown. But perception often overruns reality, and today we regard constitutional politics in Canada as inhospitable to major formal constitutional reforms due to what Michael Lusztig has described as the need for 'mass input' and 'legitimization',[86] shorthand for the nearly impossible political agreement by parties with incommensurable interests that almost inevitably doom comprehensive constitutional change involving federalism.

### *B. The new path to institutional reform*

No wonder, then, that a non-constitutional path to institutional reform has replaced the constitutional route. As Harvey Lazar observed in 1997, this is 'a

80 See Richard Albert, 'Temporal Limitations in Constitutional Amendment' (2016) 21 Rev Const Stud 37, 52–53.

81 See Richard Albert, 'The Conventions of Constitutional Amendment in Canada' (2016) 53 Osgoode Hall LJ 399, 401–402.

82 Edward McWhinney, 'Quebec and Canadian Federalism' (1994) 2 Can Parliamentary Rev 1, 3.

83 Warren J Newman, 'Living with the Amending Procedures: Prospects for the Future of Constitutional Reform in Canada' (2007) 37 Sup Ct L Rev (2d) 383, 407.

84 Ibid.

85 See David McLaughlin, *Poisoned Chalice: The Last Campaign of the Progressive Conservative Party?* (Dundurn 1994) 10–11.

86 Michael Lusztig, 'Constitutional Paralysis: Why Canadian Constitutional Initiatives Are Doomed to Fail' (1994) 27 Can J Pol Sci 747, 748.

necessary step for healing the wounds of the country',[87] certainly 'the only politically viable option for managing the federation'[88] after decades of nearly uninterrupted attention to constitution-level changes.[89] Whether on fiscal, social, environmental or aboriginal policy, constitutional actors carefully avoid the 'c' word.[90] The parliamentary recognition of Quebec as a distinct society, for instance, joins with the Regional Veto Law and the new appointment process to illustrate the 'circuitous' ways that 'changes of a constitutional character' occur now and likely into the near future[91] given the present political improbability of constitutional amendment.

Resort to sub-constitutional means is a more profitable route for constitutional actors because it requires less or even no cross-party or inter-institutional coordination. Both the Regional Veto Law and the Advisory Board for Senate appointments were the product of a majority government, meaning that neither major change confronted any substantial risk of failure. Each was promised near-certain success in light of the few veto opportunities standing in their way. Neither of these functionally constitution-level changes required support from the opposition or the provinces to become effective, though one could argue that each of them changed the basic structure of the Constitution, and therefore should have required a deeper measure of approval across political parties or levels of government.

The Regional Veto Law and the new process for Senate appointments were introduced at a much lower political cost than ordinarily required for an amendment, yet both amount to the functional equivalent of a formal amendment. Both, in fact, were part of the Meech Lake and Charlottetown Accords, though in different but recognizable forms: the precursor to the Regional Veto Law was proposed as a provincial veto and the new process for Senate appointments would have, in the case of Meech, given provinces the power of nomination, and in Charlottetown it would have created a Triple-E Senate.[92]

The Regional Veto Law, an ordinary law, has had two extraordinary consequences. First, it has achieved what Meech and Charlottetown could not—and importantly it did so outside of the formal amendment process. Quebec now has the veto promised to it. Moreover, the effect of the Regional Veto Law is substantial insofar as it effectively amends the rules of constitutional amendment by imposing formal requirements over and above those established by the

87 Harvey Lazar, 'Non-Constitutional Renewal: Toward a New Equilibrium in the Federation' in Harvey Lazar (ed.), *Canada: The State of the Federation 1997—Non-Constitutional Renewal* (IIGR 1998) 3, 28.

88 Ibid., 7.

89 See ibid., 3.

90 See ibid., 12–20.

91 Lois Harder & Steve Patten, 'Looking Back on Patriation and Its Consequences' in Louis Harder & Steve Patten (eds.), *Patriation and its Consequences: Constitution Making in Canada* (University of British Columbia Press 2015) 3, 21.

92 See Meech Lake Accord (n 78) §§ 2, 9; Charlottetown Accord (n 79) 5.

Constitution itself. What is important here is that the Regional Veto Law changes the formal amendment rules—specifically, the multilateral default procedure—by way of a simple federal law in defiance of the formal rules of amendment themselves which by their very text require the agreement of Parliament and of each provincial assembly to amend any part of the Constitution's formal amendment rules.[93] And yet the enacting Parliament expected constitutional actors to nonetheless abide by the Regional Veto Law despite its inconsistency with the formal rules of amendment and even though it is an ordinary law that did not earn its functionally special status through any of the formal routes the Constitution provides for achieving special status.

The new process for Senate appointments has likewise achieved what neither Meech nor Charlottetown could: it has changed the way senators are selected. Reading the recent *Senate Reference* would suggest that changes to the method of senator selection require a constitutional amendment. The relevant issue in the *Senate Reference* was the constitutionality of the Senate Reform and Senate Appointments Consultation bills.[94] These bills proposed to create a framework of consultative provincial and territorial elections to fill Senate vacancies. The Senate Reform bill proposed that senators 'should be chosen from a list of Senate nominees submitted by the government of the province or territory',[95] with the list of nominees 'to be determined by an election held in the province or territory'.[96] The bill furthermore insisted that the prime minister 'must consider names from the most current list of Senate nominees selected for that province or territory' when 'recommending Senate nominees to the Governor General'.[97] The Senate Appointments Consultation bill had the same objective: to constrain the prime minister to consider provincial or territorial consultative election winners for appointment to the Senate.[98]

The operative question in the *Senate Reference* was 'whether Parliament, acting alone, can reform the Senate by creating consultative elections to select senatorial nominees endorsed by the populations of the various provinces and territories … '.[99] The Court rejected the two major arguments for the bills.[100] First, the Court was not convinced by the argument that creating a framework for consultative senatorial elections does not constitute an amendment simply because the formal process for appointing individuals to the Senate—by official summoning by the Governor General on the advice of the prime minister, as required by the *Constitution Act,*

93 Constitution Act, 1982 (n 59) § 41.
94 Reference re Senate Reform, [2014] 1 SCR 704, para 2 (Can).
95 Bill C-7, An Act Respecting the Selection of Senators and Amending the Constitution Act, 1867 in Respect of Senate Term Limits, 1st Sess, 41st Parl, 2011, § 1 [Senate Reform Bill].
96 Ibid., § 2.
97 Ibid., § 3.
98 See Reference re Senate Reform, (n 94) para 62.
99 Ibid., para 49.
100 Ibid., 706.

*1867*[101]—remains unchanged.[102] The Court refused to accept this argument because, the Court observed, doing so would 'privilege form over substance',[103] and would ignore that such a change 'would fundamentally alter the architecture of the Constitution'.[104] An amendment, then, according to the Court, is more than a formal alteration to the constitutional text,[105] though the Court could have been more definitive on what in fact counts as an amendment.[106]

Nor was the Court persuaded that the text of the formal amendment rules is unclear; on the contrary, the Court noted that the multilateral default amendment procedure states plainly that it must be used for changes to 'the method of selecting senators'.[107] For the Court, this phrase 'covers the implementation of consultative elections, indicating that a constitutional amendment is required and making that amendment subject to the general procedure [in Section 38]'.[108] The Court continued: '[t]he words "the method of selecting senators" include more than the formal appointment of senators by the Governor General'.[109] It includes all changes to the method of senatorial selection, beyond and including those related directly to the act of appointment itself.[110]

Yet today senators are selected under a new process that differs from how they have historically been chosen. The Senate has been reformed, but not in the large-scale fashion many have sought since Confederation; change has instead come incrementally without engaging the formal amendment process.[111] Formal appointment continues to be made by the Governor General, but the selection process itself has changed as a result of the Advisory Board which advises the prime minister according to public criteria that now bring to light at least part of what has in the past remained concealed. Whether the new process for Senate appointments is an improvement on the previous method of senator selection is not the point, although it does seem to democratize a body that has long been inaccessible to many Canadians.[112] The point is that senator selection

101 Constitution Act, 1867, 30 & 31 Vict, c 3, §§ 24, 32 (UK).
102 See Reference re Senate Reform, (n 94) para 52–53.
103 Ibid., para 52.
104 Ibid., para 53.
105 Ibid., para 52.
106 See Kate Glover, 'Complexity and the Amending Formula' (2015) 24 Const F 9, 11; Emmett Macfarlane, 'Unsteady Architecture: Ambiguity, the Senate Reference, and the Future of Constitutional Amendment in Canada' (2015) 60 McGill LJ 883, 900.
107 Reference re Senate Reform, (n 94) para 64 (quoting Constitution Act, 1982 (n 59) § 42(b)(1)).
108 Ibid.
109 Ibid., para 65 (quoting Constitution Act, 1982 (n 59) § 42(b)(1)).
110 Ibid.
111 Bruce M Hicks, 'Can a Middle Ground Be Found on Senate Numbers?' (2007) 16 Const F 21, 21.
112 For an argument that enhancing the democratic character of the Senate appointments process cannot justify circumventing the rigid formal amendment rules, see Richard Albert, 'Constitutional Amendment by Stealth' (2015) 60 McGill LJ 673, 678–80.

has changed in a material way. Although the prime minister retains the discretion to choose whom to nominate, the range of discretion is narrowed. The creation of the Advisory Body is a significant change that would have been appropriately passed as a constitutional amendment had it been possible to amend the Constitution without opening the door to collateral matters. Paradoxically, the choice not to formalize the new process in a law, and instead to promulgate it informally, has perhaps saved it from unconstitutionality. Yet there can be no doubt that the new process is in fact new, and that it changes the way senators are selected—for better or worse.

What remains to be seen about both the Regional Veto Law and the new process of Senate appointments is whether they will endure with time. Under the right conditions, a quasi-constitutional amendment may ultimately grow as durable as a formal amendment, and it may be that the conditions surrounding both the Regional Veto Law and the new process are right for them to endure.

There are at least three conditions that foster the durability of a quasi-constitutional amendment. First, the amendment must concern an important matter of public policy. Second, the matter must be one that has in the past proven difficult to resolve by amendment. Third, the amendment must bring relative constitutional peace to the issue, defusing the subject and removing it from the foreground of the political process. The Regional Veto Law and the new process of Senate appointments appear to meet each of these three conditions, which perhaps explains why the Quebec question has for now receded to the background of constitutional politics in Canada, as well as why perennially controversial question about the proper role, membership and function of the Senate reform may soon follow. Constitutional actors are instead focusing on other matters deemed higher priorities, at least in some part a function of the success of the quasi-constitutional amendments that were introduced outside of the formal process of constitutional amendment.

There is an important difference between the quasi-constitutional amendment resulting from the Regional Veto Law and the one resulting from the new process of Senate appointments: the former emerged from the legislative process and the latter did not. This difference—call it the difference between executive-led quasi-constitutional amendments and Parliament-led quasi-constitutional amendments—may lead us to conclude that one is more legitimate than the other insofar as the legislative process is ordinarily more public, transparent, and deliberative than the decision-making process that occurs almost exclusively internally within the executive branch.

## V. Conclusion—constitutional change and its modern forms

I have sought in this brief overview to identify a concept and to illustrate it with three examples, one prior to Patriation, and two afterwards. There may well be others, including perhaps the Clarity Act passed into law after the *Secession*

*Reference*.[113] The takeaway is that quasi-constitutional amendments occupy the space between constitutional and ordinary law. Neither constitutional nor ordinary, they float sometimes uneasily between these two worlds, complicating our understanding of how a constitution is made, what it is, and where to find it.

## A. *The paradoxes of quasi-constitutionality*

Perhaps because of their unsteady status, quasi-constitutional amendments raise two paradoxes for the theory and doctrine of constitutional change. First, although they become effective with recourse to sub-constitutional means, quasi-constitutional amendments may nonetheless over time acquire constitutional status as a result of their subject-matter or importance. This reflects a mismatch between their adoption and their effect. Ordinarily, special status derives at least in part from an equally special period of creation, whether by constitutional amendment requiring heightened legislative or popular thresholds or a self-conscious recognition and attendant declaration by the enacting body that the law or measure demands special solicitude.

Second, although quasi-constitutional amendments may rank higher than ordinary law in the constitutional hierarchy, they may sometimes be closer to unconstitutionality than constitutionality. Precisely because they arise sub-constitutionally, yet purport to and maybe in fact do enjoy special status in legislatures, in courts of law or in the public square, quasi-constitutional amendments cannot validly claim the legal, sociological, and procedural legitimacy that constitutionality requires. It is true that the absence of one form of legitimacy need not always result in unconstitutionality; for instance, the adoption of the United States Constitution in violation of the rules of change in the Articles of Confederation shows how sociological legitimacy may overcome procedural illegality.[114] This, however, is an exception to the general rule that constitutional status derives from the convergence of legal recognition, sociological acceptance, and procedural correctness. Because quasi-constitutional amendments lack these three features, they quite controversially verge on the border of unconstitutionality, and indeed courts would be justified in invalidating them even in the face of high popular and political support for these constitution-level changes made sub-constitutionally. The Regional Veto Law, for example, is quite possibly unconstitutional. I believe the same to be true of provincial laws requiring binding referenda before provincial assemblies can consider ratifying an amendment proposal.[115]

113 See An Act to give effect to the requirement for clarity as set out in the opinion of the Supreme Court of Canada in the Quebec Secession Reference, 2d Sess, 36th Parl, 1999.

114 See 2 Bruce Ackerman, *We the People: Transformations* (Harvard University Press 1998) 84.

115 See Richard Albert, 'The Theory and Doctrine of Unconstitutional Constitutional Amendment in Canada' (2015) 41 Queen's L.J. 143, 177–78 (2015).

Yet quasi-constitutional amendments have an important function in constitutional democracies. They offer constitutional actors a way to update the constitution informally without recourse to onerous rules of constitutional amendment. If these rules were followed without exception for any constitution-level change, they could effectively freeze the constitution and fate it to a chronic incapacity to respond to the modern challenges of evolving political and cultural norms and of changing social and economic conditions. This interplay between constitutional and ordinary rules of change can be understood in terms of Heather Gerken's hydraulics theory of constitutional change: where the path to formal amendment is or seems to be blocked due to its difficulty, constitutional actors redirect their energies toward alternative paths to produce the same or a similar outcome, though with a different form.[116]

## B. *Constitutional form and the rule of law*

The question, then, is whether anything of significance turns on form. In Canada, we can look to the Supreme Court for guidance as to why form matters, and the answer is quite simply the rule of law. The Court has articulated a text-centric conception of the rule of law 'requir[ing] that courts give effect to the Constitution's text, and apply, by whatever its terms, legislation that conforms to that text'.[117] These positivist foundations of the rule of law are not without normative commitments. Indeed, the Court has explained that the rule of law entails respect for three principles: the supremacy of law over both public and private actors; the legal regulation of interactions between public and private actors; and the establishment and maintenance of positive laws that reflect an order of normative values.[118] For the Court, it is the text that should drive the evolution of law. The Court has moreover suggested that normative values, however they may be discovered and applied, must cohere with the text: the rule of law, the Court wrote, 'is not an invitation to trivialize or supplant the Constitution's written terms'.[119]

Constitutional actors have pushed the boundaries of constitutional form in their pursuit of constitutional reform.[120] Whether the reforms are needed is only one question; another perhaps more important one probes the consequences of making major constitutional changes outside of the formal rules of constitutional change codified in the Constitution of Canada.

On one view, quasi-constitutional amendments undermine the integrity of the Constitution because they trade on the vulnerabilities of constitutional form.

116 *See* Heather K. Gerken, 'The Hydraulics of Constitutional Reform: A Skeptical Response to Our Undemocratic Constitution' (2007) 55 Drake L Rev 925, 929.

117 British Columbia v Imperial Tobacco Canada Ltd, [2005] 2 SCR 473, para. 67 (Can.).

118 Ibid., para 58.

119 Ibid., para 67.

120 See Mark D Walters, 'The Constitutional Form and Reform of the Senate: Thoughts on the Constitutionality of Bill C-7' (2013) 7 J Parliamentary & Pol L 37–38, 48–49.

They exploit the partially codified and uncodified nature of the Constitution of Canada to introduce from the back door changes that are not possible through the front. The long-term results are uncertainty about what has constitutional status, a disjunction between constitutional text and practice, and no clear road-map for how constitutional actors may change the constitution or whether the rules in the constitutional text reflect either the necessary or sufficient conditions for constitutional reform.

On another view, quasi-constitutional amendment is an innovative strategy to update a rigid constitution that otherwise frustrates constitutional reform. It matters less *how* we change the constitution than that it changes at all because the constitution should reflect the preferences of constitutional actors and the people they represent. Where the constitution ceases to accommodate the needs of the community it governs, it exposes itself as a tool of governance poorly designed to serve its intended function. The argument from this view would continue as follows: were constitutional actors to deny themselves recourse to innovations like quasi-constitutional amendment, the consequence could be that the constitution fails to endure in moments when the pressure for change continues to build over a long period of time without the possibility of any change ever bringing relief.

For now, the latter view is dominant in Canada.[121] Constitutional actors have forged new paths to institutional reform outside of the formal rules of constitutional change.[122] Whether these paths point the way to the future remains to be seen, but there is yet no sign to suggest otherwise. Constitutional actors have grown comfortable operating in the space between constitutional and ordinary law, though perhaps less out of preference than out of necessity. But only so much constitutional change is possible through judicial interpretation, particularly where the targets of change are 'hard-wired' into the constitution, and not as cleanly changeable by interpretation[123] as might be the case for interpreting a right cast at a high level of abstraction. On matters of constitutional structure, constitutional actors today may have no other option but quasi-constitutional amendment because the road to major formal amendment appears closed.

Many questions present themselves for future research. I raise two of them here. First, what should be the process for repealing or revising a quasi-constitutional amendment? They are ordinarily entrenched, and therefore subject to ordinary repeal or revision in terms of the parliamentary threshold required. But so are quasi-constitutional statutes, with the important wrinkle that they may be repealed or revised only with clear legislative language. Should the same rule apply to quasi-constitutional amendments? Second, given the extraordinary difficulty of formal

121 See Allan C Hutchinson, 'Constitutional Change and Constitutional Amendment: A Canadian Conundrum' in Xenophon Contiades (ed.), *Engineering Constitutional Change: A Comparative Perspective on Europe, Canada and the USA* (Routledge 2013) 51, 56–57.

122 Ibid.

123 See Sanford Levinson, *Our Undemocratic Constitution* (Oxford University Press 2006) 29.

amendment in Canada, should we not expect to see more quasi-constitutional amendments—many more than the ones identified in this chapter? The first question requires a more elaborate answer than is possible in these pages. The answer to the second likewise requires more research to explain, but is a bit less of a mystery. Much of the change we would expect to see as a result of the rigidity of the Constitution has been redirected from the channels of formal amendment to the sphere of judicial interpretation in Canadian courts. The reasons why constitutional rigidity in Canada has sometimes led to quasi-constitutional amendments, and more often to informal amendment by judicial interpretation, will have to wait for another day.

# 7 Reflecting and building asymmetries

## The role of (sub-)constitutional statutes in Spain and the UK

*Nikos Skoutaris*[*]

## 1. Introduction

There are two kinds of asymmetry between sub-state entities that may affect the operation of the relevant State. The first might be described as political asymmetry.[1] It 'arises from the impact of cultural, economic, social and political conditions affecting the relative power, influence and relations of different regional units with each other and with the federal government.'[2] For instance, the very different historical trajectories of the Spanish and UK regions have led them to very different political aspirations.

The Spanish and UK constitutional orders have attempted to accommodate those political asymmetries by creating constitutional structures that are more 'open' and flexible than the ones of mature federations such as the USA, Germany and Switzerland. In the case of the UK, this is rather unsurprising given the idiosyncratic nature of its uncodified constitution. In Spain, although there is a codified constitution, it is particularly laconic with regard to its territorial aspect. So, in both cases, one has to look at the relevant (sub-)constitutional statutes in order to understand the specific constitutional relation that exists between the respective region and the metropolitan state.

The Spanish *Estatutos* and the UK Devolution Acts try to reflect the political asymmetries that exist within those multinational States by allowing for a second type of asymmetry: constitutional asymmetry. This refers 'specifically to the degree to which powers assigned to regional units by the constitution are not uniform.'[3] Both the UK and the Spanish orders are characterised by such asymmetries. Those asymmetries are described in both the *Estatutos* and the Devolution Acts whose role in the distribution of competences is central.

* Senior Lecturer in EU law, University of East Anglia, UK.

1 Charles D Tarlton, 'Symmetry and Asymmetry as Elements of Federalism: A Theoretical Speculation', (1965) 27 Journal of Politics, 861.

2 Ronald L Watts, *Comparing Federal Systems* (3rd ed., Montreal & Kingston, McGill-Queen's University Press 2008) 125.

3 Ibid.

The current paper focuses on the role of the Spanish and the UK (sub-)constitutional statutes within the respective constitutional orders. It does so in order to understand how those texts reflect the political asymmetries that exist within those States. More importantly, it analyses how those political asymmetries are translated into constitutional asymmetries as to the level of autonomy that the various regional governments enjoy. The existence of such constitutional asymmetries is rather unavoidable if one takes into account the very diverse processes that led to the adoption of the respective *Estatutos* and Devolution Acts and how they regulate the distribution of competences and responsibilities between the various levels.

Section 2 revisits the various routes to autonomy that aimed at accommodating the demands of the *comunidades históricas* and the other communities in Spain as well as the very different historical and political necessities that led to the devolution in Northern Ireland, Scotland and Wales. It shows how the drafting processes reflect such differentiation. Section 3 explains how the (sub-)constitutional documents may account for the difference in the level of legislative autonomy that the different regional governments enjoy by analysing their pivotal role in the internal distribution of competences and responsibilities. As a final point, the paper suggests that the constitutional asymmetries that exist in those systems lead to the crystalisation if not the exacerbation of the political asymmetries.

## 2. Drafting the (sub-)constitutional documents

### *2.1 The birth of the Estado de las Autonomías*

'Historically, Spain emerged from a process that involved the unification of different kingdoms and territories [...] Its constituent units [...] had and continue to have strong cultural identities, including different languages.'[4] Especially, the Euskadi (Basque country) and Catalunya have had a tradition of nationalist movements that fought for political autonomy.[5] This is why the Second Spanish Republic (1931–1936) tried to accommodate the territorial problem by the enactment of regional Statutes guaranteeing a certain degree of political autonomy.[6] In fact, Catalunya in 1932 and the Euskadi (Basque country) four years later 'were granted self-government, after referenda [sic] were held in those regions.'[7]

4 Julio López-Laborda, Jorge Martínez and Carlos Monasterio, 'Kingdom of Spain' in Anwar Shah (ed.) *The Practice of Fiscal Federalism: Comparative Perspectives* (McGill-Queen's University Press 2007) 288.

5 Victor Ferreres Comella, *The Constitution of Spain: A Contextual Analysis* (Hart Publishing 2013) 162.

6 Ibid.

7 Ibid., 163. A regional statute was also discussed in Galicia. However, the referendum took place just a few weeks before the Civil War started and Franco's forces occupied Galicia.

However, Franco's dictatorship put a violent end to this 'regionalist spring.' Franco imposed an unbending and repressive policy of state centralism in Spain for almost four decades. So, as part of post-Franco democratisation and as a means of balancing powerful regional interests fostered by the revived Basque and Catalan nationalisms, Spain pursued anew a process of regionalisation. The result of it has been a negotiated settlement that is known as the *Estado de las Autonomías*.[8] This hybrid formula has been described by academics as a 'unitary State that is decentralised in regions,'[9] as a 'regional State,'[10] as a 'federation in all but name,'[11] as a 'federal system in practice,'[12] as an order that exhibits 'virtual federalism,'[13] 'federalism in the making'[14] and 'unfulfilled federalism.'[15]

This ambivalence with regard to the classification of the constitutional system reflects the fact that the 'Spanish constitution of 1978 omits any reference to the form of the state.'[16] Article 2 of Constitution proclaims that it 'is based on the indissoluble unity of the Spanish nation' but also 'recognises and guarantees the right to self-government of the nationalities and regions of which it is composed and the solidarity among them.' However, neither the term 'nationalities' nor the term 'regions' are defined anywhere in the Constitution.[17] Instead, the constitution provides for an 'optional autonomy system', the so-called *principio dispositivo*. According to it, certain groups of 'bordering provinces with common historic, cultural and economic characteristics, insular territories and provinces with a historic regional status' had the right to become self-governing Communities (*Comunidades Autónomas*).[18] If they decided to do so, they could

8 See *inter alia* Spanish Constitutional Court, *sentencia* no. 32/1981.

9 Manuel García Pelayo, *Derecho constitucional comparado* (Alianza Universidad Textos 1984) 242–44.

10 Ibid.

11 Daniel Elazar, *Federal Systems of the World* (Longman 1994) 222.

12 Michael Burgess, *In Search of the Federal Spirit. New Theoretical and Empirical Perspectives in Comparative Federalism* (Oxford University Press 2012) 19.

13 Esther Seijas Villadangos, 'Answers to Centrifugal Federalism: Asymmetrical Federalism versus Coercive Federalism' (2014) 6 Perspectives on Federalism, E–164.

14 Luis Moreno, 'Federalisation in the Making' in Robert Agranoff (ed.) *Accommodating Diversity: Asymmetry in Federal States* (Nomos 1999) 149.

15 Pablo Bermendi and Ramon Máiz, 'Spain: Unfulfilled Federalism (1978–1996)' in Ugo M Amoretti and Nancy Bermeo (eds) *Federalism and Territorial Cleavages* (John Hopkins University Press 2004) 123.

16 Violeta Ruiz Almendral, 'Asymmetrical Federalism in Spain: The Challenges of Financing the Autonomous Communities' in Violeta Ruiz Almendral and François Vaillancourt (eds) *Autonomy in Subnational Income Taxes: Evolving Powers, Existing Practices in Seven Countries* (McGill-Queen's University Press 2013) 13, 14.

17 Eduardo J Ruiz Vieytez, 'Federalism, Subnational Constitutional Arrangements, and the Protection of Minorities in Spain' in George A Tarr and others (eds) *Federalism, Subnational Constitutional Arrangements and the Protection of Minority Rights* (Praeger Publishers 2004) 133, 136.

18 Spanish Constitution, Art 143(1).

assume the competence to legislate over a list of areas that are enumerated in Articles 148 and 149 of the Constitution. In fact, the Constitutional Court has held that the political autonomy of the Spanish regions is reflected precisely in the fact that they may have the necessary competences to manage their own interests.[19]

In order to assume this legislative autonomy, the Autonomous Communities had to adopt a Statute of Autonomy (*Estatuto de Autonomía*). To this effect, the Constitution provided for two ways to achieve autonomy: the 'normal route' (*vía normal*) (regulated in Article 143) and the 'rapid route' *(vía rápida)* (regulated in Article 151). The 'normal route' meant that the relevant Autonomous Community that would opt for it would first assume a relatively small set of competences enumerated in Article 148 of the Constitution. It could only assume further competences and thus achieve a 'higher level' autonomy at a later stage (at least five years afterwards) by actually amending its *Estatuto*. On the other hand, an Autonomous Community that followed the 'rapid route', could reach the highest level of self-government immediately.

In order to achieve the highest level of autonomy, the relevant region had to surpass a number of procedural hurdles. Most importantly, according to Article 151, the citizens in the region had to support in a referendum the initiative to follow the 'rapid route.' If the initiative received the necessary support, the voters would also have to ratify the Statute of Autonomy in a second subsequent referendum. However, this cumbersome procedure did not apply to the three regions that had enjoyed self-government during the Second Republic. By virtue of a special transitional rule in the constitution (*Disposición Transitoria 2a*), the regions that had already approved a regional statute during the Second Republic, i.e. Catalunya, Euskadi (Basque Country) and Galicia could achieve the highest level of autonomy by a simplified procedure that just required the approval of the *Estatuto* in a referendum. Unsurprisingly, those three regions opted for this procedure.

Despite the fact that this was only an 'optional autonomy system', it actually led to the division of the whole Spanish territory into 17 Autonomous Communities (*Comunidades Autónomas*)[20] and 2 'autonomous cities.'[21] Apart from the three ***nacionalidades históricas*** that followed the exceptional transitional procedure, Andalucía opted for the cumbersome 'rapid route' of Article 151 as well. Finally, Navarra had access to autonomy through a special organic law adopted by the Spanish Parliament (*Cortes Generales*), 'after negotiation with the *Diputación foral* of that province.'[22]

19 Spanish Constitutional Court, *sentencia* no. 4/1981.

20 They are: Andalucía, Aragón, Asturias, Baleares, Canarias, Cantabria, Castilla-La Mancha, Castilla y León, Catalunya, Comunidad Valenciana, Euskadi (the Basque Country), Extremadura, Galicia, La Rioja, Madrid, Murcia and Navarra.

21 The two Spanish enclaves in Africa are Ceuta and Melilla.

22 Ferreres Comella (n 5).

Despite the procedural differences that every route entailed, the approval of the Spanish Parliament (*Cortes Generales*) through the enactment of an 'organic law'[23] was a necessary requirement for the establishment of a certain *Comunidad Autónoma*.[24] The approval of the *Cortes Generales* is also necessary for the amendment of an *Estatuto*,[25] although the initiative for the procedure to start lies with the regions. The requirement for approval from the *Cortes* is in accordance with the view that the drafting of a given *Estatuto* is an act emanating from the wills of both the State and the respective region. The *Tribunal Constitucional* has underlined that an *Estatuto* is an act that cannot be disposed of by the sole will of the national State or of the respective *Comunidad Autónoma*.[26] So, within the Spanish constitutional order, the Statutes of Autonomy are both the 'highest norm of the region[27] and a government law subject to the constitution.'[28] They are an integral part of what has been called as the '*bloque de constitucionalidad*' (constitutional bloc).[29]

In that sense, the *Estatutos* as the 'basic institutional rule of each Self-governing Community'[30] may include additional contents but they still have to comply with the provisions of the Constitution.[31] In its famous decision on the 2006 Catalan *Estatut*,[32] the Constitutional Court made clear that

> statutes of Autonomy are rules subordinated to the Constitution, as it [sic] corresponds to normative provisions that are not an expression of a sovereign power, but of a devolved autonomy based on the Constitution, and guaranteed by it, for the exercise of legislative powers within the framework of the Constitution itself.[33]

And although the *Estatut* had obtained the support of the people in a regional referendum,'[34] the *Tribunal Constitucional* 'rejected 14 and read down 27 out of the 114 articles.'[35]

23 According to Spanish Constitution, Art 81 organic laws can be passed by an absolute majority of the Congress of Deputies. They are 'related to the development of fundamental rights and public liberties, those that approve Statutes of Autonomy and the general electoral regime, and others foreseen in the Constitution.'
24 Spanish Constitution, Art 144.
25 Spanish Constitution, Art 147(3).
26 Spanish Constitutional Court, *sentencia* no. 247/2007.
27 Spanish Constitution, Art 147.
28 Ruiz Almendral (n 16).
29 See, for instance, Spanish Constitutional Court, *sentencia* no. 76/83.
30 Spanish Constitution, Art 147(1).
31 Spanish Constitutional Court, *sentencia* no. 31/2010.
32 Ibid.
33 Dirk Hanschel, 'The Role of Subnational Constitutions in Accommodating Centrifugal Tendencies within European States: Flanders, Catalonia and Scotland Compared', (2014) 6 Perspectives on Federalism, E-244, E-252.
34 Ferreres Comella (n 5).
35 Hanschel (n 33) E-252.

## *2.2 The UK devolution acts*

The UK constitution has gradually evolved over centuries without having ever been codified in one single document. 'It represents a cluster of statutes, treaties, common law and constitutional conventions.'[36] It consists of

> the set of laws, rules and practices that create the basic institutions of the State, and its component and related parts, and stipulate the powers of those institutions and the relationship between the different institutions and between those institutions and the individual.[37]

Within this rather fluid constitutional landscape it is important to note that the UK judiciary has recognised the 'fundamental constitutional nature' of the UK Devolution Acts,[38] which are the foundational documents of the three devolved legislatures and executives of the UK. Having said that, the demands and the processes that led to the establishment of those devolved administrations are very different. As in the case of Spain, this explains -at least partially- the asymmetrical nature of the arrangement.

### *2.2.1 Scotland*

Scotland and England were 'united into One Kingdom by the Name of Great Britain'[39] by virtue of two legislative acts: the Union with Scotland Act 1706 passed by Westminster and the Union with England Act 1707 passed by the Parliament of Scotland. Since then, and until the end of the 20th century the UK was governed as a centralist State. Notwithstanding, the region managed to retain its own legal system and different system of education. And because Scotland's distinct system of law, education and church have been 'allied to a tradition of nationalism, with a minority seeking independence',[40] the devolution process was particularly welcomed there. In fact, in the Scottish devolution referendum of 1997 3 out 4 voters voted in favour of the establishment of a Scottish Parliament.

The Scottish Parliament and the Scottish Government in their modern form were founded by the Scotland Act 1998. Unlike, the Spanish case, where the regions had a very significant role in the drafting of the Statutes of Autonomy, this Act has been the product of a rather top-down process. This was changed

36 Ibid, E-254.

37 House of Lords Constitutional Committee, <www.publications.parliament.uk/pa/ld200102/ldselect/ldconst/11/1103.htm> accessed December 1, 2017.

38 See *H v Lord Advocate* [2012] UKSC 24; *Robinson v Secretary of State for Northern Ireland* [2002] UKHL 32.

39 Treaty of Union 1706, Art I.

40 Peter Leyland, *The Constitution of the United Kingdom: A Contextual Analysis* (2nd ed., Hart Publishing 2012) 246.

during the first major amendment of the statute. Westminster took into account the suggestions of the Commission on Scottish Devolution also referred to as the Calman Commission when it adopted the Scotland Act 2012.

The Scottish political community became even more involved during the process that led to the drafting and adoption of the Scotland Act 2016. In the wake of the Scottish independence referendum of 2014, the UK Prime Minister announced the establishment of the Smith Commission. The establishment was part of the process of fulfilling 'The Vow' made by the three main unionist parties promising more powers for Scotland in the event of a No vote. Following the rejection of independence, the Smith Commission that comprised of representatives of all five parties represented in the Scottish Parliament was asked to produce recommendations for further devolution, which were published in November 2014. Most of the recommendations of the Commission have been adopted in the Scotland Act 2016 underlining the fact that the revision of the Scottish constitutional act is not a top-down process any more. In fact, the Scotland Act 2016 goes a step further in allowing the regional legislature to have a more active role with regard to amending provisions of its own constitutional charter that relate to its operation including the control of its electoral system.[41]

What is more interesting is that before the enactment of both the Scotland Acts 2012 and 2016, the Scottish Parliament passed legislative consent motions with regard to the passage of the Bills. This was in agreement with the so-called 'Sewel convention.' According to it, the Westminster 'would not normally legislate in areas devolved to Scotland without the consent of the Scottish Parliament.'[42] Since its inception, 'the scope of the convention has evolved so as to require the consent of the Scottish Parliament not only where the UK Parliament seeks to legislate in devolved policy areas, but beyond that where a UK bill seeks to vary the legislative competence of the Scottish Parliament or the executive competence of the Scottish Ministers.'[43] The consent motion concerning the passage of the Scotland Bill in 2011 was 'worded in *conditional* terms, inviting the UK Government first to consider the amendments and proposals made by the Scotland Bill Committee at Holyrood and then later to return with an amended bill for further debate in a second legislative consent motion.'[44] The result was a new bill which sought conciliation between the two positions and which led to the successful grant of a consent motion.

The new Scotland Act sets the 'Sewel convention' into statutory footing[45] and declares that the Scottish Government and Parliament are 'a permanent part of the United Kingdom's constitutional arrangement.'[46] With regard to the

41 Scotland Act 1998, Sections 12 and 12A.
42 Leyland (n 40) 250.
43 Chris McCorkindale, 'Echo Chamber: The 2015 General Election at Holyrood – A Word on Sewel' <goo.gl/XpNKw8 > accessed December 1, 2017.
44 Ibid.
45 Scotland Act 1998, s 28.
46 Scotland Act 1998, s 62A.

former, there was a question whether the codification of the convention meant that the Westminster was constitutionally obliged to ask for the consent of the Scottish Parliament in order to trigger Article 50 of the Treaty on European Union, which will lead to UK's withdrawal from the EU. The eleven judges of the UK Supreme Court unanimously decided in *Miller* that the statutory footing of the convention does not change its legal nature. It is still a political convention. As such, judges 'cannot give rulings on its operation or scope, because those matters are determined within the political world.'[47]

Be that as it may, still, those developments can be seen as 'significant cracks in what has traditionally been a monolithic acceptance [...] of Westminster's untrammeled legislative power.'[48] In fact, one might wonder whether those new provisions challenge somehow the traditional Diceyan view expressed by the Supreme Court according to which '[s]overeignty remains with the United Kingdom Parliament.'[49]

### 2.2.2 *Wales*

'Wales has been closely integrated with England for the purposes of law and administration since the late Middle Ages.'[50] This explains to a certain extent why there has never been an equivalent level of popular demand for devolution as existed in Scotland. In fact, the initial attempt to establish a devolved legislature in the 70s failed. Nearly 80% of the Welsh voters that voted in the referendum voted against that prospect. Notwithstanding, the Labour Party prior to the May 1997 election committed itself to meeting the demand for decentralisation of power not only to Scotland but also to Wales. In the subsequent referendum, only 50% of Welsh voters turned out. Out of them only 50.3% voted in support of the establishment of a Welsh legislature.

The drafting of the Government of Wales Act 1998 was largely a top-down process. The main difference was that the little demand for significant political autonomy was reflected in the very limited competences of this devolved legislature as we shall see in the next section. Four years after the creation of the National Assembly of Wales, the then First Minister Ivor Richard created a Commission to consider whether the powers of the Assembly were adequate to the people of Wales. The Richard Commission was partly comprised of independent Commissioners and partly of appointees from the four elected parties to the Assembly. Westminster took into account the report of the Commission

47 *R (on the application of Miller and another) v Secretary of State for Exiting the European Union* [2017] UKSC 5, para. 146.

48 Stephen Tierney, 'Quiet Devolution: Sub-State Autonomy and the Gradual Reconstitution of the United Kingdom' in George A Tarr and Michael Burgess (eds) *Constitutional Dynamics in Federal Systems: Sub-National Perspectives* (McGill-Queen's University Press 2012) 195, 205.

49 *AXA General Insurance Limited and Others* [2011] UKSC 46, para. 46.

50 Leyland (n 40) 253.

when it decided to enhance the Assembly's powers by enacting the Government of Wales Act 2006. In order the Assembly to obtain an enhanced level of autonomy, two-thirds of its members had to pass a resolution requesting that primary-law making powers are transferred to it. In addition, this proposal had to gain the support of the Welsh voters in a referendum.[51] Indeed, in February 2010 the Assembly passed such resolution and one year later the Welsh voters supported such initiative by 63.5%.

The regional political community became even more involved in the next amendment of the Welsh arrangement. The coalition government of Conservatives – Liberal Democrats suggested the establishment of yet another Commission, which would look at the case for devolution of fiscal powers and whether there was support for further modifications to the then constitutional arrangements. The Silk Commission, much like the Smith Commission in Scotland comprised of representatives of the elected parties to the National Assembly. It produced two reports: one on finance published in November 2012 and one on legislative matters published in March 2014. The former led to the adoption of Wales Act 2014, which contains very similar provisions to the Scotland Act 2012. The latter led to the St David's Day process and the Wales Act 2017. That cross-party debate put forward a number of recommendations. Those include 'the devolution to the National Assembly of the power to determine its own size electoral arrangement […] along with putting the Sewel convention into statute and recognising the Assembly's permanence (as in Scotland).'[52]

From a modest top-down initiative, the Welsh devolution has become a constitutional arrangement that encompasses mechanisms for the enhancement of its own constitutional space. In 2011, such enhancement took place through a referendum while the latest Wales Act includes a number of provisions similar to the Scotland Act 2016.

### *2.2.3 Northern Ireland*

Unlike Scotland and Wales, the devolution in Northern Ireland was not a free-standing policy coming out of a political party's manifesto. It is one facet of the 'Good Friday Agreement' (also known as 'Belfast Agreement'), a peace settlement intended to bring an end to an era of political violence also known as 'The Troubles.' Neither does it signify the first time that devolution has been used in this troubled part of the world. In fact, the Government of Ireland Act 1920 set up the Stormont Parliamentary system of devolved government that functioned until March 1972. Having failed to effectively address the needs of the nationalist community, it was suspended by Westminster during the first

51 Government of Wales Act 2006, ss 103–106.

52 Bingham Centre for the Rule of Law, *A Constitutional Crossroads: Ways Forward for the United Kingdom* (British Institute of International and Comparative Law 2015) 6.

years of 'The Troubles' and Northern Ireland was directly governed by London since then.

So, one of the goals of the 'Belfast Agreement' was to restore devolved government.[53] However, this new devolution arrangement had 'to ensure that all sections of the community [could] participate and work together successfully in the operation of these institutions and that all sections of the community are protected.'[54] This meant that the Northern Irish devolution would function very differently from the other similar arrangements in the UK. As Lord Bingham has recognised:

> The 1998 Act ... was passed to implement the Belfast Agreement, which was itself reached, after much travail, in an attempt to end decades of bloodshed and centuries of antagonism. The solution was seen to lie in participation by the unionist and nationalist communities in shared political institutions, without precluding ... a popular decision at some time in the future on the ultimate political status of Northern Ireland.[55]

Starting from the latter, it is important to point out that 'Westminster has formally conceded that Northern Ireland can secede from the United Kingdom to join a united Ireland, if its people, and the people of the Irish Republic, voting separately, agree to this.'[56] Section 1 of the Northern Ireland Act 1998 is a rare example of a provision of a constitutional statute explicitly recognising the right of secession of a region. It was the only Devolution Act that contained such a provision underlining the very distinctive character of the Northern Irish arrangement. In contrast, the absence of an analogous provision in the Scotland Act meant that the 'two governments of Scotland' had to reach a political agreement (the *Edinburgh Agreement*), in order an independence referendum to be lawfully organised on September 18, 2014. According to it, Westminster conferred the power to Holyrood to organise an independence referendum in 2014.

The most striking difference, however, between the Northern Irish arrangement and its counterparts has to do with its consociational characteristics.[57] The

53 Christopher McCrudden, 'Northern Ireland, The Belfast Agreement and the British Constitution' in Jeffrey Jowell and Dawn Oliver (eds) *The Changing Constitution* (6th ed., Oxford University Press 2007) 227.

54 HM Government, *Agreement Reached in Multiparty Talks* (London, HMSO 1998) Strand One, para. 5.

55 *Robinson v Secretary of State for Northern Ireland* [2002] UKHL 32, para. 10.

56 John McGarry, 'Asymmetrical Autonomy in the United Kingdom' in Marc Weller and Katherine Nobbs (eds) *Asymmetric Autonomy and the Settlement of Ethnic Conflicts* (University of Pennsylvania Press 2010) 148, 156.

57 For an analysis, see among else Arend Lijphart, *Democracy in Plural Societies* (Yale University Press 1977); Arend Lijphart, *Patterns of Democracy: Government Forms and Performance in Thirty-Six Countries* (Yale University Press 1999).

requirements for cooperation between the two ethno-religious segments is evident *inter alia* in the government formation provisions[58] and in the special arrangements that govern how legislation is made. 'Various measures, such as financial legislation[59] (and, indeed, any legislation which 30 or more [Members of the Assembly] express concern over),[60] can only be passed if they gain "cross-community support."'[61]

## 2.3 Comparative remarks

Both the Spanish and the UK (sub-)national constitutional statutes consist of an integral part of the territorial constitution of those States. In Spain, the *Tribunal Constitucional* has recognised them as part of the '*bloque de constitucionalidad*' (constitutional bloc),[62] while in the UK, the Supreme Court has spoken about their 'fundamental constitutional nature.'[63] Having said that, one has also to appreciate that their autonomy is not unconstrained. In its famous decision on the Catalan *Estatut*, the *Tribunal Constitucional* reinstated that the statutes of Autonomy have to conform with the provisions of the constitution.[64] Given the idiosyncratic character of the uncodified UK constitution, there is no constitutional text that the Devolution Acts have to comply with as such. If one follows, however, a traditional Diceyan view of parliamentary sovereignty, then s/he might say that – in theory at least – Westminster can intervene in all areas and even abolish the devolved institutions. Politically speaking, this would be unthinkable given the democratic legitimacy with which those arrangements have been endowed. But even constitutionally speaking, this position has become somewhat untenable given that the new Scotland Act provides for the permanence of the Scottish institutions. However, the recent decision in *Miller* casts some doubt as to what is the added value of the legal codification of those political conventions.

Be that as it may, those (sub-)constitutional statutes play also a pivotal role in accommodating the different political aspirations of the various ethnic, religious, political, linguistic communities that live in those pluri-national States. They reflect a *de facto* political asymmetry that exists. Especially, the drafting processes that have been used for the constitutional statutes of the various Spanish and UK regions have taken into account the particular set of conditions that have led to the quest for legislative autonomy of those regions.

58 See Northern Ireland Act 1998, Part III.
59 Northern Ireland Act 1998, s 63(3).
60 Ibid, s 42(1).
61 Roger Masterman and Colin Murray, *Exploring Constitutional and Administrative Law* (Pearson 2014) 358.
62 See, for instance, Spanish Constitutional Court, *sentencia* no. 76/83.
63 See *H v Lord Advocate* (n 38).
64 Spanish Constitutional Court, *sentencia* no. 31/2010.

In Spain, this has taken place through a rather more systematic process that is provided by the constitution itself. The drafters of the constitution were mindful of the different historical and political trajectories that the *comunidades históricas* have followed in comparison to the rest of the regions. In the case of the UK, the political asymmetry is primarily reflected in the fact that not all the UK regions enjoy autonomy. England that possesses 85% of the population has neither a parliament nor an assembly. More importantly, the very different political realities that led to each and every constitutional arrangement is reflected in the drafting process and the contest of the Devolution Acts. The Northern Ireland Act is part of a peace settlement plan that was negotiated between the political parties of the two main ethno-religious segments, the UK and the Republic of Ireland. The initial Devolution Acts for Scotland and Wales were a political by-product of the landslide victory of New Labour. But even between those two constitutional arrangements there were important differences. The Scotland Act 1998 provided, as we shall in the next section, for a much higher level of autonomy than the Government of Wales Acts 1998 and 2006.

What is common for all three UK arrangements is that devolution is 'a process not an event.'[65] This is reflected in the fact that the initial constitutional statutes for Scotland and Wales have been amended in order to further respond to the needs and demands of the Scottish and Welsh political communities. But also, in the case of Northern Ireland, although, the Act itself has not been significantly amended, it contained flexibility mechanisms that have allowed it to adapt to the dynamic processes of the peace settlement.

What remains to be analysed is how those political asymmetries that led to the differentiated approaches in the drafting of the various (sub-)constitutional statutes are reflected in the distribution of competences and thus have been translated into constitutional asymmetries.

## 3. Distribution of powers and responsibilities

### *3.1 The role of the Estatutos de Autonomía*

While in a number of States with legislative regions, the Constitution provides for the distribution of competences between the various tiers,[66] in Spain, 'the constitutional design is neither exact nor complete.'[67] The Constitution lists three sets of competences: those that exclusively belong to the central government;[68] those that may be assumed by the Autonomous Communities

65 Ron Davies MP, HC Debs, vol.304, col. 1108 (January 21, 1998).

66 See for instance Austrian Constitution Arts 10–15; Belgian Constitution Arts 105–114 and 127–140; German Basic Law, Arts 71–74; Italian Constitution, Art 117.

67 Enric Argullol i Murgadas and Xavier Bernadí i Gil, 'Kingdom of Spain' in Akhtar Majeed, Ronald L Watts and Douglas M Brown (eds) *Distribution of Powers and Responsibilities in Federal Countries* (McGill-Queen's University Press 2006) 239, 244.

68 Spanish Constitution, Art 149.

through their Statutes of Autonomy;[69] and those that may be devolved from the central government to the Autonomous Communities through organic laws.[70] In addition, the *Comunidades Autónomas* may also assume all those powers that are not explicitly allocated to the State.[71] Finally, '[j]urisdiction on matters not claimed by Statutes of Autonomy fall with the State.'[72]

Clearly, because of the 'open' nature of the Spanish system of competences, the Statutes of Autonomy are necessary to complement the Constitution. 'As provided in Article 147(2)(d) of the Constitution, the Statutes of Autonomy are the rules whose role it is to establish "the competences assumed within the framework established in the Constitution", articulating in this manner a system of competences based on the Constitution and the Statutes.'[73] This is why they are considered together 'with certain state laws to which the Constitution refers in order to frame the distribution of powers'[74] to form part of the so-called *bloque de constitucionalidad*. In fact, the Spanish Constitutional Court has recognised the central role of the statutes in determining jurisdiction over particular areas. According to the Court,

> in order to determine if an area falls within the jurisdiction of the State or of the Autonomous Community, or whether a system of concurrent jurisdiction applies, in principle it is the text of the Statute of Autonomy of the Autonomous Community, in which competences are assumed, that shall be decisive. [...][75]

The constitutional reliance on the Statutes of Autonomy and the political asymmetries between the *nacionalidades históricas* on the one hand and the other regions on the other have led to an asymmetrical power distribution. Practically speaking, this has meant that the central State might have a competence with regard to a certain part of the Spanish territory while a *Comunidad Autónoma* might have assumed the very same competence over another part of the State. Equally, it means that not all the regions can exercise the same amount of competences.

This was particularly evident during the first years of the *Transición* given that the Autonomous Communities that followed the 'normal route' could only assume a relatively small set of competences enumerated in Article 148 of the Constitution. On the other hand, Catalunya, Euskadi (Basque country) and Galicia that used the *Transitional Provision* and Andalucía that used the 'rapid route' could also assume the powers provided by Article 149. As time went by,

69 Spanish Constitution, Art 148.
70 Spanish Constitution, Art 150.
71 Spanish Constitution, Art 149(3).
72 Ibid.
73 Spanish Constitutional Court, *sentencia* no. 76/1983.
74 Argullol i Murgadas and Bernadí i Gil (n 67) 244.
75 Spanish Constitutional Court, *sentencia* no. 18/1982.

and after the period of five years elapsed, even the low autonomy regions have progressively assumed the vast majority of the available competences. So, the constitutional asymmetry has been reduced between those regions which assumed their powers through the 'rapid route' and the rest. This does not mean, however, that they are extinct.

The prime example of constitutional asymmetry in Spain relates with the financing system of the Basque Country and Navarra. The common regime for financing the *Comunidades Autónomas* does not apply to those two regions. Their special financing arrangements of those two regions are called the *Convenio* in Navarra and the *Concierto* in the Basque Country. They provide for the most extensive revenue raising powers in Spain.

Additional provision One (*dispocisión adicional primera*) of the Spanish Constitution of 1978, 'protects and respects the historic rights of the territories with traditional charters (*fueros*).' The key feature of the foral system is that it provides for a higher level of fiscal autonomy given that those two *Comunidades Autónomas* 'regulate, manage and collect their own taxes as well as those taxes that are levied in their area by the central government.'[76] In fact, those regional governments have full powers over all personal and corporate income taxes and have also control over the administration of the main indirect taxes, the VAT and the excise duties.[77]

The very extensive revenue raising autonomy of those regions and the relative affluence of their residents have historically guaranteed almost the full financing of their expenditure without any transfer from the central government. Instead, a fixed amount of the revenue that those governments collect has to be transferred to the central government as a contribution to general charges. These negative charges are called *cupo* [quota] in the case of the Basque country and *aportación* [contribution] in the case of Navarra.

On the other hand, under the so-called 'common system' which applies to the other 15 *Comunidades Autónomas*, those regional governments enjoy more limited taxation powers. Such asymmetry between the two systems that exist in Spain used to be even higher during the first years of the *Transición*. Although, the regions under the 'common system' have progressively increased their powers, they still face a number of limits to their tax raising autonomy. 'The most important limitation is the prohibition of double taxation (Sections 6.2 and 6.3) which prevents' those legislative regions to raise similar taxes as the ones created by the central government.[78]

But it is not only in the area of fiscal autonomy that there is an important constitutional asymmetry.

76 Fernando Toboso and Eric Scorsone, 'How Much Power to Tax do Regional Governments Enjoy in Spain since the 1996 and 2001 Reforms?' (2010) 20 Regional and Federal Studies 157, 160.

77 López-Laborda and others (n 4) 302.

78 Ruiz Almendral (n 16) 20.

Even in the area of external relations there are asymmetries largely because of the expansive approach that has been used in some Statutes of Autonomy. According to the Spanish Constitution the central government has exclusive competences over international relations,[79] including treaty-making,[80] and the sub-state level lacks powers to sign international agreements or treaties. Notwithstanding, different Statutes of Autonomy have included special provisions on the foreign promotion of culture or vernacular languages,[81] international contacts with overseas migrant communities[82] and foreign aid.[83] The Basque government has gone as far as openly arguing 'for a limited understanding of the concept of international relations that reduces it to formal diplomatic representation, war and peace issues and the signing of treaties.'[84] It considers most of everything else as domestic activities and thus that it is entitled to be active. Equally, Chapters II and III of the Catalan *Estatut* that came into effect in August 2006 provide for quite an ambitious list of competences of the *Generalitat de Catalunya* in the international sphere. For instance, Article 195 foresees that the Catalan administration 'may sign collaboration agreements in areas falling within its powers.' In spite of the fact that the majority of the provisions contained in those two chapters were challenged in front of the *Tribunal Constitucional*, the judgement did not declare any of them unconstitutional.

### *3.2 The UK devolution acts*

If there is one constitutional order where the collaboration of other norms is required in order to operate the framework of powers is the one of the United Kingdom. According to the UK 'idiosyncratic' constitution, the allocation of powers to Northern Ireland, Scotland and Wales can be found in the respective constitutive acts.

#### *3.2.1 Scotland*

The Scottish Parliament has had the power to enact primary legislation from the very beginning. Its powers are defined negatively. According to Section 29 of Scotland Act 1998, it may legislate on areas that are not considered as 'reserved'

79 Art 149 of the Spanish Constitution.

80 Arts 93, 94 and 96 of the Spanish Constitution.

81 Statute of Autonomy of Andalucía, Art 68; Statute of Autonomy of Catalunya Arts 6, 50 and 127; Statute of Autonomy of Galicia, Art 1.

82 Statute of Autonomy of Andalucía, Art 6; Statute of Autonomy of Asturias, Art 8(3); Statute of Autonomy of Catalunya, Art 13; Statute of Autonomy of the Basque Country, Art 6(5); Statute of Autonomy of Extremadura, Art 3(3); Statute of Autonomy of Galicia, Art 7.

83 Statute of Autonomy of Andalucía, Arts 220 and 245; Statute of Autonomy of Catalunya, Art 197; Statute of Autonomy of Valencia, Art 62.

84 André Lecours, *Political Issues of Paradiplomacy: Lessons from the Developed World* (Netherlands Institute of International Relations 'Clingedael' 2008) 11.

competences of Westminster. Those are enlisted in Schedule 5 of Scotland Act 1998. Thus, in a way, Scotland has residual powers over the competences that are not explicitly allocated to Westminster. The latter include: international relations, energy, aspects of road, rail and marine transport. On the other hand, the Scottish legislature has competences over education, health and policing among else. Judging from the dearth of litigation reaching the Supreme Court based on the competence of Acts of Scottish Parliament with regard to reserved matters, it rather seems that the allocation of legislative authority between the different levels has been fairly unproblematic.[85]

Devolution, however, is 'a process not an event.' So, the Scotland Act has been amended twice so far to the effect that the Scottish Parliament has increased its powers especially in the area of fiscal autonomy. The Scotland Act 2012 implemented the recommendation of the Calman Commission according to which 'a big enough part of [the] budget [of the Scottish Parliament should] come from devolved taxation for it to be genuinely accountable.'[86] To this effect, a new Section 80C was introduced into the Scotland Act 1998, 'which would allow [the Scottish Parliament] to set a "Scottish rate" of income tax which, above a minimum level necessary to pay for UK-wide expenditure administered by central government would not be tied to the UK rates.'[87] However, this important reform of the financing of the Scottish devolution did not go as far as providing for the power of the Scottish legislature to control of the rates and bands of the income tax.

It was the Scotland Act 2016 that introduced that reform recently. 'Scottish Ministers will be free to decide how many bands of income tax there should be what the thresholds between them should be and at what rate should be taxed for each band.'[88] By the same Act, a number of further powers are devolved to Holyrood.[89] This transfer of powers makes the Scottish Parliament the most powerful devolved legislature in the UK and one of the most powerful in the world.

### *3.2.2 Wales*

'Devolution in Wales has been in a constant flux since 1998.'[90] Initially, the Welsh Assembly was not a law-making body equivalent to the Scottish Parliament. Unlike its counterpart in Scotland whose competences have been defined negatively, Schedule 2 of the Government of Wales Act 1998 enumerated the very limited powers of the Assembly. More importantly, the Assembly could not

85 See for instance *Martin and Miller v HM Advocate* [2010] UKSC 10.
86 Commission on Scottish Devolution, *Serving Scotland Better: Scotland and the United Kingdom in the 21st Century* (2009) 9.
87 Masterman and Murray (n 61) 348.
88 Bingham Centre (n 52) 3.
89 Ibid., 4.
90 Ibid.

pass primary legislation, but only subordinate legislation of specific relevance to Wales.[91] This changed eight years later. The Government of Wales Act 2006 'granted the Welsh Assembly Government the power to request permission from the UK Government (by Order in Council) to make pieces of primary legislation within specified fields of devolved competence, known as "Assembly Measures."'[92]

The 2006 Act, however, did not just allow for a modest extension to the competences of the National Assembly. It also provided for a procedure according to which the Assembly could assume wider powers to make primary legislation in certain enumerated areas.[93] According to it, following a resolution passed by the Assembly requesting primary law-making powers to be devolved to Wales, the proposal had to receive the support of the electorate in a referendum. Indeed, the Assembly passed such a resolution in February 2010, and the referendum took place a year later. In March 2011, the 63.5% of the Welsh voters approved the proposal. As a result, the National Assembly for Wales was able to pass laws without first needing the agreement of the UK Parliament.

This was not the last amendment, however. As we mentioned in the previous section, the Silk Commission made a number of recommendations. Some of them were adopted in the Wales Act 2014 and some of them in the Wales Act 2017. In particular, the former parallels the tax provisions of the Scotland Act 2012 while the latter adopts a 'reserved powers model,' provides for the permanence of the Welsh institutions and codifies the Sewel convention.[94] This has led to the significant narrowing of the asymmetry between the Welsh and the Scottish arrangements.

### *3.2.3 Northern Ireland*

The Northern Ireland Act 1998 is one facet of a wider peace agreement plan. In that sense, the competences devolved to Stormont reflect the tentative nature of devolution. Section 6 of the Act provides that the Assembly has power to pass primary legislation in all matters that are not expressly excluded from its powers. So, the Devolution Act is following a similar arrangement to the Scottish and Welsh ones according to which the Assembly possesses residual powers. However, while Schedule 2 enlists those 'excepted matters' that are considered as central state powers, in the case of Northern Ireland there is also Schedule 3 that provides for a list of 'reserved matters' that may be transferred to its Assembly only if cross-party support is evident.

So, the category of 'reserved matters' encapsulates the idea of the devolution as a 'process not an event.' They can be devolved if the political parties in

91 Government of Wales Act 1998, s 22(1).

92 Masterman and Murray (n 61) 355 citing Government of Wales Act 2006, ss 93–102.

93 Government of Wales Act 2006, ss 103–116.

94 Wales Act 2017 ss 1–3.

Northern Ireland can effectively prove that they can cooperate. During the first years of the devolution that has been proved particularly difficult. In fact, the Assembly was suspended in October 2002 'amidst allegations that Sinn Féin party officials were using their access to Stormont to gain information useful to Provisional IRA.'[95] Devolution was restored in 2007 in the aftermath of the St Andrews Agreement in 2006. The restoration of powers led to further transfer of powers to Stormont. Following the establishment of the Department of Justice in April 2010, the 'reserved powers' of policing, prisons and criminal law were devolved. Despite the unstable and conflictual character of Northern Irish political system, a further Stormont Agreement in December 2014 on conflict-related legacy issues paved the way for 'legislation to devolve the power to set the rate of corporation tax in Northern Ireland'[96] in accordance with the Corporation Tax (Northern Ireland) Act 2015.

### *3.3 Comparative remarks*

In this section, we noted the significant role that the Spanish and UK (sub-) constitutional statutes play in the distribution of competences. According to Viver, there is a

> failure to complete the constitutionalisation of the system of political decentralization, that is, to incorporate into the Spanish Constitution provisions pertaining to the territorial power structure. Whereas in other constitutions such provisions normally appear in the federal constitution, in Spain they are relegated above all to the statutes of autonomy and to legislation.[97]

Equally, in the UK, the competences of each and every devolved administration can be found in the respective (sub-)constitutional statutes.

In both cases, this has led to constitutional asymmetries. Different regions have assumed different legislative competences. In a way, the *de facto* asymmetry which is a result of the pluri-national character of those States has led to a *de jure* asymmetry 'which implies the setting-up of legal-formal differences between the' sub-state entities.[98] To highlight this point, we have used the area of fiscal autonomy as an example. In the Spanish case, we have underlined the difference between the so-called foral Autonomous Communities and the rest.

95 Masterman and Murray (n 61) 362.

96 Bingham Centre (n 52) 7.

97 Carles Viver, 'Spain's Constitution and Statutes of Autonomy: Explaining the Evolution of Political Decentralization' in George A Tarr and Michael Burgess (eds) *Constitutional Dynamics in Federal Systems: Sub-National Perspectives* (McGill-Queen's University Press 2012) 218, 220.

98 Víctor Cuesta-López, 'Intergovernmental Relations in Spain and the United Kingdom: The Institutionalization of Multilateral Cooperation in Asymmetric Polities', (2014) Perspectives on Federalism, E-299, E-303.

Asymmetries in this area are also evident in the UK. In the aftermath of the Scottish independence referendum, the new Scotland Act has transferred significant powers to the Scottish Parliament that are not shared by the other devolved administrations. On the other hand, the Northern Irish managed to achieve some autonomy with regard to setting the corporation tax that may make them competitive to their Southern neighbours.

## 4. In *lieu* of a conclusion

'[F]ederalism provisions of constitutions are often peculiarly the product of political compromise in historically situated moments, generally designed as a practical rather than a principled accommodation of competing interests.'[99] This is even more so in the case of States, which have not adopted a fully federal model but have opted for a system of asymmetrical devolution such as Spain and the UK. The pragmatic constitutional solutions that characterise both the Spanish and the UK systems represent an attempt to reconcile calls for regional autonomy with a desire to retain the borders of the Nation-State.

In order to achieve this important goal, the Spanish and UK constitutional orders have used the instrument of (sub-)constitutional documents to allow for some 'site-specific' decentralisation/devolution. Each and every one of the Spanish *Estatutos* and the UK Devolution Acts is a by-product of the very different set of political and historical conditions that led to its adoption. At the same time, those statutes can be also read as an attempt to accommodate the very different aspirations of their regions.

So, the paper has shed light on how those (sub-)constitutional statutes reflect the political asymmetries and translate them into constitutional ones. Those constitutional asymmetries, however, may also lead to the crystalisation if not the exacerbation of the political asymmetries, completing a vicious circle. One may observe that in the area of intergovernmental relations for instance.

The reason being that in those States, there is a lack of robust mechanisms for the collegiate representation of the regional tier in the way that the Austrian and the German *Bundesräte* may be deemed as such. The House of Lords is by no means a territorial chamber while the *Senado* is not a mechanism for the representation of the regional interests given its composition and its very limited significance in formulating the policy of the 'central State.' The lack of such mechanisms has pushed certain regions to introduce into their constitutive documents provisions for the creation of bilateral cooperation commissions between themselves and the metropolitan State. An example of that is the *Generalitat* – State Bilateral Commission that the 2006 Catalan *Estatut* provided for. This Commission that was envisaged and designed solely by the Catalan political community had as its main purpose to provide for a forum for

99 Vicki C Jackson, 'Narratives of Federalism: Of Continuities and Comparative Constitutional Experience', (2001) 51 Duke Law Journal, 223, 273–274.

policy coordination and dispute resolution. Innocuous as it may sound, it could clearly also function as a lobby mechanism for the representation of the Catalan interests. The fact that it is one of the only four similar Commissions[100] that exist in Spain show how the establishment of such mechanism through a (sub-) constitutional statute might lead to political asymmetries. A similar suggestion was made by the St David's Day process for Wales.[101]

At the same time, one might see the aforementioned example as a 'success story' of those orders and the particular role that the (sub-)constitutional statutes play in them. Because of their 'open' and 'flexible' character, they are able to adapt to the ever-changing political necessities of a multi-national State better than if they had adopted a more 'rigid' and 'formalised' approach and accommodate such initiatives that create even further differentiation between the regions. It remains to be seen whether the political developments in Catalunya and Scotland will cast doubt over this 'optimist' reading of the Spanish and UK constitutional orders.

100 The others are with Andalucía, Aragon and Castilla y León.
101 Bingham Centre (n 52) 6.

# 8 Quasi-constitutionality in armed conflict detention

*Jonathan Hafetz**

## I. Introduction

The legal framework for detention in non-international armed conflict (NIAC) remains relatively unsettled compared with that for international armed conflict (IAC). IACs describe conflicts between or among states. They are the principal context within which the law of armed conflict historically developed and provide a detailed regulatory framework. NIACs describe all other conflicts—wars between a state and non-state actor or between non-state actors. Today, most armed conflicts are classified as non-international and involve a state (or coalition of states) fighting against non-state actors. These conflicts are increasingly transnational in nature and involve non-state actors accused of engaging in terrorism. Debate centers on basic issues such as the source of legal authority to detain individuals, the permissible grounds of detention, and the procedural safeguards that must accompany it.

These issues are typically resolved through a conflict-of-laws analysis that turns on the relationship between international humanitarian law (IHL), which applies to situations of armed conflict, and international human rights law (HRL), which governs outside such situations. The competing positions that NIAC detentions should be governed exclusively by IHL, on the one hand, or exclusively by HRL, on the other, occupy opposite ends of the spectrum. Approaches that emphasize areas of convergence between the two occupy the middle ground. Convergence-based approaches generally seek to adapt and translate HRL's more stringent restrictions on a state's power to detain to this increasingly prevalent form of armed conflict. While a gradual process of convergence between IHL and HRL has been underway since the 1970s,[1] that process has accelerated in recent years in response to what former International Committee of the Red Cross (ICRC) President Jakob Kellenberger called 'an urgent need to explore new ways' for addressing perceived gaps or

* Professor of Law, Seton Hall University School of Law.

1 Theodore Meron, 'The Humanization of Humanitarian Law' (2000) 90 AJIL 239.

weaknesses in the international legal framework for the detention of individuals in NIAC.[2]

The closely watched joined appeals of *Al-Waheed v. Ministry of Defence* and *Serdar Mohammed v. Ministry of Defence* (*Al-Waheed/Mohammed*)[3] offer a window into these issues. In January 2017, the UK Supreme Court ruled that UN Security Council Resolutions for Iraq and Afghanistan[4] provided legal authority for UK forces to engage in security detention during the NIACs in those countries, but that both the grounds and procedures must accommodate the requirements of HRL and more specifically, the European Convention on Human Rights and Fundamental Freedoms (ECHR).[5] The Supreme Court declined to decide whether IHL authorizes detention in NIAC, as the UK government had urged. It did, however, reject the ruling by the UK Court of Appeal of England and Wales in *Serdar Mohammed v. Ministry of Defence* that HRL exclusively determines the grounds and procedures for detention by UK forces of suspected insurgents in Afghanistan.[6]

This paper argues that convergence-based models that seek to adapt HRL to accommodate an international law power of security detention in armed conflict may be understood as a form of quasi-constitutional lawmaking. As the UK Supreme Court's decision in *Al-Waheed/Mohammed* suggests, the question of what primacy to give IHL, with its more permissive approach to a state's power to detain, relative to HRL, with its more restrictive approach, resembles debates over the prioritizing of the relative interests of states and individuals familiar to constitutional interpretation. The effort to derive minimum grounds and procedures for armed conflict detention shares features of constitutional decision-making aimed at providing baseline requirements in areas that implicate fundamental rights.

More broadly, the paper explores how notions of quasi-constitutionality—typically applied in the domestic sphere—can help inform developments in international law. In particular, the paper describes the development of fundamental norms outside traditional channels of international lawmaking—treaty and customary international law. Like quasi-constitutional norms in domestic settings, emerging quasi-constitutional norms of international law may be said to occupy a middle ground, sharing an elevated status and degree of entrenchment that

2 Jakob Kellenberger, 'Official Statement of ICRC: Strengthening Legal Protection of Victims of Armed Conflicts' (21 September 2010) <www.icrc.org/eng/resources/documents/statement/ihl-development-statement-210910.htm> accessed 18 June 2017.

3 *Al-Waheed v. Ministry of Defence* & *Serdar Mohammed v. Ministry of Defence* (*Al-Waheed/Mohammed*) [2017] UKSC 2.

4 UN Security Council Resolutions 1546 (2004) and 1723 (2006) for Iraq and UN Security Council Resolutions 1386 (2001), 1510 (2003), and 1890 (2009) for Afghanistan.

5 European Convention for the Protection of Human Rights and Fundamental Freedoms (ECHR) (4 November 1950) 213 UNTS 232.

6 *Serdar Mohammed v. Secretary of State for Defence* [2015] EWCA Civ. 843.

distinguishes them from ordinary law, while remaining subject to override, thus distinguishing them from formal constitutionality.

## II. Detention in armed conflict under international law

IHL provides the primary source of legal authority for detention during armed conflict. IHL's content, however, varies depending on the classification of the conflict. In general, IHL provides far more comprehensive and detailed rules for detentions in IAC than NIAC. Today, however, most conflicts are non-international in character because they are waged by states against non-state actors. The evolving nature of armed conflict has prompted extensive discussion and debate on how best to interpret IHL's relative silence on detentions in NIAC. This section provides a brief overview of the law of detention in armed conflict. It then examines the different approaches to NIAC detentions and the UK Supreme Court's decision in *Al-Waheed/Mohammed*.

### *A. Detention in international armed conflict*

The 1949 Geneva Conventions supply the principal legal framework for international armed conflict, including for situations of occupation. The Third Geneva Convention (GC III) covers prisoners of war (POWs),[7] while the Fourth Geneva Convention (GC IV) covers civilians.[8] Together, they provide legal authority, grounds, and procedures for detention in IAC as well as limitations on such detention, including durational parameters, review procedures, and guarantees of humane treatment. GC III, for example, confers on states the authority to intern (or detain) POWs[9] until 'the cessation of active hostilities.'[10] It also describes the basic requirements for tribunals established to review an individual's status as a POW.[11] GC IV confers on states the authority to intern civilians where that detention is necessary for security purposes, but only for as long as the reasons that necessitated the internment continue to exist.[12] GC IV

7 Geneva Convention [III] Relative to the Treatment of Prisoners of War (12 August 1949) 6 UST 3316, 75 UNTS 135 (entered into force 21 October 1950) (Geneva III).
8 Geneva Convention [IV] Relative to the Protection and Treatment of Civilian Persons in Time of War (12 August 1949) 6 UST 3516, 75 UNTS 287 (entered into force 21 October 1950) (Geneva IV).
9 GC III (n 7) art. 21.
10 ibid. art. 118(1).
11 ibid. art. 5.
12 GC IV (n 8) art. 42(1) (authorizing a state to detain a protected person found in the territory of a party to the conflict where 'absolutely necessary' to the security of the detaining power); ibid. art. 78(1) (authorizing a state to detain protected persons in occupied territory 'for imperative reasons of security'). Protected persons generally include non-combatants (i.e., individuals not protected by GC III) who at any moment during armed conflict or occupation find themselves in the custody of a party to the conflict or an occupying power of which they are not nationals. ibid. art. 4.

also sets forth review procedures for interned civilians, including periodic review of continued detention by a court or administrative board.[13] GC III and GC IV both mandate the humane treatment of detainees and prohibit torture and other mistreatment.[14]

The 1977 Additional Protocols supplement and extend the 1949 Conventions. Additional Protocol I (AP I) increases humanitarian protections for victims of international and interstate violence and broadens the rules governing international armed conflicts to non-international wars of national liberation, including by relaxing the requirements for obtaining lawful combatant and POW status.[15] Additional Protocol II (AP II) mainly amplifies the protections of Common Article 3 of the 1949 Geneva Conventions, which supplies baseline protections for the treatment and trial of detainees in situations of non-international conflict. AP II extends those protections where the non-state group satisfies certain criteria by reclassifying such conflicts as international.[16] However, unlike the 1949 Conventions, whose acceptance by states is universal, a number of states have not ratified the Additional Protocols.[17]

Today, most armed conflicts are non-international in character because of the relative decline in interstate armed conflict covered by GC III and IV and wars of national liberation addressed by AP I. NIACs increasingly involve multiple states engaged in hostilities against non-state actors and are transnational in scope.[18]

### B. Detention in non-international armed conflict

IHL addresses detention in NIAC in far less detail.[19] States that negotiated the text of the 1949 Geneva Conventions intentionally declined to extend their provisions on detention authority and review procedures to NIACs.[20] Only one provision of the 1949 Geneva Conventions, Common Article 3, specifically

13 ibid., arts. 43, 78. See also Jean Pictet, *Commentary IV on the Geneva Conventions Relative to the Protection of Civilians in Time of War* (ICRC 1958) 260.

14 GC III (n 7) arts. 3, 17, 87; GC IV (n 8) arts. 3, 32.

15 Protocol Additional to the Geneva Conventions of 12 August 1949, and Relating to the Protection of Victims of International Armed Conflicts, June 8, 1977, 1125 UNTS 3 (AP I); Derek Jinks, 'The Declining Significance of POW Status' (2004) 45 Harv Intl LJ 367, 385.

16 Protocol Additional to the Geneva Conventions of 12 August1949 and Relating to the Protection of Victims of Non-international Armed Conflicts, June 8, 1977, 1125 UNTS 609 (AP II).

17 Gabor Rona, 'Is there a Way Out of the Non-International Armed Conflict Dilemma' (2015) 91 Intl L Studies 32, 37.

18 International Committee of the Red Cross, Report, *32nd International Conference of the Red Cross and Red Crescent; International humanitarian law and the challenges of contemporary armed conflicts* (ICRC 2015), <www.icrc.org/en/document/international-humanitarian-law-and-challenges-contemporary-armed-conflicts> accessed 18 June 2017.

19 Kevin Jon Heller, 'The Use and Abuse of Analogy in IHL' in Jens Ohlin (ed.), *Theoretical Boundaries of Armed Conflict and Human Rights* (CUP 2016).

20 Rona (n 17) 33.

addresses NIACs. Common Article 3 has been described as a 'convention in miniature' for establishing baseline protections for individuals detained in a NIAC.[21] It prohibits 'the passing of sentences and the carrying out of executions without previous judgment pronounced by a regularly constituted court affording all the judicial guarantees which are recognized as indispensable by civilized peoples.'[22] It further prohibits torture and other forms of mistreatment.[23] Article 75 of AP I, widely recognized as customary international law, specifies additional fair-trial requirements.[24] Common Article 3 does not, however, authorize or prescribe rules for detention. While the 1949 Geneva Conventions and the 1977 Additional Protocols contemplate the detention of enemy fighters in NIACs, and while they impose minimum guarantees of humane treatment, they do not expressly authorize such detention or provide standards or procedures for evaluating it.[25] Geneva law in NIAC, in short, is silent on who may be detained, on what grounds, and according to what procedures.[26] While some argue that domestic law must therefore independently authorize detention in NIAC,[27] others maintain that IHL can still supply a legal basis for NIAC detention based on implied authority from treaties,[28] customary international law,[29] and principles of military necessity.[30]

NIACs were traditionally referred to as internal armed conflicts because they took place within the territory of a single state.[31] States historically resisted international regulation of what they generally regarded as internal matters.[32] States feared that subjecting internal conflicts to international regulation would provide

21 Jean de Preux, 'Commentary: Geneva Convention Relative to the Treatment of Prisoners of War' in Jean S. Pictet (ed.) (ICRC 1960) 34.

22 GC III (n 7) art. 3(1)(d).

23 ibid art. 3(1)(a),(c) (prohibiting, *inter alia*, torture, cruel treatment, and 'outrages upon personal dignity, in particular humiliating and degrading treatment').

24 AP I (n 15) art. 75. See also *Customary International Humanitarian Law*, Jean-Marie Henckaerts and Louise Doswald-Beck (eds) (CUP 2005) vol. 1, 19–24.

25 John B. Bellinger III and Vijay M. Padmanabhan, 'Detention Operations in Contemporary Conflicts, Four Challenges for the Geneva Conventions and Other Existing Law' (2011) 105 AJIL 201, 222.

26 Laura M. Olson and Marco Sassòli, 'The Relationship between International Humanitarian and Human Rights Law Where It Matters: Admissible Killing and Internment of Fighters in Non-International Armed Conflicts' (2008) 90 Intl Rev Red Cross 599, 621.

27 Ashley S. Deeks, 'Administrative Detention in Armed Conflict' (2009) 40 Case W Res J Int'l L 403, 413; Gabor Rona, 'A Bull in a China Shop: The War on Terror and International Law in the United States' (2008) 39 Cal W Intl LJ 135, 148.

28 Sean Aughey and Aurel Sari, 'Targeting and Detention in Non-International Armed Conflict: Serdar Mohammed and the Limits of Human Rights Convergence' (2015) 91 Intl L Studies 94. 108.

29 ibid., 116.

30 Laurie R. Blank, 'Understanding When and How Domestic Courts Apply IHL' (2011) 44 Case W Res J Intl L 205, 215.

31 David Kretzmer, 'The Application of IHL in Non-International Armed Conflicts' (2012) 42 Isr L Rev 8, 13; Rona (n 17) 36.

32 Rona (n 17) 37.

non-state forces, including rebel or insurgent groups operating on their territory, with the status of privileged belligerents under international law, thereby restricting the state's ability to subject them to domestic criminal law for taking up arms.[33]

Over time, jurisprudence from international criminal tribunals, the influence of human rights law, and treaty rules adopted by states have reduced the differences between the rules governing IAC and NIAC.[34] But the use of security detention by states engaged in NIACs against non-state actors underscores the continuing distinctions between the rules for IAC and NIAC. In short, while IHL may *permit* detention in NIAC, whether IHL also *authorizes* such detention in NIAC (as it does in IAC), or whether HRL remains the controlling framework, is still vigorously contested.

In the *Wall* case, the International Court of Justice (ICJ) outlined a basic framework for addressing the relationship between IHL and HRL. It explained, 'some rights may be exclusively matters of international humanitarian law; others may be exclusively matters of human rights law; yet others may be matters of both these branches of international law.'[35] The principle of *lex specialis* provides that in the event of a conflict, the more specific rule determines the rule's content. Thus, as the ICJ explained in the *Nuclear Weapons* case, while HRL's prohibition against arbitrary deprivation of liberty continues to apply during armed conflict, a more precise IHL rule would decide its content.[36] In IAC, IHL provides such a rule and thus governs detention in this type of armed conflict. But whether IHL similarly provides a basis for detention in NIAC and, if so, how IHL thereby affects HRL's prohibition on arbitrary detention in that context, remains controversial.

## C. *Models for applying IHL and HRL to NIAC detention*

Efforts to address the application of IHL and HRL to NIAC detention may be divided into three broad categories. These categories, and the ways in which they interact, help frame the emergence of a quasi-constitutional law of armed conflict detention.

### 1. *Strong* lex specialis *model*

First, under a strong *lex specialis* model, HRL does not apply to NIAC detention since IHL fully displaces HRL in all forms of armed conflict.[37] IHL thus provides

33 Robert M. Chesney, 'Terrorism, Prosecution, and the Preventive Detention Debate' (2009) 50 S Tex L Rev 669, 694; David Kretzmer, 'Targeted Killings of Suspected Terrorists: Extra-Judicial Execution or Legitimate Means of Defense?' (2005) 16 Eur J Intl L 171, 197.

34 Marco Sassòli and Marie Louise Tougas, 'International Law Issues Raised by the Transfer of Detainees by Canadian Forces in Afghanistan' (2011) 56 McGill LJ 959, 969.

35 *Legal Consequences of the Construction of a Wall in Occupied Palestine Territory*, Advisory Opinion [2004] ICJ Rep 136 [106].

36 *Legality of the Threat or Use of Nuclear Weapons*, Advisory Opinion [1996] ICJ Rep 226 [240].

37 Marko Milanovic, 'The Lost Origins of *Lex Specialis*: Rethinking the Relationship between Human Rights and International Criminal Law' in Jens Ohlin (ed.), *Theoretical Boundaries of*

the exclusive source of authority, grounds, and procedures for detention in NIAC. The United States has adopted this approach for detentions at Guantanamo Bay, where it argues that IHL exclusively governs the confinement of unprivileged belligerents (formerly, enemy combatants) and applies certain IHL rules for IAC by analogy.[38] Such a *lex specialis* model in which IHL displaces HRL invariably gives states greater power to detain. It generally results in laxer procedural safeguards and broader grounds for detention, including potentially status-based detention based on an individual's membership in an enemy force.[39]

### 2. *Qualified* lex specialis *or convergence model*

Second, a qualified *lex specialis* or convergence model recognizes that IHL regulates detention in NIAC, but does not fully displace HRL. This model instead seeks to identify areas of convergence and resolve conflicts between these two branches of international law. Marko Milanovic has distinguished partial displacement, under which a specific IHL rule trumps a competing HRL rule that would lead to a contrary result, and norm harmonization, under which a more specific IHL rule does not automatically override a conflicting HRL norm but instead informs its interpretation.[40] Human rights bodies have adopted the latter approach, emphasizing that IHL and HRL are 'complementary, not mutually exclusive.'[41]

As a practical matter, there is often little difference between partial displacement and norm harmonization where IHL does not provide a specific, trumping rule, as in NIAC detention. In such circumstances, both approaches look not only to IHL, but also to HRL, which, in conjunction with domestic law, help define the permissible grounds and procedures for detention. The ICRC has adopted a convergence model, explaining that while IHL authorizes and regulates NIAC detention, it must be interpreted in light of relevant human rights standards, such as the prohibition on arbitrary detention.[42] Some scholars have advocated similar approaches.[43]

### 3. *HRL exclusivity model*

A third model maintains that because IHL regulates only the treatment of individuals in custody in NIAC, it does not provide authority for or otherwise

*Armed Conflict and Human Rights* (CUP 2016) 78; Beth Van Schaack, 'The Interface of IHL and IHR: A Taxonomy' (*Just Security*, 8 October 2013) <http://justsecurity.org/2013/10/08/interface-ihl-ihr-taxonomy/> accessed 17 April 2017.

38 Olson and Sassòli (n 26) 623–24.

39 Aughey and Sari (n 28) 118.

40 Milanovic (n 37) 27–28.

41 Human Rights Comm., General Comment No. 31: The Nature of the General Legal Obligation Imposed on States Parties to the Covenant [31 August 2001] UN Doc CCPR/C/21/Rev.1/Add.11.

42 Henckaerts and Doswald-Beck (n 24) Rule 99.

43 See e.g. Ryan Goodman, 'The Detention of Civilians in Armed Conflict' (2009) 103 AJIL 48.

regulate the grounds and procedures for detention in such conflicts.[44] Because there is no competing IHL rule based on treaty or custom—no '*lex*,' as Kevin Jon Heller puts it—HRL occupies the field and no harmonization or resolution of conflicting norms is required.[45] Under this approach, security detention in NIAC, where individuals are held without criminal charge, must rest on additional legal authority, such as a UN Security Council resolution or on domestic law. Regardless of the source of authority, moreover, the grounds and procedures for detention must conform to HRL requirements. While HRL does not necessarily prohibit detention without trial, it imposes greater constraints than IHL, mandating that administrative or security detention—that is, detention without criminal charge—be strictly necessary and be accompanied by more robust procedural safeguards than under IHL. Article 9 of the International Covenant on Civil and Political Rights (ICCPR), for example, requires informing a prisoner immediately of the reasons for his detention and affording him access to prompt judicial review.[46] The European Court of Human Rights (ECtHR) has held that detention of four days without judicial review is unlawful under article 5 of the ECHR[47] absent a formal derogation by the state '[i]n time of war or other public emergency threatening the life of the nation' under article 15.[48] Even in the case of derogation, the ECtHR has permitted extrajudicial detention for up to seven days with appropriate safeguards,[49] but disallowed it for fourteen days.[50]

In sum, the opposing ends of the spectrum—the first and third models—look exclusively to IHL or HRL, respectively, for the legal authority, grounds, and procedures for NIAC detention. Convergence-based approaches (the second model) look to both IHL and HRL. The first model tends to give states the broadest power to detain, whereas the third model imposes the most restrictions on that power. Detention power under the second model varies depending on the degree to which IHL modifies HRL's more stringent requirements.

### D. *Al-Waheed/Mohammed*

The joined appeals of *Al-Waheed v. Ministry of Defence* and *Serdar Mohammed v. Ministry of Defence* involve, respectively, civil actions seeking damages for

44 UN Human Rights Committee, General Comment No. 35: Article 9: Liberty and Security of Person [16 December 2014] UN Doc CCPR/C/GC/35.

45 Heller (n 19) 10–11, 41.

46 International Covenant on Civil and Political Rights (ICCPR), art. 9(4), adopted 19 December1966, 999 UNTS. 171; Monica Hakimi, 'International Standards for Detaining Terrorism Suspects: Moving beyond the Armed Conflict-Criminal Divide' (2008) 33 Yale J Intl L 369, 387.

47 *Brogan v. United Kingdom* [1988] 11 EHRR 117.

48 ECHR (n 5) art. 15(1).

49 *Brannigan and McBride v. United Kingdom* [1994] 17 EHRR 539; Stephen J. Schulhofer, 'Checks and Balances in Wartime: American, British, and Israeli Experiences' (2004) 102 Mich L Rev 1906, 1950.

50 *Aksoy v. Turkey* [1996] 23 EHRR 553.

security detention in the NIACs in Iraq and Afghanistan in violation of the right to liberty under article 5 of the ECHR. In *Al-Waheed*, UK forces captured suspected insurgent Abd Al Hameed Ali Al-Waheed in Iraq in 2007 and detained him for approximately six weeks before releasing him. In *Serdar Mohammed*, UK forces captured a Taliban commander in Afghanistan in 2010 and detained him for 110 days prior to transferring him to Afghan custody. The central issue before the UK Supreme Court was whether UK forces had legal authority to engage in the prolonged security detention of insurgents in the respective NIACs in Iraq and Afghanistan and, if so, whether the grounds and procedures for such detention were lawful.

ECHR article 5(1) prohibits deprivation of liberty unless based on one of the six specifically identified grounds and is 'in accordance with a procedure prescribed by law.'[51] Article 5 also sets forth specific procedural requirements, including a prompt determination by a court of the lawfulness of detention and issuance of an order of release if the detention is unlawful.[52]

Previously, the Grand Chamber of the ECtHR ruled in *Hassan v. United Kingdom*[53] that in IAC, the continued military detention of individuals who pose a significant security risk satisfies the ECHR's prohibition on arbitrary detention even though article 5 does not specifically provide for security detention.[54] The ECtHR concluded that the ECHR's enumerated six permissible grounds of detention must be interpreted to accommodate the *lex specialis*—specifically, GC III and GC IV—of international armed conflict.[55] It further determined that, in such conflicts, compliance with GC IV's provision of periodic review by a competent body, even if nonjudicial, satisfies the ECHR's prohibition on arbitrary detention as long as the body provides sufficient guarantees of impartiality and fairness.[56] A key issue in *Al-Waheed/Mohammed* was whether ECtHR's ruling in *Hassan* also applied to NIACs.[57]

In *Serdar Mohammed*, the Court of Appeal of England and Wales[58] and the High Court of Justice[59] initially ruled that the claimant's security detention violated ECHR article 5 because IHL did not authorize such detention in NIAC and because the applicable UN Security Council resolutions for Afghanistan did not provide legal authority to detain. Accordingly, the claimant's detention was

51 ECHR (n 5) art. 5(1).
52 ibid art. 5(4).
53 *Hassan v. United Kingdom*, App. No. 29,750/09 (ECHR, 16 September 2014).
54 ibid. [104]–[105].
55 ibid. [102].
56 ibid. [106].
57 The claimant's detention in *Al-Waheed* occurred after the conflict in Iraq had shifted from an IAC to a NIAC due to the UK's ceasing to be an occupying power and becoming a mandatory power acting in support of the newly formed indigenous government of Iraq.
58 *Serdar Mohammed v. Secretary of State for Defence* [2015] EWCA Civ 843.
59 *Serdar Mohammed v. Ministry of Defence* [2014] EWHC 1369 (QB).

governed exclusively by the ECHR, which did not authorize security detention absent derogation.

The UK Supreme Court (by 7–2 majority) rejected that conclusion.[60] The various majority opinions did not decide whether IHL authorized security detention in NIAC, as the UK had urged.[61] The majority concluded, however, that the relevant UN Security Council resolutions supplied positive legal authority for the UK's continued military detention of the claimants if necessary for imperative reasons of security, thus providing analogous authority to that supplied by GC III and GC IV in IAC.[62] Although the majority recognized that NIAC-based security detention did not fall within any of the six permissible grounds under ECHR article 5(1), it did not regard those six grounds as exhaustive outside of peacetime conditions.[63] Instead, the majority found that article 5(1) must accommodate the broader detention power in armed conflict contemplated by IHL, and that such detention, when conducted for imperative reasons of security, does not constitute arbitrary detention under the ECHR or HRL generally. It reached this conclusion even though the relevant Security Council resolutions did not specifically confer detention authority on UK forces, relying instead on the resolutions' conferral of authority on member states to use 'all necessary measures' to carry out their mission of providing security and stability to Iraq and Afghanistan.[64]

A different majority of justices also determined that the procedures used by the UK violated article 5 by denying individuals the right to effectively challenge their detention.[65] The majority acknowledged the need to adapt article 5's procedural safeguards against arbitrary detention to the circumstances of armed conflict.[66] The majority determined that the standards of review applicable to civilians in

60 *Al-Waheed v. Minister of Defense and Serdar Mohammed v. Ministry of Defense* [2017] UKSC 2 [61] (*Al-Waheed/Mohammed*). Lord Sumption (joined by Lord Hale) provided the leading judgment, with multiple concurrences, and Lord Reid (joined by Lord Kerr) supplied the dissent. For initial commentary on the decision, see Shaheed Fatima, 'UK Supreme Court Judgment on Extra-territorial Detention in Iraq and Afghanistan' (*Just Security*, 17 January 2017) <www.justsecurity.org/36407/uk-supreme-court-judgment-extra-territorial-detention-iraq-afghanistan> accessed 16 June 2017; Fionnuala Ní Aoláin, 'To Detain Lawfully or Not to Detain: Reflections on the UK Supreme Court decision in Serdar Mohammed' (*Just Security*, 2 February 2017) <www.justsecurity.org/37013/detain-lawfully-detain-question-reflection-uk-supreme-court-decision-serdar-mohammed> accessed 10 June 2017; and Marko Milanovic, 'A Trio of Blockbuster Judgments from the UK Supreme Court' (*EJIL: Talk!*, 17 January 2017) <www.ejiltalk.org/a-trio-of-blockbuster-judgments-from-the-uk-supreme-court/> accessed 21 May 2017).

61 *Al-Waheed/Mohammed* [2017] UKSC 2, [13]–[17] (Lord Sumption).

62 ibid. [44]. In *Serdar Mohammed*, the claimant argued that his detention by UK forces was limited to the 96 hours permitted by policy of the International Security Assistance Force; in *Al-Waheed*, the issue was whether UK forces had the power to detain the claimant at all.

63 ibid.

64 ibid. [19], [26], [38]–[39].

65 Lords Sumption, Hale, Wilson, Hodge, Reed, and Kerr found a breach of article 5 based on the inadequacy of the UK's detention review procedures.

66 ibid. [66].

IAC under GC IV—and not those under ECHR article 5—represented the minimum standards necessary to ensure that detention in armed conflict is not arbitrary.[67] These minimum standards include initial review of the appropriateness of detention, followed by regular reviews thereafter, by an impartial body and based on a fair procedure.[68] The majority found that detention without prompt judicial review in NIAC would not necessarily violate article 5(4) as it would during peacetime giving the practical obstacles to such review.[69] It concluded, however, that the UK's review procedures still violated the prohibition on arbitrary detention—even as accommodated for the circumstances of armed conflict—because they lacked sufficient institutional guarantees of independence and failed to provide for the detainee's participation.[70]

In dissent, two justices found that neither IHL nor the relevant Security Council resolutions provided legal authority for detention in NIAC.[71] The dissent refused to infer positive detention authority under IHL, where treaties did not specifically provide for it and where no customary international norm had yet emerged based on *opinio juris* or state practice.[72] The dissent also disagreed with the majority that Security Council resolutions provided this authority and that the ECtHR's decision in *Hassan*, which sought to reconcile detention authority under Geneva law with the ECHR, was limited to IAC.[73] The dissent concluded that, unlike in *Hassan*, the detentions in *Al-Waheed/Mohammed* were governed exclusively ECHR article 5, which did not recognize the UK's right to engage in security detention during the NIACs in Afghanistan and Iraq.

An appeal of the *Al-Waheed/Mohammed* judgment to the ECtHR is expected. Meanwhile, the UK government has signaled its intention to derogate from certain provisions of the ECHR in future armed conflicts, partly to avoid the constraints article 5 imposes on its ability to engage in the security detention of suspected insurgents.[74]

*Al-Waheed/Mohammed*'s effort to identify the minimum grounds and core procedural requirements for NIAC detention is typically viewed as a process of harmonizing two branches of international law. But it may also be understood

67 ibid. [66], [68(3)]

68 ibid. [68(3)].

69 ibid. [102]–[104].

70 ibid. [104]–[108]. Three Justices (Lords Mance, Hughes, and Neuberger) maintained that whether the claimants had an effective right to challenge their detention should have been remitted to the trial court. ibid. [223] (Lord Mance); ibid. [227] (Lord Hughes, joined by Lord Neuberger).

71 ibid. [234] (Lord Reed, dissenting, joined by Lord Kerr).

72 ibid. [274]–[276].

73 ibid. [315], [351].

74 Silvia Borelli, 'Litigating War? UK Courts and Military Operations Abroad' (*forthcoming*) (Manuscript on File with Author); Aurel Sari, 'The UK's New Derogation Policy for Armed Conflicts: Making a Success of the European Convention on Human Rights' (*Just Security*, 5 October 2016) < www.justsecurity.org/33370/uks-derogation-policy-armed-conflicts-making-success-european-convention-human-rights/> accessed 20 May 2017.

as an attempt to develop quasi-constitutional norms for NIAC detention. The next sections examine theories of quasi-constitutionality and describe how they provide a window into competing international legal frameworks for detention in armed conflict.

## III. Theories of quasi-constitutionality

Quasi-constitutionality is commonly described as an intermediate category between the twin poles of ordinary law and higher lawmaking.[75] William Eskridge and John Ferejohn have termed quasi-constitutional law that which is 'fundamental and trumping like constitutional law, but more tentative and susceptible to override or alternation by the legislature or determined judges and administrators.'[76] They identify several manifestations of quasi-constitutionality, including traditional common law adjudication, which provides background rules and policies;[77] substantive cannons of statutory construction, such as the rule of lenity in criminal law, which are animated by constitutional principles and policies;[78] and the enactment of super-statutes, defined as laws that tackle major social or economic issues and that significantly penetrate public normative and institutional culture.[79]

As other chapters in this book suggest, quasi-constitutionality defies easy categorization or precise definition. It nevertheless usefully serves as an umbrella term, with several key features. Those features include the subject matter covered; the potential to trump ordinary law; and a degree of entrenchment that makes repeal more difficult.[80] In its subject matter, a quasi-constitutional law has been described as addressing 'a fundamental feature of a constitutional system of government, such as a bill of rights';[81] possessing such 'normative significance' that it embodies or generates 'higher order constitutional principles that weave into a common law or constitutional fabric';[82] or 'substantially influenc[ing], directly or

75 William N. Eskridge, Jr. and John Ferejohn, 'Super-Statutes' (2001) 50 Duke LJ 1215, 1275.

76 Eskridge and Ferejohn (n 75) 1216–17.

77 ibid., 1218–19, 1264

78 ibid., 164–65. See also William N. Eskridge, Jr. and Philip P. Frickey, 'Quasi-Constitutional Law: Clear Statement Rules as Constitutional Lawmaking' (1992) 45 V and L Rev 593.

79 Eskridge and Ferejohn (n 75) 1215.

80 See e.g., Scott Stephenson, 'The Rise and Recognition of Quasi-Constitutional Law,' in Richard Albert and Joel I. Colón-Ríos, *Quasi-Constitutionality and Constitutional Statutes: Forms, Functions, Applications* (Taylor & Francis, 2019); Sergio Verdugo, 'Features of Quasi-Constitutional Legislation: A Comparative Theoretical Framework and the Chilean Example,' in *Quasi-Constitutionality and Constitutional Statutes.*; Rivka Weill, 'Exploring Constitutional Statutes in Common Law Systems,' In *Quasi-Constitutionality and Constitutional Statutes.*

81 Stephenson (n 80), 2.

82 David Jenkins, 'Common Law Declarations of Unconstitutionality' (2009) 7 Intl J Const L 183, 201.

indirectly what [state] institutions can and may do.'[83] A quasi-constitutional law's elevated status is demonstrated by some degree of supremacy over regular law. An ordinary statute, for example, would be presumed not to infringe on a constitutional norm. But while such statute could not trump a formal constitutional norm, it could trump a quasi-constitutional norm through an express statement or other indicia of deliberate legislative action.[84] Further, a quasi-constitutional law remains subject to repeal through the normal lawmaking process, thus distinguishing it from formal constitutional law and its unique amendment process.[85] A law's quasi-entrenched status might be demonstrated, for example, by its exemption from the doctrine of implied repeal.[86] The presence and interplay of these features distinguish quasi-constitutional law from ordinary lawmaking.

Jurists and scholars ordinarily discuss quasi-constitutionality within the field of domestic law. Quasi-constitutionality operates in states with written constitutions, such as the United States, and unwritten constitutions, such as the United Kingdom. International law is typically regarded as achieving quasi-constitutional status through its incorporation in domestic instruments. Sergio Verdugo, for example, describes the incorporation of the American Convention on Human Rights in the domestic law of Chile.[87] Eskridge and Ferejohn include within their conception of super-statutes legislation adopted by polities without written constitutions to protect important civil rights, such as the UK's Human Rights Act of 1998,[88] which incorporates the bulk of the ECHR into UK law.[89] Other countries, such as Canada, have similarly enacted super-statutes that incorporate human rights guarantees.[90] Such statutes illustrate one way that international law—and HRL in particular—can achieve quasi-constitutional status within domestic legal systems.

Yet, notions of quasi-constitutionality can also help illuminate developments in the field of international law itself. Quasi-constitutionality is a familiar feature of legal systems without a formal constitution.[91] International law, which similarly lacks a master constitution, has two principal sources: treaties and custom.[92]

83 Farrah Ahmed and Adam Perry, 'Constitutional Statutes' (2017) 37 OJLS 461.
84 Weill (n 80) 3.
85 ibid.
86 Adam Perry and Farrah Ahmed, 'The Quasi-Entrenchment of Constitutional Statutes' (2014) 73 CLJ 514.
87 Verdugo (n 80).
88 Eskridge and Ferejohn (n 75) 1265.
89 Human Rights Act 1998, c. 42.
90 Adam Perry, 'Constitutional and Quasi-Constitutional Statutes' (*Intl J. Const. L. Blog*, 24 April 2015) <www.iconnectblog.com/2015/04/constitutional-and-quasi-constitutional-statutes/> accessed 18 April 2017; M. David Lepofsky, 'Canadian Judicial Approach to Equality Rights: Freedom Ride or Roller Coaster' (Winter 1992) 55 L Contemp Probs 167, 172.
91 Stephenson (n 80) 3.
92 *Restatement (Third) of the Foreign Relations Law of the United States* (1987), s 102(1); Richard B. Lillich, 'Invoking International Human Rights Law in Domestic Courts' (1985) 54 U Cin L. Rev 367, 368.

Treaties are made by agreement among states, typically after lengthy and complex negotiations. Customary international law (CIL) develops gradually over time based on state practice and *opinio juris* (the belief by states that this practice stems from a legal obligation).[93] Since both treaties and CIL depend on consent, they have inherent limitations in responding to rapidly developing matters of global concern.

In the past, scholars have sought to enlarge the traditional categories of international law in response to these constraints.[94] Because of its relatively recent pedigree as a branch of international law and its close association with contemporary values, human rights have been an important focus of these efforts. Some scholars, for example, have advanced the idea of human rights as a separate and distinct category of CIL.[95] This CIL of human rights differs from traditional CIL because it does not look exclusively to past practice to identify customary patterns of state practice.[96] The CIL of human rights acknowledges more rapid developments in the *opinio juris* component of CIL as a way of accommodating and incorporating emerging norms.[97]

Theories of a CIL of human rights still, however, situate themselves within traditional categories of international law (*i.e.*, treaty and custom). Other approaches seeking greater flexibility more openly contemplate new sources of international legal authority. Louis Henkin, for example, previously described a new source of international law, which he termed 'non-conventional law,' that is dependent more on 'contemporary human values' and less on custom.[98] Professor Henkin characterized this law as '"constitutional" in a new sense' because it claims to bind states by reflecting fundamental human values rather than deriving its basis from consent.[99] Jonathan Charney similarly argued that the historically sluggish development of CIL makes it ill-equipped to address global problems and requires the creation of an international law less dependent on consensus as the basis for its authority.[100] Professor Charney thus advanced the notion of a universal or general international law outside the traditional confines of CIL.[101] Such universal or general international law, he argued, reflects the contemporary practice of using multilateral fora to address global problems of

93 Statute for the International Court of Justice, art. 38, 26 June 1945, 22 U.N.T.S 993; Antonio Cassese, *International Law* (2nd edn, OUP 2004) 157.

94 Christina Ochoa, 'Towards a Cosmopolitan Vision of International Law: Identifying and Defining CIL Post *Sosa v. Alvarez-Machain*' (2005) 74 U Cin L Rev 105, 117–18.

95 ibid., 117.

96 Richard Lillich, 'The Growing Importance of Customary International Human Rights Law' (1995–96) 25 Ga J Intl Comp L 1, 12–13.

97 Ochoa (n 94) 117.

98 Louis Henkin, 'Sibley Lecture, March 1994, Human Rights and State "Sovereignty"' (1995–96) 25 Ga J Intl Comp L 31, 38.

99 ibid.

100 Jonathan I. Charney, 'Universal International Law' (1993) 87 AJIL 529.

101 ibid., 529–30

mutual concern, such as environmental harm and terrorism—a practice that includes the identification of norms of general application.[102]

These more fluid approaches to international law formation echo attempts in domestic legal systems to develop a quasi-constitutional law that instantiates fundamental human values. As in domestic law, quasi-constitutional norms in international law may be identified by their matter, elevated status, and degree of entrenchment. Such norms, however, remain subject to override by the regular international law-making process (treaties and custom). A quasi-constitutional law of armed conflict detention could thus resemble what Henry Monaghan characterized, in the domestic sphere, as 'a substructure of substantive, procedural, and remedial rules' that are constitutionally inspired, but not compelled, and that are developed in common law fashion to help protect individual liberties.[103] The UK Supreme Court's decision in *Al-Waheed/Mohammed* represents a step in this direction. While putatively addressing the interaction of IHL and HRL, the majority sought to articulate a set of baseline norms and procedures designed to protect the fundamental right of personal liberty while accommodating state demands for greater detention power in armed conflict than under peacetime conditions.

## IV. Towards a quasi-constitutional law of armed conflict detention

The prevailing methodological approaches to NIAC detention described above seek to determine which body of international law (IHL and/or HRL) should apply and, assuming both remain applicable, resolve conflicts and identify convergences between them. These approaches, however, do not necessarily resolve underlying disputes over detention standards and procedures, but rather help determine the analytical starting point and accord priority to one branch of international law relative to the other. For example, adoption of a strong *lex specialis* model under which IHL preempts HRL does not resolve important questions because of IHL's lack of rules for NIAC detention. Rather, this model provides an interpretive foothold for creating a new law of NIAC detention based on analogy to IAC rules and notions of military necessity. Convergence models that accept the applicability of both IHL and HRL likewise provides only a point of departure. The precise content—who may be detained, under what circumstances, and by what procedures—is shaped not only by which body is accorded preference—IHL, with its more permissive approach to detention, or IHR, with its more stringent requirements—but also by where the balance between security and liberty is ultimately struck. Neither IHL nor HRL alone provides a definitive answer to the question of what constitutes arbitrary detention in armed conflict under convergence models.

102 ibid., 543–44.

103 Henry P. Monaghan, 'The Supreme Court, 1974 Term—Forward: Constitutional Common Law' (1975) 89 Harv L Rev 1, 9.

Convergence models, such as that adopted by the majority in *Al-Waheed/Mohammed*, instead resorts to gap-filling to determine baseline requirements for armed conflict detention, relying on and tailoring HRL to fill in the silences in IHL. Only the approach advocated by the dissent in *Al-Waheed/Mohammed*, which measures the lawfulness NIAC detention solely against HRL's standard of arbitrariness, avoids this type of tailoring. Yet, even under this approach, sufficient positive authorization—whether by a Security Council resolution or by individual state legislation—could confer on states the power to engage in security detention in a particular NIAC and thus require accommodation of peacetime HRL guarantees against arbitrary detention. Such authorization would make it necessary to determine the minimum grounds and procedures for wartime security detention based on the combined application of IHL and HRL. Alternatively, a state could seek to derogate from its HRL obligations regarding the deprivation of liberty in armed conflict as human rights treaties contemplate[104] and as the UK has proposed doing in future armed conflicts. Any such derogation would similarly still require a determination of minimally acceptable detention review procedures.

Norm conflict models focusing on the relationship between IHL and HRL, in short, do not fully capture how uncertainties surrounding the legal framework for NIAC detention are being resolved. Quasi-constitutionality offers another way of understanding this dynamic process. In particular, it helps explain the efforts by some jurists, states, and NGOs to develop a fundamental law of armed conflict detention—one that remains subject to override by traditional channels of international lawmaking, such as treaties, but that otherwise provides a floor for states engaging in the practice. Although framed as process of resolving conflicts between two branches of international law (IHL and HRL), these efforts seek ultimately to fill perceived gaps within the existing legal framework by balancing competing demands of liberty and security in the context of armed conflict.

Balancing is a staple of constitutional jurisprudence whether under the US model of weighing competing factors or under the proportionality analysis employed by constitutional courts in Europe and various common law systems, including Canada, South Africa, Israel, and the United Kingdom, to manage rights claims.[105] In the United States, balancing is central to the Supreme Court's due process jurisprudence,[106] and the Court has engaged in balancing to resolve the procedural rights of detainees in armed conflict.[107] Balancing is also at the core of proportionality analysis, which seeks to resolve disputes either

104 ICCPR (n 46) art. 4; ECHR (n 5) art. 15; American Convention on Human Rights: 'Pact of San Jose, Costa Rica' (22 November 1969) art. 27, 1144 UNTS 123, 153.

105 Jud Mathews and Alec Stone Sweet, 'All Things in Proportion? American Rights Review and the Problem of Balancing' (2011) 60 Emory LJ 797, 799.

106 See e.g. *Mathews v. Eldridge* [1976] 424 US 319.

107 *Hamdi v. Rumsfeld* [2004] 542 US 507, 533.

between two rights provisions or between a rights provision and a legitimate government interest.[108]

The UK Supreme Court's decision in *Al-Waheed/Mohammed* suggests several features of an emerging quasi-constitutional law of armed conflict detention. One feature is the adoption of interpretive principles to guide the threshold determination of whether there is a legal basis for detention that displaces or modifies the stricter default regime of HRL that operates outside armed conflict. The majority in *Al-Waheed/Mohammed* found sufficient legal authority for states to engage in security detain in NIAC based on Security Council resolutions conferring on states authority to take all necessary measures to establish peace and security in Iraq and Afghanistan. By contrast, the dissent would have required a more explicit conferral of detention power to trigger modification of HRL requirements in NIAC. This was also the approach of Justice Leggatt of the High Court of Justice, who had refused to find legal authority for UK forces to detain suspected insurgents in Afghanistan beyond 96 hours.[109] *Al-Waheed/Mohammed* thus surfaces a debate over whether courts should adopt what might be termed a quasi-constitutional principle of interpretation that requires more deliberate action by the Security Council or by individual states to trigger IHL's more permissive detention powers in NIAC and thereby modify the stricter protections of liberty under HRL.

Insisting on more deliberate action to authorize NIAC detention would serve a function similar to that served by cannons of construction in constitutional adjudication that demand greater clarity when states exercise powers that infringe on individual liberty and other fundamental rights. These cannons are meant to enhance democratic deliberation and accountability among political decisionmakers.[110] In the context of NIAC, a clear statement canon would require the Security Council or states to act more purposefully to displace or qualify HRL's more stringent requirements and thereby activate a less liberty-protective legal framework that allows for security detention. Conversely, inferring detention power in NIAC from the more generalized language of a Security Council resolution, as the UK Supreme Court majority did in *Al-Waheed/Mohammed*, facilitates the modification HRL and use of security detention in armed conflict.

Another feature of this emerging quasi-constitutional law of armed conflict detention is the identification of minimally acceptable grounds for internment. In IAC, IHL provides for detention based on a person's status (combatants may be detained under GC III based on their membership in an organized armed group that is a party to the conflict)[111] or risk level (civilians may be detained

108 Mathews and Stone Sweet (n 105) 802.

109 *Serdar Mohammed v. Ministry of Defence* [2014] EWHC 1369 (QB) [143]–[148].

110 Dan T. Coenen, 'A Constitution of Collaboration: Protecting Fundamental Values, with Second-Look Rules of Interbranch Dialogue' (2001) 42 Wm Mary L Rev 1575, 1699; Elizabeth Garrett, 'Legal Scholarship in the Age of Legislation' (1999) 34 Tulsa LJ 679, 685.

111 GC III (n 7) art. 4.

under GC IV where they pose an imperative threat to security).[112] HRL contains much narrower grounds for security detention, although the rigor of these restrictions may vary by treaty. (The ECHR, for example, imposes more stringent requirements than the ICCPR and does not provide for continued detention based on a security threat absent derogation). Most convergence approaches to NIAC seek to accommodate HRL requirements to permit IHL-based security detention, but also impose restrictions on its exercise by requiring that such detention be necessary for imperative reasons of security. In *Al-Waheed/Mohammed*, the UK Supreme Court determined that continued military detention in NIAC had to meet this baseline requirement. The majority opinions suggest a quasi-constitutional minimum ground for continued detention in armed conflict that requires that a person pose a sufficiently severe threat to security.[113] This minimum reflects a baseline standard derived from HRL's prohibition against arbitrary detention as modified by IHL and the circumstances of armed conflict.

The elaboration of procedural safeguards represents the clearest indication of an emerging quasi-constitutional law for armed conflict detention based on the interplay of IHL and HRL. The UK Supreme Court insisted that security detention in NIAC must satisfy minimum or core procedural requirements modeled on ECHR article 5, as adopted for armed conflict, to ensure that such detention is not imposed arbitrarily.[114] The minimum conditions for fairness, Lord Sumption explained in his majority opinion, include notice to an individual of the basis for his continued internment and the opportunity to mount an effective challenge to it, including by presenting his own evidence and participating in the detention review process.[115] While such review does not necessarily need to occur before a court, he explained, it must possess sufficient guarantees of impartiality and independence.[116] This floor might be said to provide a 'substructure' of quasi-constitutional procedures for armed conflict detention, to borrow Professor Monaghan's formulation, which delineates baseline protections of a fundamental right, while still remaining subject to modification or override by the treaty-making process.

## V. Conclusion

While transnational armed conflicts against non-state actors are increasingly common, there remains significant debate over the legal framework for the detention of individuals taken into custody, a legacy of IHL's traditional silence on detention in NIAC. The models competing to fill this void either assert the exclusion of one body of international law (IHR or HRL) at the expense of the other,

112 GC IV (n 8) arts. 42(1), 78.

113 This baseline would not alter a state's authority under GC III to engage in status-based detention of POWs in IAC.

114 *Al-Waheed/Mohammed* [2017] UKSC 2 [68(3)] (Lord Sumption); ibid. [167], [204] (Lord Mance).

115 ibid. [107] (Lord Sumption).

116 ibid. [104]–[105].

or seek to harmonize the two. While they reach divergent results, these models share an assumption that a conflict-of-laws analysis will determine the legal requirements for NIAC detention. This paper suggests that this analysis does not fully capture how underlying issues are being resolved. It describes how various approaches, particularly those stressing a convergence between IHL and HRL, seek to identify and entrench minimum safeguards against arbitrary detention in situations where the ordinary peacetime rules of HRL have been modified or displaced. The effort to articulate minimum requirements on such questions as the authority to detain, the scope of that authority, and the accompanying procedural safeguards exhibits several features that might be deemed quasi-constitutional.

More broadly, the paper suggests how notions of quasi-constitutionality typically applied in the domestic sphere can help inform international legal developments. It describes attempts to develop minimum standards and procedures under international law in areas that implicate fundamental rights, such as liberty. In such circumstances, relevant actors, including courts, governments, and civil society, seek to balance competing concerns and embed what might be viewed as a quasi-constitutional floor that remains subject to override by the ordinary lawmaking process.

# Part III
# Applications

# Quasi-constitutionality and the constitutional jigsaw puzzle

## Characteristics, directionality and purpose

*Dean R. Knight*[*]

The chapters in this part present a series of case studies about quasi-constitutionality, allowing us to explore the implications of this hybrid category transcending traditional or formal constitutional hierarchies. Drawn from across the world (Japan, South Africa, Egypt and Tunisia and the United States), the constitutional settings of each are diverse but each case study identifies some role – within the constitutional twilight – for ordinary rules or statutes to assume greater constitutional significance.

Rights-implementing legislation in South Africa is examined by Lael K. Weis.[1] She contends legislation required to be enacted by the (written) constitution to elaborate human rights is drenched in some of the constitutionality of the parent empowering provision. She illustrates this by reference to legislation enacted to provide for equality, freedom of information and administrative justice. Notably, Weis argues the rights-implementing legislation 'largely displaces and even supersedes the direct judicial enforcement of the right to which it gives effect'.[2] In other words, the sharper – mere legislative – expression of rights move into the foreground and their constitutional parent slides into the background.

Sofia Ranchordás focuses on the Affordable Care Act in the United States and its enduring character.[3] She argues this informal entrenchment – social, political, or economic factors militating against repeal or reform – points to the legislation having quasi-constitutional character.

James Fisher reflects on a rule of adjudication in Japan which enables the executive's interpretation of the constitution to be authoritative, despite a provision in the written constitution providing for judicial interpretative supremacy by way of constitutional review.[4] He contends this rule is quasi-

* Associate Professor, Faculty of Law; Co-Director, New Zealand Centre for Public Law; Victoria University of Wellington (dean.knight@vuw.ac.nz).

1 Lael Weis, 'Constitutionally Obligatory Legislation: A Case Study in Legal Constitutionalism'.

2 Weis, at Ibid., 206.

3 Sofia Ranchordás, 'Quasi- Constitutionalism and Informal Legislative Entrenchment: The Case of the Affordable Care Act'.

4 James Fisher, 'The Quasi-Constitutionality of Non-Statutory Law: Executive Constitutional Interpretation in Japan'.

constitutional or, as he would prefer to characterise it, the rule forms part of Japan's 'material' constitution, even though it is not included in the 'mastertext' (written) constitution.[5] The corollary of this argument is that the allied provisions in the written constitution providing for judicial supremacy in this context must, accordingly, lose their constitutional character, effectively trumped by the rule of adjudication dictating otherwise.

The protection of human rights during constitutional design and development is considered by Franciska Coleman.[6] Here, quasi-constitutionality is presented as a means to mediate conflict and disagreement during the process of constitution making – in Egypt and Tunisia. Coleman promotes the virtue of enacting human rights protection through softer form and process – 'quasi-entrenched living statues' – than the traditional incorporation of such protections in a constitution. This less ambitious constitutionalisation of rights in new and emerging democracies avoids, she suggests, some of the conflict associated with mediating contested rights matters. Importantly, this enables more attentiveness towards the creation of political structures and carving out a more meaningful role for minorities within civic activity and institutions. In making this claim, comparisons are drawn with the United States civil rights movement.

In reflecting on this suite of case studies, we might think about their contribution to the quasi-constitutionality project in terms of three different dimensions: *characteristics*, *directionality* and *purpose*.

First, we can identify the significant *characteristics* relied on by each to justify the claim to the special status of quasi-constitutionality. In the case of the quasi-constitutionality of Japan's adjudicative rule prioritising the executive's interpretation of the constitution, Fisher latches onto the practical supremacy of the rule in order to justify its quasi-constitutionality. It forms part of the material constitution because legal actors treat it as such. In other words, as he argues, the analysis is a sociological – not a legal – one.[7] Thus, status achieved by institutional practice and acquiescence because a key indicator of a rules constitutional character. Here, too, it is notable that the rule in question is non-statutory; it is an adjudicative rule or practice which has assumed currency analogous to a rule found in a constitutional instrument. It should not surprise us that such a rule of adjudication might rise to some constitutional status. But Fisher argues the non-statutory character might challenge some of the putative indicia often slated for establishing quasi-constitutionality; for example, it is inapt to examine the process of enactment in the cases of adjudicative rules which are not 'specifically and consciously *enacted* at all'.[8] I suspect this claim is a little exaggerated, given it is still possible to reflect on the nature of process by which the legal norm is created and adopted, even if

5 Fisher, at 262.

6 Franciska Coleman, 'Quasi-Entrenched Living Statutes: Creating a Multicultural Rights Regime'.

7 Fisher (n 2) 265.

8 Ibid.

not through traditional enactment. In any event, though, his point about the necessary attentiveness to context and bespoke lines of enquiry remains a sage one. While Fisher seeks to deflect the enquiry away from a rule's subject matter, I doubt he is entirely successful in doing so. Matters of subject matter – while not necessarily determinative – still *must* influence the characterisation of quasi-constitutionality. Indeed, Fisher's definition of the material constitution, viz 'a complex body of legal rules that define and regulate public power',[9] necessarily alludes to some loose qualifying subject matter. So too does the anchoring of the analysis on the fact that quasi-constitutional rules might resemble or substitute for rules within the formal written constitution, which necessarily invites an analogue with the types of rules so provided there.

Turning to human rights implementing statutes in South Africa, Weis also downplays the focus on subject matter per se; or, rather, treats it as a given. Instead, she showcases the importance of constitutional pedigree: 'whether [the statute] originates from, or is otherwise traceable to, the written constitution'.[10] Adopting a legal constitutionalist perspective, she argues attention to source and form is relevant and, in this case, controlling. In other words, the quasi-constitutionality comes from the express constitutional imprimatur: a direction that legislation subsequently be enacted to address certain matters. But even with this focus on pedigree or source, this perspective is not entirely subject matter agnostic. In fact, subject matter is inevitably a feature of such analysis, albeit not for normative purposes; constitutionally obligatory legislation must necessarily reflect the subject matter of its empowering constitutional parent. Thus, indirectly, quasi-constitutionality reflects choices made about what matters should be incorporated in a written, mastertext constitution. But Weis rightly points to the inapplicability of a more free-floating, normative assessment of constitutionality, in terms of subject matter or function, driven by political constitutionalism. Such a perspective is inapt to deal with the deferred delegation and sequencing of matters mandated by the constitution itself; the legislative output under such increasingly common empowering provision must necessarily be cloaked by some of the parent's constitutional character.

In her case study of the Affordable Care Act in the United States, Ranchordás bases her claim for quasi-constitutionality on the legislation's durability and informal or practical entrenchment. Thus, the key characteristic is 'their long-lasting nature and the democratic acceptance'.[11] Their durability or persistence over time might be implicitly tied to a nation's 'core values'; the legislative consecration of these values, she argues, allows some statutes 'to stand up well to societal, political, judicial, and economic changes'.[12] Drawing on the idea of a 'super-statute', that is,

9 Ibid., 262.
10 Weis (n 3) 205.
11 Ranchordás (n 5) 225.
12 Ibid.

a law that seeks to 'establish a new normative or institutional framework and over time "sticks" in the public culture having a broad effect on the law',[13] Ranchordás argues the persistence of the Affordable Care Act elevates its status and is suggestive of quasi-constitutionality. Endurance, though, cannot be the sole, determinative factor in the assessment of quasi-constitutionality, as Ranchordás herself concedes. Her analysis presupposes that the legislation *is* expressive of some core values – perhaps the 'preservation of fundamental rights and principles'.[14] So, while some statutes might, over time, become practically entrenched, something more might be needed before they 'earn' their constitutional credentials.

Constitution-making in Egypt and Tunisia is explored from a different perspective by Coleman, as she assumes the quasi-constitutionality of the legislative protection of human rights and directs her attention to the virtue of such an approach as a means of mediating conflict in constitution-making in emerging democracies. Thus, we might think of Coleman's approach in terms of the constitutionality of both process and, implicitly, subject matter. Looking at the phenomenon with a broad lens, the development of legal norms through constitution-making process expresses a degree of quasi-constitutionality – even if those norms are not ultimately enacted in the formal, written constitution. And the quasi-constitutional character also comes from the subject matter: fundamental human rights protections. But departures from the traditional ideal-type of fully constitutionalised rights protection unlock some potential to avoid intractable conflict in constitutional building in pluralistic societies: Coleman instances minority empowering procedures, incorporation of enforcement restrictions and delayed entrenchment as three especially helpful features. She argues that delivery of human rights protections with these features in play does not undercut the constitutional character of the protections and provide useful safety release valves to avoid conflict which risks ruining any constitutional genesis. Faith is instead placed on animating a 'living' constitution – protection of rights through unentrenched legislation and political constitutionalism catalysed through intergenerational dialogue.

Secondly, we might reflect on the *directionality*; in other words, whether the quasi-constitutional status is claimed by elevating norms from their ordinary status or by dilution of otherwise constitutional norms. Fisher's case study largely focuses on elevation of a rule of adjudication (bureaucratic interpretative supremacy) to constitutional status. However, he also acknowledges the diminution of counterpart formal constitutional norms (legal constitutionalism and strong judicial review) – albeit the latter lessening of force is slated as constitutional redundancy, rather than lessening of status to some intermediate quasi-constitutional status. Weis' case study of constitutionally obligatory legislation is capable of being seen from either perspective. On the one hand, we might think about the constitutionally-mandated direction to enact legislation addressing

13 Ibid., 228.
14 Ibid., 239.

certain matters as a form of delegated constitution-making. That is, matters ordinarily resident in the constitution are enacted outside the constitution but retain some of the constitutional character. On the other hand, we could view such legislation as the elevation in status of ordinary legislation – catalysed by the constitutional reference anticipating its enactment. Ranchordás' case study of the Affordable Care Act is an exemplar of elevation of status: ordinary legislation elevated in status due to its apparent immutability. Coleman's case study of quasi-entrenched living statutes, and their potential in constitution-making in the Arab Spring, emphasises the virtue of carving out contested topics from a formal, written constitution and deferring work on these topics until later. Again, this connotes downplaying the formal status of matters ordinarily featuring in a mastertext constitution, rather than the elevation of otherwise ordinary statutes to some exalted status (although this might be another instance of where the directionality can be read in different ways).

Finally, we might reflect on the *purpose* of the quasi-constitutionality label. What is the effect – legal, constitutional or otherwise – of branding certain rules quasi-constitutional? Here, our case studies are pretty coy, focusing more on the project of identifying quasi-constitutionality rather than explaining what difference, if any, it leads to from an instrumental perspective. That is understandable if, as it may be, the quasi-constitutionality project is essentially an observational or descriptive endeavour. In other words, if our main task is to comprehensively describe a nation's 'constitution' – understood in a broad, non-formal sense – then each of these case studies provide us with pieces that form part of that jigsaw puzzle. Fisher is one, for example, who is candid about the fact that quasi-constitutionality's ultimate quest is to find the 'material' constitution.[15]

I am confident that there is real value in being attentive to the constitutional penumbra and gathering the pieces of each nation's constitutional puzzle, whether they be an important rule about whose constitutional interpretation prevails, instruments which protect rights from state and other attack, other long-standing legislation which is expressive of a nation's values. Or whatever. And the value of the quasi-constitutionality label is to destabilise the hegemony of written constitutions and their sacred text.

But, while this broader lens is undoubtedly important, the quasi-constitutional endeavour risks being trite, especially if it is confined to this observational dimension. And especially trite for those, like me, who come from a nation lacking a complete, supreme constitution. Because it is then simply the re-expression of thinking about a generous constitutional rule-of-recognition. Absent a complete written text, the components of the constitution are expressed generally and broadly. As Bolingbroke wrote in 1733, the constitution is the 'assemblage of laws, institutions and customs, derived from certain fixed principles of reason, directed to certain fixed objects of public good, that compose the general system, according to which the community hath agreed to be

15 Fisher (n 1) 263.

governed'.[16] Or, as Matthew Palmer recently proposed, 'a rule should be regarded as constitutional if it plays a significant role in influencing the generic exercise of public power – whether through structures, processes, principles, rules, conventions or even culture'.[17] We can see echoes of these definitions in the case studies in this Part.

I repeat, though, there is value in using this broad lens to complete the constitutional jigsaw puzzle, especially for the expressive, educational or sociological functions of a constitution. However, there might be dangers in approaching this task like a constitutional magpie, seizing on instruments which attract our attention on an ad hoc basis. If our endeavour is about completeness, regardless of form, then it might be helpful to adopt a robust framework for that taxonomy. Here, I am drawn to Matthew Palmer's systemic approach.[18] He partners his broad rule-of-recognition with conceptual categories which encourage comprehensive collection of constitutional rules: the instruments of each branch of government; the interpretations of the instruments of each branch of government; the common law, including the common law of Parliament; and constitutional conventions. Our search for (quasi-)constitutionality should be thorough across those categories.

I suspect, though, the quasi-constitutionality project has more ambition. That is, it is expected that the application of the brand is meant to have some normative force, to the extent that treating something as (quasi-)constitutional triggers different legal or constitutional treatment.[19] The context of these case studies mean that dimension is not deeply explored and the possibilities are only alluded to. A couple of the case studies hint at the idea that quasi-constitutional status enables rules that are not formally constitutional to overshadow constitutional ones, animated by deference towards the administration. Witness the rule of adjudication about interpretative supremacy in Japan effectively supplanting the equivalent formal rules in the constitution. Or the rights-implementing legislation effectively taking over from the generalised commitment in the constitution, if only due to the greater specificity and richer elaboration of rights. Similarly legislative endurance is identified as a possible feature, which is suggestive of the quasi-constitutional instrument being more difficult to repeal or amend. The difficulty with these observations is that they are generally self-fulfilling – because these consequences are the very characteristics on which the quasi-constitutional character is claimed!

16 Henry Bolingbroke, *A Dissertation upon Parties* (1733), referred to in AW Bradley and KD Ewing, *Constitutional and Administrative Law* (14th ed., Pearson Longman, New York, 2007) at 4.

17 Matthew SR Palmer, 'What Is New Zealand's Constitution and Who Interprets It? Constitutional Realism and the Importance of Public Office- Holders' (2006) 17 PLR 133 at 137.

18 Palmer, at 138.

19 For example, modification of the doctrine of implied repeal is one consequence often pointed to: *Thoburn v Sunderland City Council* [2003] QB 151.

Despite these quibbles, the quasi-constitutionality project offers a different way of reflecting on a nation's constitutional fabric. And that different lens might cause us to rethink our constitutional hierarchy, whether by blurring the distinction between the ordinary and the constitutional or by admitting a previously unspoken constitutional hierarchy. Ultimately, the rich case studies that follow provide concrete examples which support this search for nuance.

* * *

# 9 Constitutionally obligatory legislation

## A case study in legal constitutionalism

*Lael K. Weis*

MELBOURNE LAW SCHOOL

## 1. Introduction

In recent years there has been increasing interest in the study of the boundary space between constitutional law and legislation from scholars working within the tradition of legal constitutionalism. In navigating this conceptual space, it makes sense to look to political constitutionalism for resources. Interrogating and negotiating the boundaries between constitutional law and legislation is part and parcel of political constitutionalism: within that tradition all constitutional law is (and always has been) at the same time legislation. By contrast, the same task presents new challenges for the tradition of legal constitutionalism. Entertaining the possibility that certain legislation has constitutional status of some kind appears to require reimagining the supremacy that constitutional law is thought to have over legislation. Indeed, it appears to require rethinking what makes constitutional law 'constitutional'—a matter often taken for granted in the presence of an entrenched, master text ('written') constitution.

The study of the conceptual space explored in this collection thus invites a fruitful exchange between legal and political constitutionalism. However, there are important limitations to this cross-fertilization, which arise from the different identifiers that each tradition has standardly used to demarcate constitutional law from non-constitutional law: *subject-matter* or *function* for political constitutionalism, and *pedigree* for legal constitutionalism. For instance, while the term 'quasi-constitutional' may be apt when deployed within the domain of legal constitutionalism to describe legislation that concerns constitutional subject matters or that performs constitutional functions, the term seems wholly inappropriate to political constitutionalism. Within the domain of political constitutionalism, legislation of this kind *is* constitutional law. To deploy the qualifier 'quasi-' is simply to misunderstand political constitutionalism, or even to deny its possibility.

Similarly, looking to political constitutionalism for guidance also has limitations for an understanding of the conceptual space between constitutional law and legislation within legal constitutionalism. In particular, it may result in overlooking phenomena within this conceptual space that are unique to legal constitutionalism, and the significance of which can only be understood in terms of a legal constitutionalist perspective: where constitutional law is identified primarily on the basis of its 'pedigree' (i.e., whether it originates from, or is otherwise traceable to, the written constitution) rather than by its subject matter or its function.

This chapter offers a case study in legal constitutionalism that concerns a phenomenon of this kind: 'constitutionally obligatory legislation.' I use this term to refer to legislation that a constitution requires the legislature to enact to give effect to constitutional rights and obligations. The notion that legislation may be enacted to give effect to constitutional rights—whether in order to complement, supplement or even supersede direct judicial enforcement of the right—is a familiar even if under-theorized idea. In recent years, however, constitutional rights provisions have increasingly been drafted in ways that not only contemplate legislation rather than direct judicial enforcement as the primary means of implementation, but that *require* the enactment of rights-implementing legislation. Constitutionally obligatory legislation is distinct in this respect from legislation that gives effect to fundamental social values in the absence of a constitutional obligation requiring its enactment.

This chapter provides a single-jurisdiction study examining constitutionally obligatory legislation in South Africa. Its objective is twofold: to identify constitutionally obligatory legislation as a distinctive category of rights-implementing legislation, and to demonstrate the need for a perspective *within* legal constitutionalism that takes seriously the possibility that such legislation has constitutional status of some kind in virtue of serving as an independent source of constitutional legal norms. Constitutionally obligatory legislation complicates the paradigmatic understanding of the relationship between constitutional law and legislation in the legal constitutionalist tradition. For reasons that we shall see, however, it does so in a way that is largely consistent with the thesis that pedigree distinguishes constitutional law from ordinary legislation. In this respect, constitutionally obligatory legislation is a phenomenon that must be approached by occupying a legal constitutionalist perspective: not only because it represents a development in written constitutions, but because appreciating its significance requires analytical tools only offered by a legal constitutionalist frame.

My focus on South Africa is strategic. Within the global constitutional law literature, South Africa is most commonly invoked as a case for examining the direct judicial enforcement of social rights. It is a jurisdiction that is thought to provide fertile ground for issues concerning the justiciability of social rights and the forms of judicial review appropriate to them. Scholarly focus on this set of issues has overshadowed issues concerning constitutionally obligatory legislation. Although it is acknowledged that legislation is often the most effective and most desirable means of realizing social rights, the potential role of constitutionally obligatory legislation as an independent source of fundamental values and legal norms has yet to be appreciated. This oversight has resulted in an inadequate and incomplete picture of how social values are given constitutional effect.

I begin by briefly surveying three areas of South African constitutional law where it is well-established and widely accepted that constitutionally obligatory legislation largely displaces and even supersedes the direct judicial enforcement of the right to which it gives effect. These areas concern familiar political and civil rights: equality (Section 9), access to information (Section 32), and just administrative action (Section 33). I then raise the question of whether such legislation can or should be viewed as having constitutional status in virtue of its potential role as a source of fundamental values and legal norms, despite the fact that those values and norms are *legislatively*-defined. In the South African context, this role is made possible by a set of interpretive practices where courts give an extraordinary degree of deference to legislative determinations regarding the manner of giving effect to constitutional rights and obligations.

Finally, I extend this analysis to the context of social rights. Here I examine environmental rights and obligations under Section 24 of the Constitution. The Section 24 context demonstrates the importance of developing a legal constitutionalist perspective that identifies constitutionally obligatory legislation as a special category of legislation, and that contemplates the possibility that such legislation has constitutional status of some kind. In particular, examining this area helps isolate the difficulties that must be addressed address in order for this to remain a legal constitutionalist perspective, and at the same time demonstrates why constitutional theories of social rights and obligations are incomplete without such a perspective.

## 2. Constitutionally obligatory legislation in South Africa

The 1996 Constitution of South Africa is celebrated for its transformative, social justice-oriented character. Its ambition to rectify past injustices and establish a new social ordering grounded in fundamental principles of human dignity and equality is reflected in a highly progressive Bill of Rights. The constitutional entrenchment of social rights in particular has attracted a great deal of international attention. An important formal feature of these provisions is that many are drafted in ways that not only expressly contemplate legislation as the principal means of giving effect to social rights, but that *require* the enactment of rights-implementing legislation. For instance, many couple a right to the provision of a particular basic good (e.g., housing, health care, food, water, and social security) with a separate clause providing that: '[t]he state *must take* reasonable legislative and other measures, within its available resources, to achieve the progressive realisation' of the right in question.[1]

In making sense of the significance that these ambitious social rights provisions have for our evolving understanding of constitutionalism, then, one plausible set of scholarly inquiries might concern the role of constitutionally obligatory legislation in giving effect to fundamental values and transforming outdated values and

1 Constitution of the Republic of South Africa 1996 s 26, s 27 (emphasis added).

legal norms in existing bodies of law. To date, however, issues concerning the justiciability of and forms of judicial review appropriate to social rights have dominated the literature. By contrast, issues concerning the potential role of constitutionally obligatory legislation as an independent source of constitutional legal norms, and the appropriate role of the judiciary in relation such legislation and the constitutional obligations that it gives effect to, are topics that have yet to receive examination.

In order to motivate the case for a perspective that identifies constitutionally obligatory legislation as a distinctive category or kind and that pursues these alternative lines of inquiry, I begin by examining some areas of South African constitutional law where it is well-established that such legislation plays the predominant role in defining fundamental values and legal norms, and that direct judicial enforcement of the corresponding constitutional right plays very little role at all. Of particular interest are the right to equality (Section 9), the right to access to information (Section 32), and the right to just administrative action (Section 33).

Starting with the right to equality, the non-discrimination clause, Section 9(4), provides that '[n]o person may unfairly discriminate directly or indirectly against anyone' on a list of specified grounds, and then further provides that '[n]ational legislation *must be enacted* to prevent or prohibit unfair discrimination.' Sections 32 and 33 have a similar structure: each first sets out the subject matter of the constitutional right in question, and then sets out state obligations to enact right-implementing legislation. Section 32 provides that:

(1) Everyone has the right of access to—

  (a) any information held by the state; and
  (b) any information that is held by another person and that is required for the exercise or protection of any rights.

(2) National legislation must be enacted to give effect to this right, and may provide for reasonable measures to alleviate the administrative and financial burden on the state.

Section 33 provides that:

(1) Everyone has the right to administrative action that is lawful, reasonable and procedurally fair.
(2) Everyone whose rights have been adversely affected by administrative action has the right to be given written reasons.
(3) National legislation must be enacted to give effect to these rights, and must—

  (a) provide for the review of administrative action by a court or, where appropriate, an independent and impartial tribunal;
  (b) impose a duty on the state to give effect to the rights in subsections (1) and (2); and

(c) promote an efficient administration.

Item 23 of Schedule 6, which concerns transitional arrangements for the new Constitution, further provides that the legislation contemplated in these three sections '*must be enacted* within three years of the date on which the new Constitution took effect' (i.e. by 3 February 2000).[2]

The formal design of each provision reflects considerations of institutional competency. All three areas present complex policy issues that require making contestable determinations about values, priorities, and resource-allocation. As such, it is arguably more plausible and more desirable to allocate the primary institutional responsibility for implementation to the political branches. Notably, the versions of each provision contained in the Interim Constitution *did not* include an obligation to enact right-implementing legislation. The inclusion of an obligation to legislate in the final Constitution could be viewed as responsive to concerns about the limitations of constitutional rights litigation as a means of giving effect to the rights in question: concerns that might otherwise be raised as objections to constitutional entrenchment.[3]

In all three contexts, Parliament has responded to its constitutional obligation by enacting detailed legislation: the *Promotion of Equality and Prevention of Unfair Discrimination Act 2000* ('Equality Act'),[4] the *Promotion of Access to Information Act 2000* ('PAIA'),[5] and the *Promotion of Administrative Justice Act 2000* ('PAJA').[6] The express purpose of all three Acts is to fulfil the state's obligation to enact legislation that gives effect to the right in question.[7] Each

2 In the case of Sections 32 and 33 there is an additional set of transitional arrangements, which provide that the constitutional description of the right in question be suspended, and another description substituted in its place, '[u]ntil the legislation envisaged in Sections 32(2) and 33-(3) … is enacted'. It is further provided that if the relevant legislation is not enacted within the required timeframe, the constitutional obligation to enact such legislation lapses: schedule 6, item 23(3). These transitional arrangements thus contemplate direct judicial enforcement of these rights almost exclusively by way of transition, or in the event that Parliament fails to fulfil its constitutional obligation in a timely manner.

3 In the case of the parallel right to access information in the Interim Constitution, Section 23, the constitutional obligation to enact legislation to give effect to the right is linked to a widening in the scope of the right. Section 23 provided that:

> Every person shall have the right of access to all information held by the state or any of its organs at any level of government *in so far as such information is required for the exercise or protection of any of his or her rights.*

By contrast, Section 32 does not contain this qualifying language, and extends the right to information held by private persons.

4 Act 4 of 2000.

5 Act 2 of 2000.

6 Act 3 of 2000.

7 For instance, the Equality Act states that its objects are 'to enact legislation required by Section 9 of the Constitution' and 'to give effect' to the rights contained therein: Section 2(a), 2(b).

Act defines the scope and content of the right and prescribes the mechanisms for its realization, including enforcement procedures and remedies.

Since enactment of the Equality Act, PAIA, and PAJA, the corresponding constitutional rights have 'retreat[ed] to a background role.'[8] These rights continue to 'exist independently of the statute that gives effect to them', but the role of courts in giving effect to them is predominantly an exercise in applying *legislatively-defined* values and legal norms rather than an exercise in constitutional interpretation that gives them independent, judicially-defined content. Direct judicial enforcement is still possible but highly 'exceptional',[9] and in all three contexts there are 'few remaining instances in which the constitutional right may be directly invoked in litigation.'[10] Thus, although traceable to the text of the constitution, it can be said that these rights have a legislative basis.[11]

To understand why this is so, constitutionally obligatory legislation must be viewed in the context of two important interpretive principles in South African constitutional law: the 'principle of avoidance', and the 'principle of subsidiarity'. Both interpretive principles are reflected in the wider constitutional principle that South Africa has 'only one system of law ... shaped by the Constitution'.[12] Taken together, they favour the *indirect* application of constitutional rights over direct judicial enforcement: which is to say, rights are given effect through the application of ordinary law, interpreted to 'promote the spirit, purport and objects of the Bill of Rights'.[13] The somewhat misleadingly named principle of avoidance requires both that legislation be interpreted in a manner that is compatible with constitutional rights (where it is possible to do so), and that the interpretation that *best* advances the spirit, purport, and object of the Bill of Rights be adopted (in circumstances where multiple, rights-compatible interpretations are available).[14] The principle of subsidiarity—also somewhat misleadingly named[15]—goes further. It requires that the direct judicial enforcement of constitutional rights be invoked only as a last resort: whenever

8 Cora Hoexter, 'Just Administrative Action', in Iain Currie & Johan de Waal eds., *The Bill of Rights Handbook* (6th ed., Juta 2015) 649 (discussing the PAJA). See also Currie & de Waal, ibid., 695–96 (discussing the PAIA).

9 Hoexter, ibid., 649, Currie & de Waal, ibid., 245.

10 Currie & de Waal, ibid., 695 (on the PAIA).

11 Hoexter (n 8) 646 (on the PAJA); Currie & de Waal, ibid., 244–245 (on the Equality Act), 695 (on the PAIA).

12 *Pharmaceutical Manufacturers Association of SA: In re Ex parte President of the Republic of South Africa* 2000 (2) SA 674 (CC) [44]. As commentators have noted, this principle effectively erodes the distinction between the indirect and direct application of rights.

13 The interpretive mandate in s 39(2) of the Constitution.

14 *Wary Holdings (Pty) Ltd v Stalwo (Pty) Ltd* 2009 (1) SA 337 (CC) [46], [84] and [107]. Currie & de Waal, 57–58.

15 Insofar as the label suggests that it pertains to the distribution of powers and responsibilities between different levels of government.

possible, ordinary law is applied to resolve the dispute.[16] Although distinct, these two principles are both commonly classified as aspects of a 'subsidiarity' approach.[17] In what follows, I shall use the term 'subsidiarity approach' to refer to both principles in the aggregate, as they apply specifically to legislation.

An important consequence of the subsidiarity approach is that, where enacted, right-implementing legislation—and *not* direct judicial enforcement—is the principal means of giving effect to constitutional rights. This is so even where the right-implementing legislation is *non*-obligatory: i.e., where the right provision does not require the enactment of implementing legislation. Application of the subsidiarity approach to non-obligatory legislation is consistent with the normative basis for the interpretive principles, which is institutional: they reflect the view that Parliament plays 'an indispensible role in fulfilling constitutional rights',[18] and in many cases is 'better equipped to ascertain the needs of society and to respond to those needs' than the judiciary.[19]

Nevertheless, legislative power to define fundamental values and the legal norms that they require through right-implementing legislation is not unlimited. That power is constrained by the independent, constitutional content of the right in question, and the corresponding obligations that it imposes on the state. These are matters of constitutional interpretation ultimately determined by the Constitutional Court. The interpretive process thus proceeds in a 'top-down' direction. Right-implementing legislation is 'read down' in light of the judicially-determined constitutional content of the substantive obligation that the constitutional obligation to enact legislation 'attaches' to.

In the context of constitutionally obligatory legislation, however, a question arises about whether there are circumstances where this interpretive process is effectively reversed. Such legislation receives special solicitude in virtue of its status *as* constitutionally obligatory. As the authors of the leading text on the Bill of Rights remark, 'courts must assume that the ... Act is consistent with the Constitution and claims that ... rights have been infringed must be decided in terms of [its] substantive provisions'.[20] Moreover, although the Act can be challenged on the basis that it is constitutionally invalid, it nevertheless 'must be treated as the principal legal instrument defining and delineating the scope and content of the right ... , establishing the mechanisms and procedures for its enforcement and limiting the right where necessary.'[21] This highly deferential approach gives normative weight to the fact that, as a matter of formal constitutional design, rights provisions that mandate the enactment of implementing

16 See Currie & de Waal, (n 8) 56–57, 68–70.

17 See *My Vote Counts NPC v Speaker of the National Assembly and Others* 2016 (1) SA 132 (CC) (Cameron J) [44]–[66]; Andre J van der Walt 'Normative pluralism and anarchy: Reflections on the 2007 term' (2008) 1 Const Ct Rev 77, 99 (n 99).

18 *My Vote Counts* (n 17) (Cameron J) [62].

19 Currie & de Waal, (n 8) 69.

20 Ibid., 244–245 (discussing the Equality Act).

21 Ibid., 695 (discussing the PAIA).

legislation allocate the primary institutional responsibility for giving effect to social values to the political branches.

In light of its special status, then, might there be circumstances where application of the subsidiarity approach to constitutionally obligatory legislation results in a 'bottom up' approach to interpretation? In other words, might courts—in the name of subsidiarity principles—use legislatively-defined fundamental values and legal norms to define the constitutional rights and obligations that the legislation purports to give effect to? Strictly speaking, such an approach is impermissible. It is inconsistent with the basic legal constitutionalist thesis that constitutional law is fundamental law.[22] Nevertheless, as I shall suggest in the following sections, there is reason to think that this interpretive process may well describe the application of the subsidiarity approach to constitutionally obligatory legislation in at least some circumstances. This possibility is presented by the 2015 Constitutional Court decision in *My Vote Counts*.

## 3. Constitutionally obligatory legislation as a source of constitutional legal norms

The principle that South Africa has 'only one system of law ... shaped by the Constitution' necessarily blurs the operational boundaries between legislation and constitutional law.[23] However, embedded in this principle is the foundational proposition that the Constitution 'is the supreme law', meaning that 'all law ... derives its force from the Constitution and is subject to constitutional control'.[24] As a matter of constitutional principle, then, constitutionally entrenched rights and obligations have independent, judicially-determined constitutional content. That content limits legislative power to define the scope and content of rights, their method of implementation, and remedies for their breach via legislation. Parliament cannot therefore simply define constitutional rights however it sees fit. Nevertheless, the Constitutional Court's recent application of the subsidiarity approach in *My Vote Counts* casts some doubt on the degree to which the *substantive* constitutional obligation that corresponds to a right can or does function as a meaningful limitation on legislative power to define fundamental values and legal norms where Parliament is also under a constitutional obligation to enact right-implementing legislation to fulfil that substantive obligation.

In that case, a majority of the Constitutional Court dismissed an application to directly enforce Parliament's obligation to enact right-implementing legislation pursuant to Section 32, the informational right. That right derives part of its content from other rights, guaranteeing 'a right to access ... any information that is held by another person *and that is required for the exercise or protection*

22 See Currie & de Waal, ibid., 60 (observing that Section 39(2) is not meant to have any bearing on Constitutional interpretation).
23 *Pharmaceutical Manufacturers Association* (n 12) [44].
24 Ibid.

*of any rights*.'[25] It was alleged that the right to vote, Section 19(3), requires access to information about the private funding of political parties: something that was not provided for under PAIA, or under other legislation. It was not, however, alleged that PAIA was constitutionally invalid: only that the Act was *insufficient* to fulfil Parliament's substantive obligations under Section 32, meaning that Parliament must either amend PAIA to extend its coverage or else enact other right-implementing legislation.

The application was rejected on subsidiarity grounds. The majority refused to consider the content of Parliament's substantive constitutional obligation, holding that the applicant's proper recourse was to challenge the constitutional validity of PAIA in the High Court.[26] The subsidiarity principle was said to leave no conceptual space for an independent question about whether an Act, once deemed to be constitutionally obligatory legislation, *fulfils* the substantive constitutional obligation that it was enacted to give effect to: *either* the Act must be relied upon to give effect to the right, *or else* the Act must be challenged as constitutionally invalid.[27] Permitting the direct enforcement of the substantive obligation once right-implementing legislation has been enacted, the majority reasoned, would pay inadequate respect to Parliament: opening the floodgates of litigation, and giving rise to '*ad hoc* and possibly nit-picking individualised claims' complaining about Parliament's method of implementation.[28]

This analysis is indicative of an approach to constitutionally obligatory legislation that goes well beyond what is standardly contemplated by subsidiarity. This approach appears to collapse Parliament's obligation to enact legislation to

25 Section 32(1)(b) (emphasis added).

26 At [122]. Following the Constitutional Court's decision, a frontal challenge to PAIA was brought in the Western Cape High Court (Cape Town). In September 2017, the High Court found PAIA invalid to the extent that it fails to provide for the disclosure of information about private funding of political parties, which was found to be reasonably required to exercise the right to vote: *My Vote Counts NPC v President of the Republic of South Africa* 2017 (6) SA 501 (WCC). The High Court's declaration of invalidity was suspended for an 18-month period to give Parliament the opportunity to respond. Just prior to the High Court's judgment, Parliament introduced a Bill addressing the private funding of political parties which includes reporting requirements: Parliament of South Africa, 'Draft Political Party Funding Bill, 2017', Government Gazette vol 627, no 41125 (19 September 2017). This legislation is still pending (at the time of writing, the Bill has been adopted by Parliament but is awaiting Presidential assent). In June 2018, the Constitutional Court affirmed the High Court's judgment: *My Vote Counts NPC v Minister of Justice and Correctional Services and Another* (CCT249/17) [2018] ZACC 17 (21 June 2018). In doing so, the Court did not take the opportunity to clarify or address concerns about the application of subsidiarity principles.

27 To be fair, the Majority alludes to a third possibility, at 75 [127], which is the possibility briefly mentioned by Van der Walt: namely, that direct application is possible in case where a 'special constitutional remedy' is called for because 'indirect protection … proves impossible for some reason': (n 17) 126. However, if *My Vote Counts* is not such a case, it is difficult to imagine what is.

28 At [180].

implement a right with the substantive obligation that Parliament is required to fulfil by enacting that legislation, leaving no 'middle ground' to litigate the content of the substantive obligation. This aspect of the majority's reasoning suggests that, once a court has determined that Parliament's purpose in enacting legislation is to implement a right—thus fulfilling its constitutional obligation to enact legislation—there no further question about whether the Act fulfils the substantive obligation. But this would have the effect of permitting Parliament to define the content of its own constitutional obligations, in contradiction of the basic commitments of legal constitutionalism.

As Cameron J observes in his dissenting judgment, such an approach is both implausible and highly problematic. It effectively renders constitutional rights that are coupled with a requirement to enact right-implementing legislation unreviewable where Parliament has enacted such legislation—save, perhaps, in cases where that legislation falls so egregiously short of implementing the right in question, or else invokes right-implementation as pretext for some other rights-incompatible legislative purpose, that it can indeed be said to be 'invalid' (rather than simply 'inadequate' or 'partial').[29] Even more contentiously, the majority's approach appears to render legislative power to define the scope and content of the constitutional right being implemented practically unreviewable. Here it is important to observe that although all three examples of constitutionally obligatory legislation discussed in the previous section unquestionably implement the rights in question, and are relatively broad and comprehensive in their coverage, all three Acts nevertheless narrow the scope and content of the rights that they implement in ways that are not obvious from the constitutional text.[30]

In summary, the Constitutional Court's approach in *My Vote Counts* demonstrates the possibility that constitutionally obligatory legislation may function as a source of constitutional legal norms not only in the usual sense of subsidiarity—where interpretation proceeds in a 'top down' direction—but also in the contentious 'bottom up' sense of subsidiarity, where legislatively-defined values and legal norms inform constitutional content. In light of this possibility, I suggest, there is a need to develop a perspective *within* legal constitutionalism that identifies constitutionally obligatory legislation as a special category of legislation, and that contemplates the possibility that such legislation has constitutional status of some kind in virtue of the type of interpretive approach just described.

29 This was the High Court's finding with regard to PAIA: see (n 26). Arguably, the fact that Section 32(1)(b) incorporates the content of other constitutional guarantees was of assistance here: because there is a separate question concerning what the right to vote requires, it is slightly less awkward to say that PAIA's shortcomings make it constitutionally 'invalid'. Even so, the oddity remains that Parliament could (presumably) fulfil its obligations in respect of the information required to exercise the right to vote by enacting *different* legislation.

30 For example, PAJA narrows the scope and content of the right to reasons in Section 33(2) by providing that reasons for administrative decisions are only required upon request, and by placing a time bar on such requests: C Hoexter, (n 8) 650, n 27.

This perspective is needed not simply in order to preserve consistency with the thesis that constitutional law has foundational priority over ordinary law, but in order to provide a better understanding of the appropriate role of the judiciary in this context. As *My Vote Counts* illustrates, even if there is agreement about the basic parameters of the subsidiarity approach and its underlying justification, there is confusion about how courts ought to review constitutionally obligatory legislation when that legislation is alleged to fail to fulfil Parliament's substantive obligation.

In developing this perspective, however, it is important to bear in mind that this is not a purely functionalist story. The legislation's *pedigree*—which is to say, the fact that it is referable to an obligation to enact right-implementation legislation that is contained within the text of the written constitution—*matters* to its function as a source of constitutional legal norms. In this respect, constitutionally obligatory legislation does not so much invert the foundational hierarchy of constitutional law over legislation as it complicates it. It is not, in other words, a full rejection of legal constitutionalism orthodoxy—or, at least, not so long as the obligation to enact right-implementing legislation retains independent, judicially-determined constitutional content.

In order to further motivate the case for developing this perspective, I now turn to an area of South African constitutional law where the role of constitutionally obligatory legislation has yet to be appreciated: Section 24, which concerns environmental rights and obligations.

## 4. Section 24: environmental rights and obligations

In its original form in the interim constitution, the environmental provision guaranteed that: 'Every person shall have the right to an environment which is not detrimental to his or her health or well-being.'[31] Its revised and current formulation in the 1996 Constitution is more complicated. Section 24 provides that:

Everyone has the right—

(a) to an environment that is not harmful to their health or well-being; and
(b) to have the environment protected, for the benefit of present and future generations, through reasonable legislative and other measures that—

  (i) prevent pollution and ecological degradation;
  (ii) promote conservation; and
  (iii) secure ecologically sustainable development and use of natural resources while promoting justifiable economic and social development.

Section 24(a) is a conventional right provision, similar to the provision in the interim constitution, with independent, judicially-determined constitutional

31 Section 29.

content. Section 24(b) is structurally distinct, however. Unlike subsection (a), the 'right' to which subsection (b) refers appears to have no content apart from the content given to it by 'legislative and other measures'. In other words, the 'right' in Section 24(b) simply *is* a state obligation to give effect to the objectives set out in subsections (i), (ii) and (iii).

Despite its distinctive formulation, some commentators have suggested that Section 24(b) should be regarded as a justiciable social right.[32] The better view, however, is that the provision is in substance a directive principle.[33] Directive principles are a type of non-justiciable or else unenforceable constitutional provision.[34] They are not merely declaratory or aspirational, but place binding obligations on the state to promote social values. However, they are given effect by means other than by direct judicial enforcement: predominantly, by legislation. Many expressly require the enactment of legislation, 'directed legislation', to give effect to the obligations that they entrench. Directed legislation is thus a kind of constitutionally obligatory legislation.

My objective in what follows is to further motivate the case for pursuing the suggestion advanced in the previous section: namely, that legal constitutionalism requires a perspective that identifies constitutionally obligatory legislation as a special category of legislation, and that takes seriously the possibility that such legislation has constitutional status of some kind. I propose to do this by demonstrating how legislation enacted pursuant to Section 24(b) is a potentially significant source of constitutional legal norms in ways that are analogous to the 'bottom up' approach to subsidiarity suggested by the majority approach in *My Vote Counts*.

In order to demonstrate this possibility, a helpful place to look is cases where legislation enacted pursuant to Section 24(b) comes into conflict with the constitutional protection of property rights under Section 25. Section 25 protects property in two ways: Section 25(1) prohibits the 'arbitrary deprivation of property', and Section 25(2) requires that property be 'expropriated' only for a 'public purpose or in the public interest' and 'subject to compensation'. Legislation implementing social rights and obligations frequently results in a reconfiguration of property rights, and therefore could be alleged to effect an 'arbitrary deprivation' or 'expropriation' of property: a possibility contemplated by Section 25's formal design.[35] Although it is uncontroversial that Section 25

32 See e.g., Anél Du Plessis, 'South Africa's Constitutional Environment Right (Generously) Interpreted: What Is in It for Poverty?' (2011) 27 S Afr J Hum Rts 279, 300.

33 This interpretation has some judicial support and is endorsed by leading commentators: see *HTF Developers (Pty) Ltd v. Minister of Environmental Affairs and Tourism* 2006 (5) SA 512 (T), [17]; Michael Kidd, *Environmental Law* (2nd edn, Juta 2011) 22, 23; Michael Kidd, 'Environmental Justice—A South African Perspective' (1999) 142 Acta Jur 154 (1999) 142.

34 See Lael K Weis, 'Constitutional Directive Principles' (2017) 37 OJLS 916, 919–923 <https://doi.org/10.1093/ojls/gqx015>.

35 See Section 25(8) ('No provision of this section may impede the state from taking legislative and other measures to achieve land, water and related reform, in order to redress the results

obligations to protect property must be interpreted in light of other constitutional obligations,[36] it is a further question what role constitutionally obligatory legislation plays in this context.

In *First National Bank*, the leading case interpreting Section 25(1), the Constitutional Court suggested that a more deferential standard of review applies to right-implementing legislation.[37] As a result, where the purpose of a law that effects a 'deprivation' is to fulfil a constitutional obligation to enact right-implementing legislation, it is unlikely to be found 'arbitrary'.[38] As a consequence, the burden that constitutionally obligatory legislation imposes on property will typically fall outside the ambit of constitutional protection afforded to property, and will not require proportionality-based justification under Section 36. In this respect, there is a sense in which the scope and content of constitutionally protected property rights are redefined to accommodate legislatively-defined fundamental values and legal norms. This includes environmental values and legal norms.

As with the rights considered in Section 2 of this chapter, this possibility poses questions concerning *how much* deference ought to be given to these legislative determinations. Is it sufficient that the legislation purports to give effect to a constitutional obligation? Or should courts scrutinize legislatively-defined fundamental values and norms in light of the relevant constitutional obligation? And if so, to what extent should courts give substantive constitutional obligations independent, judicially-defined content where Parliament is required to enact legislation implementing those obligations and such legislation has been enacted?

In the case of Section 24(b), however, these questions become more complicated. The obligation to enact implementing legislation does not attach to a judicially enforceable right, but to a *directive principle*. This makes it less obvious that the substantive obligation has constitutional content that is capable of

of past racial discrimination, provided that any departure from the provisions of this section is in accordance with the provisions of Section 36(1)', the general limitations clause).

36 *First National Bank of SA Limited t/a Wesbank v. Commissioner for the South African Revenue Services and Another; First National Bank of SA Limited t/a Wesbank v Minister of Finance* 2002 (4) SA 768 (CC) ('*FNB*') [50], [100] (holding that '[t]he purpose of Section 25 has to be seen both as protecting existing private property rights as well as serving the public interest', and emphasizing the need to consider constitutional provisions that place 'positive obligations on the state in regard to various social and economic rights').

37 Ibid., [66], [70], [77].

38 See e.g., *Transfer Rights Action Campaign and Others v. MEC for Local Government and Housing Gauteng and Others* [2004] ZACC 23, *Bissett and Others v. Buffalo Municipality and Others* [2004] ZACC 16, *Mkontwana v. Nelson Mandela Metropolitan Municipality* [2004] ZACC 9, [38] (per Yacoob J, Chaskalson CJ, Langa DCJ, Madala, Moseneke, Ngcobo, Skweyiya, and Van der Westhuizen JJ concurring), [105] (per O'Regan J) (a series of cases concerning the constitutional obligation of local governments 'to ensure the provision of services to communities in a sustainable manner' under Section 152 of the Constitution).

independent judicial determination. Arguably, then, Section 24(b) presents an even greater risk of inverting the principle of constitutional supremacy, where legislative power to define fundamental values and legal norms effectively collapses into political constitutionalism.

This risk is illustrated by the 2013 case *Agri South Africa v Minister for Minerals and Energy* ('*Agri SA*').[39] *Agri SA* concerned the *Mineral and Petroleum Resources Development Act* ('MPRDA'), directed legislation that gives effect to Section 24(b)(iii). Enacted in 2002, the MPRDA brought about a wholesale transformation in mineral and petroleum resource rights. The Act eliminated private ownership of those resources, vested them in the state as 'custodian' (or 'trustee'[40]) on behalf of the South African people, and replaced private ownership with a regime of more limited state-issued licences. It was alleged that these changes 'expropriated' resource rights held under the old private ownership regime within the meaning of Section 25(2), thereby enlivening the constitutional requirement to provide compensation. Although the Constitutional Court was unanimously of the view that no compensation was required, the judgments diverged in approach.

A majority of the Court held that property is 'expropriated' for Section 25(2) purposes only where a property interest is *acquired* by the state and, in applying that criterion, found that the MPRDA merely *extinguished* property rights.[41] The reasoning on both points not only reflects extraordinary deference to Parliament's obligation to enact legislation under Section 24(b)(iii),[42] but to Parliament's specific legislative determinations concerning *how* to give effect to that provision's substantive obligation.

Starting with the adoption of the acquisition criterion, the crux of the majority's reasoning was that a constitutional imperative to provide compensation in circumstances where property rights are extinguished but not acquired 'disregards the … constitutional imperative to transform and facilitate equitable access to our mineral and natural resources.'[43] As the judges who dissented on this point observed, however, a contradiction between these competing constitutional imperatives arises only if one assumes that Parliament must be able to determine the precise manner in which its Section 24(b)(iii) obligation is given effect.[44] But such an assumption elevates legislative contingency to constitutional necessity. In doing so, it effectively permits Parliament to define the scope and content of its own constitutional obligations—including an obligation that corresponds to

39 *Agri South Africa v Minister for Minerals and Energy* [2013] ZACC 9; 2013 (4) SA 1 (CC).

40 See Elmarie van der Schyff, 'Who "Owns" the Country's Mineral Resources? The Possible Incorporation of the Public Trust Doctrine through the Mineral and Petroleum Resources Development Act' (2008) 4 J S Afr L 757; Andre van der Walt, *Constitutional Property Law* (3rd ed., Juta 2011) 410–418.

41 *Agri SA* (n 39) [58]; see also [48], [59].

42 Ibid., [60–62].

43 Ibid., [69].

44 Ibid., [93–94], [100–105] per Froneman J.

a justiciable right that is meant to function as a constraint on the exercise of legislative power.

The majority's application of the acquisition criterion is similar in this regard. Even if there are independent reasons for adopting the acquisition criterion, it is difficult to understand why it does not apply to the state's assumption of 'custodianship' of resources, which includes the power to grant others resource-rights that previously only could have been granted by holders of the extinguished resource-rights.[45] This aspect of the reasoning appears to have far-reaching implications for the constitutional protection of property. It suggests that Parliament could abolish the private ownership of *any* category of 'thing' that is capable of being 'property' in the same manner without constitutional consequence.[46]

The crucial limiting principle in play in the majority's reasoning that avoids this radical implication is the status of the MPRDA as constitutionally obligatory legislation. Abolishing the private ownership of resources falls outside the ambit of the constitutional protection that Section 25(2) affords to property *not* because Parliament has an unfettered power to extinguish private property rights by assuming 'custodianship', but rather because the MPRDA gives effect to constitutional obligations under Section 24(b)(iii). As the Act indicates, the *purpose* of the state's assumption of custodianship is to act as 'a facilitator or a conduit through which broader and equitable access to mineral and petroleum resources can be realised.'[47]

Here too, however, the majority gives an extraordinary amount of deference to specific legislative determinations about what the constitutional obligation requires. There is no independent judicial assessment of the constitutional content of the substantive Section 24(b)(iii) obligation. This similarly has the consequence of permitting Parliament to define the scope and content of its own constitutional obligations. For the judges in dissent on the acquisition issue, this approach gets things backwards. The dissenting judges do not reject the proposition that the MPRDA is constitutionally obligatory legislation.[48] Nevertheless, on their view it cannot properly inform the scope and content of constitutionally entrenched rights and obligations. *Qua* legislation, the MPRDA must conform with the independent requirements of Section 25, and cannot be viewed as a source of constitutional meaning that bears on the interpretation of Section 25 requirements.[49]

The majority reasoning in *Agri SA* thus illustrates the same kind of 'bottom up' subsidiarity approach that we saw in *My Vote Counts*, but without the benefit of a discussion of subsidiarity principles. Indeed, conspicuously absent from

45 Ibid., [68] (Mogoeng CJ).
46 Ibid., [105] (Froneman J).
47 Ibid., [68] (Mogoeng CJ) (referring to the preamble of the MPRDA, which states that the law is enacted to give effect to the policy set out in Section 24(b)(iii)).
48 Ibid., [81] (Froneman J) (referring to the preamble of the MPRDA, which states that the law is enacted to give effect to the policy set out in Section 24(b)(iii)).
49 Ibid., [85] (Froneman J).

*all* of the judgments in *Agri SA* is any mention (let alone analysis) of subsidiarity. Nor is there any discussion of what implications the formulation of Section 24(b) as a directive principle rather than a justiciable right has for how courts are to evaluate the manner in which Parliament legislates to give effect to its constitutional obligations—although one suspects that such considerations must be in play in the majority's approach.

In this respect, the unique formal structure of Section 24 helps isolate the challenge that application of the subsidiarity approach to constitutionally obligatory legislation presents for the basic commitments of legal constitutionalism. The constitutional content of Section 24(b) obligations are less obviously capable of independent judicial-determination than obligations that correspond to justiciable rights provisions. Application of the subsidiarity approach in this context thus presents a greater risk of collapse into political constitutionalism. This underscores the need to develop an account of judicial role in relation to constitutional rights and obligations that require Parliament to enact implementing legislation.

At the same time, and more broadly, Section 24 demonstrates why constitutional theories of social rights and obligations are incomplete without the perspective contended for: a perspective that identifies constitutionally obligatory legislation as a special category of legislation and a potential source of constitutional legal norms. The formulation of Section 24(b) as a directive principle indicates that, like the rights provisions examined in Section 2 of this chapter, legislation is likely to be the predominant way of giving effect to fundamental environmental values. Indeed, this should be apparent even absent an awareness of the subsidiarity approach: directive principles are designed to be given effect by the political branches, and not by direct judicial enforcement. And yet, the promise of Section 24 has generally been thought to lie in direct judicial enforcement of the right contained in Section 24(a).[50]

Evaluated from a perspective that privileges Section 24(a) and that makes direct judicial enforcement the focal point, South Africa has been regarded as cause for pessimism about the potential of environmental constitutionalism. The principal complaints are that the Constitutional Court has failed to clarify the scope and content of the environmental right,[51] and that there has been insufficient rights litigation.[52] In the few cases where litigants have successfully invoked the right, it has either been used to prevent development approval in

50 See e.g., Du Plessis, (n 32) 281–83.

51 See e.g., ibid., 281 ('South Africa still awaits the guidance of judicial decisions on the interpretation of the obligations imposed by s 24'), 289 (identifying the need for 'judicial development with regard to the normative meaning, scope and justiciability of s 24'); Loretta Feris, 'Constitutional Environmental Rights: An Under-Utilised Resource', 24 S Afr J Hum Rts 29, 38 (2008) (noting that there is 'a marked dearth in cases where the environmental right has been fully utilised and clearly interpreted'), 39–43 (criticizing the Constitutional Court for not offering clarification about what 'sustainable development' requires).

52 See e.g., Michael Kidd, 'Public Interest Environmental Litigation: Recent Cases Raise Possible Obstacles' (2010) 13 Potchefstroom Elec LJ 27 (suggesting that the potential of

order to protect private economic interests,[53] or else courts have preferred to resolve the legal dispute on different constitutional grounds.[54] On this basis, commentators have concluded that Section 24 has 'had little practical effect' on the development of constitutional legal norms, and that 'the provision's constitutional or normative status is unclear.'[55]

As the analysis provided in this chapter demonstrates, however, this evaluation of Section 24 is at best incomplete without considering directed legislation enacted pursuant to Section 24(b). In addition to the *Agri SA* case discussed above, there are several other cases that support the view that Section 24(b) legislation has special status *qua* constitutionally obligatory legislation, and that such legislation is a potentially significant source of constitutional legal norms: in particular, that legislatively-defined fundamental values and legal norms may be used to define the scope and content of constitutional property rights.[56] Perhaps most significantly, the Constitutional Court has acknowledged the special status of the *National Environmental Management Act 1998* (NEMA), South Africa's most important environmental framework legislation, as constitutionally obligatory legislation.[57]

This suggests that Section 24(b) legislation should be regarded as analogous to the constitutionally obligatory legislation considered in Section 2: the Equality Act, PAIA, and PAJA. Just as those three Acts are widely-regarded as playing the predominant role in the configuration of fundamental values and legal norms in their respective spheres, so too should Section 24(b) legislation be so regarded in the sphere of environmental rights and obligations. In addition to

environmental rights litigation has been stunted by courts failing to give effect to constitutional principles, including Section 24, in determining standing requirements and remedies).

53 This includes the leading case on Section 24, *Fuel Retailers Association of Southern Africa v Director-General, Environmental Management Mpumalanga and Others* 2007 (6) SA 4 (CC), see esp the dissenting judgment of Sachs J, at [109]. See also *BP Southern Africa (Pty) Ltd v. MEC for Agriculture, Conservation, Environment and Land Affairs* 2004 (5) SA 124 (W) (refusal of permit to build a filling station challenged on environmental grounds, alleged to be motivated by protecting existing business from competition).

54 See e.g., *Petro Props (Pty) Limited v. Barlow and Another* 2006 (5) SA 160 (W) (case resolved on freedom of expression grounds).

55 James R May and Erin Daly, *Global Environmental Constitutionalism* 265 (2014).

56 See e.g., *Khabisi NO and Another v. Aquarella Investment* 83 (Pty) Ltd and Others 2008 (4) SA 195 (T), [1], [27]; *Oudekraal Estates (Pty) Ltd v. The City of Cape Town and Others* 2010 (1) SA 333 (SCA), [76], [78–79], [82]; *Phillips v. South African National Parks Board* [2010] ZAECGHC 27 (not reported).

57 See *Fuel Retailers* (n 53) [67] (Ngcobo J); *MEC Department of Agriculture, Conservation and Environment, Gauteng v. HTF Developers (Pty) Ltd* 2008 (2) SA 319 (CC), [23]–[28] (Skweyiya J), [57]–[58], [62] (Ngcobo J). The preamble of NEMA expressly acknowledges that it is enacted to give effect to Section 24 of the Constitution. In addition, the principles listed under Section 2 of the Act give additional content to the directive principles in Section 24(b). That section expressly states that those principles are to 'guide the interpretation, administration and implementation of this Act, and any other law concerned with the protection or management of the environment': Section 2(e).

MPRDA and NEMA, Parliament has enacted at least eight other significant statutes to give effect to Section 24(b) since the 1996 Constitution came into force.[58] Thus whereas commentators have despaired the inactivity of courts in directly enforcing Section 24(a), the same commentators have acknowledged that Parliament has 'paid serious attention to the duty created in s 24(b)'.[59] Particularly when viewed in light of the subsidiarity approach, then, it should be unsurprising that the direct judicial enforcement of the environmental right in Section 24(a) has played very little role in the production of constitutional legal norms.[60]

This critical oversight in the evaluation of Section 24 by scholarship to date underscores the need for constitutional theories of social rights and obligations to examine the potential role of constitutionally obligatory legislation as a source of constitutional legal norms, and to consider the possibility that constitutionally obligatory legislation has constitutional status of some kind. Without developing this perspective, such theories do not provide an adequate picture of the manner in which the range of increasingly robust and ambitious social values, once constitutionally entrenched as 'fundamental', lead to the creation of new constitutional legal norms. The focus on justiciability and methods of judicial review, while useful in highlighting concerns about the institutional competency and legitimacy of the judiciary that caution against entrenchment, is too narrow: it assumes that direct judicial enforcement is the principal method of implementing social rights and obligations. But this evaluative perspective does not adequately reflect interpretive practices such as subsidiarity. Nor does it reflect the manner in which many, newer social values provisions are drafted.

It is possible, and should be acknowledged, that environmental rights and obligations present a special case: directive principles are the most common way that state obligations to protect the environment are formulated in constitutions worldwide—far more common than rights provisions.[61] This reflects a common

58 The following Acts expressly acknowledge the constitutional obligation under Section 24(b) as a reason for enactment in their preamble (quoting verbatim the language from Section 24): National Environmental Management Air Quality Act 2004; National Environmental Management Integrated Coastal Management Act 2008; National Environmental Management Waste Act 2008. The following acts state that giving effect to the constitutional obligation under Section 24 is a legislative objective, rationalizing the State custodianship of certain natural resources: National Environmental Management Biodiversity Act 2004, Section 3; National Environmental Management Protected Areas Act 2003, Section 3. Other examples of environmental constitutionally obligatory legislation include: Marine Living Resources Act 1998 (constitutional obligation under Section 24 listed as an objective, Section 2); National Forests Act 1998 (constitutional obligation under Section 24 acknowledged in preamble); Spatial Planning and Land Use Management Act 2013 (constitutional obligation under Section 24 acknowledged in preamble).

59 Feris (n 51) 36.

60 Michael Kidd makes this observation: see *Environmental Law* (n 33) 25.

61 Lael K Weis, 'Environmental constitutionalism: Aspiration or transformation?' (2018) 16 Int J of Const L 836 <https://doi.org/10.1093/icon/moy063>.

view that the political branches are better equipped for decision-making about environmental issues. Environmental directive principles respond to concerns about the entrenchment of justiciable environmental rights by allocating institutional responsibility for fundamental environmental values to the political branches. Even so, there are many other social values that are entrenched using provisions, including directive principles, that present an alternative to conventional rights provisions. As the South African Constitution illustrates, even social values that are entrenched as justiciable rights provisions may require the enactment of right-implementing legislation. These methods of drafting appear to accommodate similar concerns about the institutional competency and legitimacy of the judiciary that attend the entrenchment of environmental values, and that favour legislative implementation.

## 5. Conclusion

The case study provided in this chapter demonstrates the importance of the research agenda advanced in this collection. It also demonstrates the importance of the distinctive set of concepts and concerns *within* legal constitutionalism in the pursuit of that agenda. As we have seen, constitutionally obligatory legislation is a consequence of an important innovation in the design of written constitutions, where constitutional provisions that create rights and obligations are increasingly drafted in ways that not only contemplate legislation as the principal means of implementation but that require the enactment of implementing legislation.

The significance of this phenomenon, it is suggested, can only be understood by occupying a legal constitutionalist perspective. Constitutionally obligatory legislation complicates orthodox understandings of the relationship between constitutional law and ordinary legislation for reasons that are not fully reducible to subject matter or function-based criteria for constitutional status—as a political constitutionalist perspective might suggest. It is, rather, the pedigree of constitutionally obligatory legislation that appears to be the critical factor used to rationalize its use as a source of constitutional legal norms. In other words, it is judicial recognition of the fact that such legislation gives effect to a constitutional obligation requiring its enactment that is contained within the text of the written constitution that permits it to play this role.

A question remains whether this is desirable. Should the fact that legislation gives effect to a constitutional obligation requiring its enactment make any difference to its status within the hierarchy of legal norms? And if so, should the special status of constitutionally obligatory legislation be confined to its relationship to ordinary (non-obligatory) legislation—or should that status extend to its relationship to constitutional law as well? Even if it is plausible to think that constitutionally obligatory legislation provides an attractive alternative to the judicial articulation of fundamental values and legal norms through direct enforcement—at least in some circumstances—what limitations there ought to be to that role requires further consideration. As this chapter has indicated, there is a threshold where the role of constitutionally obligatory legislation as a source of fundamental values and legal norms may simply collapse into political constitutionalism: for example, where courts avoid giving, or even refuse to give, independent constitutional content to such obligations. One's overall evaluation of constitutionally obligatory legislation may therefore ultimately turn on developing an account of judicial role in relation to constitutional rights and obligations that require the enactment of implementing legislation—and, in particular, on whether it is possible to define judicial role in a manner that resists this collapse, but simultaneously accommodates the perceived value of legislative implementation. Although this chapter has not attempted to provide answers to these questions or to develop an account of judicial role, it has demonstrated why these issues merit examination.

# 10 Quasi-constitutionalism and informal legislative entrenchment: a case study

## The case of the Affordable Care Act

*Sofia Ranchordás*[*]

## 1. Introduction

"The ACA is here to stay,"[1] President Obama stated in the wake of the 2015 Supreme Court decision *King v. Burwell.*[2] In the year that two of America's most enduring social programs—Medicare and Medicaid—celebrated fifty years of existence and the presidential campaign for the next term started, the then still recent Patient Protection and Affordable Care Act (ACA)[3] aspired to become part of this panoply of long-lasting social reforms.[4] Indeed, part of the legacy of the ACA or of any significant legal reform is determined by its duration and how deeply it becomes entrenched in a legal order.[5] The entrenchment of this act would protect it partially against the winds of change and the promises of the Republican candidates to repeal this statute. Following *King v. Burwell* academic commentators discussed the U.S. conservatives' fear that the ACA would become a 'super-statute,' that is, a statute with quasi-constitutional character that is broadly accepted by the people, is able to resist reform attempts, and judicial challenges.[6] As winds of change are expected

* Chair of European and Comparative Public Law & Rosalind Franklin Fellow, University of Groningen, The Netherlands.

1 Ed O' Keefe, 'Obama: The Affordable Care Act Is Here to Stay,' *Washington Post*, 25 June 2015 at www.washingtonpost.com/blogs/post-politics/wp/2015/06/25/obama-the-affordable-care-act-is-here-to-stay/ ('The Affordable Care act is here to stay,' President Obama declared.).

2 King v. Burwell, 135 S. Ct. 2480 (2015).

3 Patient Protection and Affordable Care Act, Pub. L. No. 111–148, 124 Stat. 119 (2010).

4 Social Security Amendments of 1965, Pub. L. No. 89–97, 79 Stat. 286 (codified as amended in scattered Sections of 42 U.S.C.). Edward Berkowitz, 'Medicare and Medicaid: The Past as Prologue' (2008) 29 *Health Care Financing Rev.* 81.

5 Paul Starr, 'The Health-Care Legacy of the Great Society' 235 in Norman J. Glickman & Robert H. Vilson (Eds.), *LBJ's Neglected Legacy: How Lyndon Johnson Reshaped Domestic Policy & Government* (University of Texas Press, 2015) 235, 246.

6 Jonathan Oberlander and Eric Patashnik, 'Conservatives Worry that Obamacare is a 'Super-Statute.' It Isn't Quite Yet.' *Washington Post*, 18 June 2015 at www.washingtonpost.com/blogs/monkey-cage/wp/2015/06/28/conservatives-worry-that-obamacare-is-a-super-statute-it-isnt-quite-one-yet/ (last accessed on December 1st, 2017).

during the Trump Administration, this qualification might appear to be premature and unrealistic at the time of writing. However, the difficulties in amending the ACA and the lack of consensus in Congress on how to reform this statute has revealed thus far the existence of informal entrenchment forces that are typically observed in the context of quasi-constitutional statutes.

In theory, the phenomenon of legislative persistence or the resistance to legislative reform should not be regarded as an exceptional matter. But sometimes it is because it limits the power of newly elected parliaments to amend legislation. Indeed, legislative persistence is an important dimension of the principle of legal certainty that is regarded by many as a cornerstone of our legal orders.[7] However, our legal orders are also characterized by an important tension between past and future. On the one hand, legislators aim to secure legislative continuity and protect the legitimate expectations of citizens. On the other, if law is to remain aligned with the will of the people, legislative reform cannot be avoided. The entrenchment of quasi-constitutional statutes has a special place in this conflict.

Quasi-constitutional statutes—at the resemblance of constitutions—consecrate core values of society as they are able to stand up well to societal, political, judicial, and economic changes. Quasi-constitutional statutes are able to root these values because they persist through time. Nonetheless, the legal literature has not attended to the informal forces that explain the long-term persistence or entrenchment of legislation. These forces, however, are behind their long-lasting nature and the democratic acceptance of statutes that eventually acquire a quasi-constitutional character. In this book chapter, I draw on interdisciplinary literature to describe how these statutes become informally entrenched. Although each quasi-constitutional statute has a unique entrenchment story, several of these informal forces are visible in different fields (*e.g.*, sunk cost fallacy, bureaucracy). I rely on examples from the field of U.S. health care law to explain why certain statutes have become almost impermeable to change despite the absence of any formal or *de jure* obstacles. I discuss the entrenchment of Medicaid and Medicare as well as the conscious or unconscious attempt to entrench ACA. This subject is particularly relevant at the time of writing as the U.S. Congress has been trying to amend the ACA since the beginning of 2017. However, despite the promises of President Trump to repeal the act, this legislative change has been difficult to execute in practice. Regardless of the future outcome of this legislative reform, this academic contribution should remain relevant as it analyzes the socio-political forces that have been entrenching legislation for centuries.[8]

7 Patricia Popelier, 'Five Paradoxes on Legal Certainty and the Lawmaker' (2015) 2 *Legisprudence* 47.

8 *See, e.g.*, Niccolò Machiavelli, 'The Prince' 167, 173 in Mitchell Cohen & Nicole Fermon (Eds.), *Niccolò Machiavelli, Readings in Political Thought: Essential Texts since Plato* (Princeton University Press, 1996) ('There is nothing more difficult to carry out, nor more doubtful of success, nor more dangerous to handle, than to initiate a new order of things. For the reformer has enemies in all those who profit by the old order, and only lukewarm defenders in all those who would profit by the new order.').

In this book chapter, I draw on the antecedents of the ACA to demonstrate how the social and political processes can be conducive to informal legislative entrenchment, contributing to the qualification of a statute as quasi-constitutional. Informal entrenchment can be diagnosed not only in the context of quasi-constitutional statutes but also more generally whenever democratic or bureaucratic forces are able to resist legislative reform.[9] I argue that informal entrenchment is particularly visible in the health care sector where legislative change is generally difficult to achieve but once it is in place, adopted policies and statutes will on their turn be resistant to alterations. The informal entrenchment forces analyzed in this paper are characteristic of quasi-constitutional statutes, which tend to persist since they are legitimized by broad legislative deliberation, fundamental principles, and popular support.[10]

This book chapter is organized as follows: Section 2 distinguishes between formal and informal entrenchment; Section 3 analyzes different informal entrenchment forces in US health care law; Section 4 discusses the process of informal entrenchment in the context of quasi-constitutionalism.

## 2. Informal entrenchment

Legislative entrenchment is the long-term persistence of legislation that is rooted in either democratic or bureaucratic forces. The causes of legislative entrenchment can be either legal (formal entrenchment) or social, political, or economic (informal entrenchment). Legislative entrenchment is a cross-temporal phenomenon that limits legislative change.

The term 'legislative entrenchment' has received a great deal of negative attention in the literature in the last decades. It has been described as a 'promiscuous word' and a synonym of outdated and ineffective legislation that reduces parliamentary sovereignty.[11] While common law jurisdictions might have a natural bias toward the maintenance of the status quo, *de jure* or formal

9 Cf. Erin C. Fuse Brown, 'Developing a Durable Right to Health Care' (2013) 14 *Minnesota J. of Law, Science & Technology* 439.

10 William N. Eskridge & John Ferejohn, 'Super-Statutes' (2001) 50 *Duke L.J.* 1215, 1216. *See also* William N. Eskridge & John Ferejohn, *A Republic of Statutes: The New American Constitution* (Oxford University Press, 2013).

11 Eric A. Posner & Adrian Vermeule, 'Legislative Entrenchment: A Reappraisal' (2002) 111 *Yale L.J.* 1665; *see also* John O. McGinnis & Michael B. Rappaport, 'The Constitutionality of Legislative Supermajority Requirements: A Defense' (1995) 105 *Yale L.J.* 483, 503–507; Michael J. Klarman, 'Majoritarian Judicial Review: The Entrenchment Problem' (1997) 85 *Georgia L. Rev.* 491, 505–506; Catherine Fisk & Erwin Chemerinsky, 'The Filibuster' (1997) 49 *Stanford L. Rev.* 181, 247–249; David Dana & Susan P. Koniak, 'Bargaining in the Shadow of Democracy' (1999) 148 *University of Pennsylvania L. Rev.* 473, 526–536; Stewart E. Sterk, 'Retrenchment on Entrenchment' (2003) 71 *George Washington L. Rev.* 231, 232; John C. Roberts & Erwin Chemerinsky, 'Entrenchment of Ordinary Legislation: A Reply to Professors Posner and Vermeule' (2003) 91 *California L. Rev.* 1775, 1778.

entrenchment dispositions are void as current parliamentary majorities cannot prevent future ones from amending ordinary legislation.

Formal entrenchment is generally a premeditated and explicit practice, while informal entrenchment is often implicit and unpredictable, resulting from the well-known legislative inertia, unexpected events or an unpredictable assembly of forces that impede Congress from modifying an existing statute.[12] Legislative entrenchment implies that legislative change is difficult but not impossible. Any statute can potentially shift the burden of inertia from one legislature to the other to a greater or smaller extent.[13] Government contracts, treaties, and a number of other legislative actions with effects to third parties can impose costs on future majorities that seek to escape the consequences of the earlier action.[14]

From a functional perspective, legislative entrenchment can be divided into two categories. First, legislative entrenchment can be perceived as a part of the so-called agency problem of representative government, where elected representatives attempt to leave a legacy and perpetuate their preferences in detriment of their constituents.[15] Second, legislative entrenchment also serves cross-temporal purposes. Cross-temporal legislative entrenchment is a more neutral concept that refers sometimes to well-intended limitations on future parliaments.[16] This form of entrenchment is thus the result of the legal and non-legal instruments employed to guarantee that tomorrow's parliament will abide by the statutes enacted by today's majority. At first, this concept might seem equally objectionable on majoritarian grounds as the first type of entrenchment.[17]

The negative position of the literature toward legislative entrenchment has been explained by the need to avoid the adoption of formal legal dispositions that create formal obstacles to legislative amendment (*e.g.*, supramajoritarian requirements). These formal requirements are typically present in constitutions as they are aimed to create constitutional stability and protect fundamental rights. Despite the existence of an important body of literature on formal entrenchment, these clauses are rare sights. In the real world, legislation stays in place not because the 'law says so' but because of social, political, and economic obstacles to change.

In the scholarship of John Ferejohn and William Eskridge, informal entrenchment has been associated with the concept of super-statutes.[18] Although unknown in the international literature, the term of 'super-statute' finds its equivalent in

12 Abbe R. Gluck, 'Symposium Issue Introduction: The Law of Medicare and Medicaid at Fifty' (2015) 15 *Yale J. of Health Policy, L. & Ethics* 1, 15.

13 Eule, *supra* note 10, at 379, 384.

14 Posner and Vermeule, *supra* note 12, at 1696

15 Samuel Issacharoff & Daniel R. Ortiz, 'Governing through Intermediaries' (1999) 85 *University of Virginia L. Rev.* 1627.

16 *See* Aaron-Andrew Bruhl, 'Using Statutes to Set Legislature Rules: Entrenchment, Separation of Power, and the Rules of Proceedings Clause' (2003) 19 *J. of Law & Policy* 345, 372.

17 Klarman, *supra* note 12, at 504.

18 William N. Eskridge & John Ferejohn, *A Republic of Statutes: The New American Constitution* (Yale University Press, 2013).

comparative literature in the concept of quasi-constitutional law and, in some legal systems, in the form of organic laws. A super statute is a law or series of laws that seeks to establish a new normative or institutional framework and over time 'sticks' in the public culture having a broad effect on the law.[19] Examples of quasi-constitutional statutes that have become entrenched in the U.S. legal order are the 1965 Social Security Act, which established the Medicaid and Medicare programs, the Voting Rights Act, and the Administrative Procedure Act.

The longstanding nature of a law does not convert it automatically into a quasi-constitutional statute. As Vermeule has explained, while first degree murder rules have persisted longer than a number of laws and policies that are often qualified as entrenched statutes and super statutes (*e.g.*, the 1965 Social Security Act), this does not necessarily mean that the Congress' hands were tied regarding the amendment of those rules. In this case as in many others, legislation remains because 'people like them,' they are deemed to be still reasonably effective or there are no alternatives.

Informal entrenchment does not implicate the adoption of any formal entrenchment clause but rather that the existence of informal entrenchment mechanisms that sustain a statute beyond the ravages of time. The importance of informal entrenchment has been visible in the endurance of legislation in the health care sector. Both Medicaid and Medicare have been able to resist several repeal attempts,[20] even though the 1965 Social Security Act did not include any *de jure* entrenchment clauses.[21]

In this book chapter, I identify a number of informal entrenchment forces that typically contribute to the long-term persistence of both quasi-constitutional and ordinary statutes.

## 3. Informal entrenchment forces in U.S. health care law

The natural bias of legal orders toward the status quo can be reinforced by the characteristics of the sector. While technological and educational sectors (*e.g.*, telecommunications, biotechnology) are characterized by fast changes; others like health care, are slow-going and impermeable to sudden course corrections.[22] A change in these fields is often analyzed from the perspective of

19 William N. Eskridge & John Ferejohn, 'Super-Statutes' (2001) 50 *Duke L.J.* 1215, 1216.

20 Medicaid and Medicare are two public health insurance programs. While Medicare is a federally-run program that provides healthcare insurance primarily to the aged (65 years or older) without regard to financial need, Medicaid is a joint federal-state insurance designed to provide medical care to low-income individuals. See John E. Steiner, Jr., *Problems in Health Care Law: Challenges for the Twenty-First Century* (Jones & Bartlett, 2014) 309.

21 Ken Wing, 'The Impact of Reagan-era Politics on the Federal Medicaid Program' (1983) 33 *Catholic University L. Rev.* 1; Robert C. Lieberman, 'Ideas, Institutions, and Political Order: Explaining Political Change' (2002) 96 *American Political Science Rev.* 697.

22 *See* Lyria Bennett Moses, 'Recurring Dilemmas: The Law's Race to Keep Up with Technological Change' (2007) 2 *J. of Law, Technology. & Policy* 239.

the ordered and patterned regularity that characterizes them.[23] Health care, for example, is a 'glacial field'.[24] In the particular case of the American health care system, Theodore Ruger has explained this feature in light of the 'remarkably slow pace of change, reform, [and] systematic federal involvement.'[25] In addition, these slow changes of the American healthcare system are also attributed to the sedimentary legacy of prior legal regimes that are present in the attitudes of both physicians and patients.[26]

In 1967, *Time* magazine ironically entitled an article 'Medicare: Expensive, Successful, Medicaid; Chaotic, Irrevocable.'[27] More than fifty years later, we are able to say that some of these predictions proved to be accurate. Despite the attempted repeals and amendments of the Reagan Administration, Medicare and Medicaid are still alive and well.[28] Medicare, in particular, has become a highly popular and bipartisan program. This example introduces the essence of informal entrenchment, which refers to a situation 'in which the possibility of amendment is virtually impossible because of exceptionally high procedural [but non-legal] barriers to change.'[29] These barriers do not result from the legal text but from the social, economic, and political obstacles that I shall analyze in the following subsections.

### *3.1. Sunk costs*

Conventional wisdom in political science says that policies are hard to terminate: Once policies are introduced, they are likely to persist.[30] Policy persistence, or the tendency of policies to change slowly, if at all, is often regarded as the outcome of political inertia. As laws and policies have an instrumental relationship, a similar reasoning tends to apply to legislation. Policy persistence becomes a 'problem' when there are no rational reasons to maintain a policy in place.[31] This occurs, for example, when suboptimal policies are not timely terminated or when they become superfluous because the

23 Lieberman, *supra* note 22, at 700.

24 Theodore W. Ruger, 'Of Icebergs and Glaciers: The Submerged Constitution of American Healthcare' (2012) 75 *L. & Contemporary Problems* 215.

25 See *id.* at 219.

26 See *id* at 219.

27 'Medicare: Expensive, Successful; Medicaid: Chaotic, Irrevocable' (1967) *Time Magazine* (October 6, 2017).

28 Diane Rowland, Barbara Lyons & Jennifer Edwards, 'Medicaid: Health Care for the Poor in the Reagan Era' (1988) 9 *Ann. Rev. of Pub. Health* 427, 430.

29 Melissa Schwartzberg, *Democracy and Legal Change* (Oxford University Press, 2009) 12.

30 *See generally* Stephen Coate & Stephen Morris, 'Policy Persistence' (1999) 89 *Am. Econ. Rev.* 1327.

31 Iris Geva-May, 'When the Motto Is "Till Death Do Us Part": The Conceptualization and the Craft of Termination in the Public Policy Cycle' (2001) 24 *Int'l J. of Pub. Admin.* 263.

problem they aimed to address no longer exists.[32] The existence of monetary or psychological sunk costs is often invoked as a reason to justify the persistence of suboptimal policies.[33]

In a study on the closure of Marine Hospitals in the United States, Janet Franz demonstrated that while public policy termination can save costs in the long-run; in the short-run the termination process involves considerable and dissuasive costs to prevent damages to communities, constituents, and staff.[34] The Marine Hospitals were originally established in the eighteenth century to provide medical assistance to disabled sailors in the United States. As their work conditions improved and the economy evolved, the protection of this particular class of workers stopped being prioritized. In 1981, a program was initiated to terminate health care programs for merchant sailors. Franz found that although the termination of this program was technically successful, it came at a high cost.[35] In addition, the sunk costs related to the investment in human capital often are an important concern—despite being a typical case of a sunk cost fallacy—when agencies are terminated and highly specialized staff must be discharged or transferred to other functions.[36]

### *3.2. Path dependence in health care reforms*

The well-known theory of path dependence has explained for decades how past decisions tend to constrain our present and future. Legislators—like many of us —tend to be risk-averse and thus avoid radical policy changes. Path dependence explains the type of health care services we receive and how laws and policies evolve to meet the changing needs of society (e.g., new medical conditions associated with aging) and the sector (e.g., the rising costs of health care services). Considering this path-dependence constraint, policy and legislative changes tend to be incremental rather than disruptive.

In the 1990s, path dependence was believed to be not very auspicious for future efforts to reform American health care. Instead, it was then clear that there was a path to be followed in order to reform health care and achieve universal coverage.[37] This tendency to maintain the status quo has also been explained in light of the multiple barriers to lawmaking in Congress, namely the

32 *See* Mark R. Daniels, *Terminating Public Programs: An American Political Paradox* (Routledge, 1997) 31.

33 Peter DeLeon, 'Policy Evaluation and Program Termination' (1983) 2 *Policy Studies Rev.* 631.

34 Janet E. Frantz, 'The High Cost of Policy Termination' (1997) 20 *Int. J. of Pub. Admin.* 2097, 2010–2011.

35 *Id.* at 2109.

36 *See* Iris Geva-May, 'Till Death Do Us Part: The Conceptualization of Policy Termination' (2001) *24 Int. J. of Pub. Admin.* 263; Eugene Bardach, 'Policy Termination as Political Process' (1976) 7 *Political Science* 126.

37 *See* World Health Organization, *Health Systems Financing: The Path to Universal Coverage* (WHO, 2010) 7.

challenge of gathering political consensus, and the design of federal statutes that rely on state administration for its implementation.[38] The ACA is a good example of the tension between past paths and the wish to build a new one in order to expand access to health care.

The ACA has been characterized as the 'most monumental piece of health care legislation' in the last decades.[39] However, the ACA is not as disruptive as one might think. It does not include an explicit and public utility regulatory vision of health care at the resemblance of other countries. Citizens will not find a right to health or healthcare posited in this statute. Rather, the ACA builds upon decades of reforms by improving access to health insurance for many—but certainly not all—citizens. This improvement resides in the introduction of a subsidy program that aims to provide access to health care insurance to those who would not have the means to pay for medical care.[40] This statute fills existing gaps, namely by changing the way health care is financed.[41]

The ACA is new and old at the same time. The truth is that this statute had been 'in the making' for almost eighty years: In 1932, the Committee on the Costs of Medical Care released a report, recommending the creation of a program that would include the utilization of provider groups, preventive care services, universal coverage, and significant investment in provider training.[42] These suggestions were not adopted in the 1930s but they might sound familiar to us as several of them were recently embraced by the ACA. However, the first steps toward the reform of the U.S. health care system were given in the 1930s during the Roosevelt Administration.[43]

During many decades, health care reforms tended to be received with animosity. Before the enactment of the ACA, there were already several programs designed to increase access to health care. This was the case of Medicare, Medicaid, EMTALA, TRICARE, COBRA, the Federal Employee Health Benefits Program, CHIP, and the Veterans Administration. Besides these federal government programs, there were also federal-state programs, the most

38 Abbe R. Gluck, 'Federalism from Federal Statutes: Health Reform, Medicaid, and the Old-Fashioned Federalists Gamble' (2013) 81 *Fordham L. Rev.* 1749, 1761.

39 Rene Bowser, 'The Affordable Care Act and Beyond: Opportunities for Advancing Health Equity and Social Justice' (2013) 10 *Hastings Race & Poverty L. J.* 69, 71.

40 Abigail R. Moncrieff, 'Regulation: What the Obama Administration Should Have Said in NFIB V. Sebelius' (2013) 39 *Am. J. of L. & Med.* 539, 541.

41 *See* Starr, *supra* note 6, at 246.

42 Simon F. Haeder, 'Beyond Path Dependence: Explaining Healthcare Reform and Its Consequences' (2012) 40 *Policy Studies J.* 65.

43 Everette James & Arthur S. Levine, 'The Inevitability of Health Reform' (2012) 50 *Duquesne L. Rev.* 235. *See also* James A. Morone, 'President and Health Reform: From Franklin D. Roosevelt to Barack Obama' (2010) 29 *Health Affairs* 1096; M. M. Matusiak, 'A National Health Insurance System/Program: A Review of US History and Current Debate' (2005) 3 *Internet J. of Healthcare Administration*, §14, at www.ispub.com/journal/the-internet-journal-of-healthcare-administration/volume-3-number-2/a-national-health-insurance-system-program-a-review-of-us-history-and-current-debate.html#e-3

significant of which is Medicaid.[44] Medicaid became the third largest entitlement program in the United States, preceded by Social Security and Medicare. This public insurance program together with Medicare replaced two previously existing programs of federal grants to states to provide health care assistance to low-income citizens.[45] One program guaranteed medical care to welfare recipients and the other to the elderly.

In 1971, President Nixon's National Health Strategy proposed new measures to improve the efficiency of the American health care system while expanding access to health care. In theory, the 'Nixon-plan' greatly resembled the ACA.[46] The proposal was however at that time not well received. An important step in the direction of the expansion of the access to health care services was given in 1986. Congress enacted the Emergency Medical Treatment & Labor Act (EMTALA) to guarantee public access to emergency services regardless of ability to pay. Section 1867 of the Social Security Act created a federal right to emergency medical treatment.[47] All these programs seem to have laid out a certain path for health care reform.

In the 1990s, President Clinton also tried to reform the American health care system. The Clinton plan was radically new and was not incremental in its design or implications for health policy. The 'Clintoncare' aimed to expand health care coverage by creating regional health alliances, imposing more burdensome employer and individual mandates. The Clinton health plan was essentially regulatory.[48] In addition, it represented a major policy change that did not fit well with American political institutions that struggle to accommodate large-scale reform.[49]

In 2009, almost 50 million persons in the United States did not have access to health insurance coverage.[50] According to recent OECD studies, even relatively advantaged and college-educated Americans seemed to be worse off than other peers in other OECD countries.[51] 'Obamacare', as it is commonly known,

44 John E. Steiner, Jr. (Eds.), *Problems in Health Care Law: Challenges for the Twenty-First Century* (Jones & Bartlett, 2014) 305.

45 Jonathan Gruber, 'Medicaid' in Robert A. Moffitt (Eds.), *Means-Tested Transfer Program in the United States* (University of Chicago Press, 2003).

46 Wesley J. Smith, 'It's Not Obamacare, It's the Nixon Plan' (2013) *National Review*, 23 October 2013 at www.nationalreview.com/corner/362362/its-not-obamacare-its-nixon-plan-wesley-j-smith (last visited July 10, 2017).

47 W. David Koeniger, 'The Statute Whose Name We Dare Not to Speak: EMTALA and the Affordable Care' (2013) 16 *J. of Gender, Race & Justice* 139.

48 Abigail R. Moncrieff, 'Regulation: What the Obama Administration Should Have Said in NFIB V. Sebelius' (2013) 39 *Am. J. of L. & Med.* 539, 543.

49 David Wilsford, 'Path Dependency, or Why History Makes It Difficult but Not Impossible to Reform Health Care Systems in a Big Way' (1994) 14 *J. of Public Policy* 251.

50 Kaiser Family Foundation, *Health Insurance Coverage in the United States* (2009), at http://kff.org/other/state-indicator/total-population/

51 Elizabeth Bradley & Lauren A. Taylor, *The American Health Care Paradox: Why Spending More Is Getting Us Less* (Public Affairs, 2013).

does not solve entirely the problem, but it makes an important incremental improvement. The enactment of the ACA is the mere starting point of a thorough reform of the American health system.[52] This begs however the following question: if the path to health reform was already being paved for decades, why was only President Obama successful in passing such a health reform and coining it? Four main reasons explain this puzzle: the economic crisis, that is, the recovery from the 2008 recession, which had exacerbated the hardship faced by a vast part of the population; the political momentum with the initial Democratic takeover of Congress; the rising costs of health care services; and the enactment of a path-dependent program.[53]

In the 1930s and the 1970s, a healthcare reform would have been too precocious as a number of required steps had to be taken first in order to pave the way for universal coverage. The system introduced by the ACA is built on existing structures, institutions and policy programs, such as health insurances, employer-based insurance, and Medicaid. This statute introduces nonetheless a number of novelties including the prohibition of discrimination on pre-existing conditions and the health insurance premiums subsidies.[54] The ACA is therefore a compromise between the new model that aims to expand coverage and guarantee affordable health care insurance and the old model governed by private and for-profit insurers as the primary providers of access to health care.[55] The ACA initiates nevertheless the realignment of the health-care system for long-term changes in health-care quality, the organization and design of health care practice, and health information transparency.

The ACA follows a long path that started being paved by President Roosevelt. There is thus a conservative and a progressive side to the ACA. On the one hand, the ACA does not change the whole system, it seeks to improve it. On the other, it tries to change the way Americans perceive health and their entitlement to health care. In this sense, the ACA aims to go further than any previous legislative act and federally-run programs such as Medicare and Medicaid; but at the same time it is path-dependent.

The historical antecedents of the ACA demonstrate the path dependence of this statute and its clear place in history. However, the resemblance of the ACA with previous Republican proposals and the limited and incremental reforms are justified not only by path dependence but also by the entrenched power of

52 Ezekiel J. Emanuel, 'The Beginning of a Health Care Revolution', *New York Times*, 20 March 2014 at www.nytimes.com/roomfordebate/2014/03/20/obamacares-four-year-checkup/the-beginning-of-a-health-care-revolution.

53 Jacob Hacker, 'The Road to Somewhere: Why Health Reform Happened' (2010) 8 *Perspectives on Policy* 861, 863.

54 Sarah Rosenbaum, 'The Patient Protection and Affordable Care Act: Implications for Public Health Policy and Practice' (2010) 126 *Public Health Reports* 130.

55 *See* Jessica L. Roberts, 'Healthism': A Critique of the Antidiscrimination Approach to Health Insurance and Health-Care Reform' (2012) *U. Illinois L. Rev.* 1159.

constituencies and institutions from past policy decisions.[56] For example, one of the pillars of the ACA is the expansion of Medicaid.[57] The ACA maintains the structure of this program as well as the traditional paths into Medicaid for pregnant women, children, caretakers of children, and disabled persons.[58] But, as Chief Justice John Roberts suggested in *NFIB v. Sebelius*,[59] the ACA abandons the traditional concept of 'the deserving poor,' that is, Medicaid is no longer a 'privilege' of the 'neediest among Americans.' Instead, it suffices to be poor—from a purely neural perspective—to be eligible for Medicaid.[60]

### *3.3. Entrenchment and interest groups*

The influence of interest groups on policies and regulation has been widely discussed in the Public Choice literature.[61] Public choice theorists have discussed how special interest groups develop rent-seeking strategies to lobby for regulation that is more favorable to them and oppose any kind of reform that would equal to loss of benefits for a special group. To illustrate, after defending universal coverage during his campaign, President Carter advanced a more modest proposal to reform the health care system by introducing a plan for an across-the-board cap on hospital charges. This would limit annual increases to one-and-a-half times any rise in the consumer index.[62] The Federation of American Hospitals rapidly formed a coalition to lobby against this plan. This Federation established a well-organized committee that sent thousands of letters to every hospital administrator in the country. In addition, this organization developed an alternative 'voluntary' cost containment plan. As a consequence of this action, the Carter plan never left the Senate Finance Committee.[63]

56 Simon F. Haeder, 'Beyond Path Dependence: Explaining Healthcare Reform and Its Consequences' (2012) 40 *Policy Stud. J.* 65, 69; Jacob Hacker, 'The Road to Somewhere: Why Health Reform Happened' (2010) 8 *Perspectives on Policy* 861.

57 *See* however Nat'l Fed'n of Indep. Bus. (NFIB) v. Sebelius, 132 S.Ct. 2566 (2012).

58 ACA 42 U.S.C. §1396a(a)(10)(A)(i), §2581 (2012).

59 Nat'l Fed'n of Indep. Bus. v. Sebelius (NFIB), 132 S.Ct. 2566, 2606 (2012). *See* David Orentlicher, 'Medicaid at 50: No Longer Limited to the "Deserving" Poor?' (2015) 15 *Yale J. of Health Policy L. & Ethics* 185.

60 The ACA expanded the Medicaid program to all persons up to 138% of the federal poverty level.

61 *See, e.g.*, Sam Peltzman, 'Toward a More General Theory of Regulation' (1976) 19 *J. of L. & Econ.* 211; George J. Stigler, 'The Theory of Economic Regulation' (1971) 2 *Bell J. of Econ. & Management Science* 3; Richard Posner, 'Theories of Economic Regulation' (1971) 5 *Bell J. of Econ. & Management Science* 335.

62 Tom Daschle et al., *Critical: What We Can Do about the Health Care Crisis* (St. Martin's Griffin, 2009) 66.

63 Jill Quadagno, 'Institutions, Interest Groups, and Ideology: An Agenda for the Sociology of Health Care Reform' (2010) 51 *J. of Health and Social Behavior* 125, 129; *See also* Jill Quadagno, 'Why the United States Has No National Health Insurance: Stakeholder Mobilization against the Welfare State, 1945–1996' (2004) 45 *J. of Health and Social Behavior* 25.

Depending on the benefits at stake, the influence of special interests on legislative entrenchment can be symmetric and it can be exerted either *ex ante* or *ex post* on any great reforms that may endanger vested interests. To illustrate, in 1965, Medicare faced fierce opposition from the American Medical Association. At that time, physicians feared that Medicare would influence general medical practices.[64] Congress responded by prohibiting Medicare of 'exercis[ing] any supervision or control over the practice of medicine or the manner in which medical services are provided.'[65] Instead, the common practices developed by the Blue Cross and Blue Shield organizations were borrowed, determining the separate payment of hospitals and physicians for single episodes of care.[66] More than fifty years later, not only is Medicare still standing but its inefficiencies have been sheltered from proposed reforms by thousands of physicians behaving like street-level bureaucrats.[67]

Legislative change can be difficult to achieve not only because of the presence of special interests but also because of the existence of divergent interest groups. Health care reforms such as the one introduced by the ACA requires extensive negotiation with a variety of self-interested groups who do not agree on a number of topics: Small businesses that do not offer or do not wish to offer health insurance to their employees; hospitals and health care providers that are skeptical of health reforms since they are afraid of repercussions on the prices of their services; religious groups and unions that seek to shape their members even through the delivered health care services; constituents with divergent preferences and needs; and pharmaceuticals that are interested in marketing their products.[68]

Despite the difficulty in uniting diverse groups, there are examples that show that when legislative change is perceived as a common enemy, more and less privileged interest groups might be more inclined to form coalitions. For example, in the 1990s, physicians joined patient groups to lobby state legislatures against managed care firms.[69] Different special interest groups have also tried to maintain the status quo in detriment of the evidence or the disclosure of information regarding the most effective treatments. In 2009, the inclusion of the so-called comparative effectiveness approach in the economic stimulus package to fund studies evaluating treatments for several diseases, became an important source of concern for pharmaceuticals and medical devices producers. Patients also feared that comparative effectiveness,

64 Nicholas Bagley, 'Bedside Bureaucrats: Why Medicare Reform Hasn't Worked' (2013) 101 *Georgetown. L. J.* 519, 521.

65 Social Security Amendments of 1965, Pub. L. No. 89–97, sec. 102(a), § 1801, 79 Stat. 291 (codified at 42 U.S. C. § 1395 (2006).

66 Bagley, *supra* note 65, at 526.

67 ibid., at 522.

68 Lawrence R. Jacobs & Theda Skocpol, *Health Care Reform and American Politics: What Everyone Needs to Know* (Oxford University Press, 2012) 57–58.

69 Quadagno, *supra* note 64, at 129.

which aims to identify the most effective treatment for a certain disease, would mean that patients would be denied specific care on the grounds of its costs.[70] A number of pharmaceuticals formed a coalition with the National Health Alliance for Hispanic Health and the National Alliance on Mental Illness, both subsidized by them, to attempt to reject the comparative effectiveness approach, arguing the underrepresentation of Hispanic in comparative effective research.[71]

### *3.4. Citizen mobilization*

Informal entrenchment tends to be a bottom-up process that can be triggered by social movements, which can both license or limit legislative change.[72] In the process of entrenchment of the ACA we observe both trends.

The ACA started developing institutions that could generate constituencies that, over time, may guarantee reiterated political support.[73] On January 2, 2014, an optimistic article in the Washington Post declared the end of the fight against Obamacare as 6 million previously uninsured citizens started to benefit from the expansion of Medicaid. In 2017, former President Obama still uses social media to urge uninsured Americans to register for a health plan. At first sight—and perhaps in a country with different demographics and political tradition—these actions could lead to a point of no return for the entrenchment of the ACA since newly registered citizens would oppose any attempt to reduce their benefits. In the United States, this number might not necessarily suffice to stop the legislative reform attempts initiated in the first year of the Trump Administration. Participatory or democratic entrenchment mechanisms are more complex than they seem. This is particularly true in the case of the ACA, which establishes a redistributive system, creating both winners and losers.[74] The ACA redistributes health costs in an attempt to concretize a universal right to basic coverage. It prohibits health insurance companies to discriminate on the grounds of pre-existing conditions and requires most Americans to obtain health insurance for themselves and their dependents ('individual mandate').[75] This imposes costs on the

70 David Orentlicher, 'Rationing Health Care: It is a Matter of the Health Care System Structures' (2010) 19 *Annals Health L.* 449, 455.

71 Barry Meier, 'New Effort Reopens a Medical Minefield', *New York Times*, 7 May 2009 at www.nytimes.com/2009/05/07/business/07compare.html?_r=0; Quadagno, *supra* note 64, at 129.

72 *See* Reva Siegel, 'Constitutional Culture, Social Movement Conflict and Constitutional Change: The Case of the de facto ERA' (2006) 94 *California L. Rev.* 1323, 1327.

73 *See* Mark Tushnet, 'The Affordable Care Act and American Constitutional Development' (2014) 62 *Drake L. Rev.* 1079.

74 *See generally* Douglas A. Kahn & Jeffrey H. Kahn, 'Commentary, Free Rider: A Justification for Mandatory Medical Insurance under Health Care Reform?' (2011) 109 *Mich. L. Rev. First Impressions* 78, 81, 84–85.

75 ACA sec. 1501 (this Section requires the 'Maintenance of Minimum Essential Coverage').

healthy citizens who could have benefited from more competitive but more discriminatory health insurance.[76]

However, informal entrenchment—in particular of quasi-constitutional statutes—can also reflect a gradual process of democratic acceptance of legislation. This acceptance or resistance to reform can be determined by citizen mobilization and other forms of formal and informal interaction between citizens and officials.[77] *De facto* entrenchment might then occur, if the statute is able to create a unified group of beneficiaries willing to express their opposition to significant future changes affecting the benefits originally conferred by this statute. The Obama Administration and a part of the literature appeared to be hopeful regarding the entrenchment of the ACA on these participatory grounds.[78] The creation of new political constituencies could theoretically be a source of opposition to any form of future repeal or amendment. This would occur since citizens who benefit from a fading policy would have incentives to become organized and try to maintain the status quo.[79]

Medicare beneficiaries, for example, have demonstrated on several occasions against the ACA, asking the government to 'keep its hands off their Medicare.' Medicare has become entrenched up to the point that senior citizens seem to be willing to mobilize against any potential change to their benefits. This discontentment resulted from the ACA plans to reduce Medicare costs over a period of ten years and the controversies surrounding the Independent Advisory Board, which rapidly and erroneously became known as 'death panels.'[80] The ACA threatened to change the structure of Medicare, allowing for the coexistence of three divergent payment models (*e.g.*, fee-for-service based on the traditional patient-health care provider relationship, and the new Accountable Care Organizations, which is being tested as a pilot and aims to integrate and consolidate services). The mentioned collective action initiated by Medicare beneficiaries translated however the concern of beneficiaries that Medicare might not be as deeply entrenched as they would like to.

Popular support and resistance to change can be translated into demonstrations, voter turnout, mass social media actions or the expression of citizens' preferences in opinion polls. These elements have been thoroughly analyzed in

76 Jessica L. Roberts, 'Healthism': A Critique of the Antidiscrimination Approach to Health Insurance and Health-Care Reform' (2012) *U. Illinois L. Rev.* 1159, 1187.

77 On public participation in the legislative process, *see generally* Peter M. Shane, 'Deliberative America' (2005) 1 *J. Pub. Deliberation* 10; Ethan J. Leib, *Deliberative Democracy in America: A Proposal for a Popular Branch of Government* (Penn State University Press, 2004). Cf. Reva Siegel, 'Constitutional Culture, Social Movement Conflict and Constitutional Change: The Case of the de facto ERA' (2006) 94 *California L. Rev.* 1323.

78 *See* Bowser, *supra* note 40.

79 Christoph Knill & Jale Tosun, *Public Policy: A New Introduction* (Palgrave, 2012) 264.

80 Paul Starr, 'Law and the Fog of Healthcare: Complexity and Uncertainty in the Struggle over Health Policy' (2013) 6 *Saint Louis U. J. of Health L. & Policy* 213.

the literature on popular constitutionalism, where popular mobilization is regarded as a driver of constitutional change.[81] Rebecca Zietlow has argued that the ACA can be qualified as a product of popular constitutionalism since it expands access to health care paving the way for the acceptance of the right to health care.[82] This claim would also support the idea that the ACA could be qualified as a quasi-constitutional statute. Nevertheless, the ACA might encounter obstacles in conquering weaker forms of social mobilization and voter turnout since it is in general difficult to guarantee the creation of new political constituencies when a policy program has an unclear identity and diffuse or ill-defined population of beneficiaries.[83] One of the weak points of the ACA is precisely that 'it treats different groups of Americans in different ways at different times, which complicates efforts to mobilize public support.'[84] While a number of citizens now has access to health insurance, another group of citizens benefiting from the former health insurance policies became displeased with the ACA since it raised the underlying costs of less expensive health insurance policies.[85]

Although the popularity of 'Obamacare' grew in the last year of President Obama's Administration, the public support of this statute has not increased dramatically in the last years. In 2013, opinion polls revealed that the greatest beneficiaries of the ACA, low and middle income citizens, were very skeptical of some aspects of the system established by the ACA, notably the health insurance exchanges.[86] A number of reasons explain this lack of strong support. First, partisanship still seems to determine citizens' opinion on equal access to health care services.[87] Second, only a small part of the voting population has been positively affected by the ACA.[88] However, despite the small victories and changes, the political support of the ACA is not sufficient to argue that citizens might be willing to mobilize to protect the statute in the future, at the resemblance of what might happen to Medicare if the danger of repeal would arise.

81 *See generally* Mark Tushnet, *Taking the Constitution Away from the Courts* (Princeton University Press, 1999). Larry D. Kramer, *The People Themselves: Popular Constitutionalism and Judicial Review* (Oxford University Press, 2005).

82 Rebecca E. Zietlow, 'Democratic Constitutionalism and the Affordable Care Act' (2011) 72 *Ohio St. L.J.* 1367, 1368. Cf. David Orentlicher, 'Rights to Healthcare in the United States: Inherently Unstable' (2012) 38 *Am. J. of L. & Med.* 326.

83 Jonathan Oberlander, 'The Future of Obamacare' (2012) 367 *New Eng. J. Med.* 2165.

84 *Id.*

85 Mark Blumenthal & Jonathan Colin, 'The Surprising Reason So Many People Still Don't Like Obamacare', *Washington Post*, 20 June 2015, at www.huffingtonpost.com/2015/06/21/obamacare-approval-polls_n_7632070.html

86 Sarah Kliff, 'Poll: Obamacare's Biggest Beneficiaries Are Skeptical of Obamacare', *Washington Post*, 22 February 2013 at www.washingtonpost.com/news/wonkblog/wp/2013/02/22/poll-obamacares-biggest-beneficiaries-are-skeptical-of-obamacare/.

87 *Id.*

88 Blumenthal & Colin, *supra* note 86.

### *3.5. Agency implementation*

Professors Eskridge and Ferejohn have argued that single-agency implementation is a requirement for the qualification of a law as a super-statute.[89] The ACA has also embraced the potential entrenchment force resulting from agency insulation by creating the controversial Independent Payment Advisory Board (IAB). This independent agency was created to control the costs of Medicare and it was granted powers to require the Secretary of Health and Human Services (HHS) to implement its recommendations unless Congress passes an alternative plan to reduce Medicare costs. This agency has received great opposition and there have been recent Congressional attempts to repeal the IAB. At the time of writing, an important actor in the American health care system is the Center for Medicare & Medicaid Services (CMS), previously known as Health Care Financing Administration (HCFA), which is located within the HHS. The CMS implements policy changes through regulations and manages day-to-day program operations.

## 4. Informal legislative entrenchment and quasi-constitutionalism

At the quasi-constitutional and constitutional levels, formal entrenchment has been regarded as a synonym of widespread public consensus and preservation of fundamental rights and principles. The attempt to entrench constitutions and constitutional and quasi-constitutional statutes has not only been common but it has also been welcomed in several jurisdictions where rigid constitutions, eternity clauses, and complex amendment procedures are institutionalized in order to limit constitutional change.[90] This has been argued not only in the United States but also in other common law jurisdictions such as Canada, New Zealand, and the United Kingdom, in the context of the consolidation of fundamental rights, free exercise of religion and protection of minorities, particularly in times of economic distress and emergencies.[91]

Constitutional entrenchment performs a preservationist function, safeguarding against the usurpation of constitutional principles by ordinary legislation.[92] It generates legal pre-commitment to constitutional values not only by explicitly limiting constitutional change but also through the delegation of the enforcement of self-binding mechanisms to external agents, in particular judges that

89 William N. Eskridge, Jr. & John Ferejohn, *A Republic of Statutes: The New American Constitution* (Yale University Press, 2010) 115.

90 *See, e.g.*, David Landau and Rosalind Dixon, 'Constraining Constitutional Change' (2015) 50 *Wake Forest L. Rev.* 859; Richard Albert, 'The Difficulty of Constitutional Amendment in Canada' (2015) 55 *Alberta L. Rev.* 86.

91 *See, e.g.*, Douglas A. Schmeiser, 'The Entrenchment of a Bill of Rights' (1981) 19 *Alberta L. Rev.* 381; Ian McLean & Scott Peterson, 'Entrenching the Establishment and Free Exercise of Religion in the Written U.K. Constitution' (2011) 9 *Int. J. Const. L.* 230; Jerome B. Elkind, 'A New Look at Entrenchment' (1987) 50 *Modern L. Rev.* 158.

92 *See* Richard Albert, 'Constitutional Handcuffs' (2010) 42 *Arizona State L.J.* 663, 678.

guarantee the preservation of the People's will. As Bruce Ackerman explains, ordinary legislation does not echo the People's will but that of political agents who speak while 'We the People' is silent.[93]

In the last decade, British courts have acknowledged that constitutional statutes are more difficult to repeal than ordinary statutes.[94] In 2012, the Administrative Court decided in the case of *Thoburn v Sunderland City Council* that, contrary to ordinary statutes, constitutional statutes can only be repealed expressly or by necessary implication, raising the bar in comparison to the ordinary repeal by implicit implication.[95] In the 2012 decision of *H v Lord Advocate*, the Supreme Court remarked that the Scotland Act, qualified as a constitutional statute, could not be altered by any type of implication. Adam Perry has explained that this "does not mean constitutional statutes are fully entrenched, because they can still be repealed expressly. Instead constitutional statutes are 'quasi-entrenched'".[96] Entrenchment is accepted in this context to preserve the fundamental values set forth in several fundamental statutes, including the Petition of Right 1628, the Bill of Rights 1689, the Act of Settlement 1701, the Act of Union 1707, the Treaty of Union with Ireland Act 1800, the Representation of the People Acts 1832–84, and the Human Rights Act 1998.[97]

At the level of quasi-constitutionalism, Professors Eskridge and Ferejohn have contributed to the study of non-legal dimensions of entrenchment in the United States with their research on 'super-statutes.'[98] These statutes are fundamental pillars of the U.S. legal order that have acquired a quasi-constitutional status by resisting judicial challenges and being able to establish a new normative or institutional framework for state policies.

As Professors Eskridge and Ferejohn explain in their scholarship on 'super-statutes,' quasi-constitutional statutes become entrenched not because they were granted a constitutional or quasi-constitutional status *ab initio* but because they 'earned it.' In other words, the ability to resist reform shows broad social, political, and judicial consensus about the fundamental value of these statutes. While this last perspective offers a useful framework to understand legislative continuity of quasi-

93 *See* Michael J. Klarman, 'Review: Constitutional Fact/Constitutional Fiction: A Critique of Bruce Ackerman's Theory of Constitutional Moments' (1992) 44 *Stanford L. Rev.* 759, 761; Bruce Ackerman, *We the People: Foundations* (Harvard University Press, 1993) 262.

94 Adam Perry, 'Constitutional and Quasi-Constitutional Statutes' (2015) *Int. J. of Const. L. Blog* at: www.iconnectblog.com/2015/04/constitutional-and-quasi-constitutional-statutes

95 [2002] EWHC 195 (Admin), [2003] QB 151, [2002] 3 WLR 247.

96 Adam Perry, 'Constitutional and Quasi-Constitutional Statutes' (2015) *Int. J. of Const. L. Blog* (2015) at: www.iconnectblog.com/2015/04/constitutional-and-quasi-constitutional-statutes. *See* Farrah Ahmed & Adam Perry, 'The Quasi-Entrenchment of Constitutional Statutes' (2014) 73 *Cambridge L.J.* 514.

97 For a thorough analysis of constitutional statutes, *see* Farrah Ahmed & Adam Perry, 'Constitutional Statutes' (2017) 37 *Oxford. J. Legal Studies* 461.

98 William N. Eskridge & John Ferejohn, *A Republic of Statutes: The New American Constitution* (Yale University Press, 2010).

constitutional statutes, not all statutes that endure fulfil Eskridge and Ferejohn's criteria. In addition, it is unclear whether this perspective on entrenchment should always have a normative value and will either improve lawmaking or favor the development of quasi-constitutionalism.[99] Moreover, the qualification of a law as a super-statute does not guarantee full judicial impermeability: in *Shelby County v. Holder*, the U.S. Supreme Court struck down the important coverage formula of Section 5 of the Voting Rights Act, limiting the practical implementation of parts of this super-statute. Therefore, even if the ACA is partially revised in the coming years, its ability to resist reform and maintain its core values (e.g., prohibition to discriminate on the grounds of preexisting conditions) might mean that the ACA has acquired a quasi-constitutional character. This entrenchment does not mean that the problems that characterize U.S. health care have been solved but rather that 'Obamacare' has captured the main institutions, constituencies, and stakeholders in this field.

## 5. Conclusion

In this book chapter, I have drawn on the case of the U.S. health care system and particularly on the Affordable Care Act to discuss the social, political, economic, and bureaucratic forces that contribute to the entrenchment of a statute. The long-term persistence of a law is one of the features of quasi-constitutional statutes, which shows that legislative entrenchment is not necessarily a problematic phenomenon. Rather, a certain degree of stability is required to guarantee structural reforms and allow for the gradual democratic acceptance of quasi-constitutional statutes.

The ACA was the result of a long path of legislative reforms that sought to change the US health care system and expand access to health care. This act offered small incremental changes that were likely to assist millions of Americans. A future classification of the ACA as a quasi-constitutional statute remains uncertain but at the time of writing it is clear that a number of informal entrenchment forces have been active and have made legislative reform more difficult than the Trump Administration could have predicted.

Legal scholarship still lacks an overarching theory of legal change applicable to constitutional, quasi-constitutional, and legislative entrenchment. Constitutional entrenchment is accepted because the traditional idea of a constitution implicates the long-term persistence of constitutional values and principles that inform the legal order. By contrast, ordinary legislation is traditionally expected to change in the aftermath of policy reforms and elections. Quasi-constitutionalism is situated somewhere in the middle. The long-term persistence of quasi-constitutional statutes is often the result of social, political and economic forces that are active when formal or legal entrenchment forces are not allowed to be.

99 Mathew D. McCubbins & Daniel B. Rodriguez, 'Superstatutory Entrenchment: A Positive and Normative Interrogatory' (2011) 120 *Yale Law Journal Online* 387, 404.

# 11 Quasi-entrenched living statutes

## Creating a multicultural rights regime

*Franciska Coleman*[*]

In the Spring of 2011, the term 'Digital Revolution' acquired new meaning as individuals across the Arab world used social media to organize protests, share information, and create national networks of citizens demanding change. Stories and videos of Mohammed Bouazizi's self-immolation in Tunisia[1] and of Khalid Said's murder by security forces,[2] spread across Twitter, Facebook, and even SMS platforms like wildfire, awakening the political consciousness of numerous communities and spurring them to action.[3]

As a result, after just twenty-eight days of protests, President Zine El Abidine Ben Ali, who had ruled Tunisia for twenty-three years, resigned and fled the country.[4] Similarly in Egypt, eighteen days of mass protest resulted in the resignation of Hosni Mubarak after almost three decades in power.[5] In Yemen, Morocco, Libya, and all across the Arab world, protestors began to demand international human rights and a greater voice in their governments. The Fourth Wave of democracy had begun.[6]

Most observers would agree that one of the greatest successes of the Egyptian and Tunisian revolutions was the ouster of longstanding dictators through relatively non-violent grassroots protests. After that was achieved, however, the protestors faced the far more formidable task of creating a new government and uniting around a constitution embodying their democratic aspirations. For, unlike the first wave of democracy—when the social and legal exclusion of

* Assistant Professor, Yonsei Law School; Visiting Assistant Professor, University of Kansas Law School. My sincere thanks to the editors and to the participants in the Symposium on Quasi-Constitutionality and Constitutional Statutes for their helpful comments.

1 Philip N. Howard and Muzammil M. Hussain, *Democracy's Fourth Wave? Digital Media and the Arab Spring* (Oxford University Press, 2013) 19.

2 Ibid., 21.

3 Ibid., 50.

4 Ayodeji K. Perrin, 'Introduction to the Special Issue on the Arab Spring' (2013) 34 UPAJIL i, i.

5 Charles Levinson, Margaret Coker, Matt Bradley, Adam Entous and Jonathan Weisman, 'Fall of Mubarak Shakes Middle East' *The Wall Street Journal* (New York, 12 February 2011) <www.wsj.com/articles/SB10001424052748703786804576137543866154926> accessed 25 April 2016.

6 Howard and Hussain (n 2).

women, minorities and the poor from the constitution making process allowed nations to avoid addressing the explosive potential inherent in racial, religious, and economic diversity[7]—inclusion is the hallmark of legitimacy for modern constitution writers.[8] However, the theories of constitutionalism that worked so well in the first wave of democracy have changed very little to accommodate later waves. Though few democracies, old or new, can be characterized as John Jay once characterized the U.S.—'one united people ... descended from the same ancestors, speaking the same language, professing the same religion, attached to the same principles of government, very similar in their manners and customs,'[9]—constitutional theory remains embedded in approaches to rights articulation that presuppose a super-consensus largely unobtainable under modern conditions of heterogeneity.

This is not surprising, for the conjunction of democracy and diversity is a relatively recent phenomenon. Democracy originated in societies with very restrictive notions of citizenship, and diversity within such citizenries was quite limited. Moreover, when citizenship was finally extended to minority groups, their differences were often required to be masked under melting pot theories of assimilation and social cohesion.[10] Thus, it is only in recent years that diversity has become something to be both celebrated and accommodated. Traditional approaches to fundamental rights protections in these new, inclusive multicultural contexts have had limited success.

This chapter will use comparisons between the recent constitutional revolutions in Egypt and Tunisia and the civil rights revolution in the U.S. to argue that quasi-entrenched statutes are often better vehicles for articulating the rights aspirations of multicultural societies than more traditional approaches to fundamental rights protections. The first part of this chapter will discuss the rights articulation attempts in the recent revolutions in Egypt and Tunisia and the influence of traditional approaches to constitutionalism on the drafting process and on contemporaneous critiques of the drafting process. The second part of this chapter will discuss the choice of the U.S. Civil Rights Movement as an explanatory foil and seek to identify the characteristics of the Civil Rights Act which enabled it to create a multicultural rights regime where formal

7 Akhil Reed Amar, *America's Constitution: A Biography* (Turtleback, 2005) 18–21 (noting that the new world ideals of opportunity and mobility were limited to White males).

8 Darin E. W. Johnson, 'Beyond Constituent Assemblies and Referenda: Assessing the Legitimacy of the Arab Spring Constitutions in Egypt and Tunisia' (2015) 50 Wake Forest L Rev 1007, 1010 (noting that 'An inclusive and broadly participatory constitution-drafting process, known as participatory constitution-making, is a hallmark of legitimacy for modern constitutions.')

9 *The Federalist Papers*, No. 2.

10 See e.g., Christine E. Sleeter and Carl A. Grant, *Making Choices for Multicultural Education: Five Approaches to Race, Class and Gender* (6th edn, Wiley, 2007) 44, 45; Helen Russon, Rethinking the Melting Pot; Diversity Is Here to Stay. How Do We Make It Work for Everyone? (1994) or St B Bull. 9.

constitutionalism had consistently failed. It will argue that the characteristics of quasi-entrenched statutes—minority empowering procedures, enforcement restrictions, and delayed entrenchment—promote the resolution of rights disagreements through existing political institutions rather than through resort to extra-legal measures. The third part of this chapter will consider the strengths and limitations of a new approach to constitutionalism in multicultural societies centered upon quasi-entrenched living statutes. It will explore the implication of this approach for emerging multicultural democracies.

## I. Constitution making in Egypt and Tunisia

Ash-sha`b yurid isqat an-nizam ('The people wants to bring down the regime.')

> *What is the Third Estate?*
> *Everything.*
> *What has it been until now in the political order?*
> *Nothing.*
> *What does it ask?*
> *To become something.*[11]

In the eyes of many observers, the Arab Spring was the awakening of the Middle East's Third Estate. After so many decades as the objects of tyranny, colonization, and others' governance, the people in Arab nations suddenly began to imagine themselves as the subjects of governance, possessing rights of self-determination.[12] This new collective consciousness of their existence and autonomy as 'the people,' spread across the Middle East like wildfire, leaving in its wake the ashes of several dictatorships. In nation after nation, the people took to the streets to reject nothingness and to lay claim to their right 'to become something.' But hard as it was to reject the mantle of nothingness, it proved even harder to concretize the vision of 'somethingness' in the form of a national constitution.

This section begins by briefly discussing the three traditional principles of constitution making that seemed to be presupposed by both the authors of the new constitutions in Egypt and Tunisia and their critics. These principles are 1) constitutional rights should be entrenched, 2) constitution making should be inclusive and participatory, and 3) constitutional substance should conform to international norms. This section concludes by discussing how these presuppositions influenced the drafting process and informed both the rhetoric and the critique of the final constitutional documents in these two nations.

11 Abbe Sieyes, What Is the Third Estate? (1789).
12 Ibid.

## *A. Traditional principles of constitution making*

Despite Jefferson's argument that constitutions are generational and naturally expire every 19 years,[13] the touchstone of modern constitutionalism is the principle of entrenchment.[14] Constitutions set forth enduring principles of government and are deliberately designed to last for an indefinite number of generations. They do not merely construct a new government; they also define the parameters within which 'all' subsequent generations of political actors will operate. Such formal constitutions are designed to preserve a specific political structure and an ideal type of citizen against the vagaries and passions of future times. In theory and occasionally in practice, entrenched constitutions are like diamonds, they are effectively forever.

The presumed permanence of constitutional identities, combined with modern conditions of heterogeneity, has given rise to a second principle of constitutionalism: Constitutions must be the product of a highly inclusive and participatory process.[15] As constitutions are higher law that will bind future generations, the process of their initial promulgation must be as democratic as possible and rooted in the consent of the whole people. Thus, the drafting and adoption of a new constitution cannot be confined to elites, and may not simply reflect the preferences of the current majority. Instead, it must be a consensus-based document that reflects the fundamental values of the whole of an informed and participating citizenry. Under modern conditions of heterogeneity, however, the twin aims of inclusion and participation may be in tension with each other, for some participatory outcomes rooted in majority rule preclude the meaningful inclusion of opposing minority viewpoints, particularly those viewed as illiberal. In addition, modern societies increasingly recognize that the bare aggregation of minority and majority preferences is not sufficient for just democratic governance. As a result, in modern approaches to democratic legitimacy, participation and inclusion are often understood to presuppose a commitment to democracy's 'internal morality.'[16] This form of democratic legitimacy recognizes that a gap may exist between what the majority wants and what justice requires.[17] Thus, inclusion and participation are not free standing variables within a system of

13 Letter from Thomas Jefferson to James Madison Paris (6 September 1789) <www.let.rug.nl/usa/presidents/thomas-jefferson/letters-of-thomas-jefferson/jefl81.php> accessed 25 April 2016 (noting that 'Every constitution, then, and every law, naturally expires at the end of 19 years. If it be enforced longer, it is an act of force and not of right.')

14 See e.g., Tom Ginsburg and Eric A. Posner, 'Subconstitutionalism' (2010) 62 Stanford L Rev 1583, 1586–1587 (noting that 'ideas of entrenchment are central to the notion of constitutions.'); Ruti Teitel, 'Transitional Jurisprudence: The Role of Law in Political Transformation' (1997) 106 Yale LJ 2009, 2057 (same).

15 See e.g., Eugene D. Mazo, 'The Upstream Problem in Constitutionalism' (2015) 50 Wake Forest L Rev 795, 825; Johnson (n 9).

16 Cass R. Sunstein, *Designing Democracy: What Constitutions Do* (Oxford University Press, 2002) 120.

17 Ibid.

popular will and compromise, but rather rest against a backdrop of higher order, supranational conceptions of substantive equality and reasonableness.

This orientation towards legitimacy leads almost seamlessly to a third principle of modern constitutionalism—national incorporation of supranational norms.[18] The proliferation of international conventions has produced a growing sense that there is a set of 'universal' human rights,[19] recognition of which has become a touchstone of democratic legitimacy. For example, gender equality, racial equality, and freedom of conscience are increasingly viewed as essential components of any legitimate constitutional system, particularly with regard to minority groups.[20] New constitutions that fail to protect these and other rights considered fundamental are increasingly criticized as lacking genuine democratic processes and commitments.[21] These criticisms reflect an increasing tendency to judge multicultural societies, not by the rule of a democratic majority, but by the extent to which minorities in the nation are able to exercise those individual rights and liberties constructed as universal.

### *B. Constitution making in Egypt*

The constitution making process in Egypt implicated all three of these traditional principles. For example, in 2011, a Constitutional Review Committee (CRC) was appointed by the Supreme Council of the Armed Forces (SCAF) to amend the 1971 constitution for use during the transition period. The selection of its members seems deliberately designed to suggest a highly inclusive and participatory process.[22] For example, the CRC consisted of a member of the Muslim Brotherhood, a Coptic Christian, a former judge who had been an outspoken critic of the Muburak regime, and three law professors with no known political affiliation.[23] Moreover, both the Coptic Christian and two other members were

18 Johnson (n 9) 1012 (noting that 'The incorporation of international human rights law norms into constitution-drafting processes became commonplace in the late twentieth and twenty-first centuries.'); see also Larry Catá Backer, 'From Constitution to Constitutionalism: A Global Framework for Legitimate Public Power Systems' (2009) 113 Penn State L Rev 671, 671–72.

19 See e.g., Universal Declaration of Human Rights (adopted 10 December 1948 UNGA Res 217 A(III) (UDHR).

20 Ibid.

21 See e.g., Li-ann Thio, 'Constitutional Accommodation of the Rights of Ethnic and Religious Minorities in Plural Democracies: Lessons and Cautionary Tales from South-East Asia' (2010) 22 Pace Int'l L. Rev. 43, 49–50.

22 Dunne and Radian, 'Egypt: Why Liberalism Still Matters' in Larry Diamond and Marc F. Plattner (eds.), *Democratization and Authoritarianism in the Arab World* (Johns Hopkins University Press, 2014) 255.

23 David D. Kirkpatrick and Kareem Fahim, 'In Egypt, a Panel of Jurists is Given the Task of Revising the Country's Constitution' *The New York Times* (New York, 16 February 2011) <www.nytimes.com/2011/02/16/world/middleeast/16egypt.html?pagewanted=all> accessed 25 April 2016.

judges on Egypt's Supreme Constitutional Court.[24] Many commenters were pleasantly surprised by the make up of the committee, as it seemed to reflect a deliberate attempt to include all the major groups who had participated in the January 25th movement.[25]

This initial attempt at inclusion was supplemented by a public referendum on the nine amendments recommended by the CRC.[26] Forty-one percent of eligible voters went to the polls, and seventy-seven percent of them voted to approve the new amendments.[27] This initial emphasis on inclusion and participation was undercut two weeks later, however, when SCAF unilaterally declared the 1971 constitution void and issued an anonymous constitutional declaration.[28] The Declaration, issued primarily in response to objections to the continued use of the 1971 constitution during the transition period, cobbled together select provisions of the 1971 constitution and the referendum amendments.[29] The Declaration was accepted with little protest[30] due in large part to its temporary, unentrenched status.

However, a year later in 2012, when the nation began to craft an entrenched constitution, the constitution design process became mired in conflict. The newly elected parliament, charged with selecting a one hundred-member Constituent Assembly to draft the final constitution,[31] was seventy-percent Islamist[32] and chose to select half of the members of the Constituent Assembly from within.[33] Almost immediately, the composition of the Assembly was challenged

24 Johnson (n 9).

25 Johnson (n 9).

26 Nathan J. Brown and Michele Dunne, 'Egypt's Draft Constitutional Amendments Answer Some Questions and Raise Others' (Carnegie Endowment for International Peace, 1 March 2011) <carnegieendowment.org/2011/03/01/egypt-s-draft-constitutional-amendments-answer-some-questions-and-raise-others#> accessed 25 April 2016.

27 BBC News, 'Egypt Referendum Strongly Backs Constitution Changes' (20 March 2011) < www.bbc.com/news/world-middle-east-12801125> accessed 25 April 2016.

28 Johnson (n 9).

29 Nathan J. Brown and Kristen Stilt, 'A Haphazard Constitutional Compromise' (Carnegie Endowment for International World Peace, 11 April 2011) <carnegieendowment.org /2011/04/11/haphazard-constitutional-compromise#> accessed 25 April 2016.

30 Kristen A. Stilt, 'The End of "One Hand": The Egyptian Constitutional Declaration and the Rift between the "People" and the Supreme Council of the Armed Forces' (2012) *Faculty Working Papers*, Paper 208 <scholarlycommons.law.northwestern.edu/cgi/viewcontent.cgi?article=1207&context=facultyworkingpapers> accessed 25 April 2016.

31 Marina Ottaway, 'Who Will Write the Egyptian Constitution?' (Carnegie Endowment for World Peace, 13 March 2012) <http://carnegieendowment.org/2012/03/13/who-will-write-egyptian-constitution-pub-47523> accessed 25 July 2016.

32 David D. Kirkpatrick, 'Islamists Win 70% of Seats in the Egyptian Parliament' *The New York Times* (New York, 21 January 2012) <www.nytimes.com/2012/01/22/world/middleeast/muslim-brotherhood-wins-47-of-egypt-assembly-seats.html> accessed 25 April 2016.

33 Heba Hesham, 'Islamists Dominate Constituent Assembly, Some Elected Members Walk Out in Protest' *Daily News Egypt* (25 March 2012) <www.dailynewsegypt.com/2012/03/25/islamists-dominate-constituent-assembly-some-elected-members-walk-out-in-protest/> accessed 25 July 2016.

in court as lacking inclusiveness.[34] The first assembly was suspended by the Administrative Court,[35] and a second more diverse and inclusive assembly was elected by the parliament in June 2012.[36] Shortly after the new assembly was formed, however, representatives of various secular parties resigned, protesting the lack of women, young people and Christians in the new assembly and accusing the Islamists of monopolizing the process.[37] In addition to the resignations, lawsuits were filed urging the dissolution of the second assembly, in tandem with the dissolution of the parliament that had elected it.[38] The nature of the criticisms of the parliament and the constituent assembly presuppose the existence of the principles of inclusion and entrenchment.

Despite the criticisms, however, the constitution produced by the Second Constituent Assembly was approved by sixty-four percent of Egyptian voters in a referendum held on 15 and 22 December 2012.[39] Opponents, however, continued to oppose the Constitution as the product of an unrepresentative process and as lacking important human rights protections. The continuing debate over principles of inclusion and human rights were largely a function of the expectation of constitutional entrenchment. For, unlike the 1971 amendments and 2011 Constitutional Declaration, the document drafted by the Constituent Assembly was to be Egypt's highest and most enduring governance document. It would definitively resolve the question of the role of Islam in Egyptian society, a key issue for many of the primary players in the Egyptian revolution.[40] The answer to this question would determine, not temporarily, but seemingly once and for all, which identities would be appreciated and valued in Egyptian society and which identities would be relegated to second class status.[41] The burgeoning solidarity that had appeared in Tahrir Square seems to have been snuffed out by the high stakes of constitution making, ably abetted by SCAF and the 'deep state' political structure.[42]

34 Mohamed Fadel Fahmy, 'Court Disbands Egypt's Constitutional Group' *CNN* (11 April 2012) <edition.cnn.com/2012/04/11/world/africa/egypt-constitution/index.html> accessed 25 April 2016.

35 Kelly Buchanan, 'Egypt's New Constitution: General Overview of Drafting History and Content,' *In Custodia Legis* (15 January 2013) <blogs.loc.gov/law/2013/01/egypts-new-constitution-general-overview/> accessed 25 April 2016.

36 Ibid.

37 'Political Forces Sign on ElBaradei Call for Constituent Assembly Boycott' *Ahram Online* (29 September 2012) <http://english.ahram.org.eg/NewsRio/54250.aspx> accessed 31 July 2016.

38 Ahmed Aboulenein and Rana Muhammad Taha, 'Constituent Assembly Dodges Dissolution Bullet' *Daily News Egypt* (23 October 2012) <www.dailynewsegypt.com/2012/10/23/constituent-assembly-dodges-dissolution-bullet/> accessed 25 July 2016.

39 Buchanan (n 36).

40 Dunne and Radian (n 27) 259.

41 Franciska A. Coleman, 'Democracy and the Other: The Inverse Relationship between Majority Rule and a Heterogeneous Citizenry' (2015) 117 West Virginia L Rev 1153, 1170.

42 Sahar F. Aziz, 'Bringing Down an Uprising: Egypt's Stillborn Revolution' (2014) 30 Connecticut J Intl L. 1, 25.

As a result of the fractured unity and the deposing of the president, a third round of constitution making began in July 2013.[43] SCAF appointed a small committee of ten jurists to amend the 2012 Constitution,[44] and circulated their draft to a group of fifty primarily nonlegal scholars appointed by SCAF from various sectors of Egyptian society.[45] Supporters of the new constitution underscored that the 'Committee of Fifty' was drawn from a broad cross-section of Egyptian society,[46] while opponents noted the complete lack of representation from the Muslim Brotherhood and the under-representation of Islamists and women.[47] Similarly, observers noted that marginal increases in the human rights protections for women and minorities were offset by increased military authoritarianism.[48] A public referendum on the third constitution had a turnout of around thirty-eight percent, with ninety-eight percent of voters approving the constitution.[49] However, this high percentage of approval is likely attributable as much to the suppression of dissenting views[50] and the arrest of dissenters[51] as it is to actual public approval.

### C. Constitution making in Tunisia

Principles of entrenchment, inclusive participation and international norms also played a significant role in the minds of the drafters and critics of the Tunisian constitution, but with very different effects than in Egypt. For example, the constitution making process in Tunisia began with the High Authority for the Realization of the Objectives of the Revolution, Political Reform, and Democratic Transition (High Commission), whose primary role was to draft the election law by which members of the Constituent Assembly would be elected and to set up an independent body (ISIE) to organize the elections.[52] Thus, the debate over

43 Gamal Essam El-Din, 'Committee Begins Revision of 2012 Egypt Constitution' *Ahram Online* (21 July 2013) <english.ahram.org.eg/NewsContent/1/64/77015/Egypt/Politics-/Committee-begins-revision-of–Egypt-constitution.aspx> accessed 25 April 2016.

44 Ibid.

45 'Who's Who: Members of Egypt's 50-Member Constitution Committee' *Ahram Online* (1 September 2013) <english.ahram.org.eg/News/80519.aspx> accessed 25 April 2016.

46 Ashraf Khalil, 'Egypt's Committee of 50 Rewrites the Constitution—Again' *Al Jazeera* (11 November 2013) <america.aljazeera.com/articles/2013/11/11/egypt-constitution committeeof50.html;> accessed 25 April 2016.

47 Matt Bradley, 'Egypt Names Mostly Secular Group to Draft Constitution' *The Wall Street Journal* (New York, 1 September 2013) < www.wsj.com/articles/SB10001424127887324202304579049243097988038> accessed 25 April 2016.

48 David M. Mednicoff, 'A Tale of Three Constitutions: Common Drivers and Diverse Outcomes in Post-2010 Arab Legal Politics' (2014) 28 Temple Intl and Com LJ 215, 235.

49 BBC News, 'Egypt Referendum: "98% Back New Constitution"' (19 January 2014) < www.bbc.com/news/world-middle-east-25796110> accessed 25 April 2016.

50 Bradley (n 48).

51 Ibid.

52 Carter Center, *The Constitution-Making Process in Tunisia 2011–2014* (15 April 2015) 23 <www.cartercenter.org/resources/pdfs/news/peace_publications/democracy/tunisia-constitution-making-process.pdf> accessed 25 April 2016.

an inclusive constitutional process began with this Commission and allegations that it was unrepresentative.[53] As a result, the Commission's membership was expanded from 72 to 155, including a variety of civil society groups and even a representative of the diaspora.[54] Elections under the new law produced a reasonably diverse body, with nineteen parties and sixteen independents obtaining seats, and with women (thirty percent) and youth (ten percent) also represented.[55] Nevertheless, Ennahda, Tunisia's top Islamist party, received forty percent of the seats in the National Constituent Assembly (NCA) (89 of 217), far greater than the number of seats obtained by any other Tunisian party —but well below the supermajority obtained by Islamists in Egypt.[56] Thus, though inclusiveness was a theme in both nations, in Egypt, inclusiveness was often something imposed top down by SCAF after setting aside electoral returns, while in Tunisia, the electoral returns themselves facilitated the incorporation of diverse perspectives in the work of the Constituent Assembly. This was not sufficient in itself, however, as nearly forty members of the Constituent Assembly boycotted the vote on an interim constitution, while protests continued throughout the nation.[57] Unlike in Egypt, however, resolution of this conflict was left to civil and political society, with neither the courts nor the military intervening to rehabilitate or delegitimize the electoral results in the name of stability.

The controversies over constitutional design were exacerbated by the entrenchment question, which, as in Egypt, proved to be an almost insurmountable roadblock. Ennahda's electoral success, coupled with the Muslim Brotherhood's success in Egypt, raised the specter of an 'entrenched' authoritarian theocracy; Ennahda's inclusion-oriented coalition building could not truly assuage this fear. In fact, minor parties in the Constituent Assembly were hesitant to be seen as working with Ennahda given the high stakes at issue, while several members of the two parties that joined with Ennahda to create the coalition government, defected from their parties and created new parties.[58] Thus, while the resulting constituent assembly had a high degree of inclusiveness as a result of a nationwide election, the high stakes of entrenchment made compromise within that diverse group extremely difficult. As a result, when Chokri Belaïd, a prominent opposition leader, was assassinated in February 2013, the

53 Ibid.

54 Ibid., 23 (n 18).

55 Ibid., 24.

56 Christopher Thornton, 'The Rocky Path from Elections to a New Constitution in Tunisia: Mechanisms for Consensus-Building and Inclusive Decision-Making' Oslo Forum Background Papers (2014) 4 <www.hdcentre.org/uploads/tx_news/The-rocky-path-from-elections-to-a-new-constitution-in-Tunisia.pdf>.

57 'Tunisian Assembly Adopts Provisional Constitution' *Al Jazeera* (11 December 2011) <www.aljazeera.com/news/africa/2011/12/201112115101550490.html> accessed 25 April 2016.

58 Carter Center (n 53) 26.

entire constitution making process was derailed.[59] Later in July, when Mohamed Brahmi, the NCA deputy was also assassinated, the entire constitution making process fell apart.[60] At the height of the crisis, over seventy members withdrew from the NCA and a coalition of opposition parties demanded the dissolution of the government.[61] Here again, however, unlike in Egypt, neither courts nor the military attempted to impose a resolution in the name of stability. Instead, four organizations from civil society—the General Union of Tunisian Workers; the Tunisian Union for Industry, Trade, and Handicraft; the Tunisian League for Human Rights; and the Bar Association ('the Quartet')—became the primary mediators in the crisis resolution process.[62] The Quartet presided over a series of national dialogues and were able to convince the two sides to reach a compromise. This resulted in a new constitution being adopted by the Constituent Assembly on 27 January 2014, with 200 of 216 votes being cast in favor of the Constitution.[63]

While the Tunisian Constitution was ratified by its Constituent Assembly rather than by popular referendum, the theory of broad participation was nevertheless an animating principle, as evidenced by the frequent use of national dialogues and consultations throughout the process. Indeed, the dialogues organized by the Quartet played a pivotal role in securing the compromises necessary to finalize the constitution. Lastly, as in the Egyptian context, criticism of the Tunisian constitution by both the domestic opposition and foreign observers were frequently couched in the language of international norms.[64] For example, the Carter report urged greater attention to international obligations in domestic law and to greater protection against traditional forms of discrimination.[65]

## II. Principles from the Civil Rights Movement for the Arab Spring

This section discusses the basis for the comparison between the Arab Spring and the Civil Rights Movement and identifies the characteristics of the Civil Rights Act that enabled it to secure rights protection that had long evaded constitutionalization in the United States.

### *A. Bridging the gap between the Occident and the Orient*

One of the most enduring binaries in an increasingly global world is the division between the Occident and the Orient. From Ernest Renan's assertion that

59 Ibid.
60 Ibid., 28.
61 Ibid.
62 Ibid.
63 Ibid., 29.
64 Ibid., 98.
65 Ibid., 98.

'Islam is the most complete negation of Europe'[66] to Donald Trump's declared intention to ban all Muslims from the United States,[67] the essential alterity of Muslims is often a taken for granted assumption of both Muslims and non-Muslims alike.[68] Thus, the idea at the heart of this comparison, that oppressed peoples in the West and oppressed peoples in the East may be able to use similar tactics in the pursuit of a multicultural rights regime, seems immediately counterintuitive. The socio-historical gap between Anglo-American legal culture and Islamic legal culture presumably leaves little ground for similarity as a basis of comparison. However, as Benedict Anderson rightly suggested, comparison is not reducible to a mere method or academic technique, but often has the greatest explanatory power when it functions also as a discursive strategy.[69] In this time of increased polarization between the East and the West, with the former often constructed as an enemy of democracy and the latter as its champion, it is helpful to recall that the West has its oppressed minorities and the East has its civil rights activists. There are similarities between the abuses of the powerful and the aspirations of the powerless that transcend culture, and these can serve as useful linchpins in the dialogue that must take place between the East and the West if peace and stability are to be achieved. The comparative lens of this chapter is designed to contribute to conversations between the socially powerless in both cultures, seeing them as human beings striving for human liberation along very similar axes, but each tailoring their efforts to their unique cultural and religious heritage.

For Egypt and Tunisia, for example, the issue was not the role of race in society, but rather the role of religion. However, race and religion are both individual characteristics that have given rise to collective identities that are alternately stigmatized by wider society and defined by individuals as an important and valuable part of who they are.[70] This is as equally true of Islam stigmatized as the religion of terrorists as it is of Blackness stigmatized as the race of criminals. Both Islamic identity and African-American identity are deeply meaningful aspects of the life stories of numerous individuals in various communities. The resulting social conflicts around these identities, though different, are thus similar in many ways.

Moreover, the use of comparison as a culture bridging discursive strategy complements the real similarities between the plight, goals, and options of African-Americans during the Civil Rights Movement and those of the participants in the Arab Spring. At the heart of each movement lay concerns, not merely

66 Lecture at the Collège de France, 'De la part des peuples sémitiques dans l'Histoire de la civilisation du 23 février 1862' (1995) 27.

67 Jeremy Diamond, 'Donald Trump: Ban all Muslim Travel to U.S.' *CNN* (8 December 2015) <www.cnn.com/2015/12/07/politics/donald-trump-muslim-ban-immigration/> accessed 25 July 2016.

68 Tariq Ramadan, *Islam and the Arab Awakening* (1st edn, Oxford University Press, 2012) 16.

69 Benedict Anderson, *A Life beyond Boundaries: A Memoir* (Verso, 2016) Ch. 4.

70 Kwame Anthony Appiah, *The Ethics of Identity* (Princeton University Press, 2007) 108.

with political autonomy, but also with the lack of economic opportunities.[71] In pursuit of these opportunities, key organizers in both groups relied on a non-violent protest tradition stretching back to India, with the Civil Rights Movement being one of the first adopters of this approach and the Arab Spring being the most recent.[72] Moreover, both movements relied heavily on the media of their time to bring their protests and abuses to the attention of national and international audiences, in hopes of persuading external entities to put pressure on their oppressors. In addition, several observers have argued for a similarity between Rosa Parks and Mohamed Bouazizi—ordinary people whose individual acts of personal protest set off national conflagrations.[73] In the Civil Rights Movement, however, the idea of a new constitutional interpretation was rejected in favor of legislation,[74] while in the two Arab Spring countries discussed here, constitutional amendment was rejected in favor of drafting a new constitution. The fact of these ultimately different outcomes, apparent even in comparisons between Middle Eastern countries with contemporaneous uprisings, does not negate, and may even underscore, the utility of discussing the effects of different strategies and their suitability as methods of political change in multicultural societies. Ultimately, the human struggle for liberty has no color, religion, or nation of origin; rather, the primary bar to theorizing across, rather than merely within these characteristics are own our mental binaries. 'Within the limits of plausible argument … the most instructive comparisons … are those that surprise.'[75]

## *B. Passage of the Civil Rights Act*

In the 1950s and 60s, civil rights legislation was difficult to pass, for Southern Democrats in the Senate would consistently align themselves with conservative Republicans to block or amend into inefficacy every civil rights bill sent to Congress.[76] Such bills would pass in the House of Representatives, only to die in the Senate. The Civil Rights Act of 1964 was no different. Like its predecessors, it passed in the House of Representatives,[77] only to be filibustered in the Senate. Under the Senate rules of the 1960s, a filibuster raised the bar of support for a bill from a majority of fifty-one to a supermajority of sixty-seven (now

71 Ibid., 9; Tomiko Brown-Nagin, 'Does Protest Work?' (2013) 56 How. L.J. 721, 723–724.

72 See e.g., Ali Mirsepassi and Tadd Graham Fernée, *Islam, Democracy, and Cosmopolitanism: At Home and in the World* (Cambridge University Press, 2014) 56.

73 See e.g., Mari Ruti, *The Singularity of Being: Lacan and the Immortal Within: Lacan and the Immortal Within* (Fordham University Press, 2012) 69; Christian Fuchs, *Social Media: A Critical Introduction* (SAGE, 2013) 205; Catherine Powell, 'Libya: A Multilateral Constitutional Moment?' (2012) 106 Am. J. Int'l L. 298, 310.

74 See e.g., Bell v. Maryland 378 U.S. 226 (1964).

75 Anderson (n 70).

76 Ibid., 14.

77 Clay Risen, *The Bill of the Century: The Epic Battle for the Civil Rights Act* (Bloomsbury Publishing, 2014) 162.

sixty).[78] Such filibusters by Southern Democrats had long been a tactic guaranteed to defeat any civil rights bill, and as a result, only one civil rights bill had been passed by the Senate in the 1950s. This lone success was due to the fact that the bill had been so weakened by amendments it was virtually meaningless.[79]

The filibuster option ensured that Northern Democrats in the Senate could not pass a civil rights bill without significant Republican support. Many conservative Republican senators, however, had genuine concerns about the intrusion into property rights represented by the public accommodations provision—without which the bill would have been anathema to civil rights groups.[80] Moreover, unlike in the House, where party loyalty had made it possible to obtain 290 yes-votes primarily through compromises among the House leadership, in the Senate party leadership had much less influence. It was necessary to persuade individual senators directly. In addition, senators from the midwestern states, who held the balance of power, had traditionally sided with Southern Democrats on issues of civil rights.[81]

The legislative approach to civil rights, however, enabled a broad range of outside groups to exert meaningful influence over the process through the power of their ballots, while the extended period of debate created by the filibuster fostered a robust national dialogue that drew in a wider and more diverse range of participants over time. The President, congressional representatives, and increasing numbers of ordinary citizens began to embrace the need for a strong civil rights bill, tipping the scales against the Southern Democrats. Also, as White conservative Christians in the Midwest joined Black and White liberals and Christians in the North and South, a national racial equality norm began to emerge. Church groups and church leaders from the midwestern states[82] were able to use prayer vigils, ministerial visits, and Sunday letter writing campaigns to persuade their Republican senators to support the Civil Rights Act,[83] while civil rights activists kept the pressure on liberal Democratic senators. As a result of these coalitions, the Southern filibuster was broken by a vote of seventy-one to twenty-nine,[84] and the 1964 Civil Rights Act was signed into law by President Johnson on 2 July 1964.[85]

Unlike the huge resistance to and backlash against *Brown*, the response to the Civil Rights Act was largely peaceful, with most cities and businesses complying with the requirement of non-discrimination in Title II.[86] One reason for this was legitimacy. While the Supreme Court's decision in *Brown* was often viewed

78 Ibid., 21.
79 Ibid., 13.
80 Ibid., 63.
81 Ibid., 21–22.
82 Ibid., 149.
83 Ibid., 149.
84 Ibid., 229.
85 Ibid., 240.
86 Ibid., 247.

as unconstitutional judicial overreaching, the process leading to the passage of the Civil Rights Act was generally considered democratic and legitimate by both opponents and proponents.[87] Though the Southern Democrats lost the vote, they did not disengage from the democratic process, but rather, encouraged their states and constituents to abide by the new law—despite the way in which it completely upended the Southern way of life.[88] The next section suggests reasons why the Southern senators were able to accept their loss with equanimity, while similar losses by secular groups in Egypt and Tunisian resulted in a complete breakdown of the deliberative process.

## *C. Lessons from the Civil Rights Movement*

### *1. Minority empowering procedures*

One reason the 1964 Civil Rights Act retained democratic legitimacy in the face of seemingly intractable opposition is because Senate procedures ensured that minority voices and perspectives received a fair (and in the view of some—more than fair) hearing. This was mostly accomplished through Senate Rule 22 (also known as the filibuster rule), one of the most controversial procedural rules in the U.S. Senate. As a result of this rule, a mere thirty-four senators could block legislation desired by the majority. This ability to block legislation could force numerical majorities to the negotiating table and often gave the more moderate portions of the opposition considerable leverage in extracting concessions from the majority. Though Rule 22 can be used to frustrate the democratic process on routine issues, fundamental rights are not routine.

Thus, one of the key factors in the post-passage legitimacy of the Civil Rights Act is that the minority perspective, though it lost, was able to exercise meaningful leverage within the process by invoking supermajority procedures. In Egypt, the Islamist party received a clear supermajority, seventy-percent of the vote, and thus would have dominated the process even with a minority empowering procedure like the filibuster. However, had escalation to a supermajority procedure been available, minority forces in Egypt would have only needed to persuade three Islamists to favor their position—as opposed to twenty-three—in order to obtain enough leverage to insist on meaningful compromises. The quantitative and qualitative difference between persuading three legislators and persuading twenty-three legislators is huge, and may well have been sufficient to encourage the Egyptian secular parties to continue the dialogue over the draft constitution, rather than abandoning the process.

The Tunisian case more clearly demonstrates the difference the meaningful leverage of minority parties can make in high stakes rights negotiations. For, in

87 Ibid., 231.

88 See e.g., Todd S. Purdam, *An Idea Whose Time Has Come: Two Presidents, Two Parties, and the Battle for the Civil Rights Act of 1964* (Henry Holt and Co., 2014) 330; Risen (n 78) 246.

Tunisia, the Islamists received only forty percent of the vote, giving the minority parties automatic leverage without formal minority empowering procedural rules.[89] Though this by no means eliminated charges of majoritarian tyranny, it did create an atmosphere of sufficient compromise and deliberation to prevent the process from being permanently derailed, despite intense disagreements among various sectors of the society. This suggests that minority empowering procedures may help promote the compromises so necessary for preserving the internal morality and legitimacy of new democratic systems.

### *2. Incorporation of enforcement restrictions*

In addition to the pressure to compromise (created through minority empowering rules), the Civil Rights Act also benefitted from the capacity of the legislative form to combine broad provisions with enforcement restrictions. Thus, while the substance of controversial provisions of the Civil Rights Act, such as Title II and the Fair Employment Practices Commission, could not be compromised away without a breakdown of the process, the simultaneous limits on enforcement methods created room for compromise. For example, pro-civil rights forces insisted that the Civil Rights Act prohibit discrimination in public accommodations, the objective of numerous direct action protests in the early 1960s.[90] At the same time, however, pro-business forces opposed increased government regulation and influence over owners of private property, and wanted Title II eliminated.[91] The pro-civil rights and pro-business forces were able to reach a compromise by combining a general prohibition on discrimination in public accommodations, with provisions that limited the enforcement role of the federal government by shifting enforcement to private individuals.[92] The compromise also exempted personal service businesses from enforcement actions all together.[93] This separation of principles and their enforcement is similar to the separation of principles and outcomes advocated by Cass Sunstein,[94] as enforcement limits presuppose certain desirable outcomes. Though constitutions are traditionally preoccupied with general principles and legislation with translating those principles into outcomes, this chapter suggests that legislation is a better vehicle for instantiating principles whose potential outcomes are underdetermined and contested.

For example, the pre-Arab Spring constitutions of both Egypt[95] and Tunisia[96] acknowledged Islam as the nation's religion; however, in the drafting process

89 Thornton (n 57) 4–5.
90 Purdam (n 89) 190.
91 Ibid.
92 Risen (n 78) 218.
93 Civil Rights Act of 1964, Pub. L. No. 88–352, 78 Stat. 241 §201 b(1) (1964).
94 See generally Sunstein (n 17).
95 Mednicoff (n 49) 229.
96 Carter Center (n 53) 82.

for the new constitutions, conflict arose over efforts to elaborate and specify the meaning of these provisions. For example, Egypt's 2012 Constitution did not merely repeat that Shari'a was a source of law, but instead tried to specify the sources of Shari'a, raising fears of a shift from symbolic acknowledgment of religion to judicial enforcement of one specific type of Islam.[97] This created strong opposition from secularists and minority religions, despite the fact that the language used in the provision was the result of a compromise between Islamist and secular groups.[98] The constitutional language intended as a compromise remained controversial because of fears about the nature of its enforcement.

Enforcement issues were a similar source of controversy in Tunisia. Some drafters wanted to make 'Islam is the state religion' an unamendable article of the Constitution, while other drafters worried about the effect of the enforcement of such a provision on Tunisia's existence as a secular state.[99] Similarly, some drafters felt that the Constitution should commit the state to the protection of the sacred, while others worried about the effect of enforcement of such a provision on the freedoms of conscience and speech.[100] The drafters compromised by putting both perspectives in the constitution, perhaps hoping that they would act as enforcement checks on each other. For example, Article VI has one clause promising to protect freedom of conscience and belief and another clause which commits the state to punishing offenses against the sacred.[101] A legislative approach may have offered a clearer path to such both/and compromises; for, a statute could provide for protection of the sacred, while simultaneously restricting enforcement against journalists and artists accused of violating the provision.

### *3. Delayed entrenchment*

Lastly, but perhaps most significantly, the Civil Rights Act benefitted from a lack of entrenchment. Though today, the Civil Rights Act is a quintessential constitutional statute, at the time of its passage, its entrenchment was far from clear. On the night before the vote, the bill's Democratic sponsors did not even know whether they had secured enough Republican votes to end the filibuster. In addition, though President Johnson strongly supported the Act, his challenger (the segregationist governor George Wallace) was winning almost a third of the democratic votes in Northern primaries.[102] Moreover, the Republican presidential candidate, Senator Barry Goldwater, had made his opposition to the Act clear throughout his campaign. Thus, it was entirely possible that the Act could

97 Mednicoff (n 49) 229.
98 Mednicoff (n 49) 230–231.
99 See e.g., Mednicoff (n 49) 224–226.
100 Ibid.
101 Ibid., Art. VI.
102 Ibid.

successfully pass the Senate, only to die later of unenforcement, should Wallace or Goldwater obtain the presidency.

Additionally, though a groundswell of support from religious groups in the Midwest and civil rights groups in the South and North had facilitated the passage of the Act, the rise of Wallace and Goldwater suggested the possibility of a white backlash against civil rights. As a result, there was no reason for opponents of the Act to believe that the national dialogue over the appropriate resolution of racial discrimination ceased with its passage. In addition, the enforcement restrictions placed Southern judges and juries in charge of enforcing major portions of the Act, allowing Southern objectors to continue their battle against civil rights before peers who often shared their sentiments. These circumstances provided outlets for continued disagreement within the system, thus lowering the stakes of failure.

The passage of the Civil Rights Act in the face of deeply held opposing views suggests that successful resolution of controversial rights issues in multicultural societies may be best pursued through a form that entails minority-empowering procedures, allows for the disaggregation of principles and enforcement, and that delays the entrenchment of fundamental rights. The next section will consider the potential criticisms and practical implementation of this approach.

## III. Quasi-entrenched living statutes

This section discusses the strengths and weaknesses of a statutory approach to fundamental rights. It discusses how an approach to constitutionalism rooted in Quasi-Entrenched Living Statues (QuELS) would modify the traditional principles of constitutionalism presented in Part I, and how QuELS constitutionalism would function in practice.

### *A. Strengths and weaknesses of the QuELS approach*

QuELS constitutionalism embraces a broadly inclusive process, but would require the incorporation of minority empowering procedures, on the ground that inclusion is meaningless without influence. Minority empowering procedures are a necessary corollary if inclusion is to be a substantive guarantee that enhances democratic legitimacy, rather than a mere formality. Moreover, while minority empowering processes often result in minority victories, they can also produce minority acceptance of the democratic legitimacy of their losses. The value of this acceptance cannot be overstated. Unless the losers in a democracy remain invested in the system and believe their losses to be legitimate and appropriate, a democracy cannot survive. Moreover, though protection of minority rights is generally considered the province of the judiciary, as minorities multiply, judges are losing the ability to protect all affected minorities equally. Instead, the modern judiciary is often forced to choose between the fundamental values of competing minorities—to protect one minority, not at the expense of the majority, but at the expense of another minority. Though judicial protection of minorities is an important aspect of democracy, when the judiciary is picking winners and losers from among minorities, it becomes difficult to separate claims of justice from claims of privilege. In such a situation, there is no substitute for empowering minorities to protect themselves.

QuELS also embraces enforcement limits on controversial rights provisions as a method of compromise and consensus-building, even though such limits may dilute the effect of rights norms within a given society. Given that some of the oldest democracies on the planet are still struggling to fully secure the supranational rights of their own constituent minorities, early under-enforcement of these rights in emerging multicultural democracies should not be considered a failure. Instead, an acceptance of enforcement limits is an affirmation of the autonomy of emerging democracies. It recognizes that younger, more heterogenous democracies may need to make enforcement compromises similar to those more established and homogenous democracies made in their youths. Most international human rights instruments acknowledge rights of derogation according to local context,[103] and enforcement limits can be justified by a similar principle. They are in some respects a local 'derogation' on the ground of newness, with an expectation of increased conformity to international norms as a democracy matures and evolves. The incorporation of enforcement limits, however, is often necessary to ensure that, in the first instance, there remains a stable democratic polity that can make such forward progress.

Lastly, QuELS constitutionalism rejects *a priori* entrenchment. Constitutionalism has historically proposed to identify the fundamental values of a society in advance and to entrench those values against a tyrannical majority. A newly constituted society, however, needs time to coalesce around a shared vision of its fundamental values, for entrenched principles are only as strong as the underlying social consensus upon which they are based. Even the United States, which has one of the oldest constitutions in the world, required time to embrace an inclusive vision of rights.[104] The approach recommended in this chapter is not the abandonment of entrenchment, however, but an argument to replace legal entrenchment with a more political entrenchment. It argues against legally entrenching controversial values before there is a meaningful consensus—merely because tradition requires that these issues be settled all at once, in the beginning. In essence, this chapter proposes to replace static bills of rights, not with a 'living constitution' updated by the judiciary, but rather with statutes

103 See e.g., International Covenant on Civil and Political Rights (adopted 16 December 1966, entered into force 23 March 1976) 999 UNTS 171 (ICCPR) Art. 4, Convention for the Protection of Human Rights and Fundamental Freedoms (European Convention on Human Rights, as amended) (ECHR) art 15, and American Convention on Human Rights, O. A. S. Treaty Series No. 36, 1144 U.N.T.S. 123, Art. 27, *entered into force* July 18, 1978, *reprinted in* Basic Documents Pertaining to Human Rights in the Inter-American System, OEA/Ser.L.V/II.82 doc.6 rev.1 at 25 (1992).

104 See e.g., *Plessy v. Ferguson*, 163 US 537 (1896), *Koremastu v. United States*, 323 U.S. 214 (1944); *Buck v. Bell*, 274 U.S. 200 (1927); *Bowers v. Hardwick*, 478 U.S. 186 (1986).

that become entrenched over time through a coalescing of agreement across the citizenry. This approach supports a living Bill of Rights, not set all at once by the founders or continuously updated by the judiciary, but one that emerges over time through intergenerational dialogue and praxis.

### *B. Implementation in multicultural democracies*

In new and emerging democracies, this chapter recommends that constitutionalism focus on the structure of government and political rights, before attempting to define the dignity and social equality rights of different genders, races, and religions. If competing groups in society create political structures, before knowing how much protection their own identities and values will receive, they may be incentivized to compromise around maximum political access for all groups. While this is not a true 'veil of ignorance,' it has the potential to place the emphasis in a constitutional convention, not on who is entitled to protection from the government and to what degree, but rather on the mechanisms by which the will of the people, writ large and inclusive, will be realized.

Thus, the approach in this chapter is designed to forestall 'clashes of absolutes' in emerging multicultural democracies in favor of building strong democratic processes on the shared democratic yearnings that inspired the birth of the new government in the first instance. It advocates a bifurcated approach to constitution making that limits the mandate of constitutional conventions to defining political rights, establishing methods of voting and representation, and determining the structure of the government. (Not because such provisions are uncontroversial, but rather because they tend to be less controversial than issues of culture and identity protection.) The new structures should include minority empowering processes and should promote the participation and inclusion of all sectors of society and the election of a broadly representative legislature. It is the responsibility of that first legislature to create an unentrenched human rights statute.

## IV. Conclusion

QuELS constitutionalism is premised on the idea that minorities in a multicultural society should be the subjects of political power rather than the objects of judicial protection, and thus foregrounds empowering political structures over promises of judicial protection. It presupposes that there is no greater protection for democracy than an active and engaged citizenry. As a result, it seeks to ensure that minority citizens are included in democratic deliberations and that rights commitments flow from an emerging democratic consensus of which they are a part.

# 12 The quasi-constitutionality of non-statutory law

## Executive constitutional interpretation in Japan

*James C. Fisher*[*]

## Introduction

This chapter explores a particular quasi-Constitutional rule of Japanese law in light of some general reflections about the nature and utility of quasi-Constitutionality. It argues that quasi-Constitutionality is a meaningful descriptor only in jurisdictions containing a formal mastertext Constitution, but that within such jurisdictions it applies with equal force to legal rules created by statute and those arising in other ways. As a case-study of non-statutory quasi-Constitutional law, this chapter analyses a rule of adjudication that equips the Japanese executive to give legally authoritative interpretations of the Constitution, notwithstanding the written Constitution's provision for judicial supremacy and conventional Constitutionality review. It draws on Japanese political and institutional history to explain how this legal rule emerged with quasi-Constitutional status, and also to deduce its precise parameters.

## The contribution of "quasi-Constitutionality" to constitutional legal study

This book assembles essays on the meaning, nature and effects of "quasi-Constitutionality" on the understanding that this term represents a theoretical innovation. But it is easy to exaggerate the novelty and utility of this new addition to juristic vocabulary. Particularly, it is not correct to present quasi-Constitutionality as a unifying feature or a conceptual middle ground between mastertext and non-mastertext jurisdictions. To talk of "quasi-Constitutionality" implies two interrelated propositions: that a legal rule is in some sense "Constitutional" notwithstanding its absence from a formal Constitutional text, and

* Project Associate Professor of Law, University of Tokyo Faculty of Law & Graduate Schools for Law and Politics. I am grateful for the insightful feedback of my discussant, Professor Tony Angelo of Victoria University Wellington, and to attendees at the Symposium, whose comments and questions prompted transformative revisions to this chapter.

that such a rule is nonetheless *only* quasi- (rather than fully) Constitutional. The first proposition is complex: on what basis, and why, should certain non-Constitutional content be grouped with Constitutional provisions? But on the assumption that this is sometimes appropriate, explaining why such rules are still not quite the same as Constitutional provisions invites a simple—if formalistic—answer: because they do not form part of the Constitutional mastertext, even though they resemble in some ways the legal rules that do.

Whether or not a particular jurisdiction contains a written Constitution, it necessarily has a *material* constitution—a complex body of legal rules that define and regulate public power. Even in jurisdictions with a notionally supreme, codified Constitution, the material constitution invariably includes legal rules not contained in the written Constitution. In jurisdictions without Constitutional mastertexts, legal rules answering certain criteria are understood to be "constitutional" in that they form part of the material constitution. In such jurisdictions there is neither need nor space for the notion of "quasi-Constitutionality": while these legal rules are obviously not Constitutional—for want of a written Constitution to which they could belong—they are fully part of the material constitution, and not merely "*quasi*" constitutional.[1] The ascendant notion of quasi-Constitutionality is simply new vocabulary with which jurists can discuss the material constitutions of mastertext jurisdictions. There is therefore perfect synonymity between a non-mastertext jurisdiction's "*constitutional* statutes" and a mastertext-jurisdiction's "quasi-*Constitutional* statutes".[2] So, although quasi-Constitutionality is not precisely a unifying feature of mastertext and non-mastertext jurisdictions' public law,[3] it represents increasing

1 Sergio Verdugo's criteria for assessing the quasi-Constitutionality of a statute focus on how far that statute imitates the substance and behaviour of a given jurisdiction's written Constitution, an approach not necessarily suitable for identifying constitutional features in non-mastertext countries: Sergio Verdugo, "How to identify quasi-constitutional legislation? An example from Chile" 45–48. In fact the point deserves to be put more forcefully—the thing rendered inappropriate by the absence of a mastertext Constitution is not a particular method for identifying the quasi-Constitutionality of a given legal rule, but the very notion of quasi-Constitutionality itself.

2 This echoes Rivka Weill's distinction between the "formal" and "material" constitutions, and her argument that Ackermanian statutes must be accepted as not merely quasi-constitutional but as having "full [material] constitutional status": Rivka Weill, "Exploring constitutional statutes in common law systems", 70. It follows that a legal rule properly considered "constitutional" in the United Kingdom or New Zealand would be describable as "quasi-Constitutional" in the USA or Australia. Scott Stephenson on this basis rightly designates statutes like the United Kingdom's Human Rights Act 1998 and New Zealand's Bill of Rights Act 1990 as "constitutional": Scott Stephenson, "The rise and recognition of constitutional statutes", 33.

3 Stephenson notes that "[t]he rise of constitutional statutes across the common law world ... cuts across the traditional divide between countries with and without a capital-C constitution": Stephenson (supra, n 2), 37. Indeed, confining the "quasi-Constitutionality" label to mastertext jurisdictions does not deny a convergence in *legislative practice* across the two traditions.

sensitivity within mastertext jurisdictions to two crucial truths. The first is that the law of the constitution is not found only in Constitutions and the judicial decisions in which their meaning and effect are declared. The second is that not all constitutional law is consciously enacted as such.

The discourse on quasi-Constitutionality is still in its adolescence and remains preoccupied with the status of statute law.[4] There is no reason that quasi-Constitutionality should be limited to statute law, and many reasons why it should not. Constitutional law consists of legal rules, and the traditional foci for constitutional legal analysis—such as written Constitutions, judicial decisions, and increasingly statutes—are simply vessels for those rules. Quasi-Constitutionality can only claim to be a coherent, convincing and useful lens through which to analyse a jurisdiction's material constitutional law if it is capable of accommodating legal rules regardless of their source.[5] Whatever it means to call a rule "quasi-Constitutional", this must be the same for rules arising other than by legislation if quasi-Constitutionality is to mean anything useful at all.

## Identifying quasi-Constitutionality

While the intuitive indicator of a rule's quasi-Constitutionality is its subject matter,[6] several contributions to this volume prefer a multi-factorial enquiry. Repeatedly suggested additional factors include the context of a statute's enactment, its trumping power and degree of entrenchment, and the importance it has been afforded by legal and political actors since its enactment. Ultimately though, all these seem intimately related to the question of substance. For instance, Rivka Weill suggests that the political drama of a statute's enactment—as a manifestation of popular democratic consciousness—can militate for its recognition as a constitutional statute. This is plausible, but something resists classifying as constitutional (or "quasi-Constitutional") a statute enacted in this way if its subject-matter is too far removed from the structuring and control of

4 The quasi-Constitutionality idea arose from attempts to understand the constitutional role of certain statutory enactments: see e.g. Bruce Ackerman, *We the People: Foundations* (Belknap Press 1991); *Transformations* (1998); *The Civil Rights Revolution* (2014); and William Eskridge and John Ferejohn, "Super-statutes: The New American Constitutionalism" in Richard Bauman and Tsvi Kahana (eds), *The Least Examined Branch: The Role of the Legislatures in the Constitutional State* (Cambridge University Press 2006); *A Republic of Statutes: The New American Constitution* (Yale University Press 2010).

5 Weill correctly notes that failing to engage with constitutional statutes is "ignoring large chunks of what constitutional law is all about" (supra n 2, 86). The same is true of legal rules outside statute altogether. As Weill observes, quasi-Constitutionality is "a broader phenomenon than constitutional statutes" applicable to "judicial decisions, conventions and custom": (supra n 2, 2).

6 For instance, Stephenson suggests that a quasi-Constitutional statute will purport to alter a fundamental feature of the system of government: (supra n 2, 28).

public power.[7] Comparatists must of course beware the intellectually imperialistic assumption that the typical subject matter of Western (or Western-influenced) Constitutions is the definitive constitutional content, such that anything else is penumbral or frivolous.[8] Nonetheless comparative constitutional legal analysis is obstructed without some common understanding of constitutional substance.

Understanding that quasi-Constitutionality means nothing more than a legal rule's place in a jurisdiction's material constitution produces a powerful insight about the identification of quasi-Constitutional legal rules that partially circumvents the difficult choice between absolute and relative understandings of constitutional content: whether a particular legal rule is quasi-Constitutional is not a question answerable by doctrinal legal logic.

It might seem problematic from a legal-analytic perspective to suggest that the material constitution—as opposed to a particular formal Constitution[9]—can be affected by the creation of positive law, since it is logically prior to civic powers' authority to augment or change the system's legal rules at all.[10] But part of the distinctiveness of quasi-Constitutional rules is their intriguing double-life: although typically they are posited rules—necessarily arising under and subject to the material constitution—nonetheless their emergence does affect the material constitution itself. This is actually not theoretically remarkable: it is quite possible for the *social fact* of the emergence of particular rules of positive law to affect social consciousness and practice—the things out of which the material constitution emerges. Nonetheless it is paradoxical to attempt to deduce through doctrinal legal analysis whether a given posited legal rule has in

7 In practice, of course, it is unlikely that a statute's passage would comprise an act of constitutional drama if its content did not concern public power.

8 Attention to Franciska Coleman's chapter rightly reminds us that many international norms are not objective standards, but rather are Eurocentric in origin": Franciska Coleman, "Quasi-entrenched living statutes: creating a multicultural rights regime". A more relativist approach is suggested by Verdugo (supra n 1, 47–48), in defining constitutional substance in terms of the content of a jurisdiction's particular mastertext Constitution.

9 Notwithstanding the supposed fundamentality of written Constitutions, they remain instruments of positive law, enacted pursuant to a prior, material constitution that authorises the Constitution-making process and gives the resulting mastertext its normative force.

10 HLA Hart, *The Concept of Law* (2nd ed., Clarendon Press, 1994), 105. Presenting similar material at the 2017 WG Hart Legal Workshop at London's Institute of Advanced Legal Studies, I was invited to have the courage of my convictions and assert that bureaucratic supremacy forms—or has formed—part of the Japanese ultimate rule of recognition. As will inevitably emerge from this chapter, this is indeed my position, but for present purposes I am content to speak of the material constitution. Nonetheless this chapter's analysis at least partially conflates a jurisdiction's fundamental material constitution with its ultimate rule of recognition. To do so is not quite accurate, but space precludes a thorough treatment of the relationship between the rule of recognition and the material constitution. The concepts are alike in the sense that concerns me presently, namely that both describe norms of greater or lesser complexity that are logically prior to positive law, and which arise out of nothing more metaphysical than a critical mass of social endorsement.

fact achieved this and consequently become part of a jurisdiction's material constitution, because the content of the material constitution is not a legal, but a sociological enquiry.[11] In answering this, a holistic, best-fit approach seems inevitable,[12] not least because the appropriate indicia will vary depending on the nature of the legal rule in question.[13] For instance, analysis of a rule's process of enactment applies only to statutory rules, since rules of other kinds are hard to regard as having been specifically and consciously *enacted* at all. Importantly for this chapter's later analysis, some indication of a rule's membership of the material constitution—which is to say its quasi-Constitutionality—can be found in the consequences of that rule's violation.

The synonymity between quasi-Constitutionality and material constitutionality has another implication. Existing scholarship on quasi-Constitutionality concerns the promotion of ordinary law to a privileged status. But as a statement of the relationship between the formal Constitution and the wider, material constitution, the notion of quasi-Constitutionality is also relevant to the opposite phenomenon. Just as rules can be part of the material constitution while outside the written Constitution, it is also possible that a rule contemplated by the Constitution is in fact not materially constitutional. This chapter concerns how a rule of adjudication notionally created by Japan's formal Constitution nonetheless is not a part of the material constitution, while a directly contradictory, quasi-Constitutional rule has emerged to take its place.

## Constitutional review in Japan

Constitutions are frequently born out of crisis or conflict, but the Constitution of Japan had a particularly painful nativity. Imposed on a conquered nation by an Occupation responsible for the almost total destruction of Japan's military, economy, and infrastructure, it represented a forced transplant of a largely foreign legal and political tradition.[14] The postwar Constitution's most famous and

11 Ibid., 110.

12 Other contributors suggest multi-factorial approaches to identifying quasi-Constitutionality, but approach it as a conventional legal-analytical enquiry: see Verdugo (supra n 1), 47–50 and Weill (supra n 2).

13 Weill makes this point powerfully in relation to different kinds of constitutional statute: Weill (supra n 2).

14 There are revisionist challenges to this understanding. Especially on the origins of Article 9, see e.g. Michael J. Kelly, "The Article 9 Pacifism Clause and Japan's Place in the World" (2007) 25 Wisconsin International Law Journal 491, 493. The traditional picture of American dominance is substantially correct: see generally Kyoko Inoue, *MacArthur's Japanese Constitution: A Linguistic and Cultural Study of its Making* (University of Chicago Press 1991); Dale Hellegers, *We the Japanese People: World War II and the Origins of the Japanese Constitution*, vol 2 (Stanford University Press 2002). Nonetheless the Japanese achieved the dilution and removal of certain provisions, particularly those concerning the rights of foreign nationals: see Timothy Webster, "Legal Excisions: 'Omissions Are Not Accidents.'" (2006) 39 Cornell International Law Journal 435; James C. Fisher, "'We the *kokumin*': The

contentious provision is Article 9: a permanent renunciation of "war as a sovereign right of the nation" and a prohibition on the state's maintenance of "war potential".[15] Both the Constitution's substance and its origins make the postwar "Peace Constitution" the *bête noire* of Japan's right-wing, including influential sections of the Liberal Democratic Party, which has been in power almost continuously for the entire postwar era. Nonetheless, for various legal and political reasons,[16] the Constitution has never been amended. Although Article 9 has lost much of its practical importance through a process of creative executive reinterpretation, its language remains as originally drafted. Given the difficulty of actually amending the Japanese Constitution, it is natural that adapting it to changing exigencies would occur mostly through (re)interpretation. But Constitutional interpretation in Japan has peculiar characteristics, and provides a powerful example of the systemic superiority of the material constitution—and the non-statutory quasi-Constitutional rules that belong to it—over formal Constitutional texts.

Prewar Japanese government proceeded unencumbered by the rule of law; the use of state power was not meaningfully constrained by any logically prior, litigible rules.[17] The Occupation regime attempted to import the familiar Constitutional vision of an executive subordinate to legal rules enforced by an independent judiciary. The modern Japanese Constitution therefore vests "the whole judicial power" in the Supreme Court and subsidiary lower courts,[18] which are tasked with declaring the meaning of the Constitutional text by testing "any law, order, regulation or official act" *ex post facto* for Constitutionality.[19] However, the Supreme Court has barely ever declared laws or state acts unconstitutional, prompting its widespread reputation as "an inherently conservative institution in deferential thrall to the executive".[20] Modern Japanese

Constitution, International Law and the Rights of Foreigners in Japan" (2015) 39 Journal of Japanese Law 109.

15 Constitution of Japan (1947), Article 9.

16 Under Article 96 of the Constitution, amendment requires a two-thirds majority in both legislative houses, and approval by public referendum. Even among elected representatives open to the prospect of Constitutional amendment, there is little agreement about what shape that reform should take: see e.g. Haruhiro Fukui, "Twenty Years of Revisionism" (1968) 43 Washington Law Review 931; Thomas U. Berger, "Ripe for Revision? The Strange Case of Japan's Unchanging Constitution" in Bryce Wakefield (ed.) *A Time for Change? Japan's "Peace" Constitution at 65* (Washington DC, Woodrow Wilson International Center for Scholars 2012) 15.

17 See Kiminobu Hashimoto, "The Rule of Law: Some Aspects of Judicial Review of Administrative Action" in Arthur Taylor van Mehren (ed.), *Law in Japan: The Legal Order in a Changing Society* (Harvard University Press 1963).

18 Constitution of Japan (1947), Article 76.

19 Ibid., Article 81. All courts have the power of Constitutional review, not just the Supreme Court: Supreme Court, 8 October 1952, *Minshū* 6-9-783. However, it is especially rare for subordinate courts to engage in Constitutional review.

20 Navraj Singh Ghaleigh, "Neither Legal nor Political? Bureaucratic Constitutionalism in Japanese Law" (2015) 26(2) King's Law Journal 193, 200.

Constitutional jurisprudence begins with the *Sunakawa* case, in which the Supreme Court refused to consider whether the US-Japan Security Treaty—under which extensive American military forces were permanently stationed in Japan—was consistent with Article 9's prohibition on "war potential". Unless an act of state was "immediately [and] clearly unconstitutional and void", to review it for Constitutionality would fall "outside ... the power of judicial review granted to the court".[21] This goes substantially further than deference to democratic decision-making: the Court denies jurisdiction to consider the Constitutionality of state action unless its non-compliance with the Constitutional text is so obvious as not to require substantial legal analysis.[22] Most scholarly attention in this area predictably focuses on the jurisprudence surrounding Article 9. Certainly this has been the most prominent arena in which the Supreme Court has demonstrated its approach to Constitutional review, but this approach is not confined to Article 9 challenges. Wherever possible, the Supreme Court avoids adverting to clearly relevant Constitutional considerations,[23] deciding Constitutionally contentious cases on technical grounds instead, typically by denying standing.[24]

## Judicial conservatism: the "human story" and rules of law

Many have tried to explain why the Japanese judiciary is so reticent seriously to embrace the Constitutionality review required of it by the Japanese Constitution. Ramseyer and Nakazato allege oblique political control over judicial decision-making, claiming that Japan's political class ensures favourable judicial behaviour through its ability "indirectly [to] reward and punish judges".[25] Conversely,

21 Supreme Court, 16 December 1959, *Keishū* 13–13-3225.

22 Archival research reveals direct US pressure on the Chief Justice in advance of the *Sunakawa* judgment, reminding him of the political considerations at stake and suggesting the ideal determination of the case: Reiko Fukawa and Shoji Shinbara, *Sunagawa Jiken to Tanaka Saikosai Chokan* (Nippon Hyōronsha, 2013). But the same stance has endured without such direct interventions: see e.g. Supreme Court, 28 August 1996, *Minshū* 50–1952.

23 Ichiro Kitamura, "The Judiciary in Contemporary Society: Japan" (1993) 25 Case Western Reserve Journal of International Law 263, 276.

24 See for example the *Naganuma Nike* case, in which the claimants' standing to bring a Constitutional challenge was presented as parasitic on showing continued interference with private law water rights. Courts interpret standing so strictly that "virtually no one other than a member of [Japan's armed forces] ordered into combat could establish the narrow legal interest deemed necessary to ground a claim that government action is in violation of Article 9": Craig Martin, 'A Constitutional Case for Amending Article 9' in Bryce Wakefield (ed.) *A Time for Change? Japan's "Peace" Constitution at 65* (Washington DC, Woodrow Wilson International Center for Scholars 2012), 64.

25 J. Mark Ramseyer and Minoru Nakazato, *Japanese Law: An Economic Approach* (Chicago University Press 1999), 217. These authors identify (at 203) dire career paths for the brave judges who obstructed Prime Minister Satou's attempts to block political demonstrations in the 1970s. See also e.g. J. Mark Ramseyer and Eric Rasmusen, *Measuring Judicial Independence: The Political Economy of Judging in Japan* (Chicago University Press 2003).

Haley finds no evidence of systemic political pressure on the judiciary in their disposal of cases, explaining the courts' conservatism as a self-imposed attempt to preserve public trust in judicial impartiality.[26] However, empirical research shows that a particular political ideology permeates the Japanese judiciary. For Law, the story is one of ideological harmony between judiciary and politicians, which Japan's consistently conservative governments have cultivated through the appointment of successive Chief Justices whose ideologies match the government's own.[27] The mechanics of the judicial administration inculcate conformity with the ideological and juridical position of the Supreme Court, and particularly of the Chief Justice. Moreover, the chances of ideological outliers achieving sufficient seniority to disrupt this are staggeringly low.[28] While the judiciary is politically independent in terms of the management of its internal affairs and the disposal of cases,[29] it is certainly not an apolitical institution,[30] and lacks "the capacity to pursue policies out of sync with those favored by [the government]".[31]

For commentators like Law and Ramseyer, the Supreme Court's implicit abdication of its role as Constitutional arbiter is attributable to a mix of party politics and the judiciary's own professional culture. Such analyses are illuminating, but legal study is much impoverished if normative analysis is wholly eclipsed by reductionist behaviouralism. The lack of meaningful judicial Constitutional review in Japan may not be exclusively explicable in terms of human motives. It is also the product of a non-statutory quasi-Constitutional legal rule. Adopting this perspective is not to suggest that the behavioural explanations for judges'

26 John O. Haley, "The Japanese Judiciary: Maintaining Integrity, Autonomy and the Public Trust" in Daniel H. Foote (ed.) *Law in Japan: A Turning Point* (University of Washington Press 2008), 99, 122; "Constitutional Adjudication in Japan: History and Social Context, Legislative Structure, and Judicial Values" (2011) 88 Washington University Law Review 1467. Maintaining its independent image is clearly important to the judiciary. Foote identifies an almost militant level of enforced apoliticality among the rank-and-file judiciary: Daniel H. Foote, "Restrictions on Political Activity by Judges in Japan and the United States: The Cases of Judge Teranishi and Justice Sanders" (2009) 8 Washington University Global Studies Law Review 285; "The Supreme Court and the Push for Transparency in Lower Court Appointments in Japan" (2011) 88 Washington University Law Review 1745.

27 David S. Law, "The Anatomy of a Conservative Court: Judicial Review in Japan" (2009) 87 Texas Law Review 1545, 1549.

28 From the start, judicial training involves a "'systematic purge' of ideologically unsuitable judges". Once qualified, potential future Justices are groomed for the post from an early age, placed onto tightly managed and homogenous career trajectories, facilitated by the judicial bureaucracy's micro-management of judges' lifestyles and professional activities: ibid. 1552–1557. Focusing on the Supreme Court, Ramseyer and Rosenbluth likewise identify tactics calculated to minimise individual Justices' ability to depart from the Court's collective stance, such as appointing candidates at an advanced age to correspondingly short tenures: J. Mark Ramseyer and Frances McCall Rosenbluth, *Japan's Political Marketplace* (Harvard University Press 1993), 144, 153.

29 Law (supra n 27), 1587.

30 The judiciary's zealousness in preventing its members' engagement in politics is therefore less about ensuring neutrality than about concealing the judiciary's inherent politicality.

31 Law (supra n 27), 1587.

conduct are incorrect. The two approaches are distinct and non-rivalrous. Legal rules do not arise out of thin air but out of human action. Every legal rule is at least partially explicable in terms of human motives and behaviours, but this fact hardly excludes acknowledging the existence of a legal rule.[32]

Law emphasises that the Japanese courts have been far more interventionalist in areas of law unconnected with Constitutionality review, and considers this evidence that the weakness of Constitutional review specifically is a human rather than a juridical phenomenon. In declining to engage in searching Constitutionality review, "the judiciary acts strategically out of self-preservation": the judiciary does not fear censure for interfering in "private conduct in ways that the government can override", but tries to avoid the repercussions of attempting "to impose limits on the government's power".[33] This analysis requires careful scrutiny. Certainly, the Japanese judiciary is not uniformly facilitative of the conservative political establishment's preferences. Exploiting mandatory principles of the Civil Code, the Constitution and public international law, the judiciary has effectively reformed—in a broadly progressive direction—many areas of Japanese law, including politically contentious issues such as divorce,[34] environmental protection, public health,[35] and sexual discrimination.[36] Given the many inventive judicial efforts to reform areas of the law that Japan's conservative political

32 Nikos Skoutaris' paper describes how "(sub-)constitutional statutes reflect … political asymmetries and translate them into constitutional ones": Nikos Skoutaris, "Reflecting and building asymmetries: The role of (sub-)constitutional statutes in Spain and the UK", 174. This resonates with the emergence and effect of quasi-Constitutional non-statutory rules, which involve the transformation of political facts into legal ones.

33 David S. Law, "Why Has Judicial Review Failed in Japan?" (2011) 88 Washington University Law Review 1425, 1453.

34 Ibid., 1453; Frank K. Upham, "Stealth Activism: Norm Formation by Japanese Courts" (2011) 88 Washington University Law Review 1493.

35 John O. Haley and Daniel H. Foote, "Judicial Lawmaking and the Creation of Legal Norms in Japan: A Dialogue" in John O. Haley and Toshiko Takenaka (eds), *Legal Innovations in Asia: Judicial Lawmaking and the Influence of Comparative Law* (Edward Elgar 2014), 103.

36 See Frank K. Upham, *Law and Social Change in Postwar Japan* (Harvard University Press 1987). Before Japan's first anti-discrimination legislation, the Japanese courts engaged in a sustained practice of using Article 90 of the Civil Code (which voids juristic acts contrary to public morals) to strike down certain discriminatory employment practices by reference to Article 14 of the Constitution, which guarantees sexual equality, construing adherence to this principle as an aspect of public morality: Megan L. Starich, "The 2006 Revisions to Japan's Equal Opportunity Employment Law: A Narrow Approach to a Pervasive Problem" (2007) 16 Pacific Rim Law & Policy Journal 551. The courts have also been active in importing into domestic law the aspirations reflected in Japan's public international legal obligations, for instance by synthesising international legal norms with domestic tort law in order to patch the gap left by Japan's lack of racial discrimination legislation. A famous example is *Bortz v Suzuki*, Shizuoka District Court, 12 October 1999, *Hanrei Taimuzu* 1045–216. For commentary, see Timothy Webster, "Reconstituting Japanese Law: International Norms and Domestic Litigation" (2009) 30 Michigan Journal of International Law 211; "International Human Rights Law in Japan: The View at Thirty" (2010) 23(2) Columbia Journal of Asian Law 241, 243.

class has declined to adapt to changing social needs and values, it is too simplistic to present the Japanese judiciary in general, or the Supreme Court specifically, as invariably reactionary. Law is right then to seek an explanation for the Court's particular timidity in Constitutional cases, but cynical self-preservation is not the only, or even the best, explanation available. For one thing, it sits uneasily with Law's central claim that the courts *share* the government's conservative ideology. If this is true, courts ought not to be under any temptation to effect legal change in directions of which the government could disapprove—a temptation that the desire for self-preservation might restrain.

In fact we can account normatively for the distinctive judicial treatment of Constitutional cases, by accepting the existence of a quasi-Constitutional rule in accordance with which the courts act. This is, in jurisprudential terms, a secondary rule of adjudication empowering the executive branch authoritatively to interpret the Constitution and consequently determine the Constitutionality of legislation and acts of state.[37]

In contrast to the judiciary's deafening silence on Constitutional matters, an elite arm of Japan's civic administration, the Cabinet Legislation Bureau, has freely issued official interpretations of the Constitution and declarations of the Constitutionality of proposed legislation.[38] This practice is particularly obvious in the Article 9 context because this is the part of the Japanese Constitution under most practical pressure, given the perceived importance of Japanese defence capacity and engagement abroad. Despite General MacArthur's retrospective insistence that Article 9 was not intended to forbid a purely defensive military force, it is clear as a matter of history that it was originally intended to do just this, as its language plainly suggests to the unprejudiced reader of either the English or the Japanese text.[39] With the progress of Communism in Asia, Japan's American military rulers thought better of Japanese disarmament,[40] instructing the Japanese government to create a National Police Reserve to fill in for the American forces that would be sent from Japan to the Korean peninsula following the outbreak of the Korean War in 1950. This was ultimately reorganised into today's "Self-Defence Forces" (SDF) in 1954. To permit this development, the Japanese Cabinet adopted an official interpretation of Article 9, treating the prohibition on "war potential" as intended only to accomplish the

37 Hart (supra n 10), 97.

38 Lawrence W Beer, "Introduction: Japan's Constitutional Law, 1945–1990" in Lawrence W Beer and Hiroshi Itoh (eds), *The Constitutional Case Law of Japan, 1970 through 1990* (University of Washington Press 1996), 25.

39 This is made clear by the "MacArthur Notes" (preserved at Japan's National Diet Library and available transcribed online at www.ndl.go.jp/constitution/shiryo/03/072/072tx.html #t001), which record three principles MacArthur himself considered essential components of Constitutional reform. See also Hellegers (supra n 14), 519 and 578.

40 Ken Motoyama, "The Significance of the Provisions for the Renunciation of War and Abolition of Military Forces in the Japanese Constitution" (2015) 26(2) King's Law Journal 285, 287.

aim of renouncing war "as a means of settling international disputes". Consequently, a purely defensive military force was Constitutionally compliant. Successive interpretations have further diluted the constraints that Article 9 purports to impose, leading to an "emerging gulf between the formal requirements of the Constitution of Japan and the practices of the Government".[41]

In declining to entertain Constitutional review, the Supreme Court is not abandoning this task into a vacuum. Rather it is acknowledging the legal authoritativeness of executive Constitutionality review.[42] Executive confirmation of Constitutionality is not just factually influential on the outcome of judicial Constitutional challenges. It is legally authoritative, sanctioned by a quasi-Constitutional secondary rule of adjudication—a rule that is seldom articulated but nonetheless observable and effective.

There are important signs that Japanese legal and political actors understand this as a binding rule of law,[43] even if they would be unable specifically to articulate it. When the recent defence and security legislation was being debated in the Japanese legislature, its Constitutionality was challenged principally on the grounds that it was inconsistent with the previous Cabinet position on the meaning of Article 9. Conversely, in defending the new legislation's Constitutionality, the Minister for Defence relied on the fact that the present Cabinet had considered in depth and approved the legislation's consistency with Article 9.[44] Judges too acknowledge the normative force of the Cabinet's conclusions about Constitutionality. Certain Supreme Court Justices, interviewed anonymously by Law, expressly attributed the rarity of successful judicial review in Japan to this rule.[45]

41 Kenichi Yanai and KD Ewing, "Introduction" (2015) 26(2) King's Law Journal 185.

42 One Japanese scholar insists that the judiciary's Constitutional conservatism is a *sui generis* phenomenon, not a reaction to the activities of the civic bureaucracy. Indeed, he suggests that the bureaucrats' *ex ante* Constitutionality review is a reaction to the judiciary's own reticence to engage in these enquiries: Iwao Satō, *Iken Shinsa-sei to Naikaku Hōsei-kyoku* (2005) 56 Journal of Social Science 81. This is unconvincing; although the Bureau's work would obviously become more complex if the judiciary were to assert its own Constitutional review role, as a matter of institutional history it is abundantly clear who has made way for whom. The Cabinet Legislation Bureau was issuing formal Constitutional interpretations in the name of the Cabinet long before the Supreme Court was presented with a case ripe for searching Constitutional review. Its predecessor—the pre-war Legislation Bureau—likewise exerted massive influence on wartime government policy, enough for the American reformers to consider it a threat to Japanese democratisation and abolish it. It was resurrected as the modern Cabinet Legislation Bureau almost immediately following the end of the Occupation.

43 They demonstrate Hart's "critical reflective attitude": Hart (supra n 10), 57.

44 National Diet Library, Proceedings of the Special Committee on the Peace and Security Legislation in the 189th Diet Session, 5 June 2015, available at http://kokkai.ndl.go.jp/sentaku/syugiin/189/0298/18906050298007a.html. For a thorough explanatory account of the legislative process in between the controversial Cabinet resolution and the passage of the resulting legislative changes, see Daisuke Akimoto, "Exercising the Right to Collective Self-Defence? An Analysis of 'Japan's Peace and Security Legislation'" (2016) 41 Journal of Japanese Law / *Zeitschrift für Japanisches Recht* 137.

45 Law (supra n 33), 1451.

As described above, Law explains that the courts—never "hermetically sealed from their political environment"—have institutionalised the values of Japan's consistently right-wing political leadership.[46] However, if it is true that a non-statutory quasi-Constitutional rule has displaced the rule of adjudication contemplated by the formal Constitution, then the crucial aspect of Japan's "political environment" is probably something much more fundamental than the conservatism of the dominant Liberal Democratic Party. Although the formal Japanese Constitution clearly contemplates legal constitutionalism—wherein public power is controlled through judicial enforcement of logically prior legal rules—the material constitutional reality is the supremacy of the civic bureaucracy. This emerged out of the political and institutional history of the modern Japanese polity, and endures notwithstanding contrary aspirations in the postwar formal Constitution.

## The origins and endurance of bureaucratic constitutional supremacy

A powerful and unaccountable civic administration has characterised Japanese government since the emergence of the modern Japanese state in 1868. The civil war that ended Japan's traditional feudal government was not a popular revolution, but an elite one, and did not seek to democratise power but to concentrate it further, with a view to orchestrating the rapid modernisation necessary to resist Western designs on Japan. The new government understood itself to be legally omnipotent, exercising the delegated personal *imperium* of an absolute sovereign Emperor. Japan's first modern Constitution, proclaimed by the Emperor in 1889, gave the nation's fledgling national assembly "only the most insignificant of powers",[47] and every aspect of public policy emanated from the government ministries. However, as an historian of the Japanese state has described:

> The revolutionary condition produces ... the central problem of authority and legitimacy. If those who seize power wish to retain it, these problems can only be resolved ... by valorization of the notion of objective rationality ... Only through such concepts can the continued power and status of a small group be legitimized while at the same time maintaining that such policy-making structures meet the requirements of equality that the revolutionary seizure of power so clearly implies.[48]

Meiji Japan's omnipotent bureaucratic state legitimised itself by claiming to transcend particular social interests and values in pursuit of independent

46 Ibid., 1425, 1462.

47 Bernard S. Silberman, "The Bureaucratic State in Japan: The Problem of Authority and Legitimacy" in Tetsuo Najita and J. Victor Koschmann (eds), *Conflict in Modern Japanese History: The Neglected Tradition* (Princeton University Press 1982), 240.

48 Ibid., 256.

expertise. However, depoliticising the basis of its power by retreating into technocracy meant the state had "no inherent claim to a monopoly over the organisation of society's interests"—after all, the state could never plausibly claim a monopoly on expertise.[49] Japan's modernisation was producing powerful new interest groups, especially the organised forces of industry and commerce, which began to threaten the state's monopoly on policy making.[50] The solution was an effective "strategy of cooptation",[51] which allowed the administration to harness to its own ends the power of potential rival power bases. In return for privileged and reliable access to state decision-making—as well as subsidies, delegated powers, and legally protected status—interest groups such as industrial bodies, commercial associations, farmers' unions and youth organisations were "coopted into the administrative structure".[52] The bureaucracy successfully linked its notionally absolute legal authority—as the instruments of an omnipotent sovereign—to its practically unassailable status as the definitive forum for the distillation of competing social interests into policy, and ultimately into specific manifestations of public power. The administration's decisions became practically authoritative because the only interests with the material power to challenge them—and who might, in other regimes, have agitated through the legal or political processes—had been co-opted into their formulation and had incentives to see them effectuated.

The Occupation legal reforms contemplated the familiar American ideal in which policy was set by elected representatives and enshrined in laws that bureaucrats would faithfully execute, subject to rigorous judicial review. But revision to the formal Constitution could not hope to overcome the continuity of the social realities that produced and sustained the material constitutional supremacy of the civic bureaucracy. The American vision assumed that legislators—now for the first time elected by the population at large—would lead the formulation of public policy, but lacking expertise and experience they instead "tended to define their own role as transmitting aspirations of their constituencies to bureaucrats and began to act more like lobbyists that legislators".[53] For most of the postwar era, even members of the notionally supreme Cabinet have in practice "tend[ed] to act as representatives of bureaucrat-made policy".[54] The practical dominance of the bureaucracy survived the Occupation unscathed, allowing it to "maintain itself over time as the authoritative institution of Japanese society".[55]

49 Ibid., 237.
50 Ibid., 230.
51 Ibid., 242.
52 Ibid., 243.
53 Kazuyuki Takahashi, "Ongoing Changes in the Infrastructure of a Constitutional System: From 'Bureaucracy' to Democracy" in Daniel H. Foote (ed.) *Law in Japan: A Turning Point* (University of Washington Press 2008), 244.
54 Ibid., 244–245.
55 Silberman (supra n 47), 232.

## The most recent executive interpretation and its consequences

Deducing the precise content and parameters of quasi-Constitutional rules is problematic. It is hardest in the case of non-statutory quasi-Constitutional rules, because there is no canonical articulation of the rule even as ordinary law. As for statutory quasi-Constitutional rules, the statutory language authoritatively states the rule's effect but this cannot reveal whether, and to what extent, the rule is also part of the material constitution. Indeed that is not a legal issue at all, but a sociological one. In the case of the Japanese quasi-Constitutional rule concerning executive Constitutional interpretation, we can look to recent political and legal events to deduce its precise content and limits.

Despite the interpretive relaxation of Article 9, it has long remained settled that it permits the use of force only directly in defence of Japan—not in defence of its allies, or to promote Japan's wider interests.[56] However, in July 2014, the Cabinet issued a resolution interpreting Article 9 as permitting collective defence in certain circumstances.[57] Following this, legislation revising ten existing statutes was enacted in September 2015 to permit deployment of the Japanese armed forces in defence of Japan's allies. This produced popular and intellectual outrage of a scale last seen in Japan following the ratification of the US-Japan Security Treaty in 1960, when enormous popular opposition felled the administration of Prime Minister Kishi.[58] Perhaps most remarkably, Japan's usually quiescent student body orchestrated mass demonstrations, particularly under the auspices of Students' Emergency Action for Liberal Democracy (SEALDs). Over 200 of Japan's constitutional scholars formally objected that the new interpretation was illegitimate.[59]

Constitutional purists have consistently—and correctly—maintained that the accepted interpretation of Article 9 (permitting a defensive military force) is textually unsupported, since "the text of the 1947 Constitution does not lend itself to a less rigorous interpretation".[60] Nonetheless this has remained a juridical technicality that the body politic has preferred to ignore, with such

56 Akiho Shibata, "Japan: Moderate Commitment within Legal Strictures" in Charlotte Ku and Harold Jacobson (eds), *Democratic Accountability and the Use of Force in International Law* (Cambridge University Press 2003), 209.

57 The change was apparently required due to "shifts in the global power balance, the rapid progress of technological innovation, and threats such as weapons of mass destruction". Japanese Ministry of Defence, *The Defense of Japan: White Paper 2014*, 120 (www.mod.go.jp/e/publ/w_paper/2014.html).

58 Maternal grandfather to the incumbent Prime Minister Abe.

59 Available at http://blog.livedoor.jp/nihonkokukenpou/archives/51804812.html. Only 7% of the 422 members of the Japan Public Law Association considered the changes Constitutional: Nippon Housou Kyoukai (NHK), *Kensho anpo hoan: ima nani wo toubeki ka* (Security Bill Investigation: What questions should now be asked?). Survey available at www.nhk.or.jp/gendai/kiroku/detail02=3690=all.html.

60 Lawrence W. Beer, "The Constitution of Japan: 'Pacifism' and Mass Media Freedom" in Daniel H. Foote (ed.) *Law in Japan: A Turning Point* (University of Washington Press 2008), 259; Nobuyoshi Ashibe, *Kenpō* (6th ed., *Iwanami Shoten* 2015) 57–61.

claims regarded as unconstructively pedantic. Since the 1960s, Article 9's interpretive dilution has produced very little constitutional upset, and the traditional position, although based on a plainly counter-textual Constitutional reading, enjoyed overwhelming popular and political endorsement. Why then has this latest reinterpretation had such a startlingly different reaction?

Material constitutions are in constant flux as new constitutional rules emerge and old ones decline. Determining the birth and death of quasi-Constitutional rules is difficult, even for statutory ones: although their validity as law can be established through conventional legal analysis, their constitutional status cannot. Things are even harder in the case of non-statutory quasi-Constitutional rules, which are usually neither consciously enacted nor consciously abandoned. Might the widespread sense of constitutional affront prompted by this latest Cabinet interpretation of Article 9 suggest the rule validating such interpretations is at last being rejected? If the rule validating executive Constitutional interpretations had been abandoned, this would necessitate rejection of the defensive role of the SDF, since this too is inconsistent with the literal Constitutional language and Constitutionally compliant only on the premise that executive interpretations are authoritative. Yet there have not been renewed calls for the literal enforcement of Article 9. On the contrary, evidence suggests most people continue to support the traditional position and might even support open Constitutional amendment to reflect it.[61] The novel response to this particular interpretive declaration is evidence not of the quasi-Constitutional rule's demise but of its precise parameters.

Embracing collective self-defence represents a major substantive change to the interpretation of Article 9, one widely understood as the crossing of a significant Rubicon that undermines the core pacifist ideal of the Constitution and is tantamount to its unauthorised amendment: while homeland defence is an inherently circumscribed activity, overseas military engagement is intrinsically more slippery, and the line between pre-emptive (collective) defence and aggression depends largely on perspective. Perhaps therefore the unique outrage that this particular reinterpretation provoked reveals the substantive limits of the quasi-Constitutional rule in question. Was the rule authorising executive Constitutional interpretation always—or has it become?—substantively restricted, in that certain actions and policies cannot be rendered Constitutional by executive declaration at all? Did the new interpretation violate the quasi-Constitutional rule of adjudication simply by stretching the language of Article 9 too far?

This is possible, but there is another important dimension. Although notionally issued by the Cabinet, Constitutional interpretations are traditionally the work not of politicians, but of the Cabinet Legislation Bureau. Established by primary legislation,[62] this elite bureaucratic institution is responsible for

61 Christopher W. Hughes, "Japan, Constitutional Reform, and Remilitarization" in Bryce Wakefield (ed.) *A Time for Change? Japan's "Peace" Constitution at 65* (Washington DC, Woodrow Wilson International Center for Scholars 2012), 30.

62 Cabinet Legislation Bureau Establishment Act (Law No 252 of 1952).

providing "unified government interpretations" of laws and the Constitution, and for providing "pre-legislative [C]onstitutional review".[63] Commentators have already noted that the Bureau's specific characteristics are central to its prominence in Japanese legal and political affairs.[64] It is comprised of around eighty senior government administrators seconded from various ministries. All are proven legal specialists with decades of experience in their respective areas. In all respects it is the very apotheosis of the Japanese state bureaucracy, epitomising the characteristics of the state administration central to its emergence into constitutional supremacy: independence, neutrality and expertise.

In fact, the apoliticality of the civic bureaucracy in general and the Cabinet Legislation Bureau in particular is exaggerated. Having developed in intimate symbiosis with Japan's ruling Liberal Democratic Party, the civic administration is as thoroughly politicised as the Japanese judiciary. There is much evidence that the Cabinet Legislation Bureau "has been selectively ignored (or manipulated) by skilled politicians".[65] Although it has certainly frustrated certain government ambitions,[66] in other cases Japanese politicians have exaggerated the extent to which its Constitutional interpretations restrict political decision-making, particularly to resist American demands for greater Japanese contributions to their mutual defence relationship. Conflicts between the Bureau and the political executive have often been resolved in the latter's favour,[67] and the Bureau's power to obstruct actions it considers unconstitutional has varied according to the political situation.[68]

63 Beer (supra n 38), 25; Yasuo Hasabe, "The Supreme Court of Japan: Its Adjudication on Electoral Systems and Economic Freedoms" (2007) 52 International Journal of Constitutional Law 296, 298–9. It is also reported to issue opinions even on legislative grammar and style: Ayako Mie, "Legislation Bureau Chief Abe's Window to Collective Defense", *The Japan Times* (Tokyo, 3 September 2013).

64 Hasabe (ibid).

65 Even the traditional Bureau interpretation of Article 9 (as permitting a defensive military) was authored at the request of Prime Minister Yoshida and under his close scrutiny.

66 A notable example was its refusal to change its interpretation of Article 9 to allow Japan to send combat troops during the First Gulf War: Sayuri Umeda, "Japan: Article 9 of the Constitution" (Law Library of Congress 2006) 16–18 (available at www.loc.gov/law/help/japan_art9.php).

67 For instance, Japanese troops participated in the Second Gulf War contrary to the Bureau's insistence that this was unconstitutional, although they were present only in non-combat regions and their role was restricted to rear-support for coalition troops, and humanitarian assistance. Nonetheless, this produced a rare judicial declaration that the SDF's operations breached Article 9: Nagoya High Court, 17 April 2008, *Hanji* 74–2056. This was technically *obiter*, since the court held that the claimants lacked standing to bring the claim. But it is interesting that such a startlingly rare declaration of unconstitutionality accompanied state action that the Cabinet Legislation Bureau had not approved as being Constitutionally compliant.

68 See generally Richard J. Samuels, "Politics, Security Policy, and Japan's Cabinet Legislation Bureau: Who Elected These Guys, Anyway?" (2004) Japan Policy Research Institute, Working Paper No. 99.

Nonetheless it is the *perception* of bureaucratic apoliticality that has so thoroughly defined Japan's material constitution. Particularly, it is fundamental to the quasi-Constitutional rule of executive Constitutional interpretation that the process be an administrative rather than political operation. In 2007, Abe announced the creation of an "Advisory Panel on Reconstruction of the Legal Basis for Security", whose remit was to consider an executive reinterpretation of Article 9 that would permit collective defence. The Panel was widely condemned as having "no legitimacy or authority whatsoever to engage in [C]constitutional interpretation, and … not contemplated in any manner by the Constitution".[69] Its interpretive project was thought particularly inappropriate since its decisions "will likely be used to preclude interference by the judiciary, which is the branch of government that does have constitutional authority to interpret the Constitution".[70] These criticisms are intriguing since all could fairly be directed at the Cabinet Legislation Bureau. The constitutional supremacy of the civic bureaucracy, and the specific quasi-Constitutional rule of executive Constitutional interpretation, are premised on the distinctive nature of bureaucratic decision-making. The most recent Cabinet interpretation of Article 9 brazenly subverted this. The interpretation came not from the established bureaucratic protocol but from a calculated political circumvention of it. Determined to break the Bureau's entrenched refusal to endorse the Constitutionality of collective defence, in 2013 Prime Minister Abe replaced its Director General with a political crony.[71] This was an unprecedented and provocative move—it is almost unheard of for the Director to come from outside the ranks of the Bureau itself, and especially for an incumbent Director to be removed to make way for a hand-picked appointee. Abe's choice served only a short tenure before resigning for health reasons, but the disruption was successful in limiting the Bureau's obstructive capacity. The Cabinet took the opportunity to redefine the accepted balance of power between the Cabinet and the bureaucracy, with sustained insistences that the role of the Cabinet Legislation Bureau was purely advisory.[72]

## Conclusion

The Japanese judiciary has not embraced the rigorous Constitutionality review that the postwar Japanese Constitution presents as integral to the judicial role. The divergence between the Contitutional vision and practical Japanese public

69 Craig Martin, "The Case against Revising Interpretations of the Japanese Constitution" (2007) 5(5) The Asia-Pacific Journal: Japan Focus.

70 Ibid.

71 Ichiro Komatsu, former Ambassador to France, who had previously been involved with the work of Abe's 2007 "expert panel".

72 The Chief Cabinet Secretary emphasised that the interpretation of the Constitution was a decision for the Cabinet on the advice of the Bureau: Reiji Yoshida, "Abe's Man in Cabinet Law Office Steps Down", *The Japan Times* (Tokyo, 17 May 2014).

law is not just a human phenomenon explicable by reference to institutional design and judicial psychology. Rather it reflects a non-statutory secondary legal rule of adjudication authorising the Japanese executive to promulgate interpretations of the Constitution and thereby declare the Constitutionality of subordinate law, notwithstanding the written Constitution's provision for judicial supremacy and conventional Constitutionality review.

But while, on the one hand, this chapter has shown that this phenomenon concerns a legal rule rather than purely a human practice, on the other hand it demonstrates that whether a given legal rule is also a quasi-Constitutional rule is not a normative enquiry, but a sociological one. Nonetheless it argued that the legal rule under review must fairly be regarded as quasi-Constitutional—which is to say that it forms part of Japan's material constitution—despite its inconsistency with the formal Constitutional mastertext. Just as legal rules can be part of a jurisdiction's material constitution without being part of the written Constitution, rules contemplated by the Constitution may in fact never enter the material constitution. This chapter explains how a rule of adjudication notionally created by Japan's formal Constitution nonetheless is not materially constitutional: its place in the material constitution is occupied instead by a distinct, quasi-Constitutional rule.

This chapter explained how this quasi-Constitutional rule emerged by reference to Japanese political and institutional history, and how it endured within the material constitution notwithstanding the contrary aspirations reflected in the postwar formal Constitution. Written Constitutions are ultimately instruments of positive law, and as such are subject to the logically prior and more fundamental material constitution. Mere revision to the formal Constitution could not have, and did not, alter the constitutional supremacy of the Japanese civic bureaucracy, since the social realities that produced and sustained it endured. The rule this chapter analysed is therefore a powerful example of the superiority of the material constitution—and the quasi-Constitutional rules it contains—over formal Constitutional texts.

# Index